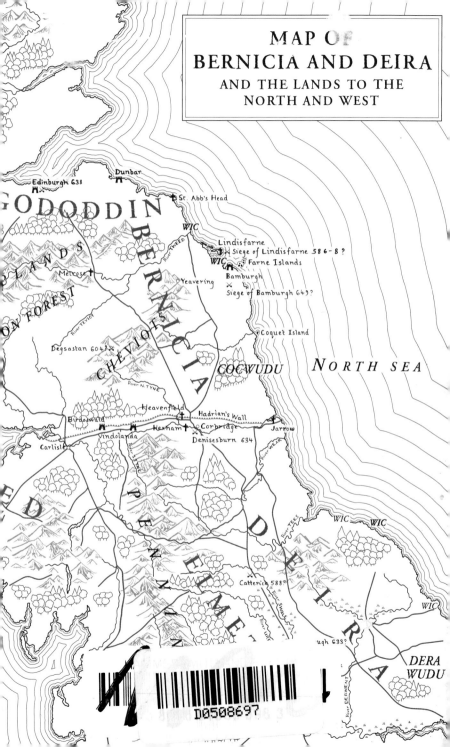

MAP OF
BERNICIA AND DEIRA
AND THE LANDS TO THE NORTH AND WEST

Edinburgh 638

Dunbar

St. Abb's Head

GODODDIN

BERNICIA

WIC

Lindisfarne

Siege of Lindisfarne 586-8?

WIC

Farne Islands

Yeavering

Bamburgh

Siege of Bamburgh 649?

River TWEED

ULANDS

Metcaud

ON FOREST

River TEVIOT

Degsastan 604?

CHEVIOT

River N.TYNE

COQUET Island

COCWUDU

NORTH SEA

Heavenfield

Hadrian's Wall

Birdoswald

Hexham

Corbridge

Jarrow

Carlisle

Vindolanda

Denisesburn 634

River IRT

River W.TYNE

PENNINE

D

ED

River TEES

WIC

WIC

ELMET

River SWALE

Catterick 588?

WIC

River URE

ugh 633?

DEIRA

River DERWENT

DERA
WUDU

D0508697

THE KING
IN THE NORTH

MAX ADAMS studied archaeology at York University and has excavated widely in Britain and abroad, publishing more than thirty papers in academic and popular journals as well as several monographs. He has made a number of television programmes as the 'Landscape Detective' and co-convenes the Bernician Studies Group in Newcastle upon Tyne where he teaches in the *Explore* Lifelong Learning programme. His active research interests include the monastic geography of County Donegal in Ireland and the Dark Age landscapes of the North of England. He is the author of *Admiral Collingwood* (2005) and *The Prometheans* (2009), which was a *Guardian* Book of the Week.

THE KING IN THE NORTH

THE LIFE AND TIMES OF
OSWALD
OF NORTHUMBRIA

Max Adams

HEAD
of
ZEUS

First published in 2013 by Head of Zeus Ltd

This paperback edition published in 2014 by Head of Zeus Ltd

1 3 5 7 9 10 8 6 4 2

A CIP catalogue record for this book is available from the British Library.

ISBN (PB) 9781781854204   ISBN (E) 9781781854174

Designed and typeset by
Ken Wilson | point918

Printed and bound by CPI Group (UK) Ltd,
Croydon, CR0 4YY

Head of Zeus Ltd
Clerkenwell House
45–47 Clerkenwell Green
London ECIR OHT

www.headofzeus.com

To lifelong learners everywhere

Contents

Maps

I
*Britain in the time of
Kings Oswald
and Oswiu*

II
*Bernicia in the time of
King Oswald*

III
*Deira in the time of
King Oswald*

Britain in the time of Kings Oswald and Oswiu

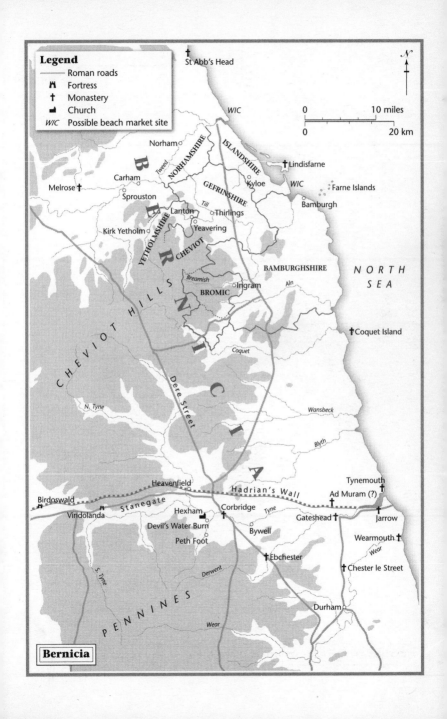

Legend
- ――― Roman roads
- ᛟ Fortress
- † Monastery
- ⌐ Church
- *WIC* Possible beach market site

0 ____ 10 miles
0 ____ 20 km

N

† St Abb's Head

WIC

B
E
R
N
I
C
I
A

NORHAMSHIRE
Norham

ISLANDSHIRE

GEFRINSHIRE

Tweed

Carham
Melrose †
Sprouston
Kirk Yetholm
YETHOLMSHIRE
Lanton
Yeavering
Till
Thirlings

CHEVIOT

BROMIC
Breamish
Ingram

BAMBURGHSHIRE
Aln

† Lindisfarne
Kyloe
WIC
Farne Islands
Bamburgh

NORTH
SEA

† Coquet Island

Coquet

CHEVIOT HILLS

N. Tyne

Dere Street

Wansbeck

Blyth

Heavenfield
Birdoswald
Stanegate
Vindolanda ᛟ
Hexham ⌐
Devil's Water Burn
Peth Foot
Corbridge
Tyne
Bywell

Hadrian's Wall
Tynemouth †
Ad Muram (?) †
Gateshead † ⌐
Jarrow

Ebchester †
Wearmouth †

Wear

† Chester le Street

PENNINES

S. Tyne

Derwent

Wear

Durham ⌐

Bernicia

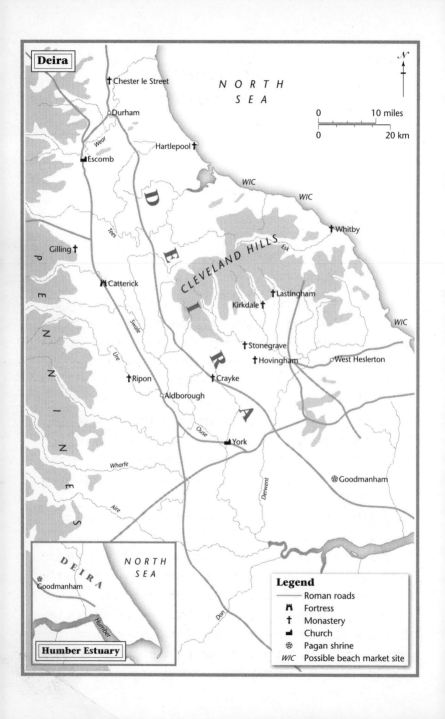

Deira

N

NORTH SEA

0   10 miles

0   20 km

† Chester le Street

○ Durham

Wear

Hartlepool †

■ Escomb

WIC

WIC

Tees

D

E

Gilling †

† Whitby

Esk

I

R

A

E

CLEVELAND HILLS

M Catterick

Swale

† Lastingham

Kirkdale †

WIC

Ure

† Stonegrave

† Hovingham   ○ West Heslerton

† Ripon

✝ Crayke

○ Aldborough

Ouse

Derwent

Wharfe

✝ York

⊛ Goodmanham

Aire

Humber Estuary

DEIRA

NORTH SEA

⊛ Goodmanham

Humber

Don

Legend
— Roman roads
M Fortress
† Monastery
◢ Church
⊛ Pagan shrine
WIC Possible beach market site

A note on dates
and timelines

THE TIMELINES I have compiled to give readers some idea of a continuous chronological narrative cannot really be reliable. The numbers will never add up because there is simply not enough accurate information to be precise about individual years. No king ever reigned for an exact number of years, so there is immediately an element of smoothing over the cracks when it comes to interpreting regnal lists. Death dates are usually more accurate than birth dates because people remembered when a famous person died whereas newborn babies were rarely famous enough for the date to matter. But even death dates were subject to political manipulation and scribal error.

Bede was a pioneer of accurate dating; he did his very best to iron out the contradictions between dates calculated from regnal lists and those from entries in Easter annals, which computed dates for the celebration of Easter and often added significant or memorable events in a side column. The Nennian Chronology (known as the *Annales Cambriae* or Welsh Annals), which survives in a famous manuscript called, with typical academic dryness, Harleian 3859, must have been drawn from such an annal. Just how many of the entries were contemporary and how many were interpolated by later copyists is a much-debated point.

Then there is the problem of when years began and ended. No-one can quite agree when Bede considered the year to begin and end; so, for example, the Synod of Whitby is recorded as having taken place in AD 664; but it may belong to autumn of the year before, if Bede was using the Roman civil year from September to September in his calculations.

Great care also has to be taken in trying to match Bede, Nennius and the Anglo-Saxon Chronicle. A great deal of superb scholarship has been applied to working out which of these major sources for the Early Medieval period borrows from which other sources and, by implication, whether any of them borrowed from lost annals which can in part be reconstructed—as it can in Ireland, where most of the chronicles derived from a lost Ionan source which can be reconstructed with some confidence.

Reconciling dates from various annals has provided doctoral theses for generations of students and much progress has been made in rationalising some of the dating systems—for example, the *Annales Cambriae* seem to more or less consistently date events three years too early; and I will show in Appendix A how fraught are the dates of the earliest Bernician kings. In the end, one either accepts that the problem is insoluble or does one's best with all the caveats that come with educated guesses. One thing is for sure: after the year 616 or 617, when Æthelfrith is defeated at the Battle on the River Idle by Edwin, dates become much more reliable. It is a great tribute to Bede to say that after his death Northumbrian chronology steadily declines to the point where a hundred years or so later it is impossible to write a continuous narrative of Britain north of the Humber. Without dates, history is lost. Without the Christian church, and writing, there were no dates.

I

QUEEN'S MOVE

Soð bið swiðlost...
and gomol snoterost

Truth is the clearest thing...
and the old man
is the wisest *

THE DARK AGES ARE OBSCURE

but they were not weird. Magicians there were, to be
sure, and miracles. In the flickering firelight of the winter's hearth,
mead songs were sung of dragons and ring-givers, of fell deeds
and famine, of portents and vengeful gods. Strange omens in the
sky were thought to foretell evil times. But in a world where the
fates seemed to govern by whimsy and caprice, belief in sympathetic magic, superstition and making offerings to spirits was not
much more irrational than believing in paper money: trust is an
expedient currency. There were charms to ward off dwarfs, water-
elf disease and swarms of bees; farmers recited spells against cattle
thieves and women knew of potions to make men more—or less—
virile. Soothsayers, poets, and those who remembered the genealogies of kings were held in high regard. The past was an immense
source of wonder and inspiration, of fear and foretelling.

* The epigraphs which head each chapter are from a work generally known as Anglo-
 Saxon Maxims II, because there is something similar in the Exeter Book known
 as Maxims I. British Library Cotton MS Tiberius B.i ff. 115r-v. The translations are
 adapted from Tom Shippey's *Poems of learning and wisdom in Old English*. Cambridge: D. S. Brewer 1976.

Historians, bards and storytellers alike were tempted to improve on the truth, as they are today. But you can forget pale hands emerging from the depths of lakes offering swords of destiny to passers-by. You can forget holy grails and messianic bloodlines. Bloodlines mattered as political reality, it is true, but they were traced from the ancestral tribal gods of Britain and Germany or the last generals of the Roman Empire, not from the crucified prophet of Nazareth.

One of The Wonders of Britain, from a list written down at the beginning of the ninth century but surely recited to children and kings for hundreds of years before and after, was an ash tree that grew on the banks of the River Wye and which was said to bear apples.[1] Such poetic imaginings are easily dismissed by academics as fancy; and yet the distinguished woodland historian Oliver Rackham has recently shown that the famous tree in question must have been a very rare *Sorbus domestica*, the true service tree, which has leaves like a rowan or ash, and which bears tiny apple- or pear-shaped fruit.[2] In 1993 one was found growing on cliffs in the Wye Valley in Wales. Early Medieval Britain was full of such eccentricities—the Severn tidal bore and the hot springs of Bath fascinated just as they do now—but the people who survived the age were, above all, pragmatists and keen observers of their world. Their knowledge of weather and season, wildflower and mammal, shames the modern native. They were consummate carpenters, builders and sailors. The monk Bede, writing in the year 731, knew that the Earth was round, that seasons changed with latitude and that tides swung with the moon's phases.

Love and romance must have played their part in life, although few men writing during the three hundred years after the end of Roman Britain thought to mention them. For the most part life was about getting by, about small victories and the stresses of fretting through the long nights of winter, about successful harvests and healthy children.

The vast majority of people in the Early Medieval British Isles, as across Europe, are invisible to us. We know farmers and craftsmen existed: we have their tools and the remains of their fields. Sometimes their houses can be located and reconstructed; rather more often we find their graves. Very, very rarely we hear their names. Sometimes they encountered seafarers and travellers from strange lands who brought tales of exotic beasts and holy places. The countryside was busy with people, nearly all of them to be found working outside in their fields or woods, or fixing something in their yards; ploughing, milking, weeding, felling, threshing and mending according to the season. We have their languages: the inflexions, word-lore and rhymes of Early English, Old Welsh, Gaelic and Latin tell us much about their mental worlds. We can guess at numbers: somewhere between two and four million people living in a land which now holds fifteen to thirty times that many. Their history is recorded in our surnames and in the names of villages and hamlets. With care, their landscapes can be reconstructed and at least partly understood. The hills, rivers, coasts, some of the woods and many of their roads and boundaries can still be walked, or traced on maps. And through pale dank sea-frets of late autumn King Oswald's Holy Island of Lindisfarne still looms mysteriously across the tidal sands of Northumberland's wave-torn coast.

Oswald Iding ruled Northumbria for eight years, from AD 634 to 642. In that time he was recognised as overlord of almost all the other kingdoms of Britain: of Wessex, Mercia, Lindsey and East Anglia, of the Britons of Rheged, Strathclyde, Powys and Gwynedd, the Scots of Dál Riata and the Picts of the far North. A famed warrior, the 'Whiteblade' or 'Blessed arm' of legend, he won and lost his kingdom in battle. He was the first English king to die a Christian martyr. He is the embodiment of a romantic hero: the righteous exiled prince whose destiny is to return triumphant to reclaim his kingdom. More than that, he is almost the first Englishman (the other candidate is his Uncle Edwin) of whom a biography might be written.

We do not know what Oswald looked like except that, like all warrior kings of the age, he probably wore his hair long and sported an extravagant moustache. Even by the standards of the day his was a short and bloody rule, his end summary and brutal. In death his severed head and arms were displayed on stakes at a place which came to be known as Oswald's Tree or Oswestry and his skull, a sacred possession of Durham Cathedral, exhibits a sword-cut wide enough to accommodate three fingers. His post-mortem career was as extraordinary as his life and death had been. Many miracles were said to have taken place where he fell and in later times his relics (rather too many of them, in truth) were valued for their virtue and potency right across Europe.

Oswald's historical significance is greater even than the sum of his parts. He forged a hybrid culture of Briton, Irish, Scot and Anglo-Saxon which gave rise to a glorious age of arts and language symbolised by his foundation of the monastery on Lindisfarne and the sumptuous manuscripts later crafted there by Northumbria's monks. His political legacy was in part responsible for the Crusades and for Henry VIII's break with Rome; and for the idea that Britain is a Christian state. He was the model for Tolkien's Aragorn in *The Lord of the Rings*. If popular history needs a heroic figure from the age of Beowulf, there is no need to invent, or re-invent one. Oswald was the real thing.

There are songs and memorial inscriptions and a substantial body of poetry surviving from the so-called Dark Ages, some of which celebrate the lives and deaths of ordinary folk: *ceorl** and *dreng*, husband and wife. The written history of the period is very much concerned with kings and queens, with exiled princes, warriors and holy men; but the politics are instantly recognisable

---

* See Glossary, Appendix C, p.409.

as that of any group of competing elite families: sibling rivalry, marital rows, betrayal and plotting for dynastic advantage are all there. Oswald was the product of such rivalries. He was born in about 604 into a family where politics were played for the highest possible stakes. For no-one were those stakes higher than for his mother.

It was not easy being a seventh-century queen—particularly so in the case of Acha Yffing. She was the mother of six sons, a daughter and a stepson. Her husband was a great, perhaps the greatest, Early Medieval warlord: Æthelfrith Iding, king of Bernicia and Deira, overlord of North Britain; but in the long campaigning summer of 616 he was far away from his Northumbrian homeland, fighting British kings and massacring Christian monks on the marches of what is now Wales. Like his father and grandfather before him, he would die sword-in-hand. The British called him, with bitter irony, *Eadfered Flesaur*: Æthelfrith the Twister.

As a woman Acha is virtually invisible. Her grave is unknown. Dr Tony Wilmott, Senior Archaeologist at English Heritage, informs me that a gravestone fragment recovered from excavations at Whitby Abbey in the 1920s bears the name AHHAE+; if this is indeed the last resting-place of Oswald's mother, it suggests that she survived until the mid-650s and was influential in the founding of the royal cult of the Idings at Whitby under Oswald's brother, King Oswiu. After the death of Æthelfrith her fate is obscure, although there are two small clues. One is the destiny of her sons. The other is a name on a map. Acha, a minuscule hamlet close to the site of an ancient *dun*, or fort, lies nestled on the sheltered south coast of the Scottish island of Coll in the lee of low hills, which protect it from the pounding swell of the open Atlantic. If the place stands as a record of her residence there it is intriguing, because at least two of her sons, Oswald and Oswiu, were educated on the island of Iona, no more than twenty miles to the south, in the famous monastery of Saint Columba (more properly Colm Cille). One of those quirks that litter our hotch-potch linguistic heritage is that the Germanic name Acha is close to the word *achaidh,* which means, in Old Scots Gaelic, 'field' or 'pasture'. So the name Dun Acha might have come into being to denote a fort with or near a field. We will never know. There are, though, good reasons for believing that Acha might have journeyed far to the north and west with her children in the after-math of her husband's violent death.

Acha was the daughter of Ælle, king of the region called Deira between the rivers Humber and Tees. We can place her birth, perhaps, at one of the royal estates of the Deiran kings on the Yorkshire Wolds within three years or so of 585. It is reasonably likely that King Ælle was deposed either by Æthelric, the father of her future husband, or by Æthelfrith himself. He was the first to join the two ancient territories of Bernicia and Deira and unite them as one kingdom of the peoples north of the Humber: the *Norðanhymbrenses* or Northumbrians.* He probably did so by force. We can place their marriage close to the year 603, and the birth of Acha's first child, Oswald, a year later. Marriages of politi-cal convenience or alliance were absolutely normal in the higher reaches of Early Medieval tribal society. Sometimes the marriage cemented an alliance ensuring the future prospects of both fami-lies and kingdoms; sometimes it reflected the superiority of one king over another, who must offer a daughter to seal his submis-sion; at other times it might be designed to put an end to a feud. The male offspring of the union might be regarded as legitimate potential rulers of a united kingdom—if they survived.

The status of potential kings, nobles of sufficiently high birth, came with the Anglo-Saxon epithet 'atheling'. It was not an equivalent to the modern concept of the heir to the throne,

---

* *Rex Norðanhymbrorum,* king of the Northumbrians: the term was first applied by Bede to King Edwin in II.5 of his Ecclesiastical History of the English People (*His-toria Ecclesiastica Gentis Anglorum*), abbreviated to EH by historians.

because on the death of an Early Medieval king all bets were off; it rather encoded the right to be considered a possible legitimate king of the future—a future which must be secured by arms or the overwhelming political will of an aristocratic elite.

That a daughter might be offered, willing or unwilling, to a future husband, especially one who was complicit in the deposition or murder of her father, is unpalatable; but it does not mean that royal women lived passive lives as mere atheling breeders and cup-bearers to their lords and masters. Far from it. The seventh century is outstanding for the number of women who played active, sometimes decisive roles in the fortunes of kingdoms, both earthly and spiritual. They are not to be underestimated. They had their own queenly agendas, engineering lines of patronage for their families, acting as brakes on hot-headed husbands, as brokers of deals, as pacifiers and landowners in their own right. Moreover, they might possess great tracts of land and wield the powers of patronage that came with such wealth. For the *Beowulf* poet the ideal was 'a noble Princess, fit to be the pledge of peace between nations'. She 'would move among the younger men in the hall, stirring their spirits; she would bestow a torc often upon a warrior before she went to her seat'. But her over-riding political role was not lost to the poet: 'She is betrothed to Ingeld, this girl attired in gold… The Protector of the Danes has determined this and accounts it wisdom, the keeper of the land, thus to end all the feud and their fatal wars by means of the lady.'[3]

Politics and status notwithstanding, in the year 617, after perhaps thirteen years of marriage, Acha Yffing found herself in a peculiarly unattractive and invidious position. We cannot know if her husband was the murderer or sponsor of the murderer of her father, even if we suspect it. But we do know who killed her husband, ambushing him on the southern borders of his lands where the old Roman Ermine Street crossed the River Idle near Bawtry in South Yorkshire.

Acha had a brother: two, in fact. Little is known about one, except that he sired two famous granddaughters and caused a small war of conquest. The other was called Edwin. As adults he and Acha can hardly have remembered each other. Edwin, born a year or so after his sister, had been in exile these many years. Deiran atheling without a homeland, freelance warrior, he sought protection and patronage where he might in the kingdoms of the Britons and the Southern English. Through all this time Acha's husband took a close, almost obsessive interest in Edwin's career: he spent some years trying to have him killed. Æthelfrith's failure to bribe Edwin's protector (the king in question, Raedwald of East Anglia, was put off by some harsh words from his queen) was fatal. Edwin lived to kill his persecutor on the field of battle and claim Northumbria for himself.

Acha may have considered waiting for her brother Edwin that late summer of 617, to ascertain his intentions towards her and her sons. That she did not speaks volumes for her state of mind and the advice of her counsellors. Shakespeare's nephew-killing Richard III was a dynastic pragmatist. So was Edwin; and so was his sister. As far as one can tell, on hearing of the death of her husband she gathered her children, her personal treasures and a group of loyal warriors and fled north. Edwin, reclaiming his kingdom, would have summarily dispatched his nephews without a thought for sisterly sentiment.

The Venerable Bede, first historian of the English and an accomplished investigator, could write only sketchily in his Ecclesiastical History of the English People of events which took place fifty years or so before his own birth:

> During the whole of Edwin's reign the sons of King Æthelfrith his predecessor, together with many young nobles, were living in exile among the Irish or the Picts...[4]

Bede had good reason to know of such things, for he had distinguished correspondents on Iona, the principal monastery and school of Dál Riata (which is what he means when he talks of the Irish); for their part, the Iona chroniclers had special reasons for recording the presence of Oswald at their monastery. He was *their* Northumbrian king. Bede does not say that their mother Acha went with them. But to risk her brother's vengeance would have been suicidal. Besides, when the boot was on the other foot—that is to say, when King Edwin was himself killed—Bede records that his queen, Æthelburh, did not hesitate to take her children with her into exile among her relatives at a very safe distance: Paris, to be exact.

Pagan queens who lost their kings in war did not necessarily find themselves disposable or politically irrelevant. Their potential role as negotiators, as counsellors or as senior representatives of their dynasties might save them. A widowed queen of Kent married her stepson on his accession, although it ended ill: Bede reported with satisfaction that the offender was afflicted by madness and possessed of unclean spirits.[5] Heathen dowagers may on occasion have been executed or left to live on the equivalent of a pension—a small estate perhaps. But the arrival of Christianity in the days of Edwin and Oswald subtly changed the status of noble women. The sanctuary of the monastery came to offer a relatively comfortable, peaceful retirement, as it also became an attractive career option for royal women who were not destined to be queens.

Acha, then, probably carried her children into exile. It is not immediately clear exactly why she chose the Scottic court of Dál Riata as a place to seek sanctuary but she was not the first Northumbrian to do so and perhaps her sons could claim paternal relations at their court.* If, as historians infer, her six natural sons were baptised and educated on Iona, she would not have been able to live with them: Iona was forbidden to women. There was an island sanctuary close by in the Sound of Iona,

* See Chapter IV.

however—Eilean nam Ban—where she and her daughter Æbbe might live in the company of other women. But there is always the chance that she was given the little *dun* on the island of Coll, facing south towards Iona and only a day's hard rowing away.

Oswald went into exile with his brothers and a group of young nobles when he was twelve years old. The Anglo-Saxon Chronicle and the Bernician king-list in the *Historia Brittonum*, both compiled a couple of hundred years later, give him five brothers and a sister, Æbbe.[6] Oswald also had a half-brother, Eanfrith. He was the son referred to by Bede as living in exile among the Picts; he married a Pictish wife and his son, Talorgen, became king of that enigmatic northern nation. Of the 'uterine' brothers—those borne by Acha—one, Oswiu, is equally certain: he succeeded Oswald as king of all Northumbria and reigned for twenty-eight hugely significant years. The four others can be permed from two lists which do not quite agree but which include: Osguid, Oswudu, Oslac, Oslaph and Offa.* In a sense, it matters little whether they were all real or not; none of them appears again in the historical record. If they survived childhood fevers and early adventures on the field of battle to return to their fatherland with Oswald, no historian recorded it. But the sums add up. Oswald was born in 604, a year or so after his parents' marriage. King Æthelfrith died in about 617, which leaves a period of twelve or thirteen years in which Acha might plausibly have borne all six alliterative sons and one daughter. Oswiu, born in about 612, would fit into that sequence as the fifth child. Oswald, Oswiu and Æbbe, the survivors, lived to play their parts on the grand stage.

There is a point at which academics run out of firm ground and either retreat or risk ridicule. Leaving them behind, the sword-and-sandal historical novelist leaps into the quicksand of imagination and uncertainty, which leads sometimes to insight, often

* Oswudu has been left out of the genealogical table In Appendix B, p.408, because I suspect him to be the same as Osguid, mis-transcribed.

to fantasy. The biographer is left beached with a risk-assessment form to fill in. The academic archaeologist or historian cannot do other than project conventional wisdom on to the unknown. They must ask what so-and-so would have done following the cultural rules of the time. They must balance probabilities and err on the side of caution. They must rationalise. They will allow an average man three score years and ten; they weigh the accidents and balls-ups and offer a balanced probability.

The real world, it is all too clear, is full of irrationality, whim, chance event and unintended consequence. Who would dare to suggest without a trustworthy record that England's seventh Archbishop of Canterbury, Theodore—a contemporary of Oswald—would be a Greek from Asia Minor, plucked from his studies in Rome at the age of sixty-seven and sent to England without knowing anything of the language or culture of the English; that he would set the essential foundations for ecclesiastical organisation which survives in the modern Anglican church; and that he would die as Archbishop twenty-one years later at the age of eighty-eight? Nobody would bet on such a thing. The academic cannot project more than ordinary likelihood on to the invisible lives of historic figures; novelists must make them up.

There is no point pretending that Oswald's childhood can be reconstructed. We do not know his birthplace; we cannot say if he was healthy or happy; there is no point picturing him gazing wistfully at the island of Lindisfarne from the ramparts of his home and wondering about his destiny as an atheling. Still, his childhood has a context and a geography that are real and tangible. The seventh-century landscape of his homeland survives in its essence: you can go there and look at it for yourself.

Oswald was a child of the Bernician royal family, which, inevitably, traced its origins to the pagan god Woden. Bede believed the Bernicians to be Angles, said to have emigrated from the ancestral lands of Angeln around the base of the Jutland

Peninsula some time in the middle of the fifth century. Their seat of power lay on the coast of north Northumberland at the fortress of Bamburgh; the lands that they claimed to rule lay broadly between the River Tyne and the River Forth. The brooding, massive castle, which stands there today on a sand-blasted outcrop of the igneous Whin Sill that forms the spine of Hadrian's Wall, is a caprice of the Victorian arms manufacturer William Armstrong (1810–1900). His grand house at Cragside near Rothbury is full of technical wonders: a pioneering hydro-electricity supply, a novel passenger lift, a water-powered roasting spit, a Turkish bath. An indefatigable industrialist, like a Bernician overlord he patronised the elite artisans and craftsmen of his day. The house is sumptuous in every detail: grotesquely so, almost. His occasional guests, who over the years included the Shah of Persia, the King of Siam, the Prime Minister of China and the Prince and Princess of Wales, might well have believed themselves transported back to the golden-gabled hall of Beowulf's Heorot.

An entry in the *Historia Regum*, a work traditionally attributed to Symeon of Durham but which may preserve parts of an eighth-century chronicle, describes the fortress as it must have been in the Early Medieval period:

> The city of Bebba is extremely well-fortified, but by no means large, containing about the space of two or three fields, having one hollowed entrance ascending in a wonderful manner by steps. It has, on the summit of the hill, a church of very beautiful architecture, in which is a fair and costly shrine. In this, wrapped in a pall, lies the uncorrupted right hand of St Oswald, king, as Bede the historian of this nation relates. There is on the west and highest point of this citadel, a well, excavated with extraordinary labour, sweet to drink and very pure to the sight.*

The entrance at the north-west corner of the castle, known as St Oswald's Gate, survives. The original wooden palisade of the British fortress, later replaced by a stone rampart and recorded in

---

* *Historia Regum* (*HR*) sub anno 774. Symeon's authorship of the *Historia Regum* is no longer acceptable. Hunter-Blair 1964.

the Anglo-Saxon Chronicle 'E' version under the year 547, must lie beneath medieval and later walls. The church of St Peter, mentioned by Bede, likely stood on the site of the present church at the east corner of the citadel. The great hall, which must have crowned the height of the stronghold, probably lay to the east of the medieval keep. A fragment of a carved stone chair discovered in the nineteenth century is likely to be part of the original throne of the Bernician kings, their 'seat of paternal antiquity'.*

That real people lived and died here is all too evident from recent excavations of an Early Medieval cemetery just to the south-east among the sand dunes that periodically swallow the coastline here. The evocatively named Bowl Hole, first revealed by chance after a great storm in 1816, has yielded more than a hundred graves dating to the century either side of Oswald's birth.[7] These were well-fed people who had grown up not at Bamburgh itself but apparently all over Bernicia; their teeth had munched on rich food, although many suffered childhood stress—scarlet fever, perhaps. Some of the men appear to have been buried with parcels of food, perhaps from their funeral feasts. Only one or two had suffered weapon injuries, which would tell of great deeds in battle; maybe the real warriors never made it home to be buried here. There is no evidence for the interment of kings; there is a royal cemetery somewhere in Bamburgh that still awaits discovery when the sands shift one more fateful time. What is so fascinating is the range of styles of burial at the Bowl Hole: some in stone-lined cists (a thoroughly British Christian rite), some flexed on their sides, some lying supine and others prone, on their faces. Not all of them were born locally, either: at least one, judging by the chemical traces left in his teeth, was born on the west coast of Scotland—on Iona, perhaps.[8] Was he a companion of Oswald?

The combination of rocky citadel, imposing location and magnificent buildings, together with the technical marvel of the

* See Chapter VII.

well (recently excavated and found to be rock-cut to an extraordinary depth of one hundred and forty-four feet) reflected the power and pretensions of the Bernician kings.[9] No child growing up there could fail to have his or her imagination stirred by such a back yard, standing indomitable against the batterings of the North Sea and all would-be invaders.

Those whose imaginations struggle with black and white plans of walls and post-holes must visit Bede's World in Jarrow where, in the shadow of Bede's own monastic church, cows, geese and pigs with convincing Dark Age grunts and smells provide the backdrop for halls and sunken huts, which would have been the entirely familiar playgrounds of the children of Æthelfrith and Acha. Literary support for the mentality and motivations of those who used them comes from the greatest early Anglo-Saxon poem, *Beowulf*; and no less a critic than the scholar J. R. R. Tolkien made the explicit link between *Beowulf* and Oswald as long ago as 1936.[10] So, if we cannot portray Oswald physically as an individual, we can at least picture his milieu and his circumstances. For a start, he was the oldest of his several natural brothers but he had a half-brother who was probably somewhat older than him—perhaps twenty years older.*

Father and half-brother spent much of the year campaigning in foreign lands for glory and the rewards of conquest. King Æthelfrith, we know, fought against the Scots of Dál Riata, the British of the Forth and of Gwynedd and the fabled King Urien of Rheged; he was a busy warlord. At other times the peripatetic Bernician kings progressed through their estates, consuming the fruits of tribute rendered from the fertile Northumbrian soil. Several of these estates can be reconstructed in outline. Their

---

* The dynamics of such families haven't changed much; my own mother was one of eleven and the second-hand mythology of that Midlands family growing up during the Second World War is enough to fill the imagination with plenty of food for thought.

principal palace site, Yeavering (Bede's *Ad Gefrin*), which lay at the foot of an imposing Iron Age hill fort and 'holy mountain' on the northern edge of the Cheviot Hills, was brilliantly excavated in the 1950s and early 1960s. The site of Old Yeavering in the dale of the River Glen is a place to pause and absorb a sense of history and myth. Glendale now is a forgotten corner of England, nestled within sight of the Scottish border in a dramatic natural amphitheatre. But it has featured in more than its fair share of history, as a strategic corridor for armies entering or leaving northern England and a bottleneck ripe for ambush. Here in 1513 an English army inflicted a terrible defeat on the Scots at Flodden Field; just to the east, below Humbleton Hill, is the site of another Anglo-Scottish conflict, immortalised in Shakespeare's *Henry IV* as the place from where noble, soil-stained Sir Walter Blunt brought news of Earl Douglas's discomfiture and Harry 'Hotspur' Percy's capture of the Earl of Fife: a 'gallant prize'.[11] Earlier, almost lost in the mists of time, the *Annales Cambriae* record the River 'Glein' as the site of the first of Arthur's legendary twelve battles.

In the days of Kings Æthelfrith, Edwin and Oswald the greatest architectural feats since the end of the Roman Empire stood here as symbols of royal power: a palace complex, noble halls of great technical complexity and grandeur and, wonder of wonders, a grandstand unique in its period. In a pagan temple offerings were made to the gods and tribal totems of the Bernicians; immense herds of cattle, the surplus wealth of the land and the tributary tax of subject kingdoms were corralled and counted; and the family of Æthelfrith could take comfort from the knowledge that the most powerful warlord in early Britain was unchallenged by any other earthly force. So complacent were the Bernician kings in their golden hall that no defences were ever constructed at Yeavering, a place of tribal assembly, judgement and ritual since time out of mind.

During great festivals, the cream of Northumbrian society gathered in the mead halls of Bamburgh, Yeavering or one of the other royal *vills*.* Mead flowed, tall tales grew taller, gifts of rings and torcs were made, alliances cemented or broken, troths plighted and promises made and regretted. Small boys being small boys, no doubt conversations were overheard which were meant to be private and neglected cups were drained by aspiring warriors who should have been in bed.

One wonders what status Oswald enjoyed with his father and half-brother. His moral authority among younger siblings was one thing, but half-siblings are another; jealousies are easily fostered. Anglo-Saxon warlords did not name heirs; kings were chosen by the political elite from a pool of athelings, those whose blood and personal attributes entitled them to be considered; those who survived. In his time Eanfrith would make one disastrous bid for the kingdom of Northumbria; Oswald would wait his turn. His relationship with his father was terminated when he was twelve. Oswald would not see his home or native land again until he was twenty-nine.

---

* *Villa regia*: a royal estate. See Colgrave and Mynors 1969, 188. See also Glossary, Appendix C, p.415.

oyster bars and the welcoming hotels of Inveraray. From there the road either hugs the sea loch contours of Knapdale towards Kilmartin and Dunadd, or tackles another pass to negotiate Glen Array, winding around the top of Loch Awe before the descent to Oban, the principal port on the west coast. Even in a modern car on modern roads one has a sense of journeying into another world, of time and history passing by.

Travel in the seventh century was a rather different matter: such a route would expose the traveller to unreasonable danger and hardship and it would take for ever. The first principle to grasp here is that water, for all the dangers of shipwreck and piracy and the vagaries of wind and wave, was a faster and more secure medium on which to travel than land. The second is to understand that Britain's coasts and her hundreds of islands were not isolated by the sea; they were connected by it. It is wrong to think of the North Sea as a separator; in the Dark Ages and before it was a natural trading basin. The same goes for the Atlantic coasts of Wales, Cornwall and southern Ireland and for the northern waters of Man, Solway and the Western Isles: these were archipelagic communities linked by sophisticated networks of trade, information exchange, kinship and geopolitics. One might, in the same sense, think of the Roman road system in Britain as providing links between sea ports just as much as joining all the towns and villages of the mainland. When a Frankish bishop called Arculf turned up at Iona in the late seventh century bearing tales from the Holy Land, he arrived by sea—blown off course, as it happened, but no-one was particularly surprised.[12] For one thing, he had self-evidently been sent by the providential whim of the Almighty. For another, seafarers from the Mediterranean were by no means unknown in these waters. Tableware, amphorae and glass from as far away as Constantinople turn up in archaeological sites on the Atlantic coast in regular—if small—numbers. This was a connected world, the more so after Oswald's reign when a

Christian elite shared a common language and culture.

The Roman road system survived substantially into Oswald's day. The fact that one can still drive along much of it should be evidence enough, but a cursory analysis of Early Medieval warfare shows that many military engagements took place on or near Roman roads, especially where they crossed major rivers. Fast-moving armies used them as highways. There is even some evidence that parts of the network were maintained by royal edict: kings, queens and the more pompous bishops liked to travel in chariots when they could, for dignity's sake. There were many hundreds of miles of ancient native trails too, used for driving cattle and sheep between farmstead and summer pasture, linking estates and strongholds, rivers, hills and coast; these are sometimes a little harder to trace on the ground but there is little doubt that they existed.

In Bernicia, with its striking north–south chains of hills and east–west river systems, the Tyne–Solway gap was the natural link between east and west coasts. Hadrian's Wall, its accompanying military road, the Stanegate, and deep, wide tidal rivers at both ends provided fast access between the North Sea ports and forts at Tynemouth and the mouth of the rivers Irthing, Esk and Eden at the head of the Solway Firth near Carlisle (Roman *Luguvalio*). From Solway to Argyll by sea was a journey of a few days by boat, starting with some hard rowing into the prevailing south-westerlies, followed by a rapid run north and west from the Mull of Galloway with the wind on the port beam.

Any overland journey undertaken fourteen hundred years ago was complicated not just by hilly, wooded and riverine obstructions, but also by the politics of its territories. Bernicia, very roughly, seems at the end of King Æthelfrith's reign to have encompassed the lands between Tyne and Forth: modern Northumberland, Berwickshire and East Lothian. The latter, the ancestral lands of the ancient tribe of Gododdin, he annexed

around the year 600. Æthelfrith seems also to have been recognised as overlord by the Britons west of the Pennines in the
obscure but poetically resonant kingdom of Rheged. North-east
of Rheged and west of Gododdin there is a hole in our knowledge of the territorial politics but Ayrshire and the Clyde Valley
were held at this period by another group of Britons, the kings
of Strathclyde, whose principal fortress was *Alcluith*, Dumbarton
Rock on the north bank of the Clyde estuary. Bernicia and the
Strathclyde Britons were old, implacable enemies.

It is very difficult to say how passage through these lands might
have been negotiated in the weeks and months after Æthelfrith's
fall. On the death of a king his writ and rule, his lines of patronage, his alliances and bonds collapsed like a captain's authority on
a sinking ship. Gododdin and Rheged may have regarded their
tributary status as having dissolved. Uncertainty and apprehen-
sion would haunt the golden halls. Harbouring a new king's enemies might be asking for trouble; on the other hand, there might
be personal loyalties, historical friendships, markers to be cashed
in. Then again, tributary nations expected and received protection from their overkings and the death of a king could expose
a tribute nation to all sorts of predations. Power vacuums always
create political instability. Rheged without Æthelfrith might be
vulnerable to attack from the Britons of Wales and Strathclyde,
the Scots of Dál Riata and from pirate attacks launched across the
Irish Sea.

There is an old saying that you need to be careful how you
treat people on the way up in case you meet them again on the
way down. The opposite works too: invest in an atheling when he
is young and weak and it might pay off in the long term. Besides,
there seems to have been a sort of code of hospitality that enabled noble and royal refugees to turn up at a king's court and
plead their case for protection. Even so, there are sufficient cases
of such supplicants being killed out of hand or turned over for

bribes to warn that refugees have never held very strong cards. Æthelfrith's widow Queen Acha, her retainers, a band of young warrior-nobles and her children might have chanced their arm in Rheged, but a pragmatic British court would encourage them to move on. It is hard to believe that they would have risked the historic enmity of the court at Dumbarton Rock.

Ultimately, the children of Æthelfrith were received at the court of King Eochaid Buide of Dál Riata, whose ceremonial seat was a tiny rocky fortress at Dunadd, near the modern village of Kilmartin at the top of the Kintyre Peninsula in Argyll. The Dál Riatan Scots were Ulstermen who had carved out a small territory on the west coast of Caledonia in the fifth century. They maintained their historic links with the great royal houses of the northern Irish and by the end of the sixth century Dál Riata held parts of Ulster tributary. Their royal house, the Cenél Gabráin, was Christian; its historical significance lies in its gift of the island of Iona to Columba in the year 565.

Today, the site of the greatest monastery of the period is reached by many thousands of tourists and latter-day pilgrims from Fionnphort (pronounced Finnafort) after a long, sometimes hair-raising passage along the single-track roads of the Isle of Mull. It is only in the context of the sea, in placing the island at its maritime heart, that one can understand Iona's geopolitical significance. Mull is one of the largest of the Scottish islands, with the soaring, cloud-wreathed step-pyramid of Ben More dominating its stream-torn boggy landscape. From Oban on the mainland it is a mere forty-minute Calmac ferry crossing to Craignure at the opposite end of Mull from Iona. At Fionnphort sleek air-conditioned coaches disgorge passengers; cars packed with children and camping equipment pull up, realising suddenly that they have reached the end of the island—practically the end of the old world, for there is almost no more land between here and the coast of Labrador three thousand miles away. There is a shop, a pub and a small visitors' centre, an RNLI second-hand bookshop and a tiny ticket office, which handles the disproportionately large number of foot passengers wishing to cross the Sound to Iona. No tourists' cars or coaches may cross to the island, as if to protect it from being sullied by the modern world.

There is no dock to speak of. The pilgrim is confronted with a concrete ramp and a breathtaking view of the medieval abbey set against the granite rump of Dun I (I from the original *Hii*). From a mile away across the clear turquoise waters of the Sound you watch the ferry rounding the sand bar which almost divides the Sound in two, its wake bowing in the strong current that runs north here, choppy white wave-crests bashing rhythmically against its side. The ferry's arrival at Fionnphort is announced by the crunch and grind of its hull engaging the ramp, where it sticks, swaying, diesel engines panting to keep it steady in the swell. It is an odd sort of anti-climax for pilgrims who have travelled halfway around the globe to visit one of the Christian world's holiest and most evocative sites.

It is nearly always windy on Iona and the seas are notorious. Two miles to the south Robert Louis Stevenson shipwrecked his young *Kidnapped* hero David Balfour on the tidal island of Erraid. The seas are littered with wrecks. Iona's monks were consummate sailors, though: Iona lay at the centre of their world. The monasteries and princely strongholds of Ireland, of Skye and Jura, of the Hebrides and Kintyre, of the Picts of the Great Glen all lay within easy reach. Those modern visitors dedicated enough to have read something of Colm Cille might hold firmly in their hand as they step on to the ferry a copy of Adomnán's Life of Saint Columba (*Vita Columbae*). They might even hold it open at the page on which Adomnán, himself an abbot of Iona in the time when Oswald's nephew was king of Northumbria, describes shouts being heard by the monks on the island from their brothers at Fionnphort for a boat to be sent to fetch them. They must have had loud voices, the monks, and none louder than Colm Cille, whose call 'could be heard sometimes as much as half a mile away, sometimes even a mile, for it was uplifted unlike any other'.[13]

As late as the nineteenth century those wishing to cross would either hail a boatman on the other side if it was a still day, or light a beacon using heather to make thick smoke.[14] A similar reply confirmed receipt of the call. The location of his fire gave each boatman a distinct call sign, so to speak. The monks probably used a similar system thirteen hundred years before. Sometimes the weather was so bad that for days on end the Sound could not be crossed unless Colm Cille called for heavenly intercession, in which case his monks would set out, in fear of their lives and perhaps in greater fear of incurring their abbot's displeasure. They were hard men; he was harder.

It was into the hands of this man's successors that Acha Yffing entrusted the futures of her sons. There can be no doubting Oswald's significance to the community of Iona: a hundred years after Colm Cille's death, the first of scores of miracles attributed to him by Adomnán in the Life of Columba was his ghostly appearance in Oswald's tent the night before the Battle of Heavenfield. That Oswald himself, in his first years as king, told the story to its abbot in person strongly suggests that the significance and empathy was mutual.

On the death of Æthelfrith Iding, Bernicia, its peasants, slaves, *drengs* and remaining thanes and *ealdormen*, its royal estates and great halls, were left to the disposal of a new king in the north, Acha's brother, Edwin Yffing of Deira. He must now impose his will and military might to keep the two kingdoms united and reconquer the lands won and lost by his predecessor. The Idings of Bernicia were now no more than strangers in a foreign land; their fates lay in the hands of kings who, on the face of it, can have had no obligations towards them. Such was the legacy of Æthelfrith, first of the Bernician kings to unite his lands with Deira.

Æthelfrith, son of Æthelric, son of Ida, son of Eobba, was a pagan in a pagan world. The bare factual bones of his career are few but they resonate with the sound of hammer on anvil. This was no ordinary man. For Bede he was *rex fortissimus et gloriae cupidissmus* (a very brave king and most eager for glory), forgiven his heathenism because he was an instrument of divine retribution, striking down the impious. The ninth-century British historian known as Nennius used the native Brythonic epithet *Flesaur* (from the Latin *flexus*): Æthelfrith the Twister. Æthelfrith had form as far as the British were concerned.

He emerges from the fuzzy boundary between myth and historical reality in the last quarter of the sixth century. Even the basic outline of the dates of his predecessors is a matter of long-nurtured debate: our few available sources seem to contradict each other; the numbers, on the face of it, simply don't add up. I have made my own attempt to untangle these chronological knots and I offer a solution; but this is tricky stuff, so I have confined it to an essay called 'The Bernician king-list problem' at the end of this book, graphically summarised in the genealogy of the Bernician royal house.*

Suffice it to say that Æthelfrith was a grandson of Ida, the legendary founding warlord of Bernicia. Ida established himself, probably at the rocky coastal fortress of Bamburgh, some time in the late 550s. No-one has been able to explain where he came from. If the Angles had come from across the North Sea a hundred years before, where had they been in the meantime?† Four of Ida's sons reigned after him, but their hold on Bernicia

* Appendices A and B, pp. 395–409.
† See p.189 for one possibility.

was tenuous for the best part of half a century. In the mid-580s, perhaps, a coalition of British forces from across the North attempted to dislodge the Idings, and to drive them back into the sea whence they came. Æthelric, father of Æthelfrith, may have been the intended victim of this campaign but he survived, apparently in exile, to fight another day. The culmination of the campaign was a siege in which his brother and successor Theodoric was blockaded with his forces on the island of Lindisfarne, called by the British *Metcaud*.*

Whatever the precise sequence and causes of the campaign which ended at Lindisfarne, it was a British disaster. The senior British warlord, the fabled Urien of Rheged, was betrayed and the alliance collapsed. Only once more did the northern British take on the growing might of Bernicia, as Theodoric and successive Bernician kings gradually established their hold over the lands between the Tyne and Tweed.

The greatest early poem in Old Welsh is Aneirin's *Y Gododdin*. It is a grand oral lament, written down long after its form was polished in firelit song, for the last great expedition of the northern British against the English. The hopeless campaign it celebrates seems to have been launched some time after the Lindisfarne siege, on the Deiran stronghold of *Catræth* (Latin *Cataractonum*, modern Catterick), whose Roman ramparts are shamelessly bisected by the line of the A1 dual carriageway where it crosses the River Swale in North Yorkshire. The assault is otherwise unrecorded in history. The names of the defenders are unknown and irrelevant to the poet who, portraying himself as the only survivor out of an army of three hundred and three score and three warriors tells a tale of feasting and drink, of boasting, of Dutch courage, of noble failure and of black ravens glutting themselves on the bodies of fallen heroes…

* See Appendix A, p.395.

The men went to Catræth; they were renowned;
Wine and mead from golden cups was their beverage;
That year was to them of exalted solemnity;

Three warriors and three score and three hundred,
wearing the golden torques.

Of those who hurried forth after the excess of revelling,
But three escaped by the prowess of the gashing sword,
The two war-dogs of Aeron, and Cenon the dauntless,
And myself from the spilling of my blood, the reward of my
sacred song.*

The raid was planned by Mynyddog Mwynfawr, Lord of *Din Eidyn*, or Edinburgh. The poet relates that it took him a whole year to rouse the passions of his warriors for one last assault on Bernicia's growing threat to the south; this may be a poetic metaphor for the time it took him to assemble the forces of other British kingdoms: Picts, Britons of Strathclyde and of North Wales (though conspicuously not of Rheged), after the failure of the Lindisfarne assault. Its destination might have been chosen from a romantic idea of revenge, because *Catræth* had been the eastern outpost of Urien's lordship. With Urien betrayed and his confederacy shattered, the English must have overrun the ancient Roman fort and now held it, defiant, against whatever depleted forces the North Britons could muster. But there may also have been a more pragmatic context. Catterick lies at the mouth of Swaledale, a location of supreme strategic value in controlling the northern Vale of York and the Swale–Tees borderlands between Deira and Bernicia. Archaeologist Andrew Fleming has convincingly argued that a series of great earthworks near Reeth, blocking the dale a few miles upstream from Catterick,

---

* *Y Gododdin* stanza XXI; Skene translation, 1868. Three hundred and three score and three might be a Brythonic trope, a symbolic number. It might also reflect very roughly the size of an army consisting of that number of noble warriors, each with his retinue.

must reflect attempts by the British of Rheged to hold that part of the Pennines against the English, preventing penetration of their heartlands from the east.[15] If this is right, the great raid of ϒ *Gododdin* may have been intended as a relieving counterpunch by Rheged's allies. Aneirin was not a historian but a poet; one must treat the details of the verse with extreme caution partly because of the inherent poetic obligation to elegise and exaggerate but also because later accretions and 'improvements' are hard to disentangle from whatever the original work sounded like. But Aneirin's reference to the warriors of Lloegr, that is to say the English, being drawn from a united Bernicia and Deira, does seem genuine. This ought to confine the date of the raid to a time when Deiran and Bernician warbands were allied, but before the kingdoms were united in about 604. The late 580s fits that bill.

The English protagonists at *Catræth* can be identified as Æthelfrith and his father. Æthelric's reign in Bernicia ended in 584 but he appears in the Anglo-Saxon Chronicle under the entry for 588 as the successor to King Ælle of Deira, reigning there for five years. I suggest that either the Bernician father-and-son deposed Ælle and then fought the British at *Catræth*; or conversely. Either way it must have been by force of arms and either way, if my resolution of the king-list problem is right, Æthelric was succeeded by Æthelfrith in Deira, not in his homeland of Bernicia, in about 592.

After twelve years of ruling Deira, that is in about 604, Æthelfrith was strong enough to attempt to reclaim the kingdom lost or given up by his father and unite all the English beyond the Humber. He accomplished this by a judicious combination of battle and marriage. The battle was waged on him by an external aggressor, King Áedán mac Gabráin of Dál Riata. Like the British confederacy before him, Áedán seems to have decided on a pre-emptive strike against the growing threat posed by the northern English. The place where the two armies met in about the year

604 was so famous that it could be identified as late as Bede's day in the early eighth century. Degsastan, that is, Degsa's stone, was sufficiently well known that Bede did not feel the need to tell his readers where it was. It is most annoying. Various locations have been put forward over the years; there is no absolute consensus, although Dawston Rigg in Liddesdale, in the grimly bleak Debatable Lands of the western Anglo-Scottish border, is the most favoured candidate. This is well outside Dál Riatan territory, in the lands that bordered Strathclyde and Rheged. The assault was carried out overland with or without the permission of the king of Strathclyde, or conducted from a sea-borne landing on the Solway Firth. It is possible that Strathclyde was, at this time, subject to Dál Riata, in which case her support would have been obligatory. Strathclyde might equally have sought the intervention of Dál Riata against her English enemies. Whichever was the case, the Scots came mob-handed and fought 'with an immensely strong army' that may have included contingents from the Irish mainland as well as, it seems, aspiring Bernician athelings. But Æthelfrith was ready for them. As Bede recorded, the whole host were cut to pieces and fled with few survivors: 'From that time no Irish king in Britain has dared to make war on the English race…'[16] Æthelfrith's victory over the kings of northern Britain was now complete but for the loss of his brother Theobald who fell at Degsastan with his entire warband. Áedán survived and ruled for another three years, but so politically weakened that one can date the decline of Dál Riata's fortunes from this time: their kings must now regard themselves as subject to Bernician overlordship. It was Áedán's son Eochaid who accepted the sons of Æthelfrith, his father's enemy, into his court in 617, which lends the events of that year a certain piquancy.

Something needs to be said about Áedán's allies at Degsastan. A version of the Anglo-Saxon Chronicle known as the 'E' recension seems to preserve an independent source for northern affairs, which was unknown to either Bede or Nennius. In its entry for 603 (more likely 604) it notes that Hering son of Hussa 'led the host thither'; that is to say, Hering led the Dál Riatan army at Degsastan. If we accept this, we ought to associate Hering son of Hussa with the Hussa who was the last on the Nennian king-list to rule the Bernicians before Æthelfrith. In my revised chronology, Hussa died (or was perhaps overthrown) in the year of Degsastan, to be replaced by Æthelfrith. Here, then, is a precedent for the athelings of Bernicia seeking the patronage of the kings of Dál Riata; and for those kings supporting exiled Bernician athelings in their pretensions to reclaim their kingdom. Hering had ample motive, as Oswald would later, for allying himself with Dál Riata in order to recover his father's kingdom and perhaps avenge his death at his cousin's hands. We might even suggest that Hussa's death precipitated Æthelfrith's bid to unite the kingdom and that Hering, wishing to succeed his father, instigated or encouraged Áedán's pre-emptive strike to prevent it.

The English triumph at Degsastan enabled Æthelfrith, finally, to consolidate his position as overlord of northern Britain. The Deiran nobility could not now deny his claim to a Northumbrian imperium. The Northern History* dates his unification of the two kingdoms to the year after Degsastan, and that this was the year in which he married Acha, daughter of Ælle of Deira, links these events with near certainty. With Scots, British and Picts all subdued and rendered tribute, Æthelfrith's claim to overlordship of all the lands north of the River Humber was irresistible. Now his Deiran wife would bear sons fit to rule all the English north of the Humber. Her brother Edwin, the Deiran atheling, must already have been in exile for many years among the Britons and

---

* Part of the British Historical Miscellany (Harleian MS3589) compiled by the ninth-century British historian often referred to as Nennius. *Historia Brittonum* (*HB*), which includes the Northern History and the Kentish Chronicle, is the major element; but it also includes the Welsh Annals and The Wonders of Britain.

southern English but would yet make his own bid for that throne.

Warrior kings like Æthelfrith had as much to gain materially from warfare as they did politically. Thanks to the sensational discovery of a hoard of battle-booty in a field near Lichfield in Staffordshire in 2009, we now have an idea of just what the spoils of Dark Age warfare looked like. Here are more than seventeen hundred objects of gold and silver, precious stones, millefiori and cloisonné, the peak of Early Medieval craftsmanship, equal in artistry to almost anything from the Sutton Hoo ship burial. Many of them are tiny: the total weight of metal and other objects is less than thirteen pounds; but even in their fractured state they are objects of the most marvellous beauty. This is a military assemblage: almost all the items come from equipment worn in battle or parade by a warrior elite, such as buckle and sword fittings, helmet cheek-pieces and the like. There are no domestic items at all. These are not trophies to be displayed or passed on as gifts. Those—the swords of conquered heroes, the mail shirts, the brooches and severed heads—had already been distributed among a victorious army. This is scrap metal, to be melted down and recycled by a king's smiths, reworked as rings and new military fittings which the king might dispense as gift, exchange or reward.

Three items show that at least some of the participants in the battle or battles from which the hoard came were Christian. Two are crosses of marvellous workmanship, made of thin sheets of Byzantine gold and Indian garnets, both folded as if to compress them. The other is a strip of gold on which the following inscription was written in Latin in an uncial form which dates from somewhere between the middle of the seventh and the end of the eighth century:

> Rise up, Lord; may Your enemies be scattered and those who hate You be driven from Your face[17]

The text is taken from the Old Testament, *Numbers* 10:35, and also appears in *Psalm 68:1*.[18] The sentiment could not be clearer: the power of the new Christian god of war was being invoked in the crushing of his enemies. But it could just as well apply to Woden, the Germanic god of war and tribal progenitor of the Idings. It might be Æthelfrith's or Oswald's motto. It does not look as if, on this occasion, it was effective.

From its location six miles south of the Mercian heartland of Lichfield, it seems as if the hoard was dumped or concealed after a bloody encounter that resulted in Mercian victory, perhaps over the Northumbrians; the research is ongoing. It had already been stripped of its lesser metals in a workshop, perhaps the royal Mercian workshops at Lichfield. Conceivably, though, the original owner of the material was Æthelfrith's son Oswiu who, we know, was forced to surrender a great quantity of treasure in the 650s to the pagan Mercian warlord Penda, in whose territories the hoard was buried or hidden before lying there vainly awaiting the return of its owner for fourteen hundred years.

If Æthelfrith took such a hoard away from the field of Degsastan, he was not careless enough to lose it. It would have been taken to his great stronghold at Bamburgh, sorted, every item stripped down to its metallic, stone or glass components and reworked by the finest smiths of the day, perhaps at the workshops recently excavated at Lanton Quarry in Glendale.* All the warriors who fought for him would have been rewarded with gifts; those who had proved themselves worthy and now wished to marry would be endowed with lands 'suitable to their rank' from the estates of the defeated and the dead; yet more aspiring Beowulfs would be attracted to Æthelfrith's battle-standard. This earthly glory was the life-blood of the pagan warlord, his burial place unknown, his long-sung heroism lost in the values of a new world dawning.

---

* See below, Chapter XI.

Behind all this lay Northumbria's other wealth: her farmlands and rivers, forests and lakes, her lush upland pastures where thousands of cattle and sheep grazed during the summer months. The fruits of this landed wealth were consumed by its peripatetic king and his growing retinue; they were also invested in the greatest palace of the period at Yeavering, where acres of trees were felled, hauled and shaped to build the greatest of halls.

For a decade after the great battle at Degsastan, Æthelfrith's expansionist activities, if any, are invisible. What was he doing in these years? Bede did not often record the secular activities of kings unless it affected his providential view of history; unless it bore on his narrative of the ultimate triumph of the Church of Rome. Æthelfrith yet had his part to play in that narrative, a part so important to Bede that he deployed it to end the first book of his Ecclesiastical History.

Timeline: AD 547 to 604

ABBREVIATIONS

EH—Bede's Ecclesiastical History
HB—Nennius's *Historia Brittonum*
AC—*Annales Cambriae* or Welsh Annals
incorporated into Nennius
ASC—Anglo-Saxon Chronicle
AU—Annals of Ulster

Names of battles are shown in **bold**

547   Traditional date of Ida's arrival at Bamburgh (ASC; EH).

—?Death of Maelgwyn, king of Gwynedd in plague (*AC*).

552   **Battle of Seaorburgh** (Old Sarum); Cynric of Wessex beats Britons (ASC).

556   **Battle at Beranburgh** (Barbury Castle); defeat of British by West Saxons (ASC).

559   Picts under Bruide mac Maelchon drive Dál Riata Scots back to Dunadd. Gabrán killed. Succeeded by Conall mac Comgaill.

560   Revised date for the beginning of Ida's hegemony as he seizes kingdom of Bernicia and founds Iding dynasty (to ?572).

—?Ælle son of Yffi succeeds to Deira (ASC).

—Probable date of death of King Gabrán of Dál Riata.

563   Colm Cille exiled from Ulster and lands in Iona (*AC*).

565   Founding of monastery at Iona (ASC).

571   **Battle at Bedcanford** (N. of Luton) implies surviving British presence (ASC).

572   ?Succession of Glappa/Adda to Bernicia.

573   **Battle of Arfderydd** (Arthuret in Cumbria) between British sub-kings in Rheged; legendary madness of Merlin (*AC*; probably should be 576).

574   Death of King Conall of Dál Riata. Succession of Áedán mac Gabráin to Dál Riata after a vision by Colm Cille of Iona.

575   Conference of Druim Cett (modern Limavady) in Ulster between Áedán mac Gabráin and Aed mac Ainmerech confirms

independence of Scottic Dál Riata from the Irish kingdoms. Possibly mediated by Colm Cille (AU).

577   **Battle of Deorham**; Ceawlin's victory over the British expands (or re-expands) Wessex to include Cirencester, Gloucester and Bath (ASC).

580   Áedán mac Gabráin fights sea war against Picts or Irish near Orkney.

      —Possible accession of Æthelric in Bernicia.

582–3   Áedán mac Gabráin fights battle against either Man or Manau of Gododdin.

584   Death of Bruide mac Maelchon, king of the Picts.

      —**Battle of Fethanleag**: Ceawlin and Cutha (Wessex) fight against the Britons (ASC).

      —Possible deposition of Æthelric; accession of Theodoric; British war.

586   Birth of Edwin of Deira.

586–8   ?**Siege of Lindisfarne** by British confederacy.

      —Possible date of **Battle of Catræth**: defeat of Rheged and Gododdin warband by combined Deiran/Bernician army.

588   Ælle of Deira dies (*AC*), ?deposed by Æthelric, who succeeds him in Deira.

588–90   Gregory the Great becomes pope.

590+?   Possible date of Dál Riatan **Battle against Miathi**: two of Áedán mac Gabráin's sons killed.

591   ?Accession of Freodwald to Bernicia.

592   Death of Ceawlin of Wessex (overlord of southern English).

592/3   ?Death of Æthelric; succession of Æthelfrith to Deira.

597   Death of Colm Cille at Iona; succeeded by Baithne as abbot.

      —Arrival of St Augustine's Christian mission to Kent (EH, ASC and others).

      —?Death of Freodwald; accession of Hussa to Bernicia.

598   Possible date of **Battle of Circenn** (unknown location) between Áedán mac Gabráin and Angles (of ?Northumbria) in which two more sons of Áedán die.

601   Paulinus is sent by Pope Gregory to accompany Mellitus to Britain; brings pallium for Augustine.

604   Æthelfrith defeats Dál Riata at the **Battle of Degsastan** as culmination of long-running war. Dál Riata now tributary to Northumbria.

—Death of Hussa; Deira and Bernicia united as single kingdom when Æthelfrith marries Acha of Deira.

—?Edwin exiled in Gwynedd (Reginald of Durham; Welsh Triads).

—Augustine meets British bishops at Augustine's Oak in Hwicce; Synod held at Bangor-on-Dee by British bishops and 'wise men'.

—Oswald, son of Æthelfrith and Acha, born.

—Death of Pope Gregory the Great.

—?Death of Augustine (before 610); succeeded at Canterbury by Laurence (to 619).

—Sæberht ruling East Saxons from London; converts to Christianity (EH V.24).

—?King Æthelberht of Kent founds St Paul's in London.

III

PRIDE AND PREJUDICE

Leoht sceal wið þystrum...
fyrd wið fyrde

*Light against darkness...
army against army*

THE REAL DARK AGE IN

British history, the yawning gap in its continuous narrative history, can be found in Book I of Bede's Ecclesiastical History, between Chapter 21, in which the fifth-century Gaulish bishop Germanus puts down a heresy among British Christians, and Chapter 23 which opens with events in 582. Germanus's visit is generally dated to the year 429 and marks an early attempt by Rome to impose orthodoxy on the British church.* The intervening Chapter 22 covers about a hundred and thirty years in seventeen lines. Bede had nothing to fill them with except the most generalised account, copied almost verbatim from the work of Gildas,† of a series of civil wars followed by a licentious, impious peace among the Britons. Bede's contempt for the indigenous inhabitants is all too clear:

---

* The heresy in question was inspired by the writing of a British monk, Pelagius, who preached against the teachings of St Augustine of Hippo. Pelagius argued that moral perfection could be attained via man's free will without the intervention of divine grace; such ideas were regarded as dangerously egalitarian.

† Gildas: *De Excidio et Conquestu Britanniae*, a letter of complaint to the British clergy and 'five tyrants', written by a clergyman some time between 490 and 540.

To other unspeakable crimes, which Gildas their own historian describes in doleful words, was added this crime, that they never preached the faith to the Saxons or the Angles who inhabited Britain with them. Nevertheless God in His goodness did not reject the people whom he foreknew, but He had appointed much worthier heralds of the truth to bring this people to the faith.*

So far as Bede was concerned the British, nominally Christians since the reign of Constantine the Great in the early fourth century, had failed as instruments of God's providential design. They had cast out the civilising administrators of Rome, fatally opened the island to the predations of the heathen; had indulged in civil war, tyranny and heresy. They had failed in their Christian duty to evangelise among the Germanic immigrants. Now, at the beginning of what became the continuous narrative history of the island, the heathen English were to be offered salvation direct from the mother church in Rome. English history proper, then, begins with 'the Conversion'.

The underlying purpose of Bede's history was to account for the triumph of the Roman church among His chosen people and in particular to show how good kings had been rewarded and bad kings punished by divine will. To this end, the last eleven chapters of the first book of the Ecclesiastical History, were dedicated to an account of the arrival of the first Christian mission among the English. To reinforce a message of British perfidy and Anglo-Saxon virtue, Bede used the last chapter of Book I to set up a heathen king, Æthelfrith of Northumbria no less, as God's agent in that mission. But his narrative begins in Kent.

Kent was unlike the other kingdoms of Britain. Its modern

---

* EH I.22. Imperial Rome called the natives generically Britons, among whom they recognised many tribes like the Cantiaci in Kent or the Votadini (Gododdin) of Lothian. The Britons called themselves *Cumbrogi* and later, as Welsh speakers still do, *Cymry*, meaning 'fellow-countrymen'. The English called them *Wealas*, or Welsh, 'foreigners' or more pejoratively 'slaves'.

name is little changed from the tribal folk-name *Cantium* by which Julius Caesar knew it.[19] It maintained close links with the Continent and the courts of the Frankish kings. Its land-holding structures were different from elsewhere in English-held territories—East Kent was divided into units called *lǽð* or lathe, rather than the more common shire—and its Early Medieval estate centres have been closely identified with the sites of Romano-British villas.[20] Æthelberht, the king to whom the first Roman Christian mission was sent, was the earliest English king to issue a law code that survives. And there is something else that has puzzled historians: Æthelberht was listed by Bede and recognised by the Pope as overlord of the southern English in the years around 600, and yet there is no record of him ever having won a battle. Glorious victory in war seems to have been a near-universal prerequisite to render other kingdoms tributary. It begs the question, what was so special about Kent, or Æthelberht?

Its natural wealth as a 'garden of England' is one explanation; its geographical proximity to the kingdom of Frankia is another. The lands ruled by the Merovingian dynasties had never entirely shaken off their Romanitas; by comparison with the earliest English kingdoms they were urbane and politically sophisticated, and before the year 600 they already had a developed concept of statehood. By far the majority of exotic imported goods which arrived from Europe into Early Medieval Britain came from Frankia through Kent, so its kings had access to a source of wealth and prestige independent of booty won in battle. Unsurprisingly, Kent possessed a number of ports from which cross-Channel trade operated. These are the so-called *wics*. The suffix *wic*— Sandwich on the East Kent coast is a prime example—seems to reflect the sites of beach or estuarine markets.* When kings began

---

* The *wic* suffix was also applied to farms and other settlement sites but emerging research is showing that *wics* on estuarine or coastal sites were probably associated with trading.

to see opportunities for controlling and taxing them in the seventh century they were given royal protection and patronage and developed into what have become known as emporia. Hamwic, near Southampton, is the most completely excavated of these. Other early emporia on this side of the Channel included Ipswich (*Gipeswic*) and Dunwich (probably *Dommoc*). *Lundenwic*, what was left of Roman *Londinium*, was named by Bede[21] as a market where goods came from many nations, even though archaeological evidence to back his claim has been slow in coming; York, then called *Eoforwic*, may have been another. There are hints of such emporia developing in Northumbria later in the seventh century.* On the other side of the North Sea/Channel famous Frisian trading centres existed at Dorestad on the Rhine and *Quentovic* (another *wic* name; probably sited at Montreuil on the River Canche). Most of the early *wic* sites probably owed their origins to markets held periodically on beaches, where opportunistic Frisian traders could haul their boats up beyond the tideline; or at fairs held to mark important festival dates such as the four quarter days.

Kent's connections with Continental traders does not completely explain its apparently unique status among the English kingdoms and there may also be a historical tradition behind its eminence. The so-called Kentish Chronicle, which forms part of the Nennian compilation, describes the disastrous invitation that the Britons made to Germanic warbands in the 430s after Britain's civitates, her tribal councils, had been given apparent permission by Emperor Honorius to look to their own defences.† Vortigern, the leader of the tribal councils that inherited the administrative functions of the British state, made a fatal pact with the legendary Hengest and Horsa by which they would protect Britain

* See Chapter V.
† The so-called Honorian rescript of 410. Zosimus, *Historia Nova*, Book VI, chapter 10.2.

from the predations of her traditional enemies, the Irish and the Picts, in return for possession of the Isle of Thanet.[22] Hengest and Horsa were Jutish: that is, from the peoples of the Jutland Peninsula said by Bede to have settled in Kent and the Isle of Wight in the fifth century. The coasts of the English Channel (known as the *Oceanus Britannicus* to the Romans and perhaps *Minch* to the natives, as it is still called *La Manche*—the Sleeve— by the French) were familiar to North Sea traders and raiders in their sleek, shallow-draughted rowing keels or *cyuls*. The Straits of Dover were, as they are today, the shortest crossing point for those wishing to exploit markets and vulnerable peoples along Britain's south and east coasts.

At some point, perhaps five or ten years after the initial treaty, the Jutish warlords decided that the balance of the deal was not quite to their liking:

> Hengest was an experienced man, shrewd and skilful. Sizing up the king's impotence, and the military weakness of his people, he held a council, and said to the British king [Vortigern], 'We are few; if you wish, we can send home and invite warriors from the fighting men of our country, that the number who fight for you and your people may be larger.' The king ordered it to be done...[23]

The Nennian version has it that, when reinforcements arrived, there was a great feast and that, having been made exceedingly drunk by the cunning and wily Hengest, Vortigern became enamoured of the Jutish chief's daughter and offered to swap her for the whole kingdom of Kent whose incumbent, Gwyrangon, was summarily deposed. This is legendary and not very histori- cal, but it echoes the sort of political marriage alliance that sealed many a treaty in the Early Medieval period. If this garbled tale records faint traces of reality, Kent—or perhaps more pragmati- cally the right to tax the peoples of Kent—was the price the Britons thought it worth paying for the Jutes, who must have been little more than Channel pirates, to keep all the other pirates at bay. They were setting a thief to catch a thief. The British probably had little choice, because Vortigern was politically weak. He was forgiven neither by the chronicler whose records underlay Nennius's compilation, nor by Gildas, who heaped infamy on the stupid Britons and their 'Proud Tyrant'.

Kent, perhaps specifically East Kent, was the earliest English kingdom granted in toto by treaty, disregarding any other parts of the eastern seaboard that might have been affected by the arrival of North Sea traders/raiders or settlers. Such treaties were not new. *Foederati*, as the Romans called such military clients, were employed widely by an imperial administration engaged in strategic military plate-spinning from Cornwall to Constantinople. This was not the land-grab beloved of Dark Age fantasy, but a legal treaty; and the self-confidence of later Kentish kings, one suspects, reflects that. The unexplained oddity has always been the idea that Germanic naval mercenaries were based in Thanet to counter the predations of the Irish and Picts. It seems as though the priority in the south-east of Britain was to protect Channel trade, never mind what the Picts and Irish were up to. Keeping the seaways open here kept Britain (especially Kent) in contact with what remained of the Empire and her traders. Any half-decent wartime leader, from Vortigern to Churchill via Queen Elizabeth I and Pitt the Younger, knows that the Channel is the key to Britain's back door. What would Philip II of Spain or Bonaparte or Hitler have given to keep the Royal Navy away for a week in good weather in 1588, 1805 or 1940?

The idea that Kentish kings regarded themselves as direct inheritors of the late Roman state is reinforced by the minting of coins in the late seventh century at Canterbury. One, found in a hoard at Crondall, Hampshire, bears the inscription DOROVERNIS CIVITAS.* That a Canterbury mint of that late date should call

---

* Arnold 1988, 58. Canterbury was *Durovernum Cantiacorum*.

Canterbury a *civitas*—an explicitly Roman administrative name for a British tribal capital—is telling. So too is Bede's testimony that when Augustine arrived at Canterbury in 597, at least two churches of Roman construction were to be found near the city, still standing and in reparable condition. Kent may, then, have been regarded as having a sort of residual primacy among the English kingdoms, to which was added the cachet of some continuity of Roman civic life, such as a theatre, and its continuing relations with the more sophisticated Merovingian court at Paris (the English have remained in awe of Paris ever since). Æthelberht's father, Irminric, bore a suspiciously Frankish-sounding name. Even Oswald's Deiran uncle Edwin thought it expedient to marry the king of Kent's daughter.

In far-distant Rome, Pope Gregory himself knew of Deira. It was he, in the days before his papacy, who noticed in a Roman slave market a blond-haired youth. On enquiring where the child came from he was told that he was an Angle from the far north, from the kingdom of Deira.[24] The Pope's awful puns on Angles/angels and Deira/*de ira* are probably bad enough to be authentic.* Gregory had intelligence of the English, knew that they were heathen; he probably also knew that Kent, the most continental of its kingdoms, might be the most receptive to a mission from the mother church, for not only had Æthelberht of Kent married into a Frankish royal family, he had married a Christian princess, one Bertha, the daughter of Charibert of Paris.

Hengest and Horsa and their original three boatloads of men were said to have landed on the Isle of Thanet, that north-east corner of Kent which in those days was detached by the wide

---

* Bede and the author of the Whitby Life of Gregory give slightly different versions. In essence, Gregory saw some pale-skinned, fair-haired slave boys being sold in the market in Rome and enquired where they were from. He was told that they were *Angli* and replied that they were surely *non Angli sed angeli* (not Angles but angels). On being told that they had been taken from Deira he offered the bon mot that they had been plucked *de ira*—from the wrath of God.

channel of the River Wantsum. It was on Thanet, also, that Gregory's missionaries landed in the year 597. The mission got off to a shaky start. The monks, understandably apprehensive about being sent to convert a barbarous people on the edge of the world, faltered in their purpose on the long journey through the kingdom of the Franks. Augustine, the leader of the mission, returned to Rome to try to beg them off what must have seemed an impossibly daunting task. He was 'encouraged' by his master to carry on in somewhat forceful terms and the mission resumed its journey. Bede's account of subsequent events is a great set-piece of English history. It also has the stamp of authenticity provided by his quotation verbatim of letters between the Pope, Augustine and Æthelberht which can hardly reflect anything but the essence of the mission's arrival and reception. And yet, the letters do not tell the whole truth—not by a long shot.

To begin with, one wonders about the relationship between Æthelberht and the Franks. His marriage to a Merovingian princess and the political and material sophistication of the Franks at this period strongly suggests that if Æthelberht was overlord of southern Britain, Charibert of Paris and his successors were in turn his overlord. In which case, why did the Christianising mission not originate with the king of the Franks? Was Æthelberht trying to assert his independence from a now-partitioned Frankia by accepting a mission direct from Rome, as it were above Frankish heads? Was he expecting the mission; had he been warned of its impending arrival? Or was he, as Bede suggests, responding to opportunity as it arose?

Bede has it that when Augustine and his forty-strong party landed on Thanet they sent to Æthelberht asking him to receive them. Æthelberht ordered that the party await him on the island, either so that he might take counsel with his advisors on what to do with them or, if he had foreknowledge of their arrival, while he prepared some sort of formal reception. He agreed to hear the papal embassy on condition that they met in the open air, so that no devilment should take place. There is more to this than mere pagan superstition on his part. Thanet was the site of one of the major *wic* settlements in Kent. At Sarre, the first crossing-point to the mainland to be bridged (as late as the fifteenth century), a richly furnished cemetery was excavated in the nineteenth century revealing a sixth- to eighth-century settlement there, populated by traders. Many of the graves contained such items as weights and balances, and large numbers of exotic and highly valuable imports were also recovered.[25] Sarre was, in fact, an emporium, perhaps one of the main ports of entry for Kent. Another, Fordwich, lay on the River Stour close to Canterbury—perhaps too close for comfort for Augustine to be allowed to land there.

Recent study suggests that these emporia offered a sort of duty-free quarantine status for foreigners, not unlike the conference facilities of global airport hubs like Schipol or Charles de Gaulle, full of bustle and exotica, people as well as goods.[26] One is almost tempted to think of something like the Casablanca of Rick's Café Américain, where almost anything, including men's souls, might be bought and sold. Augustine, it seems, was initially to be treated as a trader/diplomat, permitted to come to the international port of arrival where his credentials and the bona fides of his mission could be scrutinised 'for some days'.[27] Æthelberht had every reason to be cautious: after all, a party of forty, in other circumstances, might constitute an invading army and he evidently anticipated some sort of hocus-pocus from Augustine, a man elevated enough in rank to bring a splendid retinue with him. Æthelberht, despite or perhaps because of his wife's devotion to the Christian faith, was determined to treat Augustine's arrival with all the pomp and suspicion with which mob-handed Continental suitors would later be received at the courts of England's medieval kings and queens. In this case the only weapons on display were ceremonial: a silver cross and an image of the Lord painted on a wooden panel. These were the sword and shield of Augustine the warrior of Christ. What was Æthelberht to make of them? Had his queen prepared him for such disarming oddities?

So far, nothing in Bede's story suggests Æthelberht had asked for, or been prepared for, the papal mission; it seems Augustine was by no means sure of his reception. Bede's tone further implies that the king took his time to calculate the political pros and cons of allowing, or fostering, the objectives of the mission. In the Ecclesiastical History I.25 Bede relates how, with the aid of interpreters picked up in Frankia, Augustine told Æthelberht of the good news (the Gospels) which he brought from Rome with the promise of everlasting life. Æthelberht, from a personal point of view, was sceptical. As king of Kent and overlord of southern Britain he fulfilled the role of chief priest of the obscure heathen ceremonies practised by the English. A king's success in battle depended on propitiating the Germanic gods of war to fight for his side. Dare a king surrender this power? This was no light matter. But then, Æthelberht was no battle-fighter.

Perhaps in consultation with Queen Bertha, who had her own priest in the form of the Frankish bishop Liudhard, and certainly with the advice of his *gesiths*,* his elite household of warrior nobles, the king allowed the Christians freedom to preach, offering them provisions and giving them a dwelling in the city of Canterbury. Whatever his personal reaction to Augustine's mission, Æthelberht had to weigh carefully the political implications of allowing himself to be converted. This was not an issue for hasty judgement. Letting Christian preachers evangelise among the people was one thing; Augustine's mission, and the essence of Æthelberht's dilemma, was the conversion of the king and the nobility of Kent. This was as much to do with the acquisition of

* See Glossary, Appendix C, p.413.

diplomatic relations with Rome as it was with personal salvation. It was about being part of something bigger. Were the kings of the English to acknowledge the spiritual overlordship of the Bishop of Rome? It is the ever-interesting British question: to join and be part of the European club, to surrender a part of one's independence; or to remain aloof and excluded. For Bede, who belonged firmly to the Roman Catholic family, this was about the heathen English grasping the opportunity that the stupid Britons had rejected: the chance of salvation and re-integration into an idea of Empire and of civilisation.

Augustine and his fellow-missionaries settled in Canterbury, as Bede says, according to the way of life of the apostles and of the primitive church: that is to say, according to monastic rule, even though they did not immediately establish a monastery. They 'preached the word of life to as many as they could'.[28] This is intriguing. Were their new converts the rural poor of Kent? Were they members of the nobility, testing the waters? Could they even have been a community of Christians already worshipping in Canterbury, survivors of the congregations belonging to the old Roman buildings in what was left of the city? This potential con-tinuity of Roman Christianity in Britain is one of the key ques-tions in Early Medieval studies. In the British West a monastic movement had established itself on the Atlantic coast of Wales, and in Ireland in the sixth century there was a flourishing culture of tribal monasticism, but neither of these movements had been inspired by the diocesan church of Rome. Their spiritual inspi-ration came from the desert fathers, from St Anthony and his fellow ascetics. There is some evidence of British Christian com-munities hanging on in the Pennines and further north right into the seventh century; but it has been hard to demonstrate their survival in any English kingdom, unless that is what Bede alludes to in this enigmatic passage.

In the same chapter Bede hints at other fascinating aspects

of the conversion, or reconversion process that the new Roman mission triggered. Æthelberht, he says, was at last persuaded to convert although the suggestion that he was 'attracted by the pure life of the saints' does not really ring true. The king rejoiced, says Bede, as increasing numbers of his subjects followed him. We are told that he did not compel anyone to accept the new faith, 'though none the less he showed greater affection for believers since they were his fellow citizens in the kingdom of heaven'. The historian's ears prick up at this sort of reference: it is as clear a sign as Bede could make of the political implications of the conversion. The lines of patronage which flowed down from a king through the distribution of favours, land, gifts and alliances were to be closed to those who did not accept the new faith; the Whips' office is not an invention of twentieth-century party politics. Pope Gregory and Augustine were perfectly well aware of the pragmatic necessity for a conversion from the king down, that embracing existing systems of patronage was a key to success. Bede knew it too.

There is another phrase in the Ecclesiastical History I.26 of immense significance to understanding the impact Christian patrons would have on history. 'It was not long,' Bede says, 'before he [Æthelberht] granted his teachers a place to settle in, suitable to their rank, in Canterbury, his chief city, and gave them possessions of various kinds for their needs.' Here is the beating heart of the Anglo-Saxon tribal system. When young noble warriors like the legendary Beowulf came to offer their swords to a great king, they were without lands of their own. Only after they proved themselves loyal, brave and successful in battle did the king grant them lands 'suitable to their rank'. So here in this key phrase we have Æthelberht recognising Augustine as the leader of a *de facto* warband (albeit that his warriors were soldiers of Christ) who, swearing to fight for his salvation and bring him the gifts of everlasting life, was rewarded with the possessions due to a proven, eligible *gesith*, or household companion. Bede uses the same phrase of Benedict Biscop in his *Historia Abbatum*, the Lives of the Abbots of Wearmouth and Jarrow. In his case it was because Biscop had reached the proper age of about twenty-five and had served his time as one of King Oswiu's thegns.[29] Biscop rejected the earthly reward 'for the sake of Christ'. In Æthelberht's gift lies the first hint of the relationship that bishops and abbots would forge with their kings in the seventh century; it was a relationship adapted from secular tribal custom, with mutual benefits that came to be recognised and exploited with increasing cunning by both parties. Its long-term, unforeseen, dramatic implications for the English state only became apparent in the next three generations, in the policies of Oswald, his brother and his nephews. Although it is not possible to reconstruct the delicate negotiations which must have preceded Æthelberht's and his household's conversion, King Edwin's subsequent personal and political agonisings over the same issue were to be cast in a riveting, if typically frustrating, Bedan narrative.

Pope Gregory was quick to capitalise on the initial success of Augustine's mission to Kent. In 601 he sent letters of support and encouragement to Augustine and to Æthelberht (whom he cannily compared to the Emperor Constantine), welcoming the king into his community. He sent gifts. Gregory also dispatched a support group of senior priests, carrying with them the pallium* that conferred metropolitan status on Augustine: the first Archbishop of Canterbury. In response to a list of questions posed by Augustine relating to the subtleties of adapting to local custom, Gregory sent a lengthy reply of which perhaps the most significant aspect is his attitude to pagan shrines and idols. His unequivocal advice to Augustine and to Æthelberht was that these were to be suppressed and destroyed. Within a month he had changed

---

* Pallium: a band of white cloth worn across the shoulders.

his mind and decided to propose a more subtle approach which, in today's politico-military parlance, would be called a hearts-and-minds strategy:

> I have decided after long deliberation about the English people… that the idol temples of that race should by no means be destroyed, but only the idols in them. Take holy water and sprinkle it in these shrines, build altars and place relics in them. For if the shrines are well built, it is essential that they should be changed from the worship of devils to the service of the true God. And because they are in the habit of slaughtering much cattle as sacrifices to devils, some solemnity ought to be given them in exchange for this. So on the day of the dedication or the festivals of the holy martyrs, whose relics are deposited there, let them make themselves huts from the branches of trees around the churches which have been converted out of shrines, and let them celebrate the solemnity with religious feasts.[30]

Gregory was designing his conversion policy on the hoof. First his missionaries are to wreck the pagan shrines; now they are to place altars in them. They are not to ban the heathen practice of sacrifices, they are to adapt them; the heathen festivals are to be realigned with Christian festivals and the sacrifices turned into celebratory feasts. Not for nothing are our Christmas and Easter amalgamations of pagan and Christian tradition. But whatever instructions were now issued by Gregory, he had already advised Augustine to use his own discretion in adapting to local conditions with which the Pope recognised he was unfamiliar.

Gregory's liberal pragmatism contrasts sharply with Augustine's apparent rigidity of style and lack of self-assurance. The fact is that very few, if any, pagan shrines of the small number which have been excavated and the larger number identified from historical or place-name evidence, have ever been shown unequivocally to have been converted into Christian churches. If it happened, it was a rare event. It is as if Gregory's first advice, to destroy, to suppress and to found new churches on new sites, became the modus operandi of the Roman party.

The impact of the mission was greatest at the high table of

politics, where endowments of bespoke churches on royal lands became the fashion. Those for whom conversion carried no political weight—in other words, most of the population—probably underwent little or no spiritual transformation in the seventh century. As many as four hundred years later the Archbishop of York could complain that the peasantry were still practising pagan rituals at sacred groves and springs, and that local priests were either turning a blind eye or indulging in such rituals themselves.[31]

The first phase of Augustine's mission took three or four years. By 601 he had gained the trust and support of the political elite of Kent, the most influential kingdom in Anglo-Saxon Britain. Bishoprics were to be founded at Rochester, to serve East Kent, and in Essex. Ultimately, having founded the site of the future St Paul's Cathedral in London, the Archbishops of Canterbury would transfer their metropolitan see there.

At about the same time that King Æthelfrith of Bernicia was consolidating his position as the new power in the land at Degsastan far to the north, Augustine embarked on the next, most risky phase of the Gregorian mission. With Æthelberht's help, Bede wrote, Augustine summoned the bishops of the British churches to a meeting on the borders of Hwicce and Wessex at a place which in Bede's day was called *Augustinaes Ac*—Augustine's Oak. Despite the full weight of Early Medieval scholarship behind the search, the actual site has not been discovered, although somewhere in the region of Worcester is likely and a Roman road crossing of a river in the area south or west of Cirencester would be plausible.[32] In a sense it does not matter. The meeting, or series of meetings, must have taken place within or on the edge of the so-called imperium of Æthelberht, because it was arranged under his protection. Augustine urged the British bishops, representatives of an imperial Roman church now hopelessly out of step with contemporary practice, to realign themselves with their mother church. It is the Europe question again.

There is little doubt that the British bishops were stubborn in their refusal to accept Rome's, Augustine's and Æthelberht's authority. That Augustine was lacking in the more subtle and persuasive aspects of diplomacy there is a strong suspicion. The British, a subject nation, were not inclined to be lectured on the subject of religion by the come-lately Lloegr. The core issues under scrutiny seem to modern sensibilities trivial in the extreme: calculation of the date of Easter, details of church liturgy and canon law, the shape of a monk's haircut. However that may be, these were issues of the greatest importance for Christian communities for at stake was the unity of the Universal Church. The dispute was long and tedious and in the end Augustine was forced to produce a miracle of healing (blind man's sight restored) to convince the British of his credentials. Finally they agreed to hold a conference, which all the senior figures of the British movement should attend. This in itself must have been problematic, for the British diocesan church had been based on urban Roman civil life. It was a religion of estate owners, magistrates, senior military officers and perhaps the mercantile classes. The monastic movement, which had penetrated Wales from the sixth century, owed its origins and loyalties to the desert fathers for whom diocesan urbanity was more or less anathema. For these self-denying seekers of solitude the hermit, not the bishop, stood alone as the exemplar of ascetic spirituality. And somewhere in the mix were the British kings who, if they were nominally Christian, were interested in a tribal variant of the faith, something like that practised by the Irish. How could these disparate factions be united?

The conference was held at a place called by Bede *Bancornaburg*, identified as Bangor Is-coed (Bangor-on-Dee) on the banks of the River Dee. The British party consulted with a famous wise man who advised that Augustine, should he prove to be godly and true, ought to be listened to and treated with respect. To the question, how shall we know if he is godly and true, the wise man suggested that the British set him a test: they should arrive after the Kentish party. If Augustine rose to greet them he would prove himself meek and gentle of heart, a true servant of Christ; if not, it would demonstrate his arrogance. The British came. Augustine remained seated.

The tale as Bede tells it suggests that he got his information from a British, perhaps a poetic, source; it also sounds like retrospective simplification of a more complex set of events; and yet, it seems to capture the essence of the thing. Augustine mishandled the conference; he disregarded or was ignorant of protocol-obsessed British sensitivities and by the time he came to offer his most generous concession to the British church it was too late. The outcome was disastrous for the Roman mission and such was Augustine's frustration with his seemingly inflexible opposite numbers that he ended his participation with an invective against the British: a warning that their churchmen would suffer death at English hands.

The fulfilment of Augustine's prophecy-cum-curse cannot be precisely dated but it can be firmly laid at King Æthelfrith's door. The *de facto* unification of Bernicia and Deira after the Battle of Degsastan in 604 did not satisfy his appetite for expansion; indeed, that appetite could not be satisfied, for the only way to reward his ever-expanding warrior elite was to endow them with the fruits of fresh conquest: it was a self-sustaining cycle which only stopped when there was no more *lebensraum*. Early Medieval kings had not yet begun to understand the political economics of agricultural profit or bulk trade. They were warlords whose wealth was counted in cattle on their lands and in the scrap metal of war booty hoarded in iron-bound chests in their golden halls. Æthelfrith had no concept of statehood, of a society proof against the death of its warrior king. His ambition was to be glorified in song and saga, to defend his dynasty against competition, to fight enemies abroad and feast on the produce of his kingdom in the mead halls of his estates. The evidence for these years of accumulation is to be found in the palace at Yeavering, where increasing architectural splendour and pretension are written in the design, construction and geography of its buildings. But Early Medieval kingdoms were ephemeral: no political institution, no infrastructure, no fortification apart from Bamburgh survives to testify to Æthelfrith's greatness. If there was a Northumbrian emporium, history records nothing of it. No poetry of praise to this most aggressive and successful warrior king has come down to us.

Bede's measure of the man is his slaughter of the monks who rejected Augustine's civilising proposals. We do not know when the slaughter happened, but it was remembered by British, English and Irish sources, somewhere between 612 and 616. Bede tells us that Æthelfrith collected a great army against the 'city of the legions which is called *Legacæstir* by the English and more correctly *Caerlegion* by the Britons'.[33] This is Chester. Bede, almost certainly drawing on British sources preserved by a later Mercian monastery, says that before the battle Æthelfrith saw a group of priests standing apart from the armies of the Britons, in a safe place. These priests came from the same monastery at Bangor-on-Dee where Augustine had been rebuffed a decade or so before. Æthelfrith can have had no interest in fulfilling a prophecy; he was curious, though, to know what these monks, numbering as many as a thousand, were doing there. He was told that they were praying for their soldiers. Understanding only too well the value of having an effective god on one's side in the hour of battle, Æthelfrith pragmatically had the lot of them slaughtered, before attacking and defeating the main army. Archaeologist David Mason believes that the burials discovered at the Roman site of Heronbridge just to the south of Chester, during excavations in the 1930s and 2000s, laid out in orderly fashion in mass graves and exhibiting a preponderance of fatal sword wounds, provide evidence for mass battle-graves of the victorious dead.[34]

Coming of age
in Dál Riata

Mæst sceal on ceole...
sweord sceal on bearme

*The mast belongs on the ship...
the sword belongs
in the lap*

....

British Annalists called

Oswald Iding *Lamnguin*—'Whiteblade'—but this is not a British epithet, like *Flesaur*. It is Irish, and must have been given him during his exile among the Scots of Dál Riata.* Between the ages of twelve, when he fled Bernicia, and thirty, when he returned, Oswald was transformed from an English heathen refugee into a crusading Irish Christian prince.

The cultural adventure shared by Northumbrians and Irish, which was to have such profound effects on Early Medieval European culture, had its origins in the exile of an Irish prince, Colm Cille. In 563, at the age of about forty-one, he sailed from his homeland in Tír Conaill, now County Donegal, to Iona and founded a monastery there under the patronage of the king of Dál Riata. Colm Cille, or Columba as later Latin writers called him, belonged to the Cenél Conaill, a branch of the powerful Northern Uí Néill clan. He is supposed to have been born in the village of Gartan in the rolling green cattle country of the

---

* I am indebted to Herman Moisl for this information. *Lamnguin* has otherwise been variously translated as 'Blessed hand' and 'Flashing blade'.

extreme north-west of Ireland. It is a land of great beauty and around every corner, it seems, lies the site of an ancient church, a holy well, a cross. It has been brutalised by successive invaders and tyrants and yet something of its early landscape is recognisable in its townlands, ballyboes and raths, embellished by the haunting and affecting art of their high crosses and the tumbledown remains of early monastic burial grounds.

By virtue of his father's ancestry Colm Cille was eligible for the kingship of the Uí Néill—the Irish term is *rígdomna*, equivalent to the English atheling—but from an early age he was trained for the priesthood. Irish society in the sixth century was intensely tribal and competitive. Its hundreds of warlords and high kings were peripatetic, always on the move, living off the fruits of labour of those tied to the soil just as Bernicia's kings did. Ireland's social structure was a complex hierarchy of ancient customary rights and obligations with varying grades of free and unfree farmers and a warrior class bearing strong similarities to the thegns and *gesiths* of the early English kingdoms; indeed, the Irish *gaescedach*, meaning spear and shield, to denote a noble warrior, is demonstrably the same word as Old English *gesith*.[35]

Wealth came from the land: cattle especially, because the mild, wet Irish climate offers lush pasture year-round; but in the plains between its mountains, woods and bogs the land of Ireland also produced cereals, flax for linen and wool from sheep. The common dog whelk, an inhabitant of its more sheltered coasts, yielded a famous and immensely valuable purple dye which was a mark of rank and wealth across Europe. Christianity arrived in Ireland in the fifth century in the missions of Patrick, the northern British slave and self-appointed apostle, and Palladius, the Gaulish bishop. Their legacy was an Irish diocesan church adapted to mirror its tribal affiliations and which developed alongside a strong monastic movement so that bishop and abbot competed for the patronage of kings and for control over large tracts of productive farms, sometimes across tribal boundaries. Such was the status of Ireland's senior churchmen, themselves drawn from the ranks of tribal elites, that their legal value was on a par with those kings. But Ireland was not exclusively Christian by any means. Colm Cille himself may have been born a pagan (Colm Cille means 'Dove of the Church'; his given name seems to have been the more earthly Crimthain, or 'Wolf') and at least one high king, his contemporary King Diarmit, was probably unbaptised.

Colm Cille was more than mere aristocratic deacon, more than just a founder of monasteries: he was a giant among the figures of his heroic age, a broker and wielder of power beyond his apparent means, a man of immense charisma and political influence whose personal achievement leaps from the pages of his hagiographer. Whatever the truth behind his exile—interference in a battle for the high kingship of Ireland or the illegal copying of a book—the idea that he came to Iona by chance is hard to credit. He was said to have sailed in a curragh with the obligatory twelve companions from his native shore until he could no longer see Ireland. This story follows the traditional Irish form of maritime pilgrimage familiar to those who know the account of Saint Brendan's epic journey across the North Atlantic. The ideal for the Irish monk was *peregrinatio*, the devotional journey abroad for Christ, looking back not just on his homeland but also on material wealth, family and comforts.

Colm Cille and his companions, mainly young, unmarried male nobles of his own kin with little chance of inheriting wealth of their own, are supposed to have landed on the southernmost point of Iona,* still called Port na curraich, the harbour of the curragh. In Greencastle's Inishowen Maritime Museum, on the banks of Lough Foyle, contemplating the sea-going characteristics of one of these tarred-canvas and oak lath marvels, the author

* Iona was originally, and up to Bede's day, called *Hii*; it acquired its more famous moniker through a scribal error on the part of a monk misreading the Latin *Iova*.

met a man who had rowed in a curragh with Wallace Clark, the great historian of the traditional Irish craft. These boats were and are so flexible, he told me, that oars with very thin blades have to be used because anything larger imparts too much torque on a frame designed to give with the waves, to ride them like a porpoise. In 1963, fourteen hundred years after Colm Cille's departure, Clark and a group of fellow-enthusiasts re-enacted his journey in their own craft, an open vessel appropriately furnished with twelve oars. The coast of the Kintyre Peninsula lay just a day's rowing away to the east, clearly visible from as far west as Mallin Head; Iona had been reached within a week.[36]

Adomnán, kinsman and successor as abbot on Iona, believed that the island was granted to Colm Cille by the Dál Riatan king Conall mac Comgaill (558–74). Although Bede says that it was a gift of the Pictish king Bruide, this probably reflects Bede's respect for his contemporary Pictish correspondents rather than a genuine tradition.[37] The likelihood is that Colm Cille knew Conall, that he travelled first to Dunadd, as Oswald would fifty-odd years later, and asked for the king's protection and patronage. Conall's motive for granting Colm Cille a landed estate, even one as apparently modest as Iona—just three miles or so in length—suggests that Colm Cille's reputation as a powerful holy man and senior scion of the Cenél Conaill preceded him; accepting such a man into his sphere conferred kudos on him and his court. Colm Cille was said to have banished evil spirits from the island on landing there; it is unlikely that such a fertile strip of land had not previously been settled and so presumably he dispossessed and deported its heathen inhabitants too. There is a sinister story, not written down until the twelfth century but sufficiently wide-spread in oral tradition to give it some credence, which suggests that Colm Cille maintained at least one foot in the pagan Irish past. It relates how the saint asked one of his companions to vol-unteer to be the first to be buried on the island, as it were to

consecrate the soil, to put down roots. The monk Odhráin duly
volunteered and, according to the most lurid account, was buried
alive in a grave with Colm Cille's blessing.[38] This idea of a blood
sacrifice to consecrate holy ground is not unique in Irish mythology; heathen rituals were not easily discarded. The Abbey's cemetery is to this day called Relig Oran, the burial site of more than
forty Scottish kings and one or two other important personages
from Oswald's nephew King Ecgfrith of Northumbria to John
Smith of the Labour Party. The place has a potent sense of time-
lessness, despite the casting of many of its ancient stone crosses
into the Sound by the agents of Protestant English tyrants.

The original monastery on Iona was built within a vallum, or
bank, more or less on the site of the present, more recent and
much more imposing structure. The cells, churches and guest
houses were built of wood, probably hewn oak, and roofed with
heather, turf or thatch as some Donegal houses are to this day.
The monks cultivated the machair on the west side of the island
and probably kept sheep, but they must have had access to a
range of resources on Mull and the mainland: there are many
references in the Life of Columba to monks fetching timber and
other materials from across the seas of the Inner Hebrides. The
island community also had a forge and was capable of building
both wooden ships and curraghs. In time, the mother-house on
Iona gave birth to other foundations, on Tiree and the Garvellach
Islands, on Jura and perhaps elsewhere. These, like the original
foundation, must have been gifts of the king. Considering that
these were the lands of the Cenél Loairn means that King Áedán*
was capable of granting lands that lay outside his own immediate
tribal territory in Kintyre. His growing power and Colm Cille's
career seem to run on parallel tracks. Adomnán mentions more
than thirty Columban foundations, spread through the islands

---

* Áedán mac Gabráin, late contemporary of Colm Cille and king of Dál Riata between
about 574 and his death in 606-8.

of the Inner Hebrides and on the Scottish mainland. Many of them must have been located to take advantage of fertile soils like those on Iona. How many involved the displacement of indigenous inhabitants is not clear, although Adomnán makes reference to a disgruntled farmer to whose coppice-wood the monks had helped themselves:

> Once St Columba sent his monks to bring bundles of withies from a plot of ground belonging to a layman so that they could be used in building a guest-house. They went and did this, filling a boat with withies. On their return they came to the saint and told him that the layman was much distressed...[39]

The rest of the episode relates how Colm Cille, equally distressed at this public relations faux pas, sent the farmer some miraculous grain, which he sowed and harvested within three months. It implies tensions between Iona and the population of its hinterland; it also suggests that the monks were enterprising in their use of local resources. Since they were after coppice-wood, cut every eight to ten years or so, they cannot have been ignorant of the fact that it was owned and managed by someone, although Colm Cille was canny enough to ensure a more than adequate compensation for the offence. It shows too that the monks had craft that could carry freight. There is the implication, furthermore, that the strains of corn grown by the monks were superior to those grown by the natives of the region: monks were the great agricultural innovators of their day. Elsewhere in the Life they carried structural timber over the sea to Iona, towing it on rafts: no mean feat in those waters.[40]

Colm Cille is supposed to have returned to Ireland and founded other monasteries at Derry, which seems to have been an early emporium, and Durrow, probably in order to maintain economic and diplomatic links with his kin in the hinterland of Ireland. He made an expedition up the Great Glen to convert the Picts, during which time his legendary battles with King Bruide's chief druid Broichan gave rise to many miracles, including banishing a monster from the River Ness (not the Loch, as is commonly supposed). Colm Cille and his successors, like their secular counterparts, travelled widely, visiting and living off their subordinate foundations. Unlike secular lords, however, they established permanent, settled estates, lands held in perpetuity. In time these came to represent a threat to royal authority, but in the late sixth and seventh centuries they functioned as stable economic *caputs* or estate centres and may have played a substantial role in increasing the agricultural productivity of the land in Ireland and in Britain.

Out of Colm Cille's friendship with King Áedán and his successors and his increasing authority and reputation among monks grew a Columban imperium or paruchia. Iona became a centre of learning and of a sort of tough-love monastic ideal which won many disciples and admirers, among them Bede. Colm Cille's uncompromising but humane sense of moral authority, backed up by his judicious employment of miracles, curses, prophecies, medicinal cures and native wisdom, made him a religious and political force to be reckoned with in brokering relations between the kings of Ulster and Dál Riata, Pictland, Strathclyde and beyond. In 575 he was present at, and may have convened, a conference at Druim Cett, now an uninspiring low mound on a golf course outside Limavady near Derry/Londonderry. This momentous meeting between King Áed mac Ainmirech (a distant cousin of Colm Cille) of the Northern Uí Néill and Áedán mac Gabráin of Dál Riata confirmed the latter's primacy in its relations with the Uí Néill. At the same time Colm Cille predicted, effectively ordained, Áed's son Domnall as royal heir.[41] That Colm Cille and his successors as abbot, nearly all of them of the Cenél Conaill, should constitute in effect the royal church of the Dál Riatan kings and play a part in brokering their relations with the kings of Ulster, demonstrates the continuing status of the foundation on Iona. The iconic showpiece of this relationship was Colm Cille's blessing of Áedán as king of Dál Riata after the death of his predecessor in 574 and before the meeting at Druim Cett.[42] Colm Cille was at first reluctant to ordain Áedán, preferring his brother, until a persistent vision persuaded him to accept Áedán as God's choice. Such a story was a necessary part of the narrative theatre which Adomnán felt appropriate to this momentous event. The ceremony was performed on Iona, rather than at the secular royal site of Dunadd where a legendary rock-cut footprint, still to be seen, was the traditional stage for the ceremonial inauguration of kings. So we have king and patron travelling all the way to Iona to be endorsed by its holy man. If this represents the sort of biblical anointing which Saul underwent at the hands of Samuel in the Old Testament, then it is the first such coronation in Europe (long predating that of Wamba in Visigothic Spain in 672 or Pippin of Frankia in 751).* The 'Dei Gratia' on our coinage, the legitimising of kings by God's top civil servants, starts here. It must be said that a number of historians doubt that so much can be read into Adomnán's account; or at least, they believe his narrative to be retrospective wishful thinking. If nothing else, the story indicates the value placed by the Columban community on its relations with kings.

Some time after this putative inauguration Colm Cille prophesied the futures of Áedán's descendants to three generations.[43] It must have come as a shock to Áedán because the saint told him that none of his three oldest sons would succeed him; instead, his youngest son, the yellow-haired Eochaid Buide, who in typically miraculous fashion ran unsolicited into the saint's arms, would become king. These accounts of Colm Cille's visionary powers

---

* Sharpe 1995, 356. Saul's anointing occurs in I *Samuel*. Collins 1977, 41–4 doubts that the biblical precedent is relevant and cites late Roman practices for the origins of the anointing ritual. Nelson 1977 urges caution on the significance of ecclesiastical aspects of an essentially secular theatre.

served two functions for his hagiographer and for later Columban tradition: they show that he was able to influence the succession of both Uí Néill and Dál Riatan kingdoms, and they proved to his contemporaries how wise was his foresight, for all three of Áedán's oldest sons were killed in battle before they could succeed their father. This potency, this *virtus*, could be transferred by the saint's blessing both during life and after his death. Its most willing and worthy recipient was Oswald Whiteblade.

For those English athelings taken into fosterage on Iona, even a generation after the death of the great holy man, the significance was equally great. Colm Cille's favour was equivalent to a badge of legitimacy for aspiring kings; it was a token of his confidence; and his blessing was a sure sign that God would aid the princes of his choice. Colm Cille's successors as abbots may not have had quite the élan and authority of the founder, but their endorsement was still of a very high value. The implication, echoed in the modern anointing of prospective political leaders by the barons of the press, is that great men of wisdom only back winners. The implied threat in that endorsement is that the withdrawal of patronage in the future would be damaging, as Yaweh warned David in the *Book of Kings* and as Colm Cille made absolutely clear to his king:

> Make no mistake, Áedán, but believe that, until you commit some act of treachery against me or my successors, none of your enemies will have the power to oppose you. For this reason you must give this warning to your sons, as they must pass it on to their sons and grandsons and descendants, so that they do not follow evil counsels and so lose the sceptre of this kingdom from their hands.[44]

᯾᯾᯾

I think that Oswald, aged twelve, his brother Oswiu, just five years old, their infant sister Æbbe and mother Acha sought protection from King Eochaid Buide at his fortress stronghold of Dunadd, as Colm Cille had from Buide's great uncle Conal. On the face of it, this is hard to credit: Æthelfrith had comprehensively defeated Áedán at Degsastan in 603/4. Áedán's forces seem to have been led to that fate by a Bernician atheling, Hering son of Hussa, whose dynastic interests the king had supported against the rising power of Æthelfrith Iding. Buide would have been acting well within the bounds of Early Medieval reason had he dispatched these refugees by the sword or refused them protection; and they in turn must have felt some foreboding about their reception. Unless, that is, there was already an understanding between these landless Bernician exiles and the Dál Riatan king.

The clue to resolving this apparent paradox lies in an entry in three of the Ulster Chronicles for the year 628 recording a battle fought at Fid Eoin on the Irish mainland, between King Conadh Cerr of Dál Riata and Maelcaith mac Scandaill, king of Cruithne.* Militarily it was a disaster for Dál Riata. Conadh Cerr was killed, along with several of the grandsons of Áedán. The crucial detail is the notice in the Tigernach annal, one of the Irish chronologies which was probably based on an original compiled on Iona, that one of these grandsons was *Oisiricc mac Albruit rigdomna Saxan*: Osric son of Ælfred, Saxon atheling. Áedán, then, had a grandson who was an English prince. Some historians have been sceptical of such notices, believing them to be unhistorical. But an Osric, son of Ælfred, can be placed on the margins of the Bernician dynasty. The Nennian genealogy discussed in the appended essay on the Bernician king-list contains an odd entry: *Ealdric genuit Ælfret. Ipse est Ædlferd Flesaur*: 'Ealdric begat Ælfred; that is Æthelfrith the Twister'.† It seems that Æthelfrith's father Æthelric

---

* Noted in the Annals of Clonmacnoise, Annals of Tigernach and *Chronicon Scotorum*. Moisl 1983, 105. Cruithne is the Ulster territory of the Dál n'Araide, long-standing rivals of Dál Riata.

† *HB 57*. 'That is', *id est* in Latin, is recognised as a gloss, or explanatory remark, later than the original; but it does not necessarily invalidate it.

had four sons: Ælfred, Æthelfrith, Theobald and Ecgulf. If Ælfred was a son of Æthelric and bore a son called Osric, then Osric was a cousin of Oswald and probably of similar age. That fits the notice of him dying at Fid Eoin, fighting alongside Oswald who was almost certainly present too. More significantly, Osric is cited as a grandson of Áedán. If his father was Ælfred, his mother must have been an un-named daughter of Áedán. Eochaid Buide, it seems, was host to several Iding athelings, one of them his own nephew. In reciprocating his patronage and protection, they fought for him in his dynastic wars.

Acha could legitimately seek protection for her sons from Eochaid Buide because they were his kin. It was of secondary importance that his father had hosted rivals for the Bernician kingship and been defeated by her husband, Æthelfrith. In the political grammar of the seventh century, they would now be brought up as his foster-sons. At appropriate ages, around sixteen (in Oswald's case from about 620 onwards), they would join his warband and fight in his army. When a suitable opportunity arose they might ask for release from his lordship and seek to press their ancestral claims in their fatherland. Osric would have done so had he survived. The quid pro quo was that on reclaiming their kingdom they would recognise their foster-parent and political patron as overlord and, perhaps, foster members of his kin in turn. They might also be expected to marry daughters of his house, to reinforce bonds tied in battle. As it happens, a late Scottish source hints at a betrothal between Buide's son Domnall Brecc and Oswald's sister Æbbe, which was unfulfilled because of the Bernician princess's desire to become a nun.[45]

Training in the skills of the warrior and the culture of the mead hall was part of the fostering process; but Oswald's apprenticeship in the warband of Buide was in striking contrast to the Germanic norm. Anglo-Saxon elite warriors rode to the battlefield but fought on foot, perhaps in the shield wall, perhaps in skirmishing formations. They used a large variety of swords, jave-lins, lances, battle knives—the famous *scramaseax** included—and the large linden shield, which suggests that there was a concomi-tant variety of battle scenarios, including single combat. The talismanic value of warrior arms should not be underestimated. Zoomorphic metal and painted ornaments on shields, typically birds, dragons and fish, gave added protection and inspired a strong sense of martial valour in a warrior;[46] the same probably applied to brooches, belt-fittings and sword embellishments, the essential trappings of masculine nobility. Some of these items ended up buried with their owners, as if to continue the symbolic value in death; others found their way into hoards of battle-scrap, like the contents of the Staffordshire hoard.

Less noble foot soldiers, over whom much speculative aca-demic ink has been spilled, are a more enigmatic component of Early Medieval armies. For them the spear and small buckler-type shield called a targe may have been the normal weapons. They are much less likely to have worn mail armour or helmets. There is little evidence that the bow, a common enough hunting weapon of the period, was deployed in military encounters, probably because of the close-fought hand-to-hand nature of the shield wall. But the whalebone Franks casket from around 700, now in the British Museum, depicts bowmen raining arrows down on a besieging army from the ramparts of a fortress like Bamburgh.

At least some elite Pictish warriors seem to have fought on horseback, if the pictorial evidence of battle scenes such as those carved on stones at Aberlemno in Angus is anything to go by.[47] Lacking stirrups, they threw their light spears or javelins before engaging closely with short swords. Picts and Irish did not pos-sess the large offensive linden shields of the English but used light

---

* A short sword or stabbing knife used in close combat and whose name gave the Saxons their tribal moniker. The Welsh *Saes* (meaning English) and Scots *Sassenach* retain the link. Neither is complimentary.

targes, round or square, which would have been useless in the shield wall. The armies of Dál Riata are likely to have specialised in amphibious assault using methods that would become familiar in the Viking Age.* Among Picts, Irish and Britons the dawn ambush was a speciality. These opportunistic tactics might later give Oswald the edge against enemies whose more static, formu-laic strategies left them vulnerable to routing. Although Oswald cannot be placed unequivocally in any one battle during his exile, it must be inferred that he played a full part in the military pro-grammes of his hosts both on the Irish mainland at Fid Eoin, and in battles against the neighbouring Picts. In one or more of these battles he earned himself the nickname Whiteblade.

In warrior society the great cattle-raid or hosting, at the very least annually, was a king's obligation; it seems, indeed, to have been part of the ritual of inauguration, a rite of arms. The pur-pose of the hosting—in Irish *slógad*—above and beyond naked blood-lust and manly high spirits, was three-fold: to plunder neighbouring kingdoms, especially for cattle but also for booty and slaves; to demonstrate the horsemanship and weapon-skills of the king and his elite warriors; and to train young nobles in the arts of war. Without such regular martial exercise a tribe could not be prepared for the predations of its enemies and neighbours or attract young warriors to its ranks. Given the inherent reci-procity of such activities, it can hardly be said to have been eco-nomically productive. Even John Wayne couldn't endow the tit-for-tat cattle raid with dignity or sense. The true extent of hosting by the kings of the British Isles in Oswald's day cannot even be estimated because raids of this sort, while they were celebrated in epics like the *Táin Bó Cúailnge* or Cattle Raid of Cooley, did not rate a mention in any of the extant chronicles or annals. In a sense, one might argue the negative: if raids for cattle and plunder

---

* See p.71; Alcock 2003, 150.

worth mentioning, they must have been at the common end of frequent.

By the end of his apprenticeship Oswald was skilled in the use of the sword and spear, and he rode a horse with neither saddle nor stirrup, a considerable skill in itself. Whether he bore into battle the heavy linden shield of his countrymen or the small targe of his hosts' army is an intriguing question, which cannot be answered. He might well have possessed a mail shirt and may, as an atheling, have been entitled to wear a helmet of the sort retrieved from Sutton Hoo or York's Coppergate. In attending the king he would be entitled to wear the full array of noble para-phernalia: silver armbands and brooch on a gold-embroidered cloak dyed purple with the mucus of the humble dog-whelk; a sword hanging at his side in a jewelled scabbard. His hair would have been worn long and he probably sported the moustache of his rank. As an exile, however, he would still be lacking the essen-tial entitlement of a great man in his own kingdom: land. The confidence with which Oswald returned to Northumbria to fight for his kingdom entitles us to paint a picture of a warrior at the full height of his martial powers.

The Iding athelings were additionally handed over to the monks of Iona for conversion and baptism. Why? The initia-tive belongs either to the king or to the abbot of Iona, probably the latter for obvious reasons. We cannot assume that Oswald, Oswiu and Æbbe were baptised on arrival, so one of two abbots might have been responsible. In 617, when the Idings arrived at Dunadd, the abbot of Iona was Fergno Brit, perhaps a Briton judging by his name. He was the fourth abbot and the first to come from a new generation who had not been the companions or kin of Colm Cille. He died in 623 and was succeeded by a nephew of Lasrén, the third abbot. Ségéne (623–52) was a kins-man of Colm Cille and one of the longest-serving of the foun-der's successors. He is credited with playing an active role among

Irish churches in the propagation of Iona's primacy, and of Colm Cille's sanctity and authority. It is tempting, therefore, to see Ségéne as the motivating force behind the Bernician conversions, especially since he and Oswald enjoyed a close friendship. That friendship might well have begun during the abbacy of Fergno while Oswald was still in his teenage years; it was close enough for Oswald to learn fluent Irish from him.

The community on Iona must by the 620s have been used to playing a fostering role in the careers of royal youths, not just from the kingdoms of the Cenél Conaill and Dál Riata, but from other royal houses: the Britons of Strathclyde, perhaps, or from Bernicia. In part their role was educational: to teach these youths discipline and the virtues of hard work. They were also acculturated, imbued with the cultural, moral and aesthetic values of Irish society and particularly those of the Columban church. There was a substantial political dimension to their fostering. In a world in which institutional Christianity still stood on fragile foundations, indoctrination in the values and political virtues of Christian kingship must have motivated the community of such a political Christian as Colm Cille. His ordination of Áedán, whether it was the first genuine anointing in Europe or not, set a deliberate precedent intended to ensure that righteous kings were those approved and legitimised by the church, as heathen kings had been by their priests. In return, abbots received appropriate patronage from their kings in the form of land grants and protection. Fostering, along with other more subtle aspects of patronage, was part of the reinforcing process of this relationship which became more complex during the seventh century but which, in essence, was that forged between Iona and Dál Riata. As part of that process Oswald, his brother Oswiu and their sister Æbbe became thoroughly Irish. In the case of Oswiu, he took his integration one step further: he fathered a child with an Irish princess, Fina, daughter of Colman Rimidh, a joint high king of the Northern Uí Néill. That child would in turn become king of Northumbria, in unconventional circumstances.

Oswald's conversion may have been a matter of formality, part of his obligation towards his hosts. But I think there is more. Many an aspiring tyrant, when in power, has conveniently forgotten promises made on the way up the greasy pole. Oswald did not. He would maintain links with his abbot, Ségéne; they were to meet again on terms of intimacy after Oswald became king. He had gone to Dál Riata as an impressionable youth, had been nurtured there, had become in effect an Ionan protégé. He was taught elements of scripture; his view of history was informed by Old Testament accounts of David and Goliath, of Saul and Elijah but also by legendary tales of great Irish high kings.

For its part, the Iona community must have seen in the Bernician athelings an opportunity both to expand the interests and influence of its church and a fulfilment of divine providence. Here were young men whose kingdom, should they reclaim it, was a rising power in the north, a heathen land ripe for conversion. In the future Christian kings of Bernicia might carry the Columban ideal to all the English: it was a potentially vast source of future patronage and prestige. And then, Oswald would not have been the first Bernician to describe his homeland: plains and hills rich in pasture and cattle, as Ireland was; a rocky royal fortress like Dunadd only on a much grander scale; and close by, a few miles to the north, a tidal island of mythical beauty. Long before King Oswald sent for an Irish bishop, the Columban community must surely have appreciated Lindisfarne's potential as a new Iona in the East, as perfect a site for a royal monastery as could be conceived. And either Oswald, his brother or his cousin Osric would become *their* Bernician king. These were young men of talent and prospects, well worth the investment Abbot Ségéne and his fellow-monks would make in their futures if they survived the more secular challenges which the king and his enemies would set them. Iona would prepare them morally and spiritually for the trials ahead, could endorse their divine claims and pray for them. Only apprenticeship as warriors and the political interests of the Dál Riatan kings would ensure their earthly success in battle.

By chance, an extraordinary and unique document survives to shed insight into the military organisation of Dál Riata within which Oswald and Oswiu were trained. It is called the *Senchus Fer n'Alban*.[48] It was compiled in Old Irish during the tenth century, but probably derives from a seventh-century Latin original. Aside from sets of Dál Riatan genealogies of patchy historical validity and a number of annalistic entries, the *Senchus* records the civil and military obligations of the three tribes of the kingdom: the Cenél Loairn, Cenél nŒngusa and the ruling Cenél nGabráin, Áedán's immediate kin. The material has been corrupted in the course of its various copyings and transmissions; even so, what emerges from the jumble is a strong sense of the customary military structure of an Early Medieval tribal kingdom, for which there is no insular parallel.

The three kin branches of Dál Riata were assessed in terms of the number of fighting men the king could raise for a hosting. The assessment is by *tech*, or 'house'. The Cenél Loairn, whose territory consisted roughly of north Argyll, including Mull and Iona, Lismore and the coast west of Loch Awe with their capital at Oban, comprised 420 *techs*; the Cenél nŒngusa, ruling the lands of Islay and perhaps Colonsay, had 430 *techs*; the ruling dynasty of Cenél nGabráin, controlling Kintyre and Cowal, with their principal stronghold at Dunadd, was assessed at 560 *techs*.*

Dál Riatan kings were able to summon their fighting levies under three circumstances: to repel an invading army; to guard their borders against a threatened invasion; and to attack a

---

* See Glossary, Appendix C, p.414.

rebellious *tuath* or tribe across a border. This seems to cover pretty much any eventuality under which a king might wish to wage war. In reality, such impositions involved some sort of give-and-take: those kings with a reputation for success in battle, and who did not attempt to keep their levies in the field past harvest time, were more likely to elicit a positive response to raising their banner than those who were poor or thoughtless commanders.

Likewise, we have to be sceptical about the actual fighting strength of the Dál Riatan kings based on the *tech* render. Between them, the three tribes were supposed to be able to raise about fifteen hundred fighting men, to be carried against their enemies in around seventy-five seven-bench boats.[49] Each *tech* rendered a warrior and an oarsman. This probably reflects an ancient concept of tribal division into sevenths or *septs*, each of a hundred *techs* rendering a man per estate; a very similar customary concept survived in Wales until quite late as the *cantref* or hundred-house system. That each *tech* should provide an armed warrior and an oarsman gives an indication of the status of the warrior as estate-owner with a life interest, tied to both land and king in a concentric web of patronage and obligation whose origins lie deep in the Iron Ages of the British Isles.

The warbands of a king, even one as powerful as Áedán, might never actually have consisted of as many as fifteen hundred men, but the impression given by historical accounts of the period of relatively small armies is broadly consistent with this scale of warfare. Áedán's warbands were also swelled by contingents led by exiles such as Osric and Oswald and their followers, obliged and willing to join in whatever dynastic scraps were justified by the king's ambitions.

The Dál Riatan system of levies was evidently adapted to its peculiarly maritime interests; its borders were primarily the beaches of its islands and if it wished to maintain its imperium over ancestral lands in Ireland it was essential for its naval capability to be maintained at strength. Whether its craft were bespoke warships or, like the little ships of Dunkirk, an allsorts of fishing and trading vessels pressed into temporary service, is frustratingly unclear. There certainly were vessels of many different designs and purposes, from river coracles and punts to ocean-going curraghs and masted wooden sailing barks. Their crews were consummate and confident sailors, as Colm Cille's monks were. In Adomnán's Life of Saint Columba alone more than fifty sea voyages of one kind or another are described.[50] That a range of such craft was familiar to the peoples of Atlantic Britain is demonstrated impressively by their maintenance of relations with the peoples not just of the northern seas, but of Frankia, Africa and the Eastern Mediterranean. These links go as far back as the Bronze Age; as far, in fact, as Continental knowledge of the existence of metallic ores in the rocks of Britain and Ireland. Through and beyond the period of Roman domination, vessels plied Atlantic waters. By the end of the seventh century bulk trade of minerals and grain, the sort of interaction we would recognise as maritime trade, was a thing of the long distant past. Deep harbours with organised facilities which we, or the merchants of Alexandria or Constantinople, would recognise did not exist on the Atlantic seaboard. The emporia of the Irish Sea basin, if they existed on anything like the scale of Sarre in Kent or *Lundenwic* (which is extremely doubtful), might be located on the Scillies, at Meols near the mouth of the River Mersey, and at Dalkey Island near Dún Laoghaire. At best they were probably beach markets which occurred as and when ships arrived: irregular, opportunistic and unregulated although watched with great acquisitive interest by kings. Bulk trade requires towns for redistribution; and there were no towns in the sense that we understand urbanism in seventh-century Britain or Ireland.

No such emporium has yet been positively identified in the lands of Dál Riata, although it is conceivable that Colm Cille's foundation at Derry might reflect the existence of a trading site there in the late sixth century. Dunadd, now more than two miles inland, might have had an Early Medieval port; it gives on to very low-lying land that might once have been open water. Beach markets almost certainly existed at Tintagel in Cornwall, where a very high proportion of 'Dark Age' Atlantic imports have been recovered; and at Whithorn in Galloway, where there was probably a monastery from the sixth century and earlier. The absence of identified emporia does not mean that the Dál Riatan kings and their fostered princelings had no access to the finer things in life. Excavations at Dunadd have shown that wheel-thrown pottery, beads, glass vessels and tessera for decorative inlays, mostly from Gaul, found their way to courts that could afford to pay high prices for luxury goods.[51] Dunadd was special because it was the place where the fruits of Dál Riata's success were recycled into items of superb metalwork: brooches and bowls, swords and military trappings, which were probably the equal of those items recovered in the Staffordshire hoard. Such items were redistributed along lines of patronage, those reflected in the detail of the *Senchus Fer n'Alban*, which reinforced the shared sense of success of the Irish diaspora as well as the power of its great kings. The closeness of Dunadd's relationship with Iona is shown both by the presence of imported pottery on Iona and by the presence at Dunadd of traces of dyes used in the manufacture of holy books. Iona, as befitted the foundation of Colm Cille, seems also to have maintained its own independent links with the Continent, evidenced by the visit of Gaulish sea captains and a Gaulish bishop, Arculf.[52]

It is tempting to think that Oswald and his companions, having fought in the battles of Eochaid Buide and his son Domnall Brecc ('Freckled Donald'), returned to their homeland wearing a share of the trappings which fame and fortune had won for them. More precious, perhaps, was the Whiteblade nickname that Oswald's hosts, or perhaps his enemies, gave him during the time in which he came of age in Dál Riata. The young Bernician atheling had proved himself a worthy soldier by the time he left the court of Domnall Brecc. Iona and the Irish left their mark on Oswald. It seems he left his mark on them too.

One vital question hangs over Oswald's exile: at no point in his sixteen years at the court of Dál Riata, so far as we know, did he attempt to raise an army against his Deiran cousin Edwin, who had ruled the Northumbrian kingdoms since the death of Æthelfrith. Was he waiting for the right opportunity? Did he fear that Edwin's power was too great to take on? Did the kings of Dál Riata advise or rule against such a move? We cannot say. If impetuosity fought with wise counsel, the counsel prevailed.

UNCLE EDWIN

Wulf sceal on bearowe,
earm anhaga

*The wolf must inhabit the forest,
wretched and solitary*

ÆTHELFRITH'S NEMESIS

Edwin had, like Oswald, spent many years in exile, from perhaps the early 590s until 617. He faced the same uncertainties and opportunities as his rival, but while Oswald was to be secure in the protection of Dál Riata in the far north, Edwin was pursued from one southern kingdom to another by a relentless foe: 'he wandered secretly as a fugitive for many years through many places and kingdoms.'[53] Æthelfrith's determination to exterminate Deiran opposition to his rule is admirable in its persistence. From Gwynedd to Mercia to East Anglia, Edwin was never safe from the bribes and threats of the mighty Bernician king. The fear of the hunted animal seems to have left its mark on Edwin, whose insecurities can be traced as a recurring subtext in Bede's exhaustive treatment of his conversion. His life reads like a three-act drama, the fate of his dynasty a tragi-comic testimony to the slings and arrows of Early Medieval fortunes.

Edwin's first exile, as a young boy, seems to have been among the British of Gwynedd. The evidence for this episode is circumstantial: a medieval Welsh Triad, in denouncing his later predations, describes him as a 'Great oppressor of Mon [Anglesey], nurtured in the Island'.[54] Reginald of Durham, writing in the twelfth century but with access to British and Mercian sources now lost, relates that Edwin was brought up, that is to say fostered, by Cadfan ap Iago of Gwynedd. Cadfan is real enough: his gravestone survives in Llangadwaladr churchyard on Anglesey. There is no doubt, either, that he was a Christian king. The Latin inscription on his memorial calls him *rex sapientissimus*—most wise—a distinction earned by clerics, which may suggest he abdicated to take holy orders. Cadfan had a son, Cadwallon. If, as is likely, Edwin was raised as his foster brother, one senses there must have been ill-feeling between them, given the bloody end their relationship would meet more than thirty years later.

Edwin, raised in one of the great courts of Britain, ought to have been converted and baptised there at an early age. Indeed, there is a curious and troublesome reference to this in two versions of the Welsh Annals, which record variously that Edwin was baptised in the year 626 (which agrees with Bede's account) by a Briton, Rhun son of Urien (which does not) or by Bishop Paulinus of the mission to Kent.[55] So the story of his long drawnout adult induction into the Roman church, described with such psychological subtlety by Bede, poses some serious questions.

If Edwin grew up on Anglesey in the court of Gwynedd he, like Oswald, must have learned to fight in the king's warband alongside those loyal Deiran *gesiths* who formed his retinue-inexile. Although there were probably others, only one major battle is recorded in this period: the Battle of Chester around the year 615/16, in which Æthelfrith fought the king of Powys and slew over a thousand monks praying for the British. Historians generally agree that this was not a battle fought for territorial advantage: Powys did not border on Northumbria. But a Welsh Annal variant records that in the battle Iago ap Beli died.[56] Iago was Cadfan's father. The obvious conclusions to draw are that

Æthelfrith was making war on the British of Wales because they were harbouring his enemy Edwin; that the kings of Gwynedd and Powys were in military alliance to defend against the Bernicians; and that Edwin survived the battle.

Why does Bede not mention Edwin's involvement in that battle, or at least his part in its cause if, as seems certain, he knew of it? The answer is that Bede's providential narrative, in which Edwin was converted by Bishop Paulinus, a member of Augustine's entourage, could not be compromised by a more equivocal portrayal of British involvement in the conversion. He had already denounced the British as wicked, their failure to convert the English their principal sin. Edwin cast as a British Christian would utterly compromise Bede's narrative purpose.

After Chester, Edwin was no longer safe in Gwynedd, having brought Æthelfrith's wrath down on his hosts and their allies. He had by now, it seems, married Coenburh, daughter of King Cearl of Mercia, and had two sons, Osfrith and Eadfrith. Given the pragmatism of seventh-century politics the straightest way to read this is that Gwynedd and Powys were keen to ally with Mercia against Northumbria and that Edwin was primed for a marriage that would cement such an alliance and give him the most powerful backers in his fight for Deira.

If Edwin had threatened Æthelfrith's dynastic poise before, now he presented a triple threat: he had sons by a Mercian princess; Mercia was a growing power on his southern borders; Mercia and the British kingdoms in Wales were in alliance. No king could allow such a threat to go unchallenged. The fact that there is no record of a campaign against Mercia in the two years after the Battle of Chester can be interpreted in several ways. Either—and it seems unlikely—Æthelfrith did not take this combined threat of Mercian power and Deiran prince seriously; or he believed that the devastation of Chester had obviated that threat for the time being. Perhaps he had taken British hostages at Chester and could consider their sting drawn. He may have already been planning a campaign against Mercia; if so, it was a campaign pre-empted by Edwin's next move. Or, his eyes may have followed Edwin's travels towards the East. The next we hear of the exiled prince is that at some time between 616 and 617 he took up residence with King Rædwald of East Anglia, who now became the focus of Æthelfrith's homicidal antipathy.

Rædwald has generally been regarded as the king of the Sutton Hoo ship burial, the unique and extraordinarily rich funerary monument near Woodbridge in Suffolk that almost defines public perceptions of Dark Age kings. He was also fourth in Bede's list of the kings who ruled over all the southern kingdoms. Once tributary to Æthelberht of Kent, he emerged in the second decade of the seventh century as an ambitious, bellicose, well-connected and capable leader, just in time for Edwin to avail himself of Rædwald's growing powers of military patronage. Rædwald's identification as the Sutton Hoo king, by a combination of religious probabilities, coin evidence and a lack of other suitable candidates, is ironic. His shadowy existence on the periphery of history is mirrored by the lack of solid evidence for a body in the famous Mound I of the royal cemetery. We do not know the exact dates of his reign, for he plays only a small, if important, bit-part in Bede's grand drama and no East Anglian chronicle survives from this period. He had certainly married and produced children by about 600, at which time his kingdom was subject to the imperium of Æthelberht of Kent. Under that Christian king's patronage he himself underwent a form of conversion but, as Bede disparagingly noted, his conversion was half-hearted: he placed a Christian altar alongside the pagan idols in his temple, a case of having one's communion cake and eating it. He was not among those converts who established a seat for a bishop. Bede blamed his half-heartedness on his wife and 'certain evil teachers' and recorded that he died, as he was born, a pagan.[57]

East Anglia was almost as well placed as Kent to take advantage of the trading basin of the North Sea. Many of the artefacts in the Sutton Hoo treasure have close parallels with finds from not just Kent and Frankia, but as far away as Sweden. It was a kingdom apparently built on robust cultural and economic foundations. The North and South folk were divided geographically by the River Waveney, as Norfolk and Suffolk—the names are first recorded in the eleventh century but are probably much older—are still. Its principal emporia were the riverine port of *Gipeswic*, Ipswich on the Orwell, and further north at *Dommoc*, Dunwich, where the first East Anglian ecclesiastical see was established in 632. They gave easy access both to North Sea coasts and Continental trading centres like Dorestad (now Wijk bij Duurstede on the Dutch Rhine), Quentovic (near modern Étaples on the River Canche) and Hedeby (near Schleswig on the German–Danish border). Ipswich lies just fifteen miles or so west of Sutton Hoo and was firmly established as a major trading centre by the middle Anglo-Saxon period, with one of the few early thriving centres of pottery production. So Rædwald, like Æthelberht of Kent, may have had a source of wealth independent of agriculture and conquest. This is reflected in the stupendous richness of the artefacts recovered from Sutton Hoo and in the longevity of the East Anglian kingdom, which survived independently until the Viking depredations of the ninth century. Between East Anglia and its expansionist neighbours to the north and west were the fenlands of the Wash, a patchwork of small kingdoms such as Gyrwe, Spalda, Wixna and Willa which would ultimately be swallowed by Mercia.* To the south was the kingdom of the East Saxons who, for much of the seventh century, were also tributary to Kent. Despite East Anglia's economic and geographical advantages, Rædwald's reputation as a great

---

* These are tributary kingdoms named in the seventh- or eighth-century Tribal Hidage. See Yorke 1990.

overlord seems not to predate his association with Edwin.

Edwin's arrival at the court of Rædwald by 616/17 came at a pivotal moment in their fortunes. Edwin had few options left to him as an exile: wherever he went Æthelfrith was determined to kill him. With Rædwald, himself protected by the greater imperium of Kent, he might be safe. Æthelfrith's first attempt to persuade Rædwald to hand him over or kill him, offering money and silver, failed. A second attempt, backed with a greater treasure, failed too. There were threats.

At some point during this year of swaying fortunes Æthelberht, Kent's great Christianising king and pseudo-imperator of southern Britain, died, precipitating a dramatic shift in the balance of power. For one thing, his son Eadbald spurned Christianity and took his stepmother as a wife (deplored by Bede). It may even have been the old king's death that determined Æthelfrith to lean on Rædwald. Rædwald must now be his own man. One of his first instincts seems to have been to follow the Kentish lead, renounce his skin-deep Christianity and apostatise, probably reflecting conservative political pressures among his nobility. Then, when Æthelfrith sent a third mission to his court 'offering even larger gifts of silver and threatening to make war on him if Rædwald despised his offer',[58] Rædwald succumbed. Without the backing of Æthelberht he was politically weak. In the aftermath of the Battle of Chester and on the back of twenty years of warmongering, Æthelfrith's reputation was sublime; his threats were to be taken seriously. Rædwald agreed to his terms. Implicit in this situation was that by handing Edwin, or his body, over, Rædwald was swapping a southern Christian overlord for a northern pagan one. On such decisions seventh-century political fortunes swung from one extreme to another.

It was now, in this moment of crisis, that Edwin is supposed to have made the Faustian pact that forms a set-piece milestone of Bede's history. Bede rightly saw Æthelberht's death and the apostasy of Eadbald and Rædwald as critical blows to the ongoing success of the Augustinian mission: its fate hung in the balance. It is entirely in keeping with his providential theme that a miraculous intervention should now alter the course of history. A 'very faithful friend'[59] of the exiled prince, on hearing that Rædwald was to betray him, came to him in his room to warn him as he was retiring for the night. Taking him outside where they might not be heard, he offered the Deiran atheling a means of escape to a place where none of his enemies would find him. One suspects this meant either a fast horse-ride to the marshy fastnesses of the fens, a sort of dress-rehearsal for Alfred's hiding in the Isle of Athelney some two and a half centuries later, or a discreet cross-channel boat to Frankia where Æthelfrith's threats would mean nothing.* But Edwin, paralysed by fear of surrendering to a sort of fatalistic ennui, refused, dismissed his friend and was left alone in the night to contemplate whatever the dawn might bring...

> He remained long in silent anguish of spirit and 'consumed with inward fire', when suddenly at dead of night, he saw a man silently approach him whose face and attire were strange to him.[60]

A desultory conversation followed: why was Edwin sitting alone outside in the night? What business was it of the stranger's? He knew the cause of Edwin's sorrow; what would the young prince give for deliverance from his perils? Anything. What would he give for the destruction of his enemies and his restoration to a kingdom that would surpass all those of the English before him? Again, anything. Then:

> If the one who truly foretold all these great and wonderful benefits could also give you better and more useful counsel as to your salvation and your way of life than any of your kinsmen or parents ever heard, would you consent to obey him and to accept his saving advice?[61]

---

* Twelve hundred years later, in similar circumstances, William Blake would warn Tom Paine of his impending arrest by Government spies just in time for him to make the same dash across the Channel to France.

Who could refuse? Edwin was only too pleased to sell his soul to the one true god. After all, he was probably already a Christian. What had he to lose the night before his betrayal? The Jesuitical stranger now made a sign, placing his right hand on Edwin's head so that he might know him again when the time came to redeem his promise, and then disappeared in an instant, so that Edwin might know that this was no ordinary man, but a spirit. Hot on the spirit's vanishing trail Edwin's friend returned to give him the news that Rædwald had changed his mind, dissuaded by his queen. She had taxed him with his friendship with Edwin, and with dishonouring himself. The king had resolved to help restore Edwin to his throne. It had been a long night.

What is to be made of this? To begin with, it is striking that Edwin is alone, unaccompanied by his wife Coenburh and their two young boys or even by his *gesiths*, his closest companions. This might be dramatic licence; it might just be inferred, though, that Edwin was isolated from his circle, for whatever reason. And then we must suspect strongly that this Bedan narrative is retrospective miracle-working, a story embroidered in its many retellings. But there is no need to doubt the essentials of it, even if the shrunken timescale is incredible and the Mephistophelian conversation apocryphal. The stranger's identity at least is clear: he is otherwise revealed, though not by Bede, as the all-too-real Paulinus, one of Augustine's companions in the mission to Kent.[62] What was Paulinus doing in East Anglia? Was he part of a diplomatic mission from Kent? If so, we must suppose that at this point Æthelberht was still alive, so Bede's timeframe is unconvincing. The geography of the story is not obvious, either. Bede has it that Edwin was living with Rædwald as a retainer; but again, if this was at court, where were Edwin's family and companions? The stone, apocryphal or not, on which Edwin sat contemplating his doom, suggests that the court was on the road, perhaps between estates. We might read this as a crisis that comes on them all unexpected, so that Edwin himself has no chance to present his case to the king or to hear beforehand of Æthelfrith's latest messenger arriving. More credibly, a series of events, times and places have been conflated to make a good story better.

One ought, perhaps, to separate the *casus belli* from the retrospective need to explain Edwin's ultimate conversion. Edwin might have met Paulinus before he became king, either at Rædwald's court before Æthelberht's death, or in Kent itself. But Bede's requirement to make prophetic capital out of the meeting, or vision, allows us to dismiss its coincidence with Rædwald's musings on his fate. That Edwin was about to be betrayed by Rædwald there is no reason to doubt, although the context and timing may be more pragmatically reconstructed. Æthelfrith's embassies forced Rædwald into a corner from which he could extricate himself either by breaking his bond with Edwin and submitting to Bernician overlordship, or by conducting a pre-emptive assault. His councillors, who may have included both his queen and Edwin, persuaded him to take the bold option; but we cannot rule out the possibility that it was Rædwald himself who led the hawks. We may allow the sequence to extend over a period of weeks or months between Edwin's arrival in East Anglia, Æthelfrith's first embassy to Rædwald, and the final decision, probably in the first months of 617.

Rædwald does not come well out of Bede's account but that is to be expected, because for Bede an apostate king was the very worst sort. If he was to become a divine instrument it was through no virtue of his own; he had none. So his vacillation, and the revelation that his wife had stiffened his resolve, suits Bede's purpose all too well. Nevertheless, it is plausible that the unnamed queen planted in her husband's mind the brilliant, pre-emptive scheme that he was to carry out with such devastating conviction late in 616 or in 617. She may even, in the heroic style of the Finnsburg episode in *Beowulf*, have literally laid his sword in his lap—a gesture no warrior could refuse.[63] In later centuries, among the warring 'surnames' of the Borders, the placing of a set of spurs on a husband's empty dinner plate was intended to produce a similar effect.

Once Æthelfrith's embassy had been rejected, blows must decide the issue. Leaving no time for the Northumbrian king to gather his army for an assault on East Anglia, Rædwald attacked him with all his available forces, including those of his son Rægenhere and Edwin's own warband, which can hardly have been very large. The place where they met and overwhelmed Æthelfrith lay on the east bank of the River Idle, which Bede describes as the border of the Mercian people. Common consensus has identified the location as Bawtry, the Roman town that straddles the Idle where it is crossed by the Great North Road between Lincoln and Doncaster. This is well to the south of Northumbrian territory among the marshy wetlands of the Humber headwaters in the marches of Mercia and Lindsey, the latter tributary to Northumbria. Æthelfrith, given the outcome, cannot have had anything like a full complement of arms. What was he doing there? Did he believe that a small force hovering menacingly a week's march from Rædwald—at Lincoln, say— would produce the desired effect? Did he completely underestimate Rædwald, or merely the political forces working on the East Anglian king? If he was advancing south when he was caught, he ought to have set up a defensive position on the west bank of the Idle. Another possibility is that he was outflanked, caught by a surprise assault from the north and found himself trapped on the east bank, as Bede says, between Idle and Trent with no hope of a retreat.

The subsidiary question is: how did Rædwald's army get there? Three routes suggest themselves as possibilities: west from, say, Ipswich to Ermine Street and then a forced march north along the old Roman road; no more than a week at most. This would have allowed Æthelfrith to dictate the site of battle. A bolder option was to take his army north through his own territory, the ancestral lands of Boudicca's Iceni, to Brancaster, then make an amphibious dash across the Wash in rowing galleys (like the one in which he was later buried) and conduct a lightning strike from Burgh-in-the-Marsh west to Lincoln and beyond. But there is a third route that cannot be lightly dismissed: a fleet, sailed right up the Humber estuary and down the Trent and Idle, the way the Vikings would later attack direct into a hinterland. That way, Æthelfrith had no line of retreat to the north, no chance of reinforcement: he must stand and fight.

These questions cannot be resolved but one might offer the following scenario. The battle will have been fought on foot. The traditional view of Early Medieval warfare would have two shield walls trying each other's resolve, noble warriors and their retainers in the front rank. The shield clash is likely to have been preceded by skirmishing at a distance with javelins or angons and archers firing arrows, before closing for sword-combat.[64] Any overwhelming disparity in numbers, as Bede suggests there was, was fatal for the defenders: sheer weight would force them into rout or destruction. There was no orderly retreat along the Roman road towards the safety of the ancient fort at Doncaster and so the possibility that the East Anglian host came out of the north must be allowed. There is no doubt that the fight was bloody. Rædwald's son fell in battle and King Æthelfrith was killed. The low rise called Barrow Hills just to the south-east of the site of the Roman fortlet at Bawtry may indicate where many of the casualties were buried. It was a coup of spectacular proportions which transformed Edwin from a wolf at bay to king of the English north of the Humber and Rædwald from a self-doubting Kentish vassal to overlord of the southern English. Edwin had avenged the death of his father and rid himself of his persecutor. Bernicia's twenty-four-year domination of the northern English,

Æthelfrith *Flesaur's* hard-won but brittle empire, dissolved overnight. That a warrior king of Æthelfrith's stature and experience
could be brought down by an apparently minor competitor shows
how fragile the military state was in the early seventh century.
There was no defensive infrastructure; no attempt after the battle
to prevent Edwin from securing the kingship of all the Northumbrians. The battle, the death of the king, was all. Æthelfrith
had not, in more than two decades, constructed the framework
of a state that might survive him; that was not the way of the warrior. His queen and their children fled to the courts of the Scots.
Edwin must now try his hand at ruling the lands of his father.

Riding north along the ancient road between Bawtry and York,
Edwin's army had successively to ford the Trent at Littleborough,
the Don at Doncaster, the Aire at Castleford and the Wharfe at
Tadcaster. It is not possible to say how many of Rædwald's warriors accompanied him; possibly his force was very small, although
it might have swelled as he progressed. At each bridge or ford
they laid themselves open to ambush. They were vulnerable to
attack from Mercian warbands and from the British king Ceretic
of Elmet, where Edwin's nephew, Hereric, had been given sanctuary. At each *villa regalis* or royal estate beyond the Humber,
king's men must have come to submit to their new Lord; many
would have done so with a mixture of trepidation and hope, for
these were Edwin's ancestral lands, the kingdom of Deira. There
had not been a Deiran king for a generation. Lines of patronage
had been monopolised by Bernicians. Aspiring warriors and time-
served landed nobles would now compete for the king's interest.

At Tadcaster the road to York veers north-eastwards to take
advantage of the higher ground provided by glacial moraines.
Something of that city's Roman grandeur survived into the

seventh century, but it was not recognisable as a functioning urban political unit like the great cities of Frankia. There was no judicial function, no military command, no authority to organise maintenance of its dilapidated defences. Under Æthelfrith's rule, indeed, it may have been to all intents and purposes ignored as a centre of royal power; effectively abandoned. Its status as an emporium serving the court and its establishment as a new seat of ecclesiastical power—not by any means unconnected developments—probably date from Edwin's reign alone, as does the attempt to restore sections of its Roman walls. The high ground of the legionary fortress and principia on which York Minster stands today were in Edwin's day surrounded by the periodically flooded plains of the rivers Ouse and Foss. Edwin's ambitions for its revival may have had much to do with its history as the city where Constantine the Great was created Emperor of Rome in 306; they may also have had something to do with the motivations of his erstwhile nocturnal visitor Paulinus, who had seen Rome and knew what an imperial city ought to look like.

Deira, the land of the peoples of the Derwent: one of a number of rivers bearing the same British name derived from the Brythonic word for oak, it seems to flow the wrong way, from the sea inland. Its headwaters are indeed close to the sea near Filey but the clue to its course is its origin as a glacial melt-water lake draining the North York Moors and the chalk Wolds. In the Mesolithic period, some several thousand years BC, it was an area rich in natural resources, exploited by hunter-gatherers. The lake drained, as the river does, westwards into the Vale of York, via the Roman cavalry fort at Malton and the village of Stamford Bridge, possibly the Roman *Derventio* and site of the dramatic pre-Hastings battle of 1066 in which Norwegian King Harald Hardrada was cut down by his ill-fated Saxon namesake.

To the east and south of the River Derwent the rolling chalk uplands of the Yorkshire Wolds were densely occupied during the

Neolithic, Bronze Age and Iron Age. By the fifth and sixth centuries AD some of the earliest concentrations of Germanic pagan cremation cemeteries were to be found here: at Sancton (the largest in England), Garton Slack and elsewhere.[65] Many Wolds burials of the Early Medieval period have been recovered from prehistoric burial mounds. Somewhere along the west edge of the Wolds was a splendid Early Medieval palace: near Goodmanham or perhaps at Place Newton near Wintringham. North of the Wolds the edge of the Vale of Pickering has revealed an extraordinary landscape of settlements of which the Anglian village at West Heslerton on the southern edge has become celebrated in archaeology for the heroic scale and excellence of its excavation and for the enormous wealth of information it has revealed about the prosaic lives of its inhabitants.

For one thing, West Heslerton gives the lie to the idea that there was any great physical invasion of Germanic peoples. Recent genetic studies have shown that, contrary to what Bede and generations of historians and archaeologists believed, most of the modern British population have been here since the dimmest days of prehistory.[66] At Heslerton this has been confirmed despite the apparently contradictory evidence of 'new' building types, foreign artefacts and a general reshuffling of landscape elements. It used to be thought that the *grubenhäuser* or sunken-floored buildings, big timber halls and village layouts typical of Early Medieval settlements must have belonged to a wave of Germanic farmer-settlers; that the exotic artefacts found in cemeteries belonged to those invaders and that their settlements gave us our English place-names. Now it seems that most of the 'new' settlements had been there all along; that the indigenous British were adopting the language and fashions of a small number of immigrants. To offer a recent example, the adoption of and enthusiasm for cricket, Western dress and the English law code ought not to be taken as evidence for a mass invasion of India by the British in the nineteenth century. Settlements like West Heslerton, especially those near the south and east coasts, were susceptible to external cultural influences; they were not over-run. And there is very little evidence, if any, that these rural settlements were destroyed by violence or even that they were routinely made defensible by ramparts or stockades.

Whatever opaque forces transformed Roman Britain into Anglo-Saxon England, it was not mass immigration or invasion. It seems more likely that the general economic and political tensions of the fourth and fifth centuries prompted a reversion to regionalism, that of the native British tribes, and even to localism. The world shrank a little. The British, having been used to more or less peace and quiet, took to hiring foreign mercenaries for their protection and it was natural that, even in relatively small numbers, those with the arms, ability and experience of authority began to assume local, then regional control. Whether or not such developments looked or felt like revolution, or anarchy, may largely depend on how long they took to come about; and that question is an enduring if potentially solvable one for archaeologists.

The Vale of Pickering and indeed a large part of the lands of Deira were agriculturally productive even if much low-lying land had become waterlogged in the fifth and sixth centuries. It was a land, as Bede himself said, rich in grain, cattle and draught animals.[67] There were no great swathes of abandoned farmland for immigrants to exploit. The rural population of the north was as it had been: static, tied to the land by bonds of service and render, and subject not to displacement but to the introduction of new ideas, styles of clothing, buildings and gods under the influence of its peripatetic lords. Some of these lords probably did come, as Hengest and Horsa had, from across the sea with their warbands: their influence seems to have been entirely disproportionate to their numbers.

Heslerton's excavator Dominic Powlesland believes that the classic diagnostic feature of early English settlements, the so-called sunken-floored building or *grubenhaus*, was not the grub-hut of early twentieth-century imagination but a grain store with a raised timber floor to protect its contents from flood and rodents.[68] His evidence of animal bones—several tens of thousands of them from this one site—is that sheep, goats and cattle were kept not so much for eating as for wool, milk, hides and traction. He thinks the inhabitants mostly ate porridge. Their settlements, which one might justifiably call proto-villages, were well laid out with clusters of buildings devoted to crafts, cereal processing and so on, and a hierarchy of housing styles. They forged their own iron and probably had a corn mill, controlled by some sort of 'manorial' centre. They were buried in a cemetery in graves that suggest family groupings, exactly as one would expect in any English churchyard. The settlement was undefended. That it represents continuity in the landscape is shown by its location at the site of a Romano-British shrine and spring. These springs are keys to the location of Early Medieval settlement in the area. On the Wolds massif itself there is only one permanent stream, the Gypsy Race; where the chalk overlies a clay band, along the north scarp of the Wolds, there is a line of springs that attracted settlement from well before the arrival of the Roman legions.

The ordinary inhabitants of Deira had access to exotica: the querns made from Niedermendig lava (imported from the Rhineland), the ivory and cowrie shells, are just the materially robust remnant of goods which might also have included imported dyestuffs and leather goods. These might have been obtained from beach markets along the Yorkshire coast: at Filey, perhaps, but also from further afield. There is a cluster of *wic*-names along the Yorkshire coast between Hornsea and Filey which seems to indicate the sites of various periodic beach-markets and which is paralleled by a cluster near Lindisfarne in

Bernicia. The essential sense of continuity of the territories and settlements in this area is shown by the remarkable coincidence of Bronze or Iron Age boundaries and medieval parishes along the north edge of the Wolds, each with its manor and village, prehistoric burial mounds and palisaded knoll site, such as that at Staple Howe.[69] Today the parish boundaries run across the grain of the land from high on the Wolds, where they link late Bronze Age burial mounds, right down to the River Derwent. This reflects an ancient division of the landscape in which each community had access to the full range of resources from hill pasture to spring, arable fields, water meadows and river.

Whatever upheavals were visited on the people of East Yorkshire by the deeds of kings, the human landscape of its indigenous people had not much changed between the rules of Constantine and Edwin. There is evidence for a decline in climate to cooler, wetter conditions; there are signs that some cultivated land was abandoned to secondary woodland; the population dropped from its late Roman peak of perhaps five million in Britain, but there is no evidence of catastrophe, no wholesale exodus of British peasants fleeing Germanic conquerors. Field, pasture, fence and hedge would be recognisable to any small-scale twentieth-century farmer from the east of Europe, as would the cycles of the year dominated by plough, sickle, grain store and sheepfold.

The scores or hundreds of West Heslertons which must have existed across Deira, evidenced by the density of early English place-names and increasing numbers of archaeologically identified settlements and cemeteries, demonstrates the competence and viability of Early Medieval life. It also highlights a negative: there is very little else in the early seventh-century landscape. There were no functioning towns, perhaps anywhere in Britain, in which civic activities we would recognise as urban—planned streets, public buildings, permanent markets and industrial zones—might have carried on between the fifth and eighth centuries. Markets were temporary, perhaps even opportunistic. Gatherings were seasonal, tribal, customary. Armies were maintained not by conscription but by personal loyalties that collapsed on the death of their lords. Bridges might be maintained in certain critical locations, but most Roman examples fell into disuse to be replaced by fords and ferry crossings. Dykes were occasionally built by collective enterprise in Yorkshire, in East Anglia and Wessex; but not many, and we cannot be sure of their function or longevity. Roman roads were, in the main, maintained by use rather than repair. Justice and the rendering of food rents and services were controlled by customary law. The only features of the human landscape that reflected the social complexity of society were the estate centres on which these functions converged. For Deira, so far, few of these have been identified, but there is no reason to suppose that they did not exist as they demonstrably did in Bernicia. They may well lie, as yet undetected, beneath the fields and farmyards of later manor houses.

Where were the borders of Deira, if indeed such a term as border is relevant in this period? It used to be thought, and quite reasonably, that the rivers Humber and Tyne, or possibly Tees, marked the Deiran marches to south and north; to the east was the sea and to the west lay the Pennine British territory of Elmet, its heartlands in the region around Leeds (*Loidis*) and perhaps defined on the east by the rivers Wharfe and Don. The extent of this enigmatic kingdom is to this day indicated by place-names like Sherburn-in-Elmet and Barwick-in-Elmet, which imply that Edwin was skirting it on his route north from the Idle. One credible suggestion is that the Roman road running north to south through Yorkshire may have been identified as a boundary, but at what period is not clear.[70] The northern edge of Deira is more problematic. This is partly because of a lack of historical references to a boundary, but also because there appears to have been a fundamental shift in the dynamics of borders between the fifth and seventh centuries. Many of the territories to emerge from the mists of the fifth century seem to have been defined by watersheds, so that major river systems were at the core of their lands. Examples that survived into the historic period include Hwicce, at the head of the Severn Estuary, and Arosæte, around the River Arrow in Wiltshire.[71] Some time between the beginning of the sixth century and the end of the seventh, rivers became boundaries, not cores; and this process is likely to have coincided with many small kingdoms being subsumed into larger territories to form the so-called Heptarchy of the middle Saxon period: Northumbria, Mercia, Wessex, Kent, East Anglia, Essex and Sussex.

In Edwin's and Oswald's day there were many more. A number of these survived to be recorded in the so-called Tribal Hidage, a list of tributary states dating to the seventh or eighth century; many others are unrecorded but can be partially reconstructed from place-name and other evidence. Between Lindsey (roughly modern Lincolnshire) and Elmet, for example, there seems to have been a small polity or petty kingdom called *Hæthfelth* or Hatfield consisting of the lower Trent and Ouse fenlands at the head of the Wash.[72] Further north, the lands to the north-east of, and including, *Catræth* may have formed a small kingdom based on the Roman fortress there (or perhaps an older fortress on the castle mound at Richmond) and the fertile lowlands of the Tees Valley.[73] A pagan Anglo-Saxon cemetery of more than a hundred and twenty individuals excavated at Norton, near Stockton-on-Tees, offers an intriguing look at a sixth-century population belonging to this putative petty kingdom, a mixture of British and 'Germanic' styles of burial and grave goods with links across and outside the region and artefacts from as far away as Frankia.[74] If nothing else, it warns us of the dangers of making any sharp ethnic or cultural divisions between native and foreigner: drinking Coke and eating McDonald's burgers does not turn a Japanese youth into an American any more than a British household furnished in a popular Swedish style makes its inhabitants ethnically or culturally Ikean.

Deira itself might have originated as the lands belonging to the River Derwent: the southern Vale of York and the Vale of Pickering along with the Wolds. The work of the historical geographer Brian Roberts suggests that what he calls cultural corelands, a similar concept to the Irish tribal *tuath* based on the *magh*, or fertile plain, help to explain the existence of these polities. Their expansion in the sixth century to the point where conflict with neighbours was inevitable can now only be speculatively reconstructed. But if that is the case, then the idea of the River Tyne as a boundary between Deira and Bernicia is a false concept, even if it might apply in a limited sense to the later Anglo-Saxon period. More likely, the Tyne Basin and Valley were the core of the British kingdom of Bryneich which later became Anglian Bernicia. That being the case, Roberts argues, the converging edges of Deira and Bernicia in Oswald's day lay somewhere in the less fertile parts of north Durham.

It is unlikely that Æthelfrith, even in his exceptionally long rule, exercised what we would recognise as administrative control over a united kingdom. These were separate states forced into a mutually reluctant marriage in which tribute flowed from Deira to Bernicia. The fact that Edwin was able to exercise a similar control, but with the tribute flowing the other way, argues against, rather than for, their interdependency as a viable single kingdom. The Deiran nobility, having no acceptable candidate of their own and having been politically allied to Bernicia by the marriage of Æthelfrith to Acha, had no choice but to accept the rule of the lord of Bamburgh. Edwin, in turn, was able to exercise tributary control over Bernicia because its nobility had no other credible candidates (they had fled to Dál Riata). Æthelfrith's sons did, at least, have a claim on Deira: their mother was a Deiran princess.

Edwin did not attempt to ally himself with the Bernician nobility by marriage. For one thing, he already had sons by a Mercian princess (no doubt a matter of distress to Bernicians); for another, when he did remarry in the tenth year of his reign—and we do not know the fate of Coenburh—he chose to marry a Kentish Christian princess. But that is another story.

King's gambit

Leax sceal on wæle mid
sceote scriðan

*Salmon must glide with
trout in the pool*

EDWIN'S FIRST TASK ON
gaining the kingship of Deira was to secure his kingdom
against its enemies, internal and external. Politics could come
later; the first decade of his rule was spent establishing his borders, subjecting states to his tributary control and demonstrating
to the world that he was the supreme military power in the land.
The swiftness with which Edwin was apparently able to assert
control over the North reflects both his own strategic abilities
and Rædwald's new-found authority as overking. Edwin might
count on his diplomatic and military support, and his reassur-
ing presence on the east flank of Mercia, although he would also
have been obliged to fight on Rædwald's behalf in the event of
war with his western neighbour; he probably rendered tribute in
the portable forms of cattle and booty to the East Anglian treasury. It is an intriguing possibility that one of the most magnificent items in the Sutton Hoo treasure, the great bronze hanging bowl, might have been a gift from Edwin to his saviour and
lord: its exquisite La Tène enamelled hook-mounts are of northern British provenance (it was recovered inside a bowl which had

come from Coptic Egypt), although in its last owner's hands it was repaired by a distinctively Anglian craftsman.[75] Ironically, the beautiful little rotating pedestal-mounted bronze trout which adorns the inside of the bowl has Christian connotations which may or may not have been lost on its ultimate recipient.

On Æthelfrith's death Oswald, at just thirteen years old, was too young to challenge for his father's kingdom and as yet unproven in battle—hence Acha's apparent determination to spirit her sons away to safety. Eanfrith, his older half-brother, was for whatever reason disinclined to try his hand. Edwin's decisive military victory on the River Idle, backed by Rædwald, ensured that Bernicia submitted to him in 617. Having received oaths from the political elite of Northumbria, Edwin's immediate priority was to secure the kingdom from pretenders. There may have been Bernician candidates, other descendants of Ida hanging around; but we hear nothing of them until a later generation, in Bede's day, brought civil strife to Northumbria.

For Edwin the most likely trouble spot was the kingdom of Elmet, where his nephew Hereric had been taken in by the British court of Ceretic. Ceretic's father was one of the four great warlords who waged war against Bernicia in the 580s. Æthelfrith had made no bid of which we are aware to annexe the Pennines; either he saw Ceretic as a negligible threat, or he was allied to him by some political bond about which we have no knowledge. If Elmet was tributary to Æthelfrith, as seems likely, it may have suited the Bernician king to keep it that way: Elmet under a client king, the way it had been under Roman imperial rule, delivering treasure and cattle annually to its military masters and acting as a buffer against hostile kingdoms to the west and south. The same might have applied to other territorial or tribal groups such as the Pecsætan, the dwellers of the Peak District on the northern edge of Mercia.

The *Historia Brittonum* records blandly that Edwin occupied

Elmet and drove Ceretic out. The Welsh Annals record Ceretic's death under the year 616, which probably equates to a true date of 619. Bede, eulogising Saint Hilda (or Hild), had intelligence that her father, Hereric, was killed by poisoning while in exile at Ceretic's court, and the distinguished Bede scholars Colgrave and Mynors inferred from this that Edwin invaded Elmet in revenge for his nephew's death.[76] Given the competitive nature of seventh-century politics, the opposite is more likely: that Edwin had Hereric poisoned and drove Ceretic from his Pennine lands on the pretext of harbouring him, thus killing two birds with one stone. It is entirely plausible that in those first months or years when Edwin was at his most vulnerable, Hereric made a bid for the kingdom with Ceretic's backing; but the truth cannot now be determined. The simple fact is that within a very few years of becoming king of Deira and Bernicia Edwin added Elmet to his territorial portfolio—not merely as a tributary kingdom but as part of a greater Northumbria—and his closest dynastic rival was dead. If it was not at Edwin's hands or at his behest, Hereric's death certainly tidied things up a bit for him.

There is a slight hint of an attempt by Dál Riatan forces to try their hand against Edwin in the late 610s or early 620s. An Irish poem, now lost, told of an attack by *Fiachnae mac Báetáin*, king of the Dál nAraidi, on Dún Guaire, which can be identified with Bamburgh.[77] Fiachnae was an ally of Eochaid Buide, Oswald's host, so he would have conducted such a bold attack—via the Clyde–Forth isthmus—with the connivance or assistance of Buide; and Oswald, if he was old enough, could well have taken part. But this is no more than a faint flicker of movement on the horizon of acceptable history.

Early in the 620s Edwin felt strong enough to make his boldest expansionist statement, the bald facts of which were manipulated by Bede so he could present them as the workings of providentiality:

The king's earthly power had increased as an augury that he was to become a believer and have a share in the heavenly kingdom. So, like no other king before him, he held under his sway the whole realm of Britain, not only English kingdoms but those ruled over by the Britons as well. He even brought the islands of Anglesey and Man [*Mevanias insulas*] under his power...[78]

This is Bede at his most uncomfortable, arguing effect before cause. At the military level it is clear that Edwin possessed a fleet or was able to command the use of one. On the Dál Riata model his ships, say seven-benchers with a single square sail, would have been manned by soldier-sailors who owed him sea service as part of the render of the land which they held. Where did these men come from? A predominantly maritime nation like Dál Riata based its military render on an amphibious capability: its chief interests focused on territories on the other side of the Irish Sea and among the Hebridean islands. But Deira? Bernicia? Landlocked Elmet? The Northumbrian kingdoms must have been able to lay their hands on ships for coastal raids; but their principal requirement was for substantial land armies to pursue their interests and rivalries among the other kingdoms. So it is worth asking how Edwin assembled a fleet which must, in forcing the submission of the two largest islands off west Britain, have been substantial: a hundred vessels... two thousand men? If this force was raised among the coastal lands of the North Sea, they must additionally have been transported across country. This seems pretty unlikely, although portage across narrow necks of land between seas—the Scottish place-name Tarbet preserves the term for such crossings—did occur.

I suggest that Edwin raised his fleet from an existing maritime territory that owed him render. The obvious candidate is Rheged, the British kingdom of the Solway coast subject to Northumbrian domination since Æthelfrith's day: Rheged boats, manned by Deiran and Bernician warriors, were based probably at the mouth of the Solway not far from Carlisle. There is no doubt that the English, or their piratical forebears, were capable and enthusiastic sailors. The near-contemporary mixture of terror and admiration which made the Germanic sea-captains masters of the Western Seas is evoked brilliantly in a late-fifth-century letter by Sidonius Apollinaris, who warns his correspondent to be...

> ...on the look-out for curved ships; the ships of the Saxons, in whose every oarsman you think to detect an arch-pirate. Captains and crews alike, to a man they teach or learn the art of brigandage; therefore let me urgently caution you to be ever on the alert. For the Saxon is the most ferocious of all foes. He comes on you without warning; when you expect his attack he makes away. Resistance only moves him to contempt; a rash opponent is soon down. If he pursues he overtakes; if he flies himself, he is never caught. Shipwrecks to him are no terror, but only so much training. His is no mere acquaintance with the perils of the sea; he knows them as he knows himself. A storm puts his enemies off their guard, preventing his preparations from being seen; the chance of taking the foe by surprise makes him gladly face every hazard of rough waters and broken rocks.[79]

Bede does not tell us when Edwin's Irish Sea invasion took place. Probably it was not his first priority and must have taken substantial planning. It was a risky operation only to be undertaken after Edwin felt secure in his borders and perhaps as the culmination of a long campaign. Edwin cannot have hoped to regard himself as king of these territories; he wanted them to submit to his imperium. This is confirmed by Bede's note of their tributary values: nine hundred and fifty hides for Man, three hundred for Anglesey.[80] That is to say, the customary render of these lands, equivalent to something like the same numbers of small land-holdings, was now owed to Edwin of Northumbria rather than the previous overlord of these islands, probably the king of Gwynedd. The benefits to Edwin were in treasure, to be distributed to his victorious warriors, and an increase in his dominion, the worldly territories over which he held sway and which, to Bede's retrospective eyes, was an indication of God's favour.

Nothing is known of the dynastic history of Man at this period, but in identifying Cadwallon of Gwynedd as overlord of Anglesey one also suggests a motivation for Edwin's maritime campaign: it was personal. Open warfare between the two former foster-brothers, probably after the death of Cadfan, Edwin's foster father, in around 625, ended in Cadwallon's virtual destruction.* The Welsh Annals record that he was besieged on the island of *Glannauc*—that is, Ynys Seiriol or Priestholm off the east coast of Anglesey. The annal entry is for 629, although the exact date of Cadwallon's political nadir could be two or three years either side of that. There is a chance that Gwynedd and Elmet, both king- doms of British Christians, had enjoyed a historic alliance, which would have added spice to whatever animosity existed between Edwin and Ceretic. That Gwynedd and Elmet enjoyed political or cultural links is indicated by a carved stone inscription from St Aelhearn's churchyard at Llanaelhaearn on the Llŷn Peninsula commemorating ALIORTUS ELMETIACO, Aliotus the Elmetian.[81]

Edwin's failure to finish Cadwallon off during this campaign would cost him his life. At the time, however, even such personal vendettas must have been peripheral to Edwin's core political ambitions and to other conflicts, martial, spiritual and political. From 617 until about 624 he remained in theory tributary to Rædwald, unable to act entirely independently but accumulating wealth and military strength through raiding and forcing submis- sions on neighbouring kings. It was the decline and death of the East Anglian overlord that seems to have triggered the second phase of Edwin's kingship. A flurry of political activity among the southern kingdoms both preceded and followed Rædwald's

---

* Alex Woolf (2004) has raised serious objections to the identification of this Cadwal- lon with the son of Cadfan and instead suggests that the destroyer of Edwin was a warlord of the Strathclyde Britons; but without any additional narrative context for this candidate, and given the location of the Battle of Hatfield Chase (see p.125), it is difficult to displace the widely accepted Venedotian Cadwallon. ('Venedotian' is the adjectival form of Gwynedd.)

magnificent nautical interment at Sutton Hoo. Edwin saw his opportunity to succeed as overlord, exercising imperium over the southern kingdoms and rendering them tributary; but the politics were complicated.

The Roman mission was plunged into crisis after the death of Æthelberht in 616. Æthelfrith's massacre at Chester precluded any chance of a rapprochement between the British and English churches. Bishop Mellitus had been expelled from the kingdom of the East Saxons and his see at London by the pagan sons of its convert King Sæberht; Mellitus and fellow bishop Justus had left for Frankia. However, King Eadbald of Kent—who had apostasised after his father Æthelberht's death, married his stepmother and, according to Bede, was afflicted by illness as a result—was then converted, probably before 620. According to Bede, Laurence, the Archbishop of Canterbury, was at his wit's end with the apparent failure of Augustine's mission and planned to return to the Continent too until a vision which he related to Eadbald changed both their minds. The Kentish–Roman axis was restored, but vulnerable in the face of surrounding pagan states and lacking Æthelberht's long-nurtured authority.

The background to Eadbald's change of heart is obscure. Historians suspect political pressure from the Merovingian court of Dagobert I—a man with his own political axes to grind among the febrile dynastic rivalries of the Franks—but the possibility of a moment of personal spiritual revelation or the fact of Laurence's traumatic nocturnal terrors should not be dismissed entirely. Enter Eadbald's sister, Æthelburh, who had been raised at Dagobert's court along with other sympathetic exiles such as Sigeberht of East Anglia. Æthelburh's mother was a Frankish princess, so the daughter's Christianity was culturally and dynastically bred in the bone. She, returning to Kent, very possibly provided the diplomatic stick and carrot that persuaded her brother to renounce his stepmother/wife and save the Canterbury mission. It was the first of two decisive moments in the legacy of Augustine. Within a year of the probable date of Rædwald's death, Christian Æthelburh was profitably betrothed to pagan Edwin of Northumbria. Negotiations between Eadbald and Edwin were delicate: Northumbria and Kent were each reluctant to accept tributary status to the other. Edwin's conquests gave him *de facto* status as the most powerful warlord of the English; Eadbald's historic cultural and political ties with the former Roman provinces across the Minch ensured that Kent retained its kudos. Æthelburh, reluctant or willing, was the currency whose rate of exchange must now be determined.

In the summer of 625 the princess travelled north with her entourage. The pre-eminent political figure in the party was Paulinus, who had been living and preaching in Kent for more than twenty years and who carried with him the authority of the original Augustinian mission. In July he was consecrated bishop in the significant surroundings of the ancient Roman principia at York, where he began to construct the first Christian church to be built in England for two-hundred-odd years, a tiny wooden oratory. Edwin agreed that Æthelburh might continue to practise as a Christian, just as Æthelberht had indulged her mother in Canterbury. Eadbald, and by implication Dagobert, insisted that Edwin promise to undergo baptism himself. Edwin agreed to consider conversion, buying time to weigh the domestic political pros and cons of such a decision against the theoretical federal benefits and disciplines of embracing Roman orthodoxy. His patron Rædwald had faced the same dilemma. The marriage was undoubtedly advantageous to Edwin: it was an alliance that linked him via Kent with Frankia and strengthened both parties against Mercia and the other emerging power in the south, the *Gewisse*, the West Saxons of the upper Thames Valley. Few Northumbrians can ever have seen such material splendours as the trappings which Æthelburh brought as her dowry and personal treasures.

Edwin had time on his side: politics do not change much and a marital bird in the hand then, as now, was worth two in the bush. Edwin had his new queen.* He could use her credentials to apply pressure on his Deiran (and Bernician) constituents and, in turn, employ their truculence (real or supposed) to delay acceptance of Eadbald's and Æthelburh's conditions on the grounds that he must achieve political consensus among the Northumbrians. Word of Edwin's tactical shufflings reached as far as the mother city and were read as procrastination. Pope Boniface wrote letters from Rome to the royal couple, copies of which Bede possessed via his Kentish correspondents and which he included in full in his Ecclesiastical History. The letter to Edwin was full of flattery and admonition, describing him as 'Illustrious King of the English' but also accusing him of spiritual delusion, adjuring him to cast out his evil demons and accept everlasting life. The letter was accompanied by a magnificent gold robe and a 'garment' from *Ancyra* (modern Ankara) in Asia Minor.[82] To Æthelburh he sent a silver mirror and an ivory comb adorned with gold, begging her to enlighten her husband, to 'inflame his cold heart'.[83] Gifts and exhortations were potent political weapons: such exotic material glories were not often seen as far north as York; later there would be gold crosses and chalices.† But not for the first or last time, one senses in the seventh-century narrative the shadowy but very real influence of a queen whose political clout was matched by personal authority in the king's household and more particularly in the bedchamber.

The implication of the Pope's intervention was that both spiritual and material glories would follow; and in handling this part of the narrative Bede must once more face up to a difficulty. It

---

* It is not known when Edwin's Mercian queen Coenburh died, or if he repudiated her.

† EH II.20 These last items were retrieved by Paulinus after Edwin's death and taken to Kent.

would have suited his purpose better if Edwin's material successes had *followed* his conversion; it was necessary for him to execute the clumsy sleight-of-hand in which he cited Edwin's territorial success as an 'augury' of his acceptance of Christ. It was not the only awkward conjuring act Bede found it necessary to resort to in bending the conversion of the English people to his providential requirements.

Who can say precisely what effect the Pope's letters had on the illiterate king of the Northumbrians; who can say whether they were read to him by his wife over breakfast, assuming that she could read Latin, or by Paulinus before his nobles in the mead hall? The timing of the letters has never been satisfactorily calculated, but they do not seem to have been decisive in Edwin's acceptance of Christianity. Rome was, after all, a distant chimera. Edwin's political intuition would decide the issue; that, and events. The pressure on Edwin to accept baptism must have increased along parallel lines. The queen's discomfort must have grown during the early part of 626 as the birth of her first child approached. Paulinus, too, was under pressure to exploit this most propitious of opportunities to bring a great warlord into the church.

At Easter 626 the king of the *Gewisse*, Cwichelm, sent an envoy named Eomer to Edwin's court while he was residing at a royal estate on the banks of the River Derwent—perhaps near Stamford Bridge or Malton. He was received at Edwin's table in a manner suitable to his political rank and chose his moment for maximum dramatic effect. As he addressed the court with his master's bogus embassy, he drew a short sword smeared with poison that he had concealed in his cloak and rushed towards the king, thrusting at him with great force.[84] It must have been an extraordinarily chaotic and violent scene: tables and benches overturned in the uproar which followed the unprovoked attack; swords drawn; panic, shouts, the barking of dogs. The boldness of this suicidal attack is breathtaking. One of the king's men, a *gesith* called Lilla, who must have been at the target's side, managed to put himself between the assassin's blade and his king and, taking the full fury of the attack, was killed. Edwin was injured by the same sword thrust, such was its ferocity, before Eomer was surrounded and brought down. In the ensuing fracas the assassin was killed but not before he had taken with him another of Edwin's *gesiths* named Forthere. Lilla's sacrifice seems to have earned him a magnificent burial, if the mound called Lilla's Howe on Goathland Moor in North Yorkshire—probably in origin a prehistoric barrow re-used as a mark of special favour—commemorates him.

The same night, as Edwin recovered from his wounds, Æthelburh was delivered of a daughter whom they named Eanflæd. For Bede, no more providential pairing of events could be imagined: God had intervened in decisive fashion to persuade the king of His powers. How could Edwin now resist such proofs of the virtues of the Christian God? One student of the period, Catherine Bridges, has rather brilliantly suggested that the traumatic events of that Easter might have induced the premature birth of the queen's first child, which would give the whole episode an additional poignancy not lost on either of its parents.[85] At Whitsun, fifty days later, Paulinus baptised the infant princess Eanflæd, whose life her father pledged to Christ as a sign of gratitude for his (and her) delivery: the Mephistophelean priest thus received his first payment in kind. Eleven others of the household were baptised in the same ceremony, which may have taken place close to the oratory built by Paulinus at York. The suitably apostolic number of baptisms—twelve—must have been suggested by Paulinus for maximum biblical effect. Even now, Edwin sought further political capital from his own prospective conversion. He would cast aside his idols and accept the word of God should his war of revenge against the West Saxons prove successful. Would the One God prove as effective in war as his own tribal totem, Woden?

Edwin's campaign against Cwichelm later in the same year, after his wounds had healed, was in the nature of a punitive raid during which no fewer than five 'kings' of the *Gewisse* were slain.[86] Cwichelm himself survived and one must infer that the kings in question were either sub-kings under tribute to Cwichelm or leaders of substantial warbands under his personal command—possibly brothers and cousins. There could now be no doubt that Edwin was the most powerful warlord among the English, able to strike at will over large distances across both land and sea. If he now chose to adopt the Christian religion, who would challenge either his authority or that of the one true God? And it has to be remembered that this was not about personal salvation, whatever the Pope had written; this was about the acceptance of theoretical Roman ecclesiastical authority over the ruling class of Northumbrians, the land-holding warriors. But, yet again, Edwin delayed. Bede's oddly split narrative of these events, which seems to preserve three incompatible accounts of Edwin's internal musings, tries to marry political, spiritual and providential anecdotes which must, I think, reflect genuine political complexities and doubts in the king's mind. We can read this in several ways. Edwin was not a rash man: all the evidence suggests that he weighed political considerations with great care before he acted. Bede describes him as a man of 'great natural sagacity' who 'would sit for long periods in silence... deliberating with himself as to what he ought to do'.[87] Is this a man of brooding self-doubt, or one deeply sensitive to the potential consequences of his political and moral decisions? It is hard to say, but the Edwin who emerges from Bede's pages, if a great warlord, is also more than that: he is a politician and a man of tangible sensibilities.

In attempting to give a consistent narrative thread to these complexities Bede would have us believe that now, after so many apparent signs of divine favour, Edwin was brought to a final understanding of his obligations by Paulinus, who at last revealed to the king that it was he who had appeared to him in the vision many years before at Rædwald's court when his fate looked so bleak at the point of betrayal. Paulinus was either a shameless opportunist who had heard Edwin's story of the vision and substituted himself for the stranger in the night; or he had in fact met and cultivated Edwin during his exile and was now calling in the marker. If the latter was the case, he had waited an improbably long time to produce his IOU and wave it in front of his patron. This is how Bede, no doubt conflating several oral versions circulating down to his own day, describes the cathartic encounter with, once again, Edwin cast as Faust:

> One day Paulinus came to him and, placing his right hand on the king's head, asked him if he recognised this sign. The king began to tremble and would have thrown himself at the Bishop's feet but Paulinus raised him up and said in a voice that seemed familiar, 'First you have escaped with God's help from the hands of the foes you feared; secondly you have acquired by His gift the kingdom you desired; now, in the third place, remember your own promise; do not delay in fulfilling it but receive the faith and keep the commandments of him who rescued you from your earthly foes and raised you to the honour of an earthly kingdom.'[88]

That Paulinus had such intimate access to the Northumbrian king is in itself remarkable, even if they had met before in other circumstances. There is no suggestion that Edwin and Paulinus enjoyed a personal friendship like that attributed to Oswald and Ségéne on Iona. Even so, Edwin's intimates might very well have resented his access to their lord. Tensions between spiritual and secular advisors have troubled many rulers over the centuries, especially if those advisors are close to the female head of the royal household. Paulinus had some experience of such tensions from his time in Kent; Bede's portrayal of Edwin suggests that he too was sensitive to the dangers of jealous interest. But his store of political capital was overflowing. Edwin, after a triumphant return from the raid on the West Saxons, now embarked on a series of political consultations culminating in a summit meeting, which forms the backdrop to the most famous passage in Bede. The strong sense of theatre that Bede conveys shows the necessity for Edwin to make a grand political event out of negotiations that must substantially have taken place in private, and over many months. The context, given Edwin's probable childhood conversion at the court of Gwynedd, is laden with irony.

The set on which the drama was played out is that of Beowulf's Heorot: a great mead hall lying at the centre of a *villa regalis* somewhere on the edge of the Yorkshire Wolds; the lighting is provided by a great fire burning in a pit at the centre, and by lamps of oil or wax. The walls are hung with banners and glittering arms, the trophies of lost companions and dead foes. Great doors at either end are embellished with carvings: dragons' heads, ravens and other serpentine beasts. Tribal totems stand grisly guard outside. In the middle of each long side there are doors too, part perhaps of the symbolic furniture of precedence and rank. The king sits at the centre with one of these doors at his back. Along the length of the hall are tables ranged in order of precedence: the king, his battle-proven, landed companions; unlanded warriors; retainers of the household. The queen and her entourage are present, Æthelburh playing the part of political hostess to perfection, judiciously flattering her male guests and sweetening them with the mead cup. The twin spiritual forces of Christianity and the heathen gods are represented by Paulinus and by Coifi, the chief priest of the Deirans.

Bede liked to portray such events as spontaneous. It is much more likely that proceedings were stage-managed, just as modern political summits are. Agendas are agreed beforehand; suitable spokesmen are chosen. Lines are rehearsed, little is left to chance and all those present know their parts. Many such councils must have met to debate alliances or prospective military campaigns.

The traditional executive role of the Germanic king was confined to his status as 'king in war'. The wholesale conversion of a kingdom's elite was a matter of great political moment. Are we seeing the emergence of a concept of statehood, an idea of an institution which might exist outwith the physical person of the king? Perhaps. If so, there is a precedent. The Early Medieval historian Edward James has identified a similar three-part process, taking place over perhaps a decade, in the conversion of the Frankish king Clovis around the turn of the sixth century.*

Coifi, the chief priest, is Bede's first witness. He is strangely keen to renounce his former religion. The core of his argument seems to be that for all Edwin's success in war and diplomacy he, Coifi, has seen little reward:

> None of your followers has devoted himself more earnestly than I have to the worship of our gods, but nevertheless there are many who have received greater benefits and greater honour from you than I do...'†

It is as if the arrivals of Paulinus and Æthelburh have cut his lines of patronage. Bede's purpose in deploying him is to show that the head of the pagan priesthood sees little value in pursuing the worship of idols and the divination of auguries. Coifi goes on to advise scrutiny of the case for Christianity and its acceptance if it should prove 'better and more effectual'. The speech may be concocted from anecdotal material circulating in Bede's day, or it may be based on notes taken by the only persons present capable of making a written record—Paulinus and his deacon James. Either way, it does not carry much conviction. Indeed, there have

---

* James 1988, 123. The three parts comprised the king's intellectual conversion, his baptism, and the public announcement, all of which incurred great political risks in pagan aristocratic societies in which Christianity was viewed with the greatest suspicion.

† EH II.13 Colgrave and Mynors 1969, 183. I have often wondered whether Coifi, with his rather un-Germanic name, might in fact have been a Christian British priest retained in Edwin's household since his days of exile and cast in the role of idolater for the occasion.

often been suggestions that the entire Bedan account is in fact that of Paulinus. The testimony of Bede's second witness has the air of a practised rhetorical form, one that a proselytising priest like Paulinus might well have rolled out as part of a sort of DIY conversion kit:

> Another of the king's chief men agreed with this advice and with these wise words and then added, 'This is how the present life of man on earth, King, appears to me in comparison with that time which is unknown to us. You are sitting feasting with your *ealdormen* and thegns* in winter time; the fire is burning on the hearth in the middle of the hall and all inside is warm, while outside the wintry storms of rain and snow are raging; and a sparrow flies swiftly through the hall. It enters at one door and quickly flies out through the other. For the few moments it is inside, the storm and wintry tempest cannot touch it, but after the briefest moment of calm, it flits from your sight, out of the wintry storm and into it again. So this life of man appears but for a moment; what follows or indeed what went before, we know not at all. If this new doctrine brings us more certain information, it seems right that we should accept it.'[89]

The third in Bede's trio of witnesses is Paulinus: tall, stooping (he must have been at the very least in his late forties), with black hair, thin features and classic Italian aquiline nose, he gave off an air of gravitas and moral authority.[90] Although Bede furnishes his account of the priest with the first pen-portrait in English history, he fails to record his words, lending weight to the idea that it was Paulinus who set down the account of Edwin's conversion. He leaves Coifi to summarise the findings of the council and to recommend with admirable zeal the destruction of the idols and temples which were the outward symbols of their worthless religion. Coifi it is who symbolically rides out from the king's palace on a stallion with spear in hand and sword at his side to defile the chief shrine of the Deirans at a place which today is called Goodmanham.

He ordered his companions to set fire to and destroy the

---

* *Ducibus ac ministris.*

shrines and enclosures. Whether that meant razing the entire temple complex to the ground is unclear; if that was the case it was in contravention of Pope Gregory's advice to convert the temples to Christian use but one doesn't imagine Paulinus demurring at such actions, instead watching with a quiet smile of satisfaction on his saturnine features. As for Edwin's chief priest, did he undergo baptism and train for the priesthood, or retire quietly on a small grace-and-favour estate for playing his part so well? As an archaeologist, I am sorely tempted to speculate on what Coifi's eventual burial might have looked like. Was he buried with spear and sword in hand, or with Byzantine Saul and Paul spoons* in his palms, gold-leaf crosses on his eyes and a chalice at his side? Or both, as ambivalent kings like Rædwald and Sæberht seem to have been furnished with. There was an intriguing burial at Yeavering which looks suspiciously like that of a heathen priest and is probably contemporary with these events. The so-called Grave AX lay at the west end, just outside the entrance to one of the great halls (Building A4). The ghost of a stain in the soil indicated the inhumation of an adult male in the flexed position—partially on its side with knees bent. Laid across the body, running the length of the grave, had been a wooden object bound with bronze fittings which seemed to designate the occupant as a person of special rank or function—as did his position of honour. Yeavering's brilliant excavator, Dr Brian Hope-Taylor, thought that the object might be a ceremonial staff and the idea that this was the grave of Coifi, Edwin's chief priest, is an attractive one.[91] The individual could equally, as Hope-Taylor himself suggested, have been a standard-bearer with his *tufa* or even the surveyor-general of the township's buildings.

Within a year Edwin, all 'his nobles and a vast number of

---

* The Sutton Hoo burial contained a pair of such silver spoons with the two names of the apostle Paul, before and after his conversion, engraved on them. They are regarded as bearing a symbolic reference to baptism.

the common people' (*gentis suae nobilibus ac plebe*) were baptised by Paulinus and his deacons. It was a political triumph for
the king and a personal one for the Italian missionary, who thus
fulfilled Gregory's original intention to install a bishop in the
ancient Roman *colonia* at York. Deira was now Christian, in name
at least. Paulinus embarked on a programme of catechism and
baptism that led to mass immersions in the swift brown waters
of the River Swale at Catterick.* Later, he built a church at a
royal residence called Campodonum, probably near Dewsbury in
West Yorkshire, while work also progressed on a stone church to
replace his oratory at York.

Now secure in the king's own territory, Paulinus and his entourage moved north into Bernicia where, Bede relates somewhat
disingenuously, the rest of the Northumbrians gladly received
the grace of baptism. It must have been a strange event; but no
Bernician ambitious to enjoy the fruits of patronage of this most
successful king could afford to spurn the chance of joining his
new club. The warrior elites of early England were nothing if not
pragmatic. The place where hundreds of Bernicians underwent
the rites of salvation was another royal residence, one with the
strongest heathen overtones: Yeavering. For thirty-six days from
morning until evening Paulinus and his deacons immersed the
prospective faithful in the River Glen, one of England's most historically blood-filled rivers.

Yeavering is pre-eminent among the excavated settlements
of Early Medieval Britain, investigated in the 1950s and 1960s
by an archaeologist of rare talents who was in many respects far
ahead of his time. Brian Hope-Taylor's exquisite monograph[92]
describes an extraordinarily detailed landscape of royal architecture and social space but also seems to bridge the often-defiant
chasm between history and archaeology. Here Hope-Taylor

---

* The author has swum there himself after long hot days excavating on the farm that
  overlooks the spot and can testify to its cleansing properties.

believed that he could actually identify structures commissioned by the historical King Edwin for precisely this Bedan scene: the wholesale conversion of the Bernician nobility. The excavations identified the literal and physical manifestation of the stage on which this Shakespearean drama was played out against a magnificent backdrop: the primeval, sensuously atmospheric hills of the Cheviot massif.

The grandstand at Yeavering is unique in archaeology. Surviving below the topsoil as a pattern of post-settings in deep arcing trenches, it has left behind the unmistakeable form of a segment of a circle, looking from the air like some sonic wave from an echo-locator. Its focal point, towards the north-east, was a dais or platform of the sort one used to see on newsreels for the ceremonial launching of great ships. Beyond that, aligned as if by a meticulous town-planner, an imposing series of magnificent timber halls, the archaeological reality of Beowulf's Heorot, stressed the royal splendour of the setting. Beyond them lay another unique structure, the great enclosure: an enormous cattle corral.* Other domestic apartments fanned out to the north while behind the grandstand, to the south-west, were an ancient pagan cemetery focused on a succession of timber posts and a complex of ritual buildings, where sacrifices were made to the gods of Bernicians and huge feasts were prepared for the visits of kings.

The bulk of the grandstand structure measured fifty feet from front to back. Nineteen feet to the rear of the widest arc four great post-holes indicated where buttresses had supported the immense weight of the back tier—an estimated twenty feet off the ground.[93] Hope-Taylor had no doubt that the whole construction

---

* Perhaps not quite unique. In 1983 the author was flying over the Yorkshire Wolds above the village of Wintringham, looking for prehistoric earthworks, when he saw the cropmark of an enclosure terminal he thought identical to that at Yeavering. Perhaps one day a royal settlement on the western edge of the Wolds, Yeavering's Deiran twin, will be properly identified and excavated.

sloped up from front to back, exactly like the terrace of a Greek or Roman theatre. No-one can say for sure why the grandstand was built, but Hope-Taylor's conclusion was that it was constructed to formalise the proceedings of Paulinus's mass conversion, in suitably impressive surroundings. Later archaeologists have approached the excavator's historical synchronisation of his findings with caution, almost with over-caution: it seems just too good to be true. But the uniqueness of the historical occasion and the singularity of the structure are hard to ignore and there are other reasons for believing Hope-Taylor's interpretation. Much discussion has revolved around the grandstand's possible precedents elsewhere in the archaeological record. There seem to be none. If the building is to be placed in Edwin's reign, one must seek its inspiration.

Two lines of thought can be traced. One is the existence of surviving Roman structures which Edwin might have seen during his years of exile, or in his own lands. York, it is true, possessed surviving Roman masonry, but no theatre. Colchester, in the kingdom of the East Saxons, had an amphitheatre and an out-of-town theatre at Gosbecks during the Roman period. Closer to home, Aldborough on the Roman road north-west of York, which had been the *civitas* capital of the Brigantes tribe, had an amphitheatre. Chester, which Edwin might have visited in his days in Gwynedd, also boasted an amphitheatre. These structures had, naturally enough, been built of stone in pure Mediterranean style; and Edwin's evident desire to embrace the trappings—or what he thought of as the trappings—of the fallen empire of the giants, might certainly have encouraged him in the desire to have his own copy. It suited his idea of imperium which, as Bede says, was expressed by the carrying of a *thuf* or *tufa*, an iron standard or staff like that from the Sutton Hoo burial, before his train, and by his royal progress with standard-bearers walking before him.[94] Not for nothing had Edwin revived York, the city of Constantine the Great's elevation to the Imperial purple, as a place of royal significance.

Another equally plausible thought is that the grandstand was inspired by Paulinus. This was a man who had spent his early life in the mother city, who would have walked among the splendours, such as they still were in the year 600, of ancient Rome. More than that, even, Paulinus had spent twenty years or so in Canterbury, where the Roman theatre (about twice as big, front to back, as the Yeavering grandstand) could still be seen, and entered, in the centre of the town right down to the early seventh century.[95] That Paulinus might have suggested the erection of the grandstand to his patron is intriguing; that he was able to commission its construction is remarkable. The builders of the palace complex at Yeavering were masters of woodcraft; did they envision Paulinus's idea from drawings, or a model? Did Paulinus bring craftsmen over from the Continent? I favour the former scenario. Probably no-one had ever built such a thing in wood, but it was certainly not beyond the capabilities of local engineers and craftsmen for whose skills Hope-Taylor's admiration leaps from the pages of his sumptuous account.

There is a third, even more intriguing context for this enigmatic structure. A recent re-evaluation of Hope-Taylor's account of the grandstand draws attention to a contemporary Frankish law code that expounds the role and use of a *staffolus*.[96] This was essentially a post, perhaps not unlike a tribal totem pole, a focal point for dispensing the king's law and for his quasi-divine role as tribal head. Yeavering's grandstand has a post-hole as its focal point, which fits perfectly the notion implied by the *Lex Ripuaria*, and the re-use of Roman theatres as places of Continental tribal assembly is well-established. What makes this proposition so apt for Yeavering is that the *Lex Ripuaria* is generally regarded as a product of the court of Dagobert I, and Edwin's queen Æthelburh was also a product of that court. Did Æthelburh's influence extend beyond her husband's conversion to its physical embodiment at the tribal assembly place of the Bernicians beneath their holy mountain of Yeavering Bell? Was the grandstand, in fact, the conception of a Frankish woman, realised by Bernician craftsmen to emphasise both her husband's imperium and her priest's spiritual hegemony over the north? It is tempting to believe that, subtle politician as he was, Edwin deployed his queen to win the hearts and minds of his subject peoples by flattering and perhaps intimidating them with magnificence—imposing on the vulgar, as a later social historian would have it.* Curious readers trying to envision this Dark Age marvel will be happy to know that in late 2012 approval was given for a project to recreate the Yeavering grandstand at Bede's World in Jarrow, in a suitably Early Medieval setting.

After fifteen years of rule over Deira and Bernicia, King Edwin might be supposed, and was certainly believed by Bede, to have laid the foundations of a Christian Anglo-Saxon state. He had successfully, it must have seemed, converted all the English peoples of the North to a more civilised spiritual code with the promise that for future generations life did not end suddenly like the flight of a sparrow into the winter storms but that believers would bathe in the warmth of everlasting salvation. More, he had played a part in rescuing the Augustinian mission; he had even persuaded the apostate king of East Anglia, Rædwald's son Eorpwald, to convert and Eorpwald had established Bishop Felix in a new see at *Dommoc*.† Paulinus went on to preach in Lindsey, constructing a church—perhaps that excavated at St

---

* Sir Richard Phillips, commenting in 1817 on the Prince Regent's new palace in St James's Park, wrote: 'The love of shew in princes... is often justified by the alleged necessity of imposing on the vulgar; but I doubt whether any species of imposition really produces the effect which the pomp of power is so willing to ascribe to it, as an excuse for its own indulgences.' From *A morning's walk from London to Kew*

† Either Dunwich, a port that was consumed by the sea, or more obviously Felixstowe.

Paul-in-the-Bail, in Lincoln—and establishing a bishopric there. York, after the gift of a pallium* sent by Pope Honorius, would became Britain's second metropolitan see, a status it did not actually acquire until 735 but which it retains today.

It remains to ask just how deep was the penetration of the Augustinian mission in Northumbria. Paulinus's stone church, which probably lies beneath the foundations of York Minster, was not completed before Oswald's day. We know of only one other church in Deira belonging to the mission. Archaeologists have, unsurprisingly, sought answers at Yeavering. Was the church constructed there in wood (Building B, the focus of an east–west aligned cemetery) a feature of Edwin's palace or was it not built until Oswald's day? Was the building identified as a heathen temple (Building D2, in which a pit contained the remains of several ox skulls) converted, as per Gregory's instructions to Augustine and Æthelbert, into a place for Christian worship? Or, as we might suspect, was Edwin's and Paulinus's conspicuous conversion of the Bernicians no more than political show?

Whatever may be said of King Edwin's attitude to the Christian God, there is no doubting his sense of pomp and state, or his idea of imperium. The archaeologist and historian Nick Higham has argued persuasively that the list of subject peoples and the renders they owed, known as the Tribal Hidage, was a product of Edwin's rule. Listing the peoples owing tribute (Deira and Bernicia are conspicuously absent from the list) to an unnamed king, it records the number of hides at which each territory was assessed, offering some clues to the relative wealth or at least punitive value of those kingdoms, great and petty, of which it is composed. It is the first document which gives us a clue to the political geography of England in the seventh century (if we

---

* The pallium was a broad strip of embroidered cloth worn as a mark of office by what would later be called an archbishop. In Paulinus's case it arrived too late (see below, p.129).

may date it so early) and the first attempt by a literate state (again one suspects the hand of Paulinus, for Edwin surely did not learn his letters) to establish by documentary record what it was owed, and by whom. It was also said that in Edwin's day…

> there was so great a peace in Britain, wherever the dominion of King Edwin reached, that, as the proverb still runs, a woman with a new-born child could walk throughout the island from sea to sea and take no harm. The king cared so much for the good of the people that, in various places where he had noticed clear springs near the highway, he caused stakes to be set up and bronze drinking cups to be hung on them for the refreshment of travellers.[97]

This was the legacy of a man who intended that he should be remembered as a great warlord, but as more than just a warlord. His ambition for a revival of Constantine's imperial legacy is breathtaking. His journey from the lonely night-before-death exiled prince to latter-day emperor was epic. And yet, his vision for a united people under one king and one religion was a chimera that did not outlive his death, following which the Northumbria state collapsed. That was the way with the early Anglo-Saxon pagan state, and Edwin's Northumbria was no different.

Timeline: AD 604 to 631

604   Oswald, son of Æthelfrith and Acha, born.
       —Death of Pope Gregory the Great.
       —?Death of Augustine (before 610); succeeded at Canterbury by Laurence (to 619).
       —Sæberht ruling East Saxons from London; converts to Christianity (EH V.24).
       —?King Æthelbert of Kent founds St Paul's in London; Mellitus is first bishop.

606   Probable date of death of Áedán mac Gabráin aged over seventy after a thirty-four-year reign in Dál Riata (*CS*; 607 in the *AC*). Succeeded by Eochaid Buide (to 629).

611   Cynegisl becomes king of Wessex until 642. Edwin probably in exile among British at Gwynedd; at some point before 616 marries Cearl of Mercia's daughter Coenburh. Has two sons, Osfrith and Eadfrith.

612   Oswiu, son of Æthelfrith, born.
       —Probable date for the death of St Kentigern, or Mungo, founder of Glasgow.

615   ?Rheged seized by Æthelfrith and annexed to Northumbria.
       —Edwin of Deira takes refuge with Rædwald of East Anglia.
       —Possible birth date of Æbbe, daughter of Æthelfrith and Acha.

615? **Battle of Chester**: Æthelfrith defeats British warbands under Solon, son of Conan of Powys. His slaughter of monks is later cited by Bede as divine retribution for their failure to agree terms with Augustine.

616 Edwin seeks refuge with Rædwald of East Anglia. Æthelberht of Kent dies. Eadbald succeeds (to 640), and apostasises; marries stepmother, converts *c.*617.

616/17 Æthelfrith is ambushed and killed by Rædwald of East Anglia at Bawtry in the **Battle of the River Idle**.

—Oswald takes refuge in Dál Riata with Oswiu and infant sister Æbbe. Half brother Eanfrith flees to Pictland.

—Edwin becomes king of Deira, having fought beside Rædwald.

619 Edwin conquers British kingdom of Elmet (*AC*), now parts of West Yorkshire; Elmet under Ceretic may have been previously tributary to Cearl of Mercia.

—Archbishop Laurence dies; succeeded by Mellitus (to 624).

—Pope Boniface V succeeds Deusdedit to 625.

622 (or later) Edwin campaigns against Man and Anglesey; besieges Cadwallon on Priestholm Island.

623 Possible campaign against Irish Dál Riata by Edwin; possible siege of Bamburgh by Irish, cited in Annals of Ulster, Annals of Tigernach and Book of Leinster.

—Dagobert I succeeds Clothar II in Austrasia; capital at Metz.

624/5 King Rædwald of East Anglia dies (probable date; likely buried at Sutton Hoo), the first English king to render all Roman provinces of Britain tributary to him. Succeeded by Eorpwald, who apostasises (but is reconverted by Edwin: see under 628).

—Archbishop Mellitus dies; succeeded by Justus (to 631).

625 King Edwin marries a Christian princess, Æthelburh of Kent (sister of Eadbald). He has previously been married to Coenburh, the daughter of Cearl of Mercia.

—Paulinus consecrated 21 July as bishop of York.

—Pope Boniface dies; Pope Honorius (to 638) consecrated.

626 Assassination attempt on King Edwin at Easter by agent of Wessex's King Cwichelm. Edwin recovers from wound and wages campaign against Cwichelm; slays five Wessex kings.

—Birth of Eanflæd, daughter of Edwin and Æthelburh, at Easter; baptised at Pentecost with eleven others.

627   King Edwin is baptised in a new wooden church at York on Easter Sunday 12 April by Bishop Paulinus. Osfrid and Eadfrith also baptised. Mass baptisms follow in the River Swale (*Catræth*) and at Edwin's refurbished palace at Yeavering. Æthelthryth, Uscfrea and Æthelhun baptised. Æthelhun and Æthelthryth die in infancy. Yffi son of Osfrith is baptised.

—Penda son of Pybba succeeds to or becomes first overlord of kingdom of Mercia (626 in ASC). ?Cadwallon returns to Gwynedd from exile.

—Possible date of conversion of Eorpwald of East Anglia, persuaded by Edwin.

—Archbishop Justus dies (between 627 and 631); succeeded by Honorius (last of the Gregorian mission: to 653).

—?Tribal Hidage (a list of tributary renders) written, possibly under direction of Paulinus.

628   Probable date of death of Eorpwald of East Anglia; killed by heathen Ricberht (who seizes throne?); East Anglia apostasises for three years.

—Cynegisl and Cwichelm fight against Penda at Cirencester (ASC); they come to 'an agreement'.

629   Death of Clothar II; succeeded by Dagobert I in all of Frankish Gaul.

—Death of Eochaid Buide, king of Dál Riata (from 608). Succeeded by son Conadd Cerr who dies the same year in **Battle of Fid Eoin** fighting against Ulster (or 628 in AU); succeeded by brother Domnall Brecc to 642/3. Saxon atheling possibly fighting in Ireland for and with Conadd Cerr. Death of Osric son of Ælfred, cousin of Oswald, in battle (ATig, CS, AClon).

*c.*630   (or 628) Domnall Brecc succeeds father Eochaid Buide as king of Scotic Dál Riata.

631   Probable date of accession of Christian King Sigeberht in East Anglia (or 629–30; previously in exile in Gaul). Bishop Felix is sent by Pope Honorius to establish see at Dunwich.

WINTER QUARTERS

Scur sceal of heofenum,
winde geblanden

*The shower will fall from the heavens,
stirred by the wind*

ONE OF THE MANY IRONIES
of Edwin's dramatic reign is that it should end barely ten miles from the place where he had won his kingdom seventeen years before. On 12 October 632 (the year, incidentally, in which the prophet Mohammed died at Medina) Edwin's army was overwhelmed at a place which the British called Meicen and the English knew as the plain of *Hæthfelth*, or Hatfield. Edwin was killed along with his son Osfrith. As it turned out, he was the last of his line to be king of the English north of the Humber.

Bede would have us believe that Edwin, in anticipation of his salvation and in reward for fulfilling his promises, had held under his dominion all of Northumbria—that is to say, that he had united two kingdoms as one. I think it possible that he had installed Osfrith or even a cousin, Osric, as his tributary king in Bernicia late in the 620s; but not until much later in the century, after 679, could Northumbria be truly called a single kingdom. Northumbria as a single entity, in fact, is a creation of Bede. Its inherent disunity was immediately exposed on Edwin's death, with Bernicia looking always to the north and west for enemies and allies and Deira looking south. Both kingdoms reverted to home-grown kings, and to paganism. Edwin's political vision failed to survive him by even a year.

The circumstances of the war that led to Hatfield are obscure; its location and the identity of the antagonists are all that historians have to go on, and even these are by no means secure. Bede records that Cadwallon, king of the Britons, rebelled against Edwin and was supported by Penda, 'a most energetic member of the royal house of Mercia'.[98] Bede casts Cadwallon in terms that make it clear he believed him to be a British tyrant in the tradition of Gildas's five kings of an earlier generation. Penda is almost new on the scene. The Anglo-Saxon Chronicle records under the year 628 that he fought two kings of Wessex at Cirencester. Bede does not allow him the title of king in 632 and so we must suppose that he is a warlord on the make; he does not seem to have been related to the Cearl whose daughter Edwin had married while in exile. The alliance with Cadwallon looks opportunistic.

That the Cadwallon with whom Edwin had been fostered as a child, and who had been humiliated during Edwin's Irish Sea campaigns of the 620s, should seek revenge against him seems perfectly natural. That he should ally with a battle-proven warlord of the Mercians makes sense too: Mercia must have been in Edwin's sights these ten years and more notwithstanding his earlier marriage. An assault on Edwin's southern borders close to where the Great North Road meets the Roman road from Lichfield at Doncaster is the classic Early Medieval location for a battle. Traditionally the as yet unidentified battle site has been accepted as Hatfield Chase, which in the later medieval period was a royal hunting park: low-lying, at the headwaters of the Humber. In the cool, wet centuries after Roman withdrawal it was frequently flooded in winter and unsuitable for agriculture. Given what we know of battle sites in this period and given that Bede qualifies *Hæthfelth* with the term 'plain' (Latin *campo*), it is worth considering an alternative. The Welsh name for the battle (and the area) is *Meicen*, of which the first part also equates to the term 'plain'. This term had a quite specific meaning, certainly in Ireland, where *Mag* (pronounced 'Mai') was strictly reserved for fertile, cultivable plains which formed cultural heartlands like those discussed in Chapter V. Historian Nick Higham[99] points out that early field systems existed around Hatfield in the late Iron Age and Roman periods, but with increasing water levels in the post-Roman centuries it was an area to be avoided by armies so late in the year. October is well outside the normal months for campaigning because roads begin to be impassable; after the *Haligmonað* of late summer when harvests were brought in, the Anglo-Saxon calendar gives us *Winterfilleð* for the first month of autumn, our October.* The name speaks for itself. Warriors and their retinues and supporters generally looked towards the fires of home and to repairing fences to keep out the beasts that roamed the woods and bare fields of winter. Surviving this season in the field was an unattractive prospect when there was little foraging to be had in the open countryside.

If the heather-and-peat lands of *Hæthfelth*, an area of sufficient historic status to be named as a small part of the tributary kingdom of Lindsey in the Tribal Hidage, had an associated fertile plain it must be sought not in the fens east of Doncaster skirted by the Roman road, but to the west and north, on the line of marching between Edwin coming from the north and his enemies approaching from the south-west: just east of a line between Sprotbrough and Brodsworth, where the land rises gently above the vale and is well-drained on fertile limestone soil. Here a triangle formed by three Roman roads has one apex in the south-east at the Roman town of Doncaster, one at the end of a great earthwork of early but not certain date known as the

---

* Bede, *De Temporum Rationem*, edited by C. W. Jones, 1943. The *ð* character is *eth*, as in brethren.

Roman Rig, and the third a few miles east of North Elmsall. As it happens, there is a Raven Hill close to the centre of this triangle on the parish boundary between Marr and Sprotbrough, which would be well-suited as a place for carrion birds to look down on the bloody field of battle where Edwin, in an age-old gesture of triumph and contempt, was decapitated by the victor.

Edwin's army was destroyed by the combined forces of Gwynedd and Mercia. It does not look as if, like Æthelfrith, he had been caught without his full host; whether he was defeated by superior tactics or by two armies acting in concert to outflank him cannot be known. Unlike the battlefields of later English wars, the sites of Early Medieval battles have never been archaeologically identified, let alone excavated: we simply do not know how their dispositions were made. If Cadwallon's forces included a complement of mounted skirmishers, as some British armies seem to have done, their participation may have been decisive, cutting off Edwin's line of retreat to the north. That both Edwin and one of his sons were killed in what Bede describes laconically as a fierce encounter suggests an overwhelming defeat. What followed makes it certain.

Bede portrays the year after *Hæthfelth* as the darkest of days in Northumbrian history. Those who compute the dates of kings, he tells us, struck the whole year from the annals; this is one reason why the chronology of these events is fluid, compounded by the timing of the battle at Hatfield in October, which may—or may not—be the start of Bede's new year: infuriating. But he portrays vividly a sense of the complete collapse of Edwin's imperium which was the inevitable outcome of his death, demonstrating the bald truth that Edwin, for all his politicking and ersatz Romanitas, had not created a state robust enough to survive him. Neither Paulinus, nor Æthelburh; neither the influence of the great Dagobert of Frankia nor his own ambitions for a Roman-style overlordship of North Britain enabled Edwin to transcend the ancient realities of Dark Age kingship. It was personal, it was based primarily on leadership in war; it was barely institutional. Five years of Christianity, embracing as it did only the line-toeing political elites of the Anglian North, left barely a mark, like straws in the wind. There was no state except the person of the king and in his passing the state also passed.

Deira and Bernicia very quickly adopted kings from their own royal stock. Eanfrith returned from exile in Pictland to claim Bernicia, while a cousin of Edwin's, Osric son of Ælfric, was chosen by the Deirans. Edwin's second son, Eadfrith, was forced to submit to Penda (having presumably survived the battle at *Hæthfelth*) in the hope that he might at least be ransomed for some fantastic treasure or perhaps be allowed to rule as a sub-king. He was later put to death during the reign of Oswald. The armies of the Northumbrians, devastated by their crushing defeat, were unable to prevent Cadwallon from ravaging the North. Bede, deeply prejudiced against a man in whom he saw the wickedest of Christians, far worse than any pagan, portrays him laying waste the lands of Northumbria:

> With bestial cruelty he put all to death by torture and for a long time raged through all their land, meaning to wipe out the whole English nation from the land of Britain. Nor did he pay any respect to the Christian religion which had sprung up among them.[100]

This was not a war of submission or annexation; it was a rampage of pillage and plunder—at least, that is what Bede wishes us to believe as he wipes his historical slate clean in preparation for the return of God's chosen king: Oswald.

Christianity's hold on the English of the North had been, it is true, skin deep. Both Eanfrith (a pagan like his father) and Osric repudiated the Roman faith, presumably as a matter of political expediency in the chaotic aftermath of defeat. Edwin had not been a Christian by conviction; nor were his immediate successors. Paulinus's career had, one suspects, more the flavour of personal ambition than the proselytising fervour with which one associates the impending Irish mission. Penda, to whom Deira must now be tributary, was an unreconstructed heathen; Cadwallon held the Roman church in absolute contempt, with the memory of the slaughter of Chester reinforcing his desire for revenge over Edwin's people. The new faith which had promised so much had conspicuously failed to deliver its most important reward: the benefits cited by the pagan chief priest Coifi of enhanced patronage for those who followed their king into catechism and the baptismal waters of Swale and Glen. One wonders with wry curiosity how Coifi, if he survived the initial disaster of *Hæthfelth*, argued his way to rebuilding the idols and temples he had defiled six years before.

In the aftermath of *Hæthfelth* Queen Æthelburh, her two surviving children Eanflæd and Uscfrea and her stepgrandson Yffi, took refuge at the court of her brother, King Eadbald of Kent, along with Paulinus and most of his followers and whatever treasure they could carry. The queen, fearing that Edwin's children were not safe from the threat which the restored sons of Æthelfrith might pose, later sent them to the court of Dagobert where, with the exception of Eanflæd, they all died in infancy; thus was the male line of the Yffings extinguished by a combination of battle and ill-fortune. Paulinus later became bishop of Rochester and lived out his years there, although the pallium the Pope sent to confer on him the metropolitan status he so craved at York arrived too late. York would not get its first archbishop for another hundred years. The only survivor of the Pauline mission in the North was James the Deacon, who ministered from a small church somewhere in the neighbourhood of Catterick* and

---

* Bede knew the name of the place but omitted to pass it on. As late as the fifteenth century it was known as *Seynt Iamestret*; its location has been much sought, but never confirmed; the *stret* element suggests it lay on or close to a Roman road. Colgrave and Mynors 1969, 207. James is also a possible primary source for much

survived long past the restoration of Christianity under Oswald to be present at the Synod of Whitby in 664.

The fates of Eanfrith and Osric were ignominious, as befitted two apostate kings. Bede has them presiding over a period of unparalleled chaos, as if God's wrath had been visited on them in a narrative which can only have been inspired by the Old Testament and the apocalyptic rantings of Gildas. Unless Bede's partisan account is to be taken literally, the background and timing of the events he describes so vividly must be teased out. First, it is worth looking at the archaeological evidence, such as it is. The few settlement sites of this period that have been investigated in Northumbria offer equivocal evidence of the sort of violence which would be compatible with Cadwallon ravaging the whole of the kingdom.[101] York offers no evidence for such a campaign; Edwin's stone church, still roofless at his death, was later completed by Oswald. At West Heslerton, in the Vale of Pickering, there is no sign of disruption to normal community life. But at Yeavering almost the entire township was burned to the ground at a time Hope-Taylor identified as the horizon between Edwin and Oswald. The Yeavering evidence comes with a health warning: there was very little independent dating for the excavations, which took place before the days of radiocarbon assays. Hope-Taylor interpreted the razing of the township at the end of what he called Post-Roman Phase IIIc as an episode of wanton destruction and very naturally, being wholly acquainted with Bede's account, associated it with Cadwallon—but it is a circular argument. As it happens, his timing of this sequence has never seriously been challenged, so compelling is the case for that phase marking the pagan/Christian boundary; and the grandstand, which was not razed but certainly damaged by fire prior to reconstruction, has only ever been realistically assigned to Edwin (or

information about the Northumbrian conversion cited by Bede, who may have been his marginal contemporary.

Æthelburh and Paulinus). That the grandstand survived might, by some, have been regarded as providential; just as likely it testifies on behalf of the excellence of Yeavering's outstanding builders.

Leaving aside the possibility that Edwin's palace at Yeavering was burned down by a successor—perhaps Eanfrith or Oswald, wanting to wipe the Deiran stain from their tribal heartland—or by an accidental fire, we must also be careful not to assume that because Yeavering was burned, the whole of Northumbria was laid waste. Only once has a comprehensive wasting been visited on historical Northumbria: the so-called Harrying of the North in 1069–70 by William I left the region practically without viable settlement or infrastructure. Some have estimated that a hundred thousand people were killed. It was afterwards and for more than fifty years a land devoid of economic potential, one reason why the Domesday surveyors did not record its renders. Not until the twelfth century did kings think it worth providing incentives for the natives to take up their ploughs and bring life back to the land.

No such genocidal wasting occurred in the year or years after Hatfield. Oswald succeeded to a functioning and economically productive kingdom. So Cadwallon's activities, brutal as they probably were, must be placed in context. And to grasp that context it is worth attempting a reconstruction of events following Hatfield, as minutely as is possible given the gaping holes in Bede's narrative. It is inevitably speculative.

ANNO 632: *Winterfilleð*

In the aftermath of the slaughter of *Hæthfelth*, Penda returns with his army to Mercia, laden with booty and glory. He uses this victory to press his claims to be accepted as king of Mercia, where he subsequently reigns for more than twenty years. Cadwallon is not satisfied. He determines to ensure that Britain (by which he means that part of Britain which we call Wales) will never again be subject to Anglian domination. He aims to terminate the lines of Northumbrian kings. So he sets up winter quarters on the southern edge of Deira, and my candidate for this overwintering site is the Roman town of *Isurium Brigantum*, Aldborough, near modern Boroughbridge. Bede, in describing the events of the following year, uses the term *oppido municipio*, a fortified town. Despite the temptation to identify the site with York, some historians are uncomfortable with such a description for the former Roman *colonia*. Other candidates that spring to mind include the ancient British stronghold at Stanwick or, indeed, Doncaster; but Aldborough, the *civitas* capital of the Brigantes, is more likely: two days' march north of Hatfield and not much more than a day from York. It enjoys lines of retreat to the south-west, controls all movement along the Great North Road and is readily defensible.

Anno 632: *Blotmonað*

Cadwallon's army needs feeding and entertaining over the winter months, so he forces the donation of the renders of royal estates within reach of his camp. Campodonum, a lost *villa regia* thought to be in the area of modern Dewsbury, is one royal site recorded by Bede that suffered such a fate and was then burned down—a precedent for Yeavering, perhaps. Cadwallon concentrates on royal estates as targets for two reasons: for their punitive value in diminishing the power, prestige and economic potential of the house of Yffing; and because these are central collection points for the renders of the royal shires—half the work of the looter has been done for him. Their barns stand full of grain and cattle, their halls hang with weaponry and embroidered cloth and their treasuries are heaving under the weight of scrap metal and jewels accumulated by Edwin's retinues over seventeen years. By November, the Anglo-Saxon *Blotmonað* (slaughter month), as winter closes in, they are well-provisioned and occupied in securing their camp. Their poets compose verses of praise and glory on a new, triumphant chapter in the history of the Britons.

Osric, Edwin's cousin, must during these months take counsel with the Deiran nobility, what is left of them. At some point over the winter he emerges as the chosen king of Deira and is inaugurated at what Julian of Toledo called, in a Visigothic setting, the 'seat of paternal antiquity'—*solium paternae antiquitas*—the *urbs regia* of the Deirans somewhere on the edge of the Yorkshire Wolds near Goodmanham—maybe *at* Goodmanham; or conceivably at York.[102] His genealogy, back through generations of Yffings and legendary heroes such as Soemil and Sigegar and culminating in the godly seed of almost all the English kings, Woden, will be recited to remind all those present that he has a legitimate claim to the kingship. Far to the north, Eanfrith is making his bid too. He receives permission from the Pictish king Bridei to leave his court and rides from Pictland to Bamburgh (or Yeavering) where he also takes counsel and is endorsed, as the eldest son of Æthelfrith, son of Æthelric, son of Ida etc., etc., kings of Bernicia time out of mind (eighty years, at least), at *his* 'seat of paternal antiquity'. He spends the winter of 632/3 in the secure, rocky fortress of Bamburgh by the sea, receiving submissions from Bernician nobles and drawing on the oaths of their sons for the warband he will soon muster.* News reaches him that Cadwallon is overwintering in Deira.

Anno 633: *Ðrimilcemonað*

In the late spring or early summer of 633 Osric moves against Cadwallon; perhaps he has been besieging him in the *oppido municipio* (Aldborough) since the melting of the winter snows. He prepares for a long wait. But Cadwallon's warriors are stir-

---

* But see p.137.

crazy and ready for action; Cadwallon, in Bede's account, 'suddenly broke out with all his forces, took Osric by surprise, and destroyed him with all his army'.[103] The surprise element may reflect the British propensity for the dawn ambush. Cadwallon has proved himself unpredictable and a flexible military strategist. The sally is brilliantly successful: Osric's host is destroyed. Incidentally, there is circumstantial support for my suggested timing in an early eighth-century calendar of saints, which gives Osric's feast day as 8 May, at the beginning of *Ðrimilcemonað* (May: the month when cows can be milked three times daily).*

At any rate, Cadwallon is not yet satisfied, for, as Bede says,

> After this he occupied the Northumbrian kingdoms for a whole year, not ruling them like a victorious king but ravaging them like a savage tyrant, tearing them to pieces with fearful bloodshed.[104]

A more realistic reading of Bede's apocalyptic prose is that Cadwallon spends the summer living off Deiran royal estates, looting treasure—not just metallic hardware but also furs of otter and marten, rich cloth, amber, ivory, dyestuffs and other portable exotics—and dispatching any pretender who is brave or foolish enough to take to the field. There is now no suitable candidate for the Deiran kingship; no great noble of the line of Yffings to raise his war-cry. But this is not a pogrom: think of the humble James the Deacon beavering away near Catterick for the souls of his small flock of Christians. Deacons, rural villages, are for the most part beneath Cadwallon's radar. What seems extraordinary, if we accept the Bedan chronology, is that Cadwallon stays in the North for a whole year without, apparently, losing half his army to homesickness and the needs of the Venedotian harvest. Two reasonable inferences can be drawn: either he declines to leave until he has dealt with the Bernician Idings or he does actually have pretensions to become king of Northumbria—or at least

---

* Chaney 1970, 80; that the apostate Osric was given a feast day is interesting in itself.

Deira. Perhaps he has no kingdom to return to in Gwynedd, having been deposed at home after the disastrous defeats at Edwin's hands in the 620s and, according to Welsh sources, time spent in exile first on Priestholm and later across the seas. We cannot tell; historians, like the hard-boiled detective, run into the mysteries of human motivation. But stay he does.

Anno 633: *Weodmonað*

August is the month for weeding fast-ripening crops. Most of the followers of an army want to be at home. Perhaps Cadwallon's warriors and their retinues are hooked on bloodlust and the acquisition of yet more treasure. It is a pity that no heroic poem survives to tell of the last great victory of the British princes over Lloegr; we have only *Υ Gododdin* to remind us of their mindset:

> Because of wine-feast and mead-feast they charged,
> Men famed in fighting, heedless of life.
> Bright ranks around cups, they joined to feast.
> Wine and mead and bragget, these were theirs.[105]

Whether through mead-soaked song and carefully calculated gift or by hard bargaining and rule of fist, Cadwallon persuades his warriors to keep going; and now they head north to confront Bernicia. This, surely, is the Britons' chance to avenge the legendary defeats of Gododdin and Chester; perhaps Cadwallon even razes the *villa regia* at Catterick, the very walls on which those poetic ravens were glutted, on his way north. By the autumn of 633 he may already have campaigned further north; may already have looted and burned Yeavering.

Anno 633: *Winterfilleð*

Cadwallon must find a defensible site for his second winter in the field, with good lines of retreat set in a fertile landscape, royal estates within reach from which to plunder and feed his host. Since there is only one location at which one can place Cadwallon with any confidence in Bernicia, I suggest that is where he sets up his camp: at Corbridge, the apparently long-abandoned Roman garrison town of *Corstopitum*.* Corbridge guards the crossroads where the Roman Stanegate leads west, parallel to Hadrian's Wall through the Pennine gap at Gilsland and where Dere Street runs north through the wild fells of Cheviot towards *Din Eidyn* and the lands of Gododdin and Strathclyde. Furthermore, the Roman bridge here commands a critical crossing of the River Tyne at its highest navigable point and is probably still functional in the early seventh century; if not, the river can be forded just downstream. It is the most strategically dominant spot in southern Bernicia and a safe distance from Eanfrith, overwintering at his tribal stronghold of Bamburgh. It is the Bernician king who must make a move. Meanwhile, Cadwallon's army plunders the royal estates of the Bernician lowlands from Newburn on the lower Tyne perhaps as far as Whittingham beyond the Simonside Hills.

ANNO 634: *Eostermonað*

This period of looting and his own military weakness prompts Eanfrith to sue for peace. What is so striking is that Eanfrith, who ought to have at his disposal retinues from both Pictland, where he has been exiled these many years, and northern Bernicia, does not seem to feel strong enough to attack Cadwallon. Given that Cadwallon is isolated in foreign territory and has been in the field for more than a year it is surprising, to say the least, that Eanfrith does not believe he can match him or is too timid to make the attempt. There must be a suspicion that Eanfrith's Pictish hosts

---

* Regrettably, most of the critical parts of the Roman town there were excavated before archaeologists thought to, or were able to, identify anything as subtle as the ephemeral traces of a Dark Age campsite. Bishop and Dore 1988.

are uncomfortable with the idea of supporting a bid for the Bernician throne against British opposition and will not back Eanfrith's bid with substantial military resources; Oswald will face the same problem. In describing Eanfrith's approach to the parley Bede uses the term 'unadvisedly'—*inconsulte*—just as he has used the term 'rashly'—*temerarie*—for Osric's assault. There is a suspicion of coupled adverbs here that has the whiff of poetry about it: are these the slight fragments of a heroic poem or a lost annal to which Bede has access? It is hard to say. Why does Eanfrith, as Bede records, so 'unadvisedly' come to negotiate with Cadwallon with a mere twelve companions? The number is biblical, to be sure; it may be meaningless in terms of real numbers. What it suggests is that Eanfrith either comes to Cadwallon's camp under an accepted flag of truce, or at least feeling reasonably secure; or that he has no other option but to attempt to play a concealed hand. It is possible that this is because it is still early in the year, before the campaigning season. If so it is a fatal miscalculation. Cadwallon has no hesitation in killing him out of hand.

There is one other possibility for Eanfrith's apparently weak hand. That is the suspicion that in warrior society (it is true of the Franks, another Germanic people) only a son born while his father is king is eligible to succeed. It may be one reason why Edwin, Oswald and Oswiu all marry—in Edwin's and Oswiu's case re-marry—and produce heirs *after* they became king. We must allow, then, for the explanation that Eanfrith was not recognised as a legitimate king by the Bernician elite and that, therefore, his really was a weak hand.

It is worth considering Cadwallon's position at this point. Bloodthirsty he may be, bent on revenge against Edwin and his house and the Northumbrians in general—he can have no love for the sons of Æthelfrith, after all. He may, as Bede suggests, desire to wipe the entire race of the Northumbrians from the face of the earth.[106] More likely, having amassed sufficient treasure and having excised the legitimate lineages of both the Bernicians and Deirans, he will now return to Gwynedd glutted and with his war chests bulging. Eanfrith's death ought to satisfy him. Unless, that is, he believes Æthelfrith's surviving son Oswald might yet pose a threat. Cadwallon, then, having dispatched Osric and fulfilled his and his warriors' lust for plunder and wasting, summons Eanfrith to Corbridge on the edge of Bernician territory where he, Cadwallon, can defend himself and maintain a line of retreat. Whether it is Oswald or Eanfrith who arrives first, Cadwallon is strategically placed to intercept either—or both. There is no suggestion, incidentally, that Deira recognises Eanfrith.

Eanfrith hopes that Cadwallon is after his submission or an equitable peace deal. Probably, in accordance with the customary nature of such proceedings, a great quantity of treasure will be negotiated and delivered, oaths sworn, hostages swapped. But Eanfrith has read the British king wrong: he does not care for mere submission; he does not care to impose his absentee rule on tributary Anglian kings of the North as an act of imperium or self-aggrandisement. In his tent, surrounded by battle-hardened campaigning veterans, Cadwallon has Eanfrith and his retinue put to the sword, probably decapitated so that their heads can be posted on stakes on the decayed ramparts of *Corstopitum* as trophies. He takes their treasure too. Now there is almost no-one left who might challenge the arbitrary military despotism of the British king. Northumbria is finished as an Early Medieval kingdom. Almost. This is the cue for Oswald *Lamnguin* to make his entry.

If Oswald and his half-brother Eanfrith were in communication between the fall of Edwin and Cadwallon's arrival in Bernicia, it has not been recorded. Of the fact that both knew of the battle at *Hæthfelth* soon after the event there can be only small doubt. Very little has been written about intelligence-gathering in the Early Medieval period, it is true. Kings picked up regional news items as they travelled; traders brought stories from far afield. There were spies, as the assassination attempt on Edwin by Cwichelm's man shows. Military scouts recruited either from natives with excellent local knowledge (King Ine of Wessex had British 'riders' among his retinues) or from the ranks of unmarried young warriors must have been kept busy. A number of unspecified journeys are to be found in the pages of Bede and Eddius Stephanus that may reflect missions of one sort or another. Pilgrims journeyed as far as Rome and beyond. The poor and unfree may have been tied to the land of their lords, but people moved around the landscape, as the early law codes testify.

The ability of armies to locate each other in the seventh century is impressive, even allowing for the obvious concentration of battles on the lines of Roman roads. In 1745 the Young Pretender's three armies failed to find each other in the Borders, never mind the enemy. Edwin's instruction to have bowls hung above water sources on roads implies that in the seventh century there was royal interest in maintaining arterial routes. The question is, was there a cadre of royal messengers whose job it was to pass diplomatic and intelligence material: offers of alliance, warnings, arrangements for meetings and so on? The answer must be a cautious yes. That there were lodgings for travellers is attested by Bede in a post-mortem story about Oswald.[107] That messages might pass very rapidly is a little harder to show, but nonetheless likely. On the death of Elizabeth I in 1603 Sir Robert Carey, who had a personal interest in the matter, rode from London to Edinburgh carrying the late queen's ring (finger still attached). The journey nearly killed him and won him few friends, but he accomplished it in three days at the end of March on roads that cannot have been very different from those used by the Anglians or British of Oswald's day. And there is a striking near-contemporary example of the speed at which news of great events could move. In 685 St Cuthbert was staying with King Oswiu's daughter Ælfflæd in the city of *Lugubalia* (Carlisle, where Roman public fountains still ran in Cuthbert's day) when he received an awful premonition of the death of King Ecgfrith in battle against the Picts in the region beyond the River Tay. Within two days a fugitive from the battle appeared and confirmed his fears.[108] In Bede's view this story was miraculous proof of Cuthbert's sanctity; but he could not have told it if the events he described were not at least credible, since they occurred well within the memory of many of his contemporaries.

Oswald, living at the court of Domnall Brecc in Argyll, will have heard soon enough that Edwin was dead, that Osric and Eanfrith had claimed the kingdoms of Deira and Bernicia respectively. He will have heard of Eanfrith's murder by Cadwallon and must at that point, if not before, have taken counsel. To suggest that more political capital had been invested in Oswald by Dál Riata than by the Picts in Eanfrith may be to read too much into Eanfrith's dismal fate; nevertheless, to say that in the four hundred days or so between Hatfield and the death of Eanfrith interested parties in Dál Riata were watching events closely and carefully considering their options is an understatement. The future of Bernicia was a matter of the greatest importance in Argyll and on the island of Iona. It is possible, with care, to reconstruct plausibly the circumstances in which Oswald was released from his obligations as a member of Brecc's household to make his own, fateful bid for Northumbria. If he were to succeed in fulfilling his ambitions and those of his sponsors and companions, the timing of his bid would be crucial: there was not a moment to lose.

VIII

THE RETURN OF THE KING

*Fyrd sceal ætsomne...
tirfæstra getrum*

*The army stays together...
a band set on glory*

THOMAS, LORD COCHRANE, the frigate captain famed for his dashing exploits in the wars against Napoleon, distributed a handbill calling for volunteer crewmen for his 1805 commission in the thirty-two-gun frigate *Pallas*. For stout hands who could handle field pieces and 'carry an hundred weight of PEWTER, without stopping, at least three miles' he offered the chance to fill their sea chests with Spanish dollars and doubloons.[109] The *Pallas* later returned to Portsmouth with gold Spanish candlesticks tied to her mastheads after a cruise that netted Cochrane something like seventy-five thousand pounds and would have made even her ordinary seamen enough to set up as tavern-keepers. After one famously successful voyage sailors were seen squatting over skillets on Portsmouth Hard, frying gold pocket-watches in a state almost of delirium.

The reciprocal ties that bonded an Early Medieval warlord and his warriors were not unlike those which held together the officers and crew of an eighteenth- or early nineteenth-century frigate. Patronage flowed downwards; wealth flowed upwards; loyalty and duty worked both ways. A successful fighting captain—and there were few more successful in prize-money than Cochrane—was able to attract the best men. These in turn were rewarded by his success in action: his fighting prowess and tactical skill, and above all his reputation for being lucky—his talismanic virtue. The one-eighth share of prize money which belonged to a post-captain is not so very far from the roughly one-tenth render which a warlord would take from his estates or, perhaps, from the great booty of a battlefield. The best crews worked, lived and fought together over many commissions; were battle-hardened, unflappable, tough and unshakeable in their desire for more treasure, more glory: it was addictive. Many a sailor sang of the deeds of his youth in doggerel less polished but no less evocative than *Y Gododdin*. Like Early Medieval warriors, the navy's elite officer cadre, recruited from the sons of those bred to fight and lead, established a literally fabulous reputation for derring-do. Similarly their weaponry, clothes, badges of honour and privileged lifestyle were supported by a much larger number of less-celebrated supporters: carpenters, bosuns, pursers, cooks and seamen who hoped, by being attached to a leader with a reputation like Cochrane's (or Oswald's), to receive their relatively pathetic share of wealth and glory and its concomitant bragging rights over their fellows. And like the fighting sailors of a frigate—two hundred and fifty-odd men largely confined to their own company within the wooden walls of their ships—the Early Medieval warrior was effectively peripatetic: the warband and the tent were their home for long periods.

Oswald *Lamnguin* had proved himself as a young man fighting in the warbands of the kings of Dál Riata. The many young nobles with whom Bede tells us the sons of Æthelfrith went into exile must have matured or died alongside him during seventeen years of exile. The twelve companions who Adomnán tells us were baptised with him on Iona must be regarded with the same scepticism as those who accompanied Eanfrith to his fatal encounter with Cadwallon; it is a symbolic number. Oswald's exploits in the field of battle may have attracted more Bernician exiles into his warband and that of his younger brother Oswiu, now twenty-two. The prospect of adventure and glory perhaps also drew young nobles of Dál Riata to Oswald's purple and gold banner. That this motley band were eager to take on Cadwallon's veteran army can be inferred; that they were equipped to do so on their own is doubtful. Eanfrith had failed in his attempt to launch an assault from Pictland: he had not been able to attract sufficient men of skill and experience to his band to take on the British army. Oswald's bid could not be allowed to fail so abjectly. In reconstructing the events of his return to Bernicia the part played by his sponsors cannot be underestimated.

In the aftermath of *Hæthfelth* and Eanfrith's disastrous meeting with Cadwallon, Oswald, bound by oath of loyalty to his lord Domnall Brecc, must have taken counsel. Who were his advisors? Brecc was the son of Eochaid Buide, Colm Cille's chosen successor to Áedán at whose court Oswald and his brothers and sister had taken refuge in 617. Brecc and Oswald may have fought alongside each other in Ireland, and were perhaps of similar age. Brecc would preside over the precipitous decline of fortune of the kings of Dál Riata and in the early 630s his position was complicated by tensions with his ancestral Ulster homeland, with the British kings of Strathclyde* and with Pictish kings to the east (both at least nominally Christian, as was Cadwallon). At the same time, his sponsorship of Oswald, if successful, would give him rights of tribute and patronage over Northumbria and the promise of reciprocal help in his dynastic wars, so he had a delicate diplomatic plate-spinning act to pull off and there may have been parties at his court lobbying for different strategies.

* His death at the hands of Eugein I of Strathclyde at the Battle of Strathcarron in 642 is versified in the Dyfnwal Frych (Domnall Brecc) stanza of *Y Gododdin* (see p.194).

If Oswald had made a bid for his father's kingdom during Edwin's reign, there is only the faintest allusion to it in the notice of the attack on Bamburgh hinted at by the Irish Annals.* Any attempt to reclaim his kingdom by battle against Cadwallon might have further complicated the politics. Much later Scottish tradition has it that Brecc forbade Oswald to deploy Dál Riatan warriors against Cadwallon, with whom he was historically allied.† Nevertheless, the complex realities of Northern politics imply that while Cadwallon was a British Christian king of the line of Cunedda of the Gododdin and might, therefore, expect sympathetic support or abstention from other historic enemies of the heathen Lloegr, his campaign in Northumbria might also be seen as destabilising established relations; in not seeking to rule but merely to plunder and kill, he had upset the natural order of things. He was a liability; he had gone rogue.

Brecc must have had a major say in Oswald's intentions, if only because Oswald required his permission to leave the court. Whom else did Oswald consult? There are several obvious candidates. If Acha, his mother, was still alive he may have sought her counsel. Her keenness to return to Bernicia can only be imagined, as can the interest with which she encouraged the careers of her sons after the death of her estranged brother Edwin. Oswald's younger brother Oswiu and his sister Æbbe may also have been privy to family debates about timing and tactics. If they had any residual loyalty to their half-brother Eanfrith, that was now irrelevant. Oswald could probably count on Oswiu's own warband—perhaps small and less experienced than Oswald's—to support him.

Maybe the most interested party in these deliberations was the abbot of Iona. Since 623 the incumbent of the mother church of

---

* See p.122, under the year 623.

† Fordun: *Chronica Gentis Scotorum*; the theme is expanded convincingly by Marsden 1992, 112ff but the lateness of the source means it must be treated with caution.

the Columban federation had been Ségéne. Iona had invested heavily in its protégé princes: not just in the education of young Idings, but in the careers of sons of the Cenél nGabráin. Ségéne's friendship with Oswald was allied to a keen interest in his career. When the opportunity arose in 634 he was prepared to back his atheling with all the resources under his control. He may have been directly involved with counselling alongside Domnall Brecc, whom he had known since birth and probably ordained in 629. Iona was by no means an insignificant party in any deliberations over the extent to which the Scotic kings and the Irish church should back the aspiring Bernician kings. Ségéne's support went beyond interceding with the king of Dál Riata. He could supply his own warriors, monks who were prepared to fight the fight for Christianity among the heathen (or the rogue Christian); who would obey their abbot. He might also invoke the potent virtues of the founder Colm Cille in support of Oswald's campaign. That there was an Ionan contingent in Oswald's forces has been the subject of a certain amount of debate, but it is now generally accepted as a serious possibility. The historical evidence relies on a very few lines in the Red Book of Hergest,* which survives only in a very late copy but which laments, in elegising Cadwallon, his final betrayal:

> From the plotting of strangers and iniquitous
> Monks, as the water flows from the fountain,
> Sad and heavy will be the day of Cadwallon[110]

It is impossible to be sure about the timing of Oswald's arrival in Bernicia. I doubt if he came with Eanfrith. More likely, he had to organise the patchwork elements of his warband and calculate their surest approach. Early in the summer of 634, I suggest,

---

* The existing manuscript dates to the fourteenth century and is evidently a miscellany of Welsh-language sources including the pre-Christian stories called the *Mabinogion*. Most historians believe the Triads, from which the Cadwallon stanza is taken, to preserve elements of authentic Early Medieval oral tradition.

Brecc gave him permission to leave the Dál Riatan court and make his bid. The timing depends largely on Oswald's means of travel. His original exile from Northumbria was probably made by boat from the Solway Firth, and I suggest that his return was effected by the same route. Brecc's Dál Riatan armies were recruited by customary render of military service as an amphibious assault force: they mustered by boat, they moved by water; like Cochrane's crews, the progenitors of the Royal Marines, they assaulted from the sea. If Brecc were to back Oswald with warriors, they were surely marines and the boats were supplied from the traditional musters of the Cenél nGabráin. Travel by sea avoided slow, awkward, potentially disastrous marching across the lands of the Strathclyde Britons and Picts; it avoided alerting Cadwallon to their movements; it was also quicker. I believe, then, that Oswald's disparate crew of exiled Bernician hopefuls, sword-wielding monks and Dál Riatan young-bloods (who had been told not to actually fight Cadwallon) sailed south from Dál Riata and landed somewhere on the upper reaches of the Solway Firth; they may even have sailed right up the River Eden to Carlisle. Perhaps, at this point, the official obligations of the Dál Riatan marines were over, since they were not supposed to fight. But fight they did.

The trigger for this enterprise was Eanfrith's death, followed by negotiations, provisioning and the muster. The window of opportunity was provided by the season. The two middle months of the Anglo-Saxon calendar were *Ærra Líða* and *Æftera Líða*. *Líða* is translated by Bede in his treatise on time, *De tempore ratione*, as 'gentle', or 'navigable': in other words, these were the prime sailing months. Oswald's window was between June and July, which is why I think it worth setting Eanfrith's death no later than the early months of 634. Cadwallon had been prepared for Osric and Eanfrith; Oswald's intention must have been to launch an assault without warning in order to compensate for the relative weakness of his army. He might have had intelligence of Cadwallon's whereabouts if I am right that the British warlord had overwintered at Corbridge and met Eanfrith there; alternatively, Cadwallon might have received word that Oswald was on his way and positioned himself strategically to intercept his army, whether it came from north or west.

There are two further reasons, aside from the Dál Riatan boat muster, for believing that Oswald came to meet Cadwallon from the west. One is that when Oswald set up his camp before the assault on Cadwallon, it was located a few miles to the north-west of Corbridge, at a place called Heavenfield. That then makes sense as the direction from which he marched—not from the north along Dere Street. The other is the nature of relations between the Bernician kings and those of Rheged. Æthelfrith, it is supposed, had annexed Rheged, the kingdom of the Solway, during his long reign. Hostages must have been exchanged; perhaps marriage alliances were brokered. One of these was later fulfilled: Oswiu, born in 612, had fathered a child with the Irish princess Fina during his Scottish exile but his first acknowledged marriage was to Rhieinmelth, daughter of Royth, son of Rhun,* son of Urien of Rheged.

Rheged was, therefore, another interested party. It had effectively lost its independence, so far as we can tell, after the death of its great hero Urien in the years before 600. And yet, its court was still sufficiently regarded to provide consorts for Bernician over-kings; or at least prospective Bernician overkings. It cannot have been oblivious to Cadwallon's depredations across the Pennines; and may have felt threatened by them even if Cadwallon was also British.† Oswiu's marriage to Rhieinmelth must date to around

---

* *HB* 57; Presumably the same Rhun attested by a gloss in the *Historia Brittonum* as the man who baptised Edwin while in exile. Rhiein means 'queen' in Brythonic.

† In my view the nationalistic interpretation of some of the politics of this period is inappropriate; it owes much to Gildas, and the actual evidence for British solidarity against Lloegr is thin.

630–5 because their son Alhfrith became sub-king of Deira under his father around the year 655 and cannot realistically have been much less than twenty years old at the time. The union of Rheged and Bernicia, then, might have taken place either side of Oswald's restoration. But that is not to say that the two houses had not arranged the marriage earlier, perhaps between 612, the year of Oswiu's birth, and 617 when Æthelfrith was killed by Edwin.

Oswald, then, if I am right and his route to Bernicia was made via Solway, must have presented himself to the court of Rheged (perhaps at Carlisle, the British *Caer Luel*, or Stanwix, just the other side of the River Eden)* and engaged the court with an ingratiating speech something like this: *does the court of Royth son of Rhun son of Urien of great fame recognise the friendship between our two peoples forged in the days of our fathers; will the warriors of Rheged stand by their allies against the perfidious apostate Cadwallon* (laying it on a bit thick, here, as one does in such situations) *who like a cursed whelp seeks only to destroy and defile the north parts of our island with rapine and slaughter* (appealing to the stability lobby); *will the King cement our friendship in the name of the True God by honouring the betrothal in Christ of our brother Oswiu with his daughter Rhieinmelth agreed upon in the time of our fathers?* etc., etc. Gifts would have been exchanged, backstage deals struck, oaths made. I am guessing, but I do not think the politics of such events has changed much; nor the florid superficiality of the language.†

What Oswald wanted was an ally, both to guard his rear—or

---

* Much debate surrounds the exact extent of Early Medieval Rheged; for a summary and opinion see McCarthy 2002.

† A letter very similar in style and intent was written by a later Northumbrian, Admiral Collingwood, to the Emperor of Morocco in 1808 asking for his help and support (especially horses) against the wicked godless Napoleon in Spain and invoking, with extraordinary prescience, the wisdom and authority of the Qur'an. The idea of appealing to enlightened self-interest has a pedigree much older than the eighteenth century.

at least abstain from joining in against him—and probably, since he had come by boat, to supply horses and provisions for his small but zealous army; goodness only knows what the proud but much-reduced court of Rheged must have thought. Probably they considered Oswald, of whose martial reputation they must have heard, a better bet than the rogue Cadwallon: a restored and powerful (and Ionan-Christian) Northumbria offered stability, protection and a measure of access to its lines of patronage.

For much later narrative histories it is possible to identify elements of charisma in individual leaders. Nelson had it in bucketloads, as did T. E. Lawrence—both of them born (in their own minds, at least) in the classical flashing-blade mould of warband heroes. Colm Cille's charismatic leadership of the community of Iona is drawn with awe and affection by Adomnán (albeit a hundred years after the fact) and Bede cannot help admiring the heathens Penda and Æthelfrith, as well as Oswald. Oswald's Irish nickname *Lamnguin* allows us to glimpse something of his reputation as a fighting man, a dashing warrior on the field of battle. To achieve that exalted status required not just charisma but luck, the facility to inspire, generosity and magnanimity; above all, perhaps, skill in arms and horsemanship—all those virtues ascribed to his poetic equivalent Beowulf.

In Oswald's case there might have been something more on which he could trade both to attract good men to his warband and convince doubters (at Dunadd; at Carlisle?) of his prospective success. *Lamnguin*, 'Whiteblade' or perhaps 'Bright arm' recalls the legendary Irish God Nuada Airgetlám, whose arm was severed in battle and replaced with a silver prosthetic which entitled him to the kingship.[111] In Rheged there had once been a cult devoted to a totemic tribal deity, known to us only from inscriptions and one or two crude but evocative representations of the naked and very evidently virile horned war god Belatucadros, spear and shield in hand, whose name, roughly translated, means 'bright, beautiful one' or perhaps 'death-decorated one'. The Roman soldiers of the Wall garrisons unsurprisingly equated him with Mars, their god of war. An atheling as canny as Oswald might well have traded on any associations made between himself, the returning Whiteblade, and these attractive, cunning, lucky gods of war.[112] This idea is reinforced by the association of a similar representation of Woden as a god with horned helmet, naked, carrying a spear in either hand.[113] If Oswald did present himself at the court of Rheged looking for support and tapping into Irish and Germanic iconography and native Christian/pagan sentiments, it also provides a plausible backdrop for his brother Oswiu's marriage to a princess of that once-proud kingdom. The success I suppose Oswald to have had in Rheged is, in a sense, attested by the outcome.

Now to war: from Carlisle, Oswald heads off to do battle with Cadwallon at a speed which is faster than news can travel towards the British host; probably with horses supplied by Rheged; perhaps even with a British contingent of young Rheged nobility among his forces. He must strike before Cadwallon is aware of his landing. East, then, at dawn's first light into the early summer sun along the Stanegate, the first-century Roman road joining Rheged to Northumbria through the Solway–Tyne gap. It predates Hadrian's Wall, keeping to lower, easier ground, and at its inception was probably intended as a frontier in its own right. It was retained as a route of supply to the Wall forts and as a means of transferring troops quickly along the Wall's length. The Roman army reckoned it a three-day march from Carlisle to Corbridge; two days at forced pace. Oswald's host, numbering perhaps in the low hundreds, is unhampered by baggage trains or booty: it travels light and fast. No shining legion had been seen in these parts for two hundred years but warbands cannot have been a strange sight. The wall of Hadrian still stood in large part, although the gates of its forts had long ago rotted on their hinges and it was no barrier to farmer or trader. At Birdoswald Fort there is archaeological evidence for some sort of establishment surviving into perhaps the sixth century, evidenced by timber halls erected over the abandonment layers of the fort. It is tempting to associate its name with a memory of an overnight camp by the Bernician atheling; but the name is all we have.* More likely Oswald camped in the Stanegate fort at Nether Denton or carried on towards Vindolanda where, in its last active days, there seems to have been a British church.[114] Despite the effective abandonment of the Solway-Tyne gap as the military frontier of an empire, this was not an empty landscape. Traders working their way from sea to sea, like the latter-day truckers winding slowly along the A69, modern equivalent of the Stanegate, must have used this route. If the old Roman forts did not support anything resembling urban communities, they were still convenient staging posts, places to build up stocks of food, fodder and ale, and probably supporting smithies where farriers could count on passing trade: the desultory remnants of once-thriving economies. Drovers and shepherds must also have been in evidence, herding their cattle and sheep on to the high pastures in early summer but otherwise uninterested in the movements of warriors except for the bartering of a night's meat ration. When new settlements developed in the Early Medieval period they were to be found along the Stanegate corridor, not on the Wall.

Rivers in mid-summer still ran with ale-coloured water draining off the high moors. At Greenhead, the highest point of the route, a narrow pass had to be scouted—a perfect place for an ambush, although it seems Cadwallon was blissfully unaware of approaching doom. If bridges survived at Chesters and elsewhere

---

* The association with Oswald may belong to a later church dedicated to the saint after the death of King Ælfwald in 788.

the army would keep its pace; otherwise, fording points must be warily scouted. Oswald surely had intelligence of Cadwallon's position: the site chosen for his last camp shows that his army avoided the last stretch of Stanegate; probably it was closely watched. At Chesters the army moved along the precise line of the Wall to within an hour's march of Corbridge at a turret three or four miles to the north-west across country and sheltered from southerly eyes by a convenient bluff. Cadwallon's apparent ignorance of Oswald's imminent arrival suggests strongly that local sympathies lay with the Bernician atheling, not with his British enemy.

There is a church at Heavenfield today: squat and domestic, no more than three hundred years old, the belfry mounted at its west end seemingly a decorative afterthought. The gnomon of its sundial dispassionately tracks the passing of daylight hours year after year. There are few dwellings nearby whose families might be summoned to prayer by its tolling bell. Beyond it to the north are bleak carrs and scattered farmsteads which have stood time out of mind, locked tight into the fabric of the land by drystone walls that tell tales of labour and self-enslavement. Almost crouching within its low encircling wall with its leaning headstones, a grove of oaks protects the modest hilltop to the north of the Wall and General Wade's eighteenth-century anti-Jacobite military road. To the south seamless hills run on for ever into the blue.

The story of the night before Oswald's defining battle of 634 was still circulating as late as a hundred years afterwards when Bede recorded it, probably from stories related by his friend Bishop Acca of Hexham. It suited Bede's providential view of Oswald's whole life to portray the mood in Oswald's camp as spiritual theatre; and it suited Adomnán, in Iona, to record the supposed influence of Colm Cille on so crucial a battle for the fortunes of the Columban church. Their accounts carry additional weight in that both authors could directly cite witnesses; and not just any old witnesses, but the testimony of Oswald himself as he told the story to Abbot Ségéne, and that of the monks who venerated the site. But Bede and Adomnán offer very different, if broadly compatible details of what happened. Here is Adomnán's version of events, given extraordinary prominence in the Life of Saint Columba by being recited in the first chapter of Book One as direct evidence of Colm Cille's earthly (or unearthly) powers:

While this King Oswald was camped ready for battle, he was asleep on a pillow in his tent one day when he had a vision of Saint Columba. His appearance shone with angelic beauty, and he seemed so tall that his head touched the clouds and, as he stood in the middle of the camp, he covered it all except one far corner with his shining robe. The blessed man revealed his name to the king and gave him these words of encouragement, the same the Lord spoke to Joshua, saying, 'Be strong and act manfully. Behold, I will be with thee.' In the king's vision Columba said this, adding:

'This coming night go out from your camp into battle, for the Lord has granted me that at this time your foes shall be put to flight and Cadwallon your enemy shall be delivered into your hands and you shall return victorious after battle and reign happily.'

Hearing these words the king awoke and described his vision to the assembled council. All were strengthened by this and the whole people promised that after their return from battle they would accept the faith and receive baptism.[115]

How clever of Adomnán to invoke the identification of Oswald with Joshua, the assistant of Moses who led the Israelites back into the land of Canaan, to victory and the recovery of the lands which God had promised them.

Bede's narrative continues in a passage that may have been intended to convey parallels with the story of the Emperor Constantine before the Battle of the Milvian Bridge in 312 and those famed Christian victories of Theodosius and Clovis.[116] In Constantine's vision, the night before his battle, he was commanded to make the sign of a cross on the shields of his soldiers.

Perhaps with this precedent in mind (and he must have heard the story of Constantine while on Iona) Oswald…

> When he was about to engage in battle, set up the sign of the holy cross and, on bended knees, prayed to God to send heavenly aid to His worshippers in their dire need. In fact it is related that when a cross had been hastily made and the hole dug in which it was to stand, he seized the cross himself in the ardour of his faith, placed it in the hole, and held it upright with both hands until the soldiers had heaped up the earth and fixed it in position. Thereupon he raised his voice and called out to the whole army, 'Let us all kneel together and pray the almighty, ever living and true God to defend us in His mercy from the proud and fierce enemy; for He knows that we are fighting in a just cause for the preservation of our whole race.'[117]

Bede was in no doubt of its significance. The historical purpose of the two accounts is to place both God and Colm Cille at Oswald's side in battle; to give the event a historical (and biblical and Roman) context and to set it within a hagiographic tradition in which signs and events portended or reflected God's special favour. The scene we are presented with also leaves us in no doubt that Oswald was fully aware of the potency of such religious and historical imagery. If, as the medieval Scottish historian John of Fordun* later believed, the Dál Riatan contingent were given instructions not to fight Cadwallon (in which case, why were they there?), Colm Cille's apparent direct intercession, effectively pre-ordaining Oswald as righteous king, was a masterstroke: the spiritual clout of Iona superseded the political interest of the court of Domnall Brecc. Oswald, it seems, had the right stuff.

Cynics might say that Oswald, and the historians and hagiographers who traded on him over the next five hundred years, were consciously manipulative; that the vision was a fabrication and the cross mere psychological hokum. That is to mistake the nature

---

* John of Fordun, who died around 1384, wrote a five-volume history called *Chronica Gentis Scottorum,* in which he seems to have drawn on independent sources now lost to us.

of the Early Medieval mindset. Oswald's and Bede's worlds *were* miraculous: without the probabilistic explanations of science, truth was constructed from a combination of practical reality and a strong belief in sympathetic magic, omen and augury. Signs were there to be read and they were taken very seriously indeed. Oswald, in a state of high excitement and, perhaps, having been warned by his friend Ségéne to look out for signs of Colm Cille's favour (so that the monks might be certain which Christian king was the more righteous), very naturally interpreted whatever dream or vision he had as just that. Moreover, there is little doubt that for all his political acumen—and he had been well taught—Oswald was a genuine spiritual convert, unlike his uncle Edwin who was baptised for political convenience. Oswald was a believer. Like Rædwald, however, he may have kept a strategic foot in each camp.*

Until the nineteenth century, Oswald's clash with Cadwallon was known as the Battle of Heavenfield; the Ordnance Survey still locates the battle site next to the church and the modern wooden cross that stands beside the road here. Bede says that in his day the site was held in great veneration; monks would process there on the eve of Oswald's feast day every year to keep vigil. People would take splinters from the cross which Oswald raised and soak them in water, before giving the drink to sick men or beasts or sprinkling them with it; such people were quickly restored to health.[118] There is some satisfaction for archaeologists in this forensic detail. It is often difficult to explain how the past operated physically in creating the archaeological record. Here is direct, compelling evidence to explain why the original cross

---

* The doyenne of Northumbrian archaeology, Dame Rosemary Cramp, has made the point that Oswald's deployment of the cross might also have tapped into Bernician sensibilities about the potency of tribal totem poles. Several examples were excavated by Hope-Taylor at Yeavering, like that which was the focal point of the grandstand. Cramp 1995, 30.

is no longer there: it was nicked, splinter by splinter. What form the original cross took is obscure. Was it hastily fashioned from local boughs and lashed together? Was it, perhaps, made from Roman floor joists pulled from the mile turret on the site? Or was it crafted in anticipation—did it in some way artistically anticipate the Irish-influenced stone high crosses of Northumbria which are the great glories of the northern Christian landscape? Turret 25b, the not very evocative name of the site where this is supposed to have happened, was excavated in the 1950s.[119] On the excavator's plan there is a rectangular hole in the centre of the floor of the turret, interpreted at the time as disturbance from a later period; but it would perfectly suit as a hole in which a cross might be raised.

So confident was Bede of the providential nature of Oswald's campsite that he regarded the name Heavenfield as having been given to the place in antiquity as an omen. By the time Bede was writing, the first church had been erected there and one has stood on the site ever since.

At dawn, the morning after Oswald's vision and his raising of the cross, the army launched its attack on Cadwallon's 'irresist-ible' army.* But the encounter was not fought at Heavenfield. The tradition of the Welsh Annals has it that the battle, recorded under the year 631, equating to 634, was called *Cantscaul*. Early writers suggested that this was derived from Brythonic *Cat*, for 'battle', and *gwal*, or 'Wall'; that the battle therefore must have taken place close to Oswald's camp. This has now been dismissed on philological grounds, and it is accepted that *Cantscaul* is a corrupt form of *Cant scaul*, which itself can be shown to precisely transliterate Old English *Hagustaldesham*: that is, Hexham.[120] That name, which intriguingly means 'enclosure of the young

---

* EH II.1 Bede says Cadwallon boasted that his army was irresistible: how would he know what Cadwallon said, unless this is another adverbial clue to a lost battle elegy?

warrior', does not seem to have come into existence until later, perhaps when the church was established there in Oswiu's reign and when its first bishop, the ambitious Wilfrid, wanted for his own reasons to trade on Hexham's associations with nearby Heavenfield. It is not really credible as the site of the battle because there is a better and more specific location on offer. Bede says that Cadwallon's destruction happened 'at a place which is called in the English tongue *Denisesburn*, that is the brook of the Denise'. Not until the nineteenth century did a historical document emerge to pin down Denisesburn. It was found in a charter, apparently by members of the Tyneside Naturalists' Field Club whose president, the indefatigable barrow-digging antiquary Canon William Greenwell, reported its significance for the location of the battle site in 1864. The charter, dating to 1233, granted one Thomas of Whittington:

> Twenty acres of land from his waste in Ruleystal, between these boundaries, namely between Denisesburn and Divelis, beginning to the east upon Divelis and rising to the great road which leads up to the forest of Lillewude.[121]

If Denisesburn is now lost, Divelis is not: it is Devil's Water, a stream which rises from the moors south of Hexham and which is joined by the Rowley Burn just below the hamlet of Steel (Ruleystal). Who the Denises were, Bede does not say and we cannot tell. Steel seems an improbable place for a battle; indeed, Bede does not say that the battle was fought here, only that Cadwallon, together with his immense force, was destroyed here. Steel lies about five miles south-west of the river crossing at Corbridge, as the crow flies. The Devil's Water enters the River Tyne a mile or so upstream. This places the action on the east bank of the Devil's Water until the road from Corbridge—anciently a drove road across the moors—crosses the gorge just below Steel, at the ford of Peth Foot where the two streams join. It is possible that there was a Roman road in the vicinity. If so, it was more pack-horse trail than metalled military road, a difficult route which led across some of the bleakest fells of the North Pennines. Its destination must have been Whitley Castle, the extraordinarily well-defended Roman hilltop fort near Alston, which seems to have been associated with state control of the Roman lead mining industry. Is it possible that Cadwallon knew of it and sought to use it as a redoubt?

The most plausible reconstruction of the battle is that Oswald, coming on Cadwallon's camp at Corbridge in the very early morning and with the British host unprepared, forced the enemy to flee either in loose formation or in a full-scale rout until they were overcome and overwhelmed at the river crossing. Here, Cadwallon was cut down, surrounded by his most loyal warriors, their bodies left to pollute the stream with blood. It is a more or less continuous climb from the haughs at Dilston all the way to the confluence of the Rowley Burn and Devil's Water; the crossing is not easy and at that precise point flight on to the moors, perhaps encumbered by four hundred days' worth of booty, was no longer possible. From Peth Foot it is a short, steep climb on to the ridge above. To the left is the tumbling course of Denisesburn; to the right, the gorge closes in on the Devil's Water. Here, perhaps, a last stand was made in a vain attempt to allow Cadwallon time to escape across the ford and on to the moors; if so, it failed. Oswald's relatively insignificant force, by a combination of stealth and impetuosity, had pulled off a most improbable victory, one of the greatest significance for the subsequent history of Northumberland and, indeed, Anglo-Saxon England.

Oswald's triumph ensured not just that he was accepted as the rightful and legitimate king of Bernicia but also, through his mother Acha's pedigree, the termination of Edwin's line and his undisputed claim as a great warrior of Deira. The two historically hostile rival kingdoms which had been held together by main force under Æthelfrith and Edwin were now united under a single house and a king with the immediate military, political and fiscal capital to create a kingdom in his own vision: one in which church and state were mutually reinforcing facets of the same divine dynastic purpose.*

* One thing niggles. Cadwallon had chosen his camp well if, as I suppose, he was stationed at Corbridge. His natural line of retreat was south and east, along Dere Street, where he knew the topography and might even have mentally envisaged tactical redoubts. Why, then, did his army cross the river and turn not left but right, to the south-west towards the fatal choke-point at Steel and their doom? Did he believe that the difficult road to Whitley Castle was a better bet for retreat than the fast road south? Did his army split into two in the fog of battle? Did Oswald's tactics include a detachment aimed at cutting of his retreat along Dere Street? I do not know.

IX

HOLY ISLANDS

Til sceal on eðle... domes wyrcean

*A good man shall gain honour
in his own lands*

IN 635 OSWALD IDING, AT

the age of thirty, was undisputed overlord of all the lands north of the Humber up to the Firth of Forth. With an impeccably legitimate claim through his parents to both Northumbrian kingdoms and with a martial reputation to match his father's, his political capital was immense, far greater than most athelings could boast on becoming king. How would he spend it? He could, like Edwin, have delayed weighty decisions on faith and politics until he felt secure within his borders, deferring the repayment of his moral debts. He might have embarked on an immediate campaign of conquest of the weak southern kingdoms. He could have allied himself by marriage to one of the northern British kingdoms, to Dál Riata or Mercia. These were the conventional tactics of a young man out to prove to himself and his subjects that he was made of the right stuff. The political reality of Oswald's first years in power shows breathtaking ambition and vision, the sureness of touch of a man with little self-doubt. It begins, though, with apparent modesty, with the establishment of a small community of monks on a windswept island off the coast of Bernicia.

As is so often the case with Bede, the story he tells is neither straightforward nor, at first sight, terribly revealing. He manipulates a seemingly simple narrative to suit his overall providential purpose; he omits much that one would like to know; and in trying to cover up those unsightly stains with which heroic tales are in reality marked, he leaves a subtle trail of clues which we have to unpick, one by one. He is at perhaps his most disingenuous when writing of Oswald.

Within months of the victory at Heavenfield the king requested from Iona a bishop to minister to him and his people. Edwin had waited a decade before paying off his Faustian debt to Paulinus. Oswald was a believer whose military triumph had been won in the name of Colm Cille and God (perhaps more than one god). He saw the conversion of his people to Christianity, if that was what it was, as a gift to them, not a political imposition. Bede is insistent that the initiative was the king's:

> Oswald, as soon as he had come to the throne, was anxious that the whole race under his rule should be filled with the grace of the Christian faith of which he had had so wonderful an experience in overcoming the barbarians.* So he sent to the Irish elders among whom he and his thegns had received the sacrament of baptism when he was an exile. He requested them to send a bishop by whose teaching and ministry the English race over whom he ruled might learn the privileges of faith in our Lord and receive the sacraments. His request was granted without delay. They sent him Bishop Aidan, a man of outstanding gentleness, devotion and moderation…

This is all very well. It sets up Bede's account of Lindisfarne, of Colm Cille and the founding of Iona and Aidan's ministry. But two chapters later Bede admits that Aidan was not, in fact, the first missionary of the Irish church to Northumbria; that the original mission had not gone according to plan. The first bishop sent from Iona found the Northumbrians resistant to the good news which he brought, as well they might—it had not done Edwin

---

* EH III.3; Colgrave and Mynors 1969, 219. Cadwallon is here a mere heathen.

or his subjects much good and their most recent experience of a Christian king was Cadwallon. The bishop was 'unreasonably harsh' on his ignorant audience, rubbing them up the wrong way and preaching over their heads.[122] Believing the pagan English to be unwilling converts 'because they were intractable, obstinate and uncivilised'[123] he returned to Iona where he was debriefed at a conference. His failure, if we accept this story, must have been of the greatest concern to Abbot Ségéne who was both a friend of Oswald and the motivating force behind the Northumbrian mission. The fact that the elders of Iona convened a summit to address the issue testifies to their concern. Bede would have us believe that a monk called Aidan, present at this conference, spoke eloquently of a more gentle, persuasive means of appealing to the heathen mind and, in the manner of such things, was unanimously chosen to head a new mission to Oswald's court, was consecrated bishop, and despatched.

Who consecrated Aidan, when there was no incumbent bishop in the community, is a nice question. It is more likely that Aidan was already a quite senior figure in the Irish church, but it makes a better story if he is plucked from the ranks of Iona's own community of monks. The Martyrology of Donegal,[124] a very late seventeenth-century compilation whose author seems to have had access to sources independent of Bede and Adomnán, lists Aidan's first bishopric as *Inis Cathaigh*—Scattery Island, a famous and early monastery and bishopric on an island at the mouth of the River Shannon in County Clare. If this is true, Aidan was no mere monk but a rather heavyweight bishop; and from a high noble family, if the Martyrology is to be believed.

This begs several more questions, though. Why does Bede bother to insert a complication in the story of Aidan's dispatch, two chapters after its natural place? Then again, why wasn't a better candidate for such a crucial posting chosen first time around? And why did that better candidate, that is to say, Aidan, not accompany the Bernician atheling on his campaign of conquest in the first place? After all, they had had seventeen years to plan the foundation of an Iona in the East; and to have their man in place alongside Oswald in the hour of triumph would have been no more than prudent. Why give the new king an opportunity to forget or defer payment on his promise?

There is another issue here. We know that Bede had specific sources for the Oswald account: Lindisfarne, where naturally enough stories of the king's reign would have been handed down as part of the lore of the founder; Iona, where Bede had correspondents and where there was substantial interest in historic ties to Northumbria; and Hexham, where the founder and first bishop of that establishment, Wilfrid, was instrumental in fostering the cult of Oswald. The insertion of a story about the failure of the first mission into an account of Aidan's ministry shows that, as in other split narratives, Bede was trying to reconcile two apparently contradictory stories. Which is which? Bede need never have mentioned the original failure; he did not even know the name of the bishop—if indeed the man was a bishop.

Bede, I think, told the story about the initial failure for two reasons. First, he took his duties as a historian seriously; he knew the story and felt he ought to tell it. Second, it redounded to Aidan's great credit that he overcame the difficulties of the challenge, just as Augustine had forty years previously. It made that mission, and Aidan, all the more special. As to how these two accounts came into his possession, the questions to pose are these: in whose interests was it to cultivate a story about a failed initiative, and in what circumstances did that earlier initiative try its hand?

There was a cult of Aidan at Lindisfarne in the late seventh century and I suspect that is where the story of the first failure came from. Since the monks of Lindisfarne were deeply implicated in the history of the Northumbrian church, Bede could hardly avoid telling their story. Further, I suspect that the mission to Northumbria, in the immediate wake of the victory at Denisesburn, may have been in some respects unofficial, focused on the site of Oswald's cross where Colm Cille had appeared to him: that is to say, at Heavenfield. As I hinted above, it would seem natural if the first missionary to Northumbria had been one of the monks in Oswald's warband, a man who remained at Heavenfield in order to cultivate the shoots of the conversion in its most holy place, but who proved unequal to the task.

Is there any evidence of an early mission at Heavenfield? There is. Bede says that many miracles occurred at the site of the cross; he narrates the story of a Hexham monk, Bothelm, whose fractured arm was cured by a poultice of moss that had grown on the cross.[125] He says that the brethren of Hexham Abbey had long been in the habit of making a pilgrimage to the site on the anniversary of Oswald's death. He also says that lately (presumably in the first quarter of the eighth century) a church had been constructed on the site. There is something else, too. From the air a striking and unusual sub-rectangular field pattern, shaped like a playing card, immediately to the south-west of the present church at Heavenfield (and centring on the site of Hadrian's Wall turret 25b) suggests an enclosure pre-dating the military road; it consists of the sort of stone field walls familiar all over Northumberland. Some of the stones are re-used Roman masonry, but that is not by any means unusual around here. It cuts across the two ditches of the Wall on the north side and straddles the Wall itself at precise right angles. The centre of the enclosure is about where the turret would have stood, and that turret is probably where Oswald made his camp and set up his cross. Without at least a geophysical survey it is impossible to determine how old the enclosure is or what it enclosed, except that it must predate the Jacobite rebellion of 1745 because it is neatly bisected by General Wade's military road. Only excavation could prove its authenticity, date and exact nature. As I noted above, the interior of the turret was excavated in the 1950s and the results are open to question: was the void in the centre a later 'disturbance', or the setting for a cross? In any case what is so absolutely striking is the enclosure's shape and size. Superimpose its outline on aerial photographs, at exactly the same scale, of the monastic enclosure at Iona and that reconstructed for Lindisfarne by Rob Young and Deirdre O'Sullivan[126] and the dimensions are very similar: six hectares internally and the same proportion of length to breadth. Dare one suggest that Iona's first mission, perhaps an informal initiative of the fighting monks in Oswald's warband, resulted in the founding of a monastery, on the Iona pattern, at the site of Oswald's vision of Colm Cille; and that, the mission having failed for the reason cited by Bede or because of a lack of official backing, the monastery lay undeveloped but the site of the cross retained its magical powers of healing and luck until the time when it became part of Wilfrid's Hexham hegemony and was revived as a royal cult site? Here is a hypothesis that might, in the foreseeable future, be tested archaeologically by geophysical prospection.

So much for the story of the first mission. There is another complication that needs to be accounted for in the story of Aidan's deployment. The crucial tale of the vision of Colm Cille appearing to Oswald the night before battle seems to have been told in person by the king to his friend Abbot Ségéne. This is the testimony of Adomnán, whose predecessor Abbot Failbe heard it from Ségéne who heard it in person from Oswald.[127] The clear implication is that at some point between 634 and his death in 642, Oswald met with his old friend and mentor. But where and when? That Oswald should travel to Iona is not, perhaps, inconceivable, but to journey so far from one's heartlands has been the undoing of many a king and I doubt if Oswald would have risked being absent for a long period in his first years. One is left with the conclusion that Ségéne travelled to Northumbria to meet with Oswald. This is not in itself surprising, given the importance already attached to the mission. Did he, perhaps, accompany the first bishop, whose name is offered in a much later Scottish source as Corman?[128] Or, more plausibly, did he travel with Corman's replacement, Aidan, to make sure that the second mission did not fail?

On the basis that it was Ségéne who travelled to Oswald and not the other way round, one might also speculate that the abbot of Iona had an ulterior motive: to ordain Oswald as king (Iona's king) on the same basis that Colm Cille had ordained Áedán, with an adjuration to foster the founding saint's interests—or else. If such an ordination did occur, the stage was Bamburgh, the 'paternal seat of antiquity' of the Bernician royal house and the place where a fragment of a stone throne, now in the castle museum, has been recovered from excavations. Bamburgh lies just a few miles south of, and in clear sight of, Lindisfarne and when Bede tells us that Aidan, on arrival, chose the mythical island as the site of his first monastery, one suspects it was not a spur-of-the-moment decision. Oswald must, during his long exile, have told his Ionan hosts about this magical spot:

> As the tide ebbs and flows, this place is surrounded twice daily by the waves of the sea like an island and twice, when the shore is left dry, it becomes again attached to the mainland.[129]

They cannot have been unmoved either by its periodic remoteness, its resemblance to Iona, or its proximity to the caput of the Bernician kingdom. I suggest, then, that one of the Ionan party who accompanied Oswald's army attempted to found a monastic establishment at Heavenfield; that this mission was unplanned, irregular and institutionally unsuccessful; that Oswald sent to Iona for a more formal mission as previously arranged and that Ségéne came to Northumbria himself, bringing the more experienced and politically astute Bishop Aidan, to lend full weight to the embassy. I suspect that his visit was additionally designed to conduct a formal ordination like those orchestrated by Colm

Cille. This is hinted at by Adomnán, who tells his readers that after Heavenfield Oswald was ordained by God as emperor of all Britain.[130] Such an ordination would have been uncomfortable for Bede to describe since, as he readily admits, he believed the Ionans of Oswald's day to be in the wrong regarding the Easter controversy and other Roman orthodoxies. Such ordinations were, even in Bede's day, probably regarded as uncanonical and perilously close to the heathen inauguration rites practised at places like Dunadd (and probably at Bamburgh or Yeavering under previous kings) in the bad old heathen days of their unenlightened forebears.

I may here be reading too much between Bede's lines. The whole thing does not quite add up. There is an awkwardness to his narrative of Oswald that masks some ambivalence on his part. The fact that in his earlier *Chronica Maiora* of 725, a sort of dry run for the Ecclesiastical History, Bede does not even mention Oswald's part in the Northumbrian conversion, leaves one with suspicions.* More than a few historians have speculated that the pagan overtones of Oswald's reign, which emerged strongly after his death, may have made him an equivocal figure for Bede to deal with. One thing seems clear: unlike his uncle and predecessor Edwin, Oswald is not recorded as having had to convene a council and go through the motions of debating the merits or otherwise of Aidan's presence in the kingdom. This was an executive decision; and who would argue?

Whatever troubles Bede had in reconciling conflicting accounts, or his own views of Oswald, his admiration for Aidan is perfectly genuine. Once the right man had been installed in the right place the mission proceeded at pace and with what Bede regarded as unqualified success:

---

* Thacker 1995, 112. My colleague Colm O'Brien suggests that Oswald's later elevation to the apogee of his narrative may have something to do with Bede's wish to enhance Aidan's reputation.

From that time, as the days went by, many came from the country of the Irish into Britain and to those English kingdoms over which Oswald reigned, preaching the word of faith with great devotion. Those of them who held the rank of priest administered the grace of baptism to those who believed. Churches were built in various places and the people flocked together with joy to hear the Word; lands and property of other kinds were given by royal bounty to establish monasteries, and English children, as well as their elders, were instructed by Irish teachers in advanced studies and in the observance of the discipline of a Rule.[131]

Make no mistake: this was the deliberate founding of an institutional church on an Irish model with the full backing of Britain's newly enthroned overlord. There is nothing here of the ambivalence of Edwin and Paulinus, no pillow talk or letters and bribes from Rome. Aidan, Oswald's bishop, was a man of exemplary faith, humility and leadership; moreover, he was not content to minister merely to the king's household and Bernicia's aristocratic elite. The failure of the first Ionan mission shows that whatever royal patronage might do, conversion of the plebs, a priority for the church of Colm Cille, was different from and much harder to accomplish than the mere political acknowledgement of the nobility. It shows how ambitious Iona was, and how much political capital they were prepared to invest, that they sent Aidan and so many others over. For more than fifteen years the Irishman and many, many more of his countrymen preached the Irish species of Christianity, a blend of desert asceticism, personal godliness and tribal affiliation, among the plains and hills of the North Sea coast. The youth of the Bernician, and perhaps Deiran, nobilities were educated in Latin and in Bible studies: the first literate English in the North. On Lindisfarne Aidan constructed a modest cluster of wooden buildings of hewn oak, roofed with thatch in the Irish style. There would have been a small church, cells for the monks, and a guesthouse for receiving visitors. On a tiny offshore isle, later associated with St Cuthbert, monks could retreat for periods of solitude and contemplation. A watchtower was built at some point during the seventh century, and a dormitory; but, in the tradition of the mother-house on Iona, architectural pretension was wholly absent. There was no pomp, no splendour, except perhaps in the possession of treasures given by the king himself. Miles to the south, and in plain view of Bamburgh, the island of Inner Farne provided Aidan and later Cuthbert and other monks seeking solitude a desert place whose only inhabitants were the seals and seabirds of that famous wildlife sanctuary.[132] As scholar Michelle Brown has suggested, the presence of fasting monks visible from the royal apartments of the Bernician kings might have been partly intended to concentrate their minds and remind them of their Christian responsibilities.[133]

There was sufficient land on Lindisfarne, some three-quarters of a square mile of farmland, to grow crops and pasture animals. There was ample fishing both inshore and offshore and seals may have been hunted in the tiny Farne archipelago. The island, like Iona, was not deserted when the monks arrived. In the late sixth century, when Lindisfarne was still known by its British name of *Inis Metcaud*, the Bernician king Theodoric had been besieged here by a British army. Excavation has shown that there had been activity on the island since the Mesolithic period, probably exploiting the rich year-round marine resources of the coast. In the Early Medieval period there was a farming settlement on the north side of the island at Greenshiel, later consumed by sand dunes; and it is quite likely that the site of the much later castle on its iconic and exotic-looking hill had been the site of a fortress—possibly that of Theodoric and possibly surviving in the late seventh century as the fortress known as *Broninis*.*

The monastic enclosure of Aidan's day has not yet been traced with certainty, although the reconstruction suggested by Deirdre O'Sullivan and Rob Young[134] makes plausible use of the topography of the island to produce a plan which would mirror in size

* See p.351.

and shape its Ionan model, focusing on the market place of the present village at the south end of the island. The church probably stood on the site of the later Benedictine abbey, close to its harbour and sheltered, like Iona Abbey, from the worst of storms. At low tide the island was reached by walking across the sands along a route still marked and known as the pilgrim's way so that in a sense Lindisfarne had two protective *valla*: the ditched and banked enclosure built by the sweated labour of the monks, and that provided by God in the form of the tides. At high tide boats might have plied the short distance to the mainland or ferried goods and monks along the coast to north or south. There is a cluster of suggestive *wic-* names on the sandy coast between Berwick-upon-Tweed, some eighteen miles to the north, and Bamburgh to the south, which suggests that beach markets may periodically have been held in the vicinity, perhaps under the protection of royal patrons at Bamburgh. Windswept it may have been, but Lindisfarne lay at the core of the Bernician kingdom.

Aidan, and the monks who joined him from Ireland, did not spend their days wholly in devotion to their own spiritual needs. Aidan himself walked among the scattered settlements of the hills and coastal plain bringing his word to the 'ordinary' people. Some of these ordinary people might already have been Christians, especially if they regarded themselves as in some way 'British'—that is to say, the *folc* of *Brynaich*, not Bernicia. If so, they are likely to have been more sympathetic to Aidan's brand of the faith than they had been to the Catholic, urbane version touted by Paulinus.

Although he had been given a horse by a Deiran sub-king, Oswine, as befitted his rank and dignity, Aidan later gave it, or one like it, away (much to Oswine's horror) to a pauper.* Aidan was by no means an unequivocal figure for Bede: his adherence to Irish practice in matters of Easter observance and the form of

* See p.265.

the monastic tonsure were inimical to the Jarrow monk's Roman orthodoxy. But:

> Such were his love of peace and charity, temperance and humility; his soul which triumphed over anger and greed and at the same time despised pride and vainglory; his industry in carrying out and teaching the divine commandment, his diligence in study and keeping vigil, his authority... All these things I greatly admire and love in this bishop and I have no doubt that all this was pleasing to God.[135]

Bede, in placing Oswald and Aidan at the heart of his conversion narrative, was speaking loud and clear to his contemporaries, both bishops and kings. The education of Christian kings was a primary function of the senior churchmen in the land. Royal power came with royal responsibility. Oswald, who had been educated by Colm Cille's successors, can have been in no doubt how those responsibilities were to be exercised.

Aidan's spiritual and moral superiority affected all those whom he met. It is quite possible that Oswald knew Aidan from his days in exile; in any case, the friendship that developed between them was mutual and genuine. Aidan was no sycophant or court groupie: he spent little time as a retainer. Bede says that if he was summoned by Oswald to feast with him at a royal estate, Aidan would attend with one or two of his monks, eat a little food for form's sake, and then hurry away to be with his people or to pray.[136] He would occasionally have entertained senior members of Oswald's retinue as a matter of formal hospitality, but evidently did not seek their company for its own sake. He gave money and gifts to the poor and disdained to curry favour with the rich, whom he was known to rebuke or correct without fear. He was also known to purchase those whom poverty, injustice or ill luck had rendered slaves, and release them or train them as priests. The Bernician nobility must, at first, have thought him a very odd fish, but can have been in no doubt of his moral authority or the favour in which he was held by the king.

Aidan's relationship with Oswald was cemented by the king's habit of acting as his translator from Irish to English. The king would spend many hours in prayer with his hands on his knees and the palms turned upward, from matins until daybreak.[137] Oswald also endeared himself to Aidan by his sympathetic behaviour. Bede's set-piece story is, as so often, staged at Easter, when Oswald and Aidan had sat down to dinner. They were eating rich foods off a silver dish, perhaps in the great hall at Yeavering or in the fortress at Bamburgh...

> They had just raised their hands to ask a blessing on the bread when there came in an officer of the king, whose duty it was to relieve the needy, telling him that a very great multitude of poor people from every district were sitting in the precincts and asking alms of the king. He at once ordered the dainties which had been set in front of him to be carried to the poor, the dish to be broken up, and the pieces divided amongst them. The bishop, who was sitting by, was delighted with this pious act, grasped him by the right hand, and said, 'May this hand never decay.'[138]

And so the seed of the later cult of Oswald was sown in an act of spontaneous generosity. Well, perhaps. The story has so many features of interest that it deserves a closer look. To begin with, Bede situates his readers (senior churchmen and, more importantly, contemporary kings) in the context of Oswald's expanding *imperium*. Oswald, as reward for his patronage of Aidan, was granted 'greater earthly realms than any of his ancestors had possessed'.[139] In contrast to Edwin's reign, the reward came after the proof of virtue, not in anticipation. By the end of his reign, Bede claimed, he held sway over all the peoples and kingdoms of Britain. That may or may not be true. His humility and kindness to strangers and the poor is set against this imperial backdrop as a moral fable which spoke loud and clear to Bede's own times.

The action takes place in a hall, the natural theatre of the Anglo-Saxons, where an Easter feast has been prepared. Bede offers few details of the scene, but it can be peopled with the ranks of the Northumbrian elite; with perhaps unmarried women of the court acting as cup-bearers and oiling the wheels of alliance and patronage; with aspiring warriors and elderly, time-expired *gesiths*, with hunting dogs and nameless children. Then there are the king's functionaries. One of these is identified, perhaps surprisingly, as an officer whose duty it was to relieve the poor. This man must be an *ealdorman*, perhaps past his military prime, an almsgiver holding in effect a sinecure of the king in return for loyal service in the past; one of his father's men, perhaps. In later years such men will be called King's Almoners. Who are the other functionaries? Elsewhere in Bede, in saints' lives and various prose and verse works, we catch sight of a few of them. Bede tells us of those whose job it was to compute the dates of kings, probably another formal function;[140] there must also have been king's messengers and couriers. King Ine of Wessex retained a group of British horsemen, perhaps for the purpose of escorting such couriers. Either formally, or as occasion arose, there must have been some sort of equivalent of ambassadors, of the sort so conspicuously portrayed in the story of Edwin's attempted assassination (also at Easter). There would have been a hunt master: kings have always been enthusiasts for the chase. Edwin also had his chief priest, Coifi, and one might speculate that for Oswald the same role was fulfilled by Aidan. In addition there were reeves, who administered royal estates, standard-bearers, bards and poets (*scops*, or praise-singers); perhaps also architects and the king's own specialist metalworker or jeweller. How many of these spent their days in the company of the king is a matter of speculation. Aidan may have been unique in choosing his own manner and timing of attendance on the king who was, after all, one of two lords whom he was required to serve.

It might come as a surprise to learn that Oswald charged an officer with almsgiving; whether this was a specifically Christian innovation is hard to say. The story suggests that as the king proceeded on his tour of royal estates, the poor of the locale would converge in the hope of having a petition heard, of receiving the leftovers of the feasting, or in expectation of a more formal distribution of alms. Early texts understandably offer little insight into poverty; the most graphic account is given in Æthelwulf's eighth-century poem *De Abbatibus* which includes the tale of an abbot who disguised himself and crept out of the monastery to give comfort to the poor who were immersing themselves in the warm rubbish (hot ashes, or worse?) discarded by the monks. That the multitude in Bede's narrative was allowed to crowd into the palace precincts is an indulgence in itself; it implies at the very least that the king did not fear popular uprising.

Oswald's response, having the silver dish on which his food was to be served cut up and distributed, sounds suspiciously like the key element in a ceremonial ritual, one which reappears in the later historical record as the Maundy service of the medieval kings, during which the monarch would also wash the feet of the poor as Christ had done in an act of penitential Easter humility. But it may be an amalgam of several ceremonials, including some variation of the Easter eucharist. Quite what the poor were supposed to do with a piece of silver is a moot point; but then, Maundy money is not exactly a negotiable food coupon. Clovis, the Frankish king whose conversion in about 500 seems to have been a well-known story (Bede certainly knew of it), showered the people of Tours with gold and silver coins on receiving the consulship from the Emperor Anastasius.[141] And the Irish monk St Gall, a companion of Columbanus on the Continent in the late sixth century, distributed to the poor a silver cup which had been destined for an altarpiece.[142] There might even have been a tradition inherited from late Roman Continental practice of provincial governors distributing largesse. Aidan, charged with educating Christian rulers in their responsibilities, may have been shepherding Oswald through a rite practised by kings in Ireland, or Dál Riata. An early fifth-century hoard of Roman silver including more than one thousand seven hundred coins, found at Ballinrees, County Londonderry, in 1854, shows that Irish kings were able to access such riches.[143] Then there is this intriguing story told by Cogitosus in his *Life of St Brigid*, one of Ireland's three great saints.

> Her miracles are great, but this one is especially admired. Three lepers came, asking for alms of any kind, and she gave them a silver dish. So that this would not cause discord and contention among them when they came to share it out, she spoke to a certain person expert in the weighing of gold and silver, and asked him to divide it among them in three parts of equal weight. When he began to excuse himself, pointing out that there was no way he could divide it up so that the three parts would weigh exactly the same, the most blessed Brigid herself took the silver dish and struck it against a stone, breaking it into three parts as she had wished. Marvellous to tell, when the three parts were tested on the scales, not one part was found to be heavier or lighter by a breath than any other. So the three poor people left with their gift and there was no cause for envy or grudging between them.[144]

Aidan probably knew this story; perhaps he had told it to Oswald with the express purpose of teaching the new king his Christian responsibilities. Equally, one might look to the gift-giving role of kings at important feasts and see more of Beowulf than Christ in the gesture. Oswald could not distribute coin; he had no mint. But he could, if tradition demanded, distribute wealth in precious metal by weight, or by division of a known quantity. Was the silver dish in question made bespoke for just such a division and given, as Bede must, a providential and divinely inspired polish? Or was it a piece of Roman tableware, recycled battle booty?

Who were these multitudes of poor? Early English, and for that matter British, society emerges from the historical and archaeological sources as socially ordered. Those who were free were valued higher than those who were unfree; the unfree belonged to the land, whose ownership might be transferred; they themselves were bound to it. Labour and patronage were opposite halves of the same equation: the lord protected the labourer in return for his or her toil. There does not seem to be much room for multitudes of dispossessed peasants. Are these the rural dwellers who, by historical accident—the death of an heirless warrior, perhaps—had been left without a lord and therefore subsisted in grinding misery outside the system so that *only* the king, as their ultimate lord, might be appealed to for succour? If this is true, the arrival of a Christian, compassionate king was timely: the Annals of Ulster recorded that in the winter of 635 a 'great snowfall killed many', a reminder that the elements wielded a power stronger than kings or holy men.

And then, what does one make of Aidan's blessing of the king's right hand? By Bede's day the story of Oswald's incorrupt arm and its adventures post-mortem was already the subject of cult attention. But Oswald's Irish moniker *Lamnguin* and its association with an Irish silver-armed god suggests that Oswald's right arm already had form. It was, to be sure, the martial arm, the sword-wielding, gift-giving and sceptre-carrying arm of the king. Dare one suggest that, like the god Nuada Airgetlám, Oswald had lost an arm or the use of it in battle; that the nickname *Lamnguin* was ironic (as most such nicknames were); that the arm in question was a prosthetic of some sort, or withered, and that Aidan's gesture was trading on that irony? This is too much to infer from the sources; nevertheless, Oswald's right arm carries a significance that predates his death in battle and Bede may have known more than he admits of its history in myth and reality.

During the fourth century various emperors, particularly Constantine, were keen to alloy aspects of both the pagan divine and the Christian in their ceremonials. The acceptance of a single, universal, omnipotent being forced compromise on secular leaders because they had been used to being treated and received as gods in their own right. Conversion seems to comprise an act of self-emasculation. The impression a king or emperor wished to make on those he visited on his peripatetic journeys was 'one of regular imperial arrival, a safeguard of general security and... interest in the various parts of the empire'.[145] Something of the ceremonial aspect of this *adventus* survived into the sixth century at least in Constantinople. One cannot directly argue from late Roman emperors to Early Medieval kings, but it is easy to imagine that pagan warlords undergoing conversion, like Oswald and Edwin, were reluctant to discard aspects of the pagan divine in their own being. Why should they? There was ample motive to retain divine elements in ceremonials of *adventus*, to maintain their propaganda value. Again, Bede's treatment of Oswald betrays discomfort in bending the oral traditions of this charismatic king to his providential purpose when Oswald, a committed Christian, was trying very hard to retain the most potent imagery of pagan tribal totemism. Bede, in fact, might be overdoing the poverty of Oswald's Easter reception party. They may conceivably have been his landed constituency: the free seekers of patronage and protection basking in his glory, rather than the unfree, unwashed masses. In that case the gift of silver can be seen not as poor relief and humility but as a token of condescending royal favour: one foot in Beowulf, one in the New Testament, with feasting, charity and the eucharist naturally enough being blended into a set of rituals associated with the arrival of the king and the consumption of the region's surplus—a dividend of royal power and prerogative. Aidan's raising of the king's right hand is as much a triumph for Aidan and his God as it is a token of the king's literally incorruptible moral virtue. Edwin emphasised his Romanitas by having standard-bearers walk in front of him; Oswald accomplished it by acts of Christian humility and largesse that Bede could not but approve of.

The most significant aspect of the relationship between king and cleric for later history is Oswald's donation of gifts and lands for Aidan's community to support themselves. In this, Oswald set

a Northumbrian precedent, the effects of which no-one anticipated at the time, although by Bede's day it had become a consuming political issue. There is nothing to suggest that Edwin
thought of such a thing. We learn very little from Bede about the
practical aspects of Oswald's patronage of the church. Church
buildings, he says, were founded in various places in the kingdom;
he does not say where and we can guess at few of them. Personal
gifts were made to Aidan, as to others of noble rank; it was part of
the tribal system of patronage and distribution. Æthelberht of
Kent had conferred on Augustine lands and estates 'suitable to his
rank'. Oswald, with the Irish example more relevant than the Kentish, regarded the church of Aidan as the Irish kings would: as a
tribally affiliated institution legitimising, supporting and ministering to the king and his family and court and with spiritual authority over the needs of the faithful (and prospectively faithful).

In the case of Bernicia, as in Kent, there is a question of the
potential survival of British Christianity. In Canterbury a Roman
church still stood; whether it retained a British congregation is
much less certain. That there were Christians in north Britain in
the Early Medieval period has long been suspected by archaeologists and historians; there were evidently still communities further
south in the Pennines in the middle of the seventh century. Bernicia
and Gododdin in particular may have had a substantially British
population, both ethnically and linguistically, even in Oswald's
day. The archaeological evidence is most obvious in the form of
long cist graves: that is, stone-lined interments, aligned east–west,
which may date from the fourth century onwards and which occur
both singly and in cemeteries from East Lothian southwards as far
as the Tweed and now, demonstrably, at Bamburgh.

The monastery to which Cuthbert first belonged, Old Melrose,
has been identified as a possible British survival on the basis that
Bede used its Brythonic name, *Mailros*, in referring to it. Two
stone inscriptions, one now missing, in the Peebles area, refer

to a *sacerdos* and an *episcopi*, both terms for a bishop.[146] Then there are the so-called *Eccles* names. These are places in which the Latin *ecclesia*, for church, has been preserved via Primitive Welsh *egles*, in names such as Eccles, just north of the River Tweed, and Eaglescairnie in East Lothian.[147] One of these, the hilltop Eccles Cairn to the east of Yetholm near Yeavering, is close to the heartland of Oswald's kingdom. There has been much speculation that the Tweed Valley was the core of a British kingdom in the fifth and sixth centuries—perhaps even the kingdom of Bryneich, which later became Bernicia. Some historians argue that this kingdom was influenced, if not wholly converted, by the mission of Ninian, the British saint of Whithorn, on the coast of Galloway; at Stobo, in Tweeddale, a church and well are associated with St Mungo, otherwise known as Kentigern, the late-sixth-century saint said to have had dealings with the semi-mythical Myrddin, or Merlin. That the Germanic kings who ruled over Bernicia in the latter part of the sixth century were heathen is attested by the direct evidence of early burials and totemic and sacrificial behaviour at Yeavering; but that is not to say that there was no residual practice of Christianity north of the River Tyne. How such populations may have reacted to the arrival of Aidan's mission (or that of Paulinus before) can only be guessed at; possibly he was just another lord, if an unconventionally benign one. In the next generation churchmen of the Roman persuasion like Wilfrid would have no compunction in depriving British churches of their lands in favour of their own foundations and communities.

It is possible, then, that the early donations of land to the Irish mission in Northumbria included lands which had been held by British monasteries and churches. More likely, such donations came from the royal portfolio. This begs a very basic question: how did kings know what they owned and, by extension, what they might give away? To suggest that kings could donate any piece of land within their kingdom is to read Early Medieval landholding wrong. Kings knew very well what they owned; or rather, what was potentially in their gift. The core of the royal property portfolio was the royal shire, with the *villa regia* at its heart collecting renders and playing host to the peripatetic king at various times during the year. Bamburgh was a likely Early Medieval shire, given—that is, its surplus in the form of a render of goods, foods and service was given—to Bebba by Æthelfrith or his family as dower.* With the render came the right to dwell in the palace or hall, to manage and administer and probably, at the local scale, to judge. There is no suggestion that the farming inhabitants of such estates moved around or, indeed, cared much in whose name they laboured. Given the multitudes of poor, perhaps lordless subjects who crowded at Oswald's Easter door, it is reasonable to suggest that the first grants to monasteries might have included lands which had no lord, that the poor were in effect being handed over to the protection of the church in return for labour. If that is the case, one begins to see an element of social progression—albeit perhaps accidental—in the extension of church lands in the later seventh century, at least in its early stages.

Generally kings gave, or 'alienated' land with only a life-interest as a reward to warriors who had served them on campaign and who were of an age, around twenty-five at least, when they required estates to provide income (in effect an army pension like that of the Roman legionary settling in his *colonia*) and an establishment in which to marry, raise children and maintain a hall. These lands were effectively held by lease and returned to the royal portfolio on the death of the 'owner'. This form of landholding ensured a more or less constant circulation of estates with which kings rewarded their warriors. Some estates in lands conquered on campaign were alienated from their native incumbents and redistributed, so that the size of the king's army might grow

* See my essay on the Bernician king-list, Appendix A, p.395.

until such time as the king died in battle, when the redistribution game was reset to zero and began again under a new lord and patron. There is a limited amount of evidence for the existence of what we would call freehold land, estates that were passed direct from father to son as customary right; but in extent such lands must, in Oswald's day, have been quite small.

Lindisfarne apart, there is no contemporary record of those lands gifted to Aidan to support his monastic mission. However, a fascinating document survives from the eleventh century which traces the history of the community of St Cuthbert from its origins in Aidan's day to its arrival in Durham in the tenth century, into whose narrative were interpolated records of lands granted by various means to the community. There are possible elements of retrospective claims here, not to say of downright fraud, in asserting historic grants after the fact. Nevertheless, the *Historia de Sancto Cuthberto*, or *HSC*, is accepted by historians as substantially reflecting the accumulation of estates by the Lindisfarne establishment, especially during the seventh and eighth centuries under Oswald and his heirs. Although the text has to be treated with caution, it is extraordinarily revealing about the process of alienation and even more so about the geography of early shires and estates.[148]

The first grant to be directly referenced, in Section Three of the *Historia*, dates to around 651 under King Oswiu; but Section Four appears to record a monastic tradition of the earliest territory of Lindisfarne, which may preserve in essence the original land grant made by Oswald in 635. It describes the 'boundary of the territory of Lindisfarne', including the lands which later became Islandshire (the townships between Berwick and Bamburgh but not including the latter) and Norhamshire (along the south bank of the Tweed). Assuming Colm O'Brien's reconstructed Gefrinshire, whose estate centre was Yeavering, to be strictly the preserve of the king, and Bamburghshire to be similarly inalienable, the remainder of the earliest grants (that is, under Oswald and Oswiu) consisted of the valley of the *Bromic* or River Breamish from its source down to perhaps the boundary formed by the Roman Devil's Causeway road (now roughly the A697 between Powburn and Wooler).* These 'shires', unlike the later county shires, seem to have consisted of groups of ten to twelve townships, or *vills*,† with a single more or less central place to which renders, in the form of food and services, were gathered for the consumption of a *gesith* and his family and retinue. One might best see them as a sort of grand estate whose social and cultural function was to support the warrior elite of the kingdom. That their boundaries can largely be reconstructed, that they still make geographic sense, is one of the more remarkable features of recent Early Medieval studies.

The fact that such units of land, carefully defined by reference to watersheds and river mouths, could be described and understood as coherent territorial units under the seventh-century kings suggests that these were already-existing economic polities. The Breamish Valley can be shown to possess the same territorial and economic coherence in the later prehistoric and Roman periods, which implies a continuity in rural land division and, perhaps, society, if not in the structures of the state. If Britannia collapsed in the decades after the withdrawal of Roman Imperial administration in around 410, perhaps no-one had told the inhabitants of the far North. Its land-holding institutions, as was realised many years ago, may substantially be British survivals.[149]

Apart from piety, what were Oswald's and his successors' motives in giving away land to the church? It must have been evident from the start that such lands could not readily be reclaimed or recycled by kings. The relationship between king, cleric and monastic establishment did not work like that. One way in which

* O'Brien 2002.
† See Glossary, Appendix C, p.414.

it was expressed was that the renders owed by those parcels of land were not lost but were 'commuted to prayer'; but the effective alienation was complete. If kings were to trade the uncertainties of pagan mortality for the everlasting joys of the next world and enjoy the stamp of legitimacy offered by the authority of God and Colm Cille, it stood to reason that the prayers offered for their salvation by the monks who enjoyed their patronage must also be everlasting. That is to say, the kings' tenure in heaven was envisioned as freehold and the monks' earthly tenure must also be freehold: as the early English put it, *bocland* or book-land as opposed to *laenland* or leasehold.* This permanent 'alienation' of land from the king's property portfolio had immediate implications. Firstly, monks and abbots, given security of landed tenure, could invest physical capital in their lands: the sweat-equity of labour—clearing scrub and woodland for fields; building barns for storage and so on—and the material equity of permanence—stone buildings with lead roofs, for example. The monastic community, unlike the heathen kingdom, did not collapse or disband on the death of the abbot. This injection of capital into the newly Christianised landscape led to economic stability and increasing surplus. It led eventually to freedom for the monks to pursue artistic and educational ambitions. One might even see in this apparently ingenuous precedent set by Oswald the beginnings of a sort of agricultural capitalism, a process which by the end of the century was to produce the scriptoria of Jarrow, Wearmouth and Lindisfarne and their magnificent, costly books.[150] Now that there was a sanctioned and protected church among the English of the north-east, monks from Iona and from the Irish mainland flocked to the region as missionaries and disciples of Aidan. The knowledge, skills and labour to exploit this new landscape of capital came freely; and they were thoroughly Irish.

---

* Old English *boc* for book derives from the same root as beech, a wood that must have been used either as a binding or for writing on.

The other implication for kings of the granting of so much land to the church was that less land was available for them to donate as *laenland* to warriors in reward for military or other service. The odd shire here or there could be lost to the royal portfolio without damage to the king's *fisc*, effectively his exchequer, especially if monasteries were responsible for agricultural innovation and if the lands they were given were not the most productive. But the wholesale alienation of royal estates, which became the norm in later decades, sowed the seeds of social, political and military disaster.* The almost inevitable inference to draw is that the Bernicia of Oswald's day was rich in agricultural holdings but, perhaps because of the second-hand patronage the kingdom had suffered under Edwin, was short of earthly warrior-tenants.

There is nothing in Aidan's career that foreshadows the Machiavellian pomp and majesty of the medieval prince-bishops of Durham, his lineal if not spiritual successors. His relationship with Oswald was one of mutual respect, even a sort of reserved friendship. As an instrument of Ionan political authority his role was to ensure the loyalty of Northumbrian kings to the paruchia of Colm Cille, although it seems unlikely that he issued Oswald with the sort of admonitory prophecy that would threaten doom to the Idings if they betrayed the founder saint; he probably did not need to. The bishop-abbot of the Irish church was a chief priest of immense authority, unafraid of kings or kingship; he served, after all, what he believed to be a greater lord. But there is no hint that Aidan or his immediate successors were intent on carving out a political hegemony for material benefit—far from it. Aidan, unlike Paulinus, saw himself both as a monk and as a missionary among the pagan English (and perhaps the indigenous Christians) with a pastoral role familiar to modern readers from the careers of Benedict of Nursia and Francis of Assisi. Until the

---

* As I will demonstrate in Chapter XX.

later seventh century Lindisfarne retained its modesty, the ideal of its monks being personal isolation and self-denial combined with benevolent pastoral work.

The churches Aidan founded outside Lindisfarne, with two possible exceptions, are unknown in both extent and location. The two exceptions are Bamburgh, where Aidan is known to have died and been buried, and probably Yeavering where Building B, constructed as part of a great expansion of the royal township in both scale and architectural magnificence and dated by Hope-Taylor to Oswald's reign, lay to the east of the great halls. It occupied the site of a former string-grave cemetery, perhaps to be associated with Eanfrith's brief tenure of the kingdom. The church was simple, a structure forty feet long by about twenty wide, set in a fenced enclosure absolutely crammed with east–west aligned graves; so crammed, in fact, that the excavator had difficulty determining where one grave ended and the next began; one interment was squeezed in so tightly between others as to be forced to fit around a buttress post. After an initial phase the church was destroyed by fire and rebuilt with a western annexe in a style closely resembling the superior domestic complex of Area C to the north-west. This was a royal church, not the ancillary structure of an outsider permitted to cling to the fringes of power. Royal, suitably imposing, but well within the aesthetic compass of Irish sensibilities. That Oswald, assuming he was the king responsible for this phase of building at Yeavering, intended Iona's influence to lie at the heart of his rule, seems a reasonable conclusion to draw.

The success of Aidan's and Oswald's mission is evident in the simple fact of its survival after the king's untimely death in battle. Oswald's reign lasted less than a decade. But his political success in that short time shows that his energies were by no means confined to the establishment of the Irish church in England.

THE NEIGHBOURS

Duru sceal on healle…
rum recedes muð

A hall needs a door…
the building's wide mouth

AS A HALL NEEDS A DOOR,
a king must have a wife. The name of Oswald's queen
was not even recorded by Bede. She is the most invisible of royal
consorts in the seventh century. We have to trust the much later
assertion of Reginald of Durham that she was called Cyniburh.
We can be reasonably sure that she was the daughter of Cynegisl,
king of the *Gewisse* or West Saxons. She bore Oswald a son,
Œthelwald, who played his own small and ignominious part in
the fortunes of Northumbria. Oswald conspicuously waited until
he was king to marry. Merovingian custom in this period was
that only offspring born to a king during his rule might succeed
him, and Oswald may have felt subject to a similar constraint
either by Irish or by Bernician precedent.* He was leaving nothing to chance. Since marriage was a political event in the seventh
century, Oswald's nuptials must be seen as part of a political and
military alliance with the king of the *Gewisse*.

At no point can the lands of the Bernician kings have bordered on those of Wessex. Their kings were not then remotely

---

* Brooks 1989a, 66; the same custom may have precluded Eanfrith from the Bernician
  succession.

the dominant force they came to be in the ninth century; not until Cædwalla (with his oddly British name) in the late seventh century were they able to impose tributary status on their southern neighbours. But Wessex was rich in resources, as the founding of the trading town of Hamwih under Cædwalla's successor King Ine implies. In the Tribal Hidage it was assessed at one hundred thousand hides, three times the tribute exacted from Mercia or East Anglia. This is not necessarily a direct reflection of wealth, because if the Hidage belongs to Edwin's reign there were obvious grounds for an extreme punitive levy on the kingdom that had sponsored his attempted assassination. Even so, Wessex might have been seen as a rising star. More importantly, it bordered Oswald's southern neighbour Mercia, whose would-be king Penda had helped dispatch Edwin and whose own rise must have been one of Oswald's principal territorial concerns.

The mechanics of this alliance, which the Anglo-Saxon Chronicle records under the year 636, are hung on Cynegisl's baptism by Birinus, a sort of freelance bishop who had been allowed to preach among the heathen *Gewisse*. The king's conversion was very likely Birinus's initiative, but its political motivation must have been the overt Christianity of the new great power in the land. Cynegisl's choice of Oswald Iding as godfather makes that clear enough. An alliance with Bernicia, on a tributary basis, was also desirable for a West Saxon king whose son, Cwichelm, had been behind the murder attempt on Edwin. So Oswald's Christian credentials already carried sufficient weight that heathen kings would undergo conversion as a corollary of alliance. It is hard to imagine that Oswald and the king's daughter were previously acquainted, so this looks like the most calculated of marriages. Given that the queen left almost no other mark on history I suggest that she was not the political or moral force her sisters-in-law became. In Bernicia it must have seemed that a long period in the shadows of Deiran domination had now given way to an age reminiscent of the glorious days of Æthelfrith. In Mercia the alliance cannot have been looked on with anything other than deep misgiving.

Bede's claim that Oswald held sway over more lands than any of his predecessors—as a result, clearly, of his Christian virtues— is worth a close look to see if it stands up. Within living memory Kent and East Anglia had claimed or been acknowledged to exert imperium over the other kingdoms. The death of Æthelberht of Kent in about 616 and the apostasy of his successor led to a decline in Kentish influence, confirmed by Bede when he records that after her flight to the Kentish court in 633, Edwin's widow 'Æthelburh, fearing kings Eadbald and Oswald... sent these children to Gaul to be brought up by King Dagobert.'[151] Eadbald of Kent had apostasised on the death of his father, married his step-mother and then undergone baptism in the early 620s. He had given his daughter in marriage to Edwin and his niece Eanflæd would become Oswiu's second (or third) wife. Kent may not have been tributary to Edwin, but Æthelburh's concerns for her children indicate that Oswald's writ ran all the way to the Channel. Oswald also held imperium over the South Saxons,[152] so that the whole south coast of England from Thanet to Poole and as far north as the Thames was tribute to him.

Lindsey, squeezed between Mercia in the west, the River Humber, the east coast and the fenlands of Anglia to the south, had a chequered history under the Northumbrian kings. It was a second-division kingdom, if its Hidage assessment of seven thousand hides is anything to go by. Its royal genealogies are thinly attested in the historical record. Its origins probably belong in the Roman province whose capital was the *colonia* at Lincoln.[153] Here, in the church of St Paul in the Bail, is some of the best archaeological evidence for the survival of Romano-British Christianity into the Early Medieval period. Paulinus preached at Lincoln and constructed a stone church there in about 627. If the

Tribal Hidage was compiled by Paulinus under Edwin, Lindsey was already tribute to Deira in his reign, when it was bundled with Hatfield. Oswald decisively conquered Lindsey, probably as part of his campaigns to shackle Mercian pretensions. Bede, in recounting the story of the translation of Oswald's bones to the Lindsey monastery at Bardney, tells us that the monks initially rejected the relics because of Oswald's aggressive treatment of their kingdom.* There might be something more. Historians have noted and rather failed to explore the obvious similarity of Lindsey's Tribal Hidage record, under which it appears as *Lindisfaran*, with the island of Lindisfarne. There is no certain historical link but there is a good chance that Lindisfarne was a primary foothold of an Anglian warband sailing up the east coast from Lindsey, lost in the mists of the early sixth or late fifth century—perhaps led by Ida, founder of the Bernician ruling dynasty. The inhabitants of Lindsey may have believed that they had, as a police officer might say of a recidivist criminal, 'previous'; Bernician kings may have believed themselves to possess residual rights over their ancestral homeland.

Lindsey never wielded great power: its princesses were not objects of diplomatic desire among the great kingdoms; it had little opportunity for expansion against more powerful neighbours; its subjugation was a military hobby for kings pursuing greater imperium and strategic domination of the Humber basin waterways; Mercia regarded it as a natural extension of its own territory to the east. That Oswald was able to conquer and control it suggests that during his reign Mercia did not yet have sufficient military strength to match him there; not, that is, until the last year of his life. But there is evidence of an attempt by the southern English kingdoms to assert their independence from Northumbria.[154] There are entries in two of the Irish annals, in

* EH III.11; and see Chapter XVIII.

the late 630s, which deserve more notice than many historians have given them. Both are derived from a lost chronicle of Iona and reflect increased interest in northern English affairs after Oswald's succession. The Annals of Tigernach record under the year 637 a 'congregation of the Saxons against Osualt'. The Ulster Annals note under the year 639 the 'battle of Oswald, king of the Saxons'. They might record two military campaigns or, more likely, both derive from mention of a single conflict. If it is the latter, then it seems that Oswald faced a combined attack from the south; and if it was a 'congregation', of which kingdoms did it consist? The specific mention of Saxons suggests that there was no British involvement. The obvious candidates are Lindsey and Mercia, perhaps supported by East Anglia. Wessex, already allied with Bernicia, can be ruled out as, I think, can Deira, Kent and the other southernmost kingdoms. Was the campaign led by the rising star of the southern English?

Mercia's great warlord Penda is an enigma, as little understood as the origins of his kingdom. Bede had no Mercian correspondents and no Mercian chronicle survives to record its genealogies or its foundation stories. It emerges as an entity in the early seventh century when its kings or war leaders are noticed in chronicles and when its princesses begin to marry well. But it does not possess the legendary narratives beloved of Bernician or Kentish genealogists; there is no Mercian historian whose work survives to do it justice, as Bede did for the Northumbrians. There is a resultant danger of underestimating the power and influence of its rulers, especially before the reign of the celebrated Offa in the eighth century. For all the power of the Northumbrian kings, none of them was ever able to strike at the Mercian heartlands in the seventh century. Mercia was not a small kingdom grown great like Wessex or East Anglia. It was not named after a people or a *civitas* capital. Mercia is a Latinised form of the Old English word *Merce*, meaning 'people of the March or border', as in the Marcher lords of the Middle Ages; and the lands on which it must have marched are those of the British of Powys and the other Welsh kingdoms. The broad consensus is that by tracing the boundaries of the surrounding territories named in the Tribal Hidage, in which the unspecified Mercian lands are rated for tribute at thirty thousand hides, the hole left in the middle must constitute the core lands of Mercia in the early seventh century. This exercise gives us roughly the modern counties of Staffordshire, Leicestershire, Nottinghamshire, the southern half of Derbyshire and Warwickshire.[155] Even then, parts of these lands must originally have been separate, if minor, kingdoms in earlier centuries. Mercia was—must have been—a confederate state, if that is not too loaded a word. If one takes its core territory to be defined by the later dioceses at Lichfield and Leicester one would probably not be too wide of the mark, with the watershed of the upper Trent as its cultural coreland, perhaps; its royal cemetery lay at Repton, its 'seat of paternal antiquity' probably at Tamworth; its diocesan seat at Lichfield.

The first hint we have of Mercia asserting independence from Northumbrian kings is in about 614–15, when King Cearl—and it is by no means certain what 'king' means in Mercia at this time—gave his daughter to the exiled atheling Edwin, a move which could not be more calculated to inflame the wrath of Æthelfrith. An entry in the Anglo-Saxon Chronicle for the late 620s has Penda fighting against Cynegisl and Cwichelm of the *Gewisse* at Cirencester, with no apparent outright winner, although Mercia seems afterwards to have been able to exact tribute from the kingdom of the Hwicce, of which Cirencester was the capital.* Before

---

* The kingdom of the Hwicce is one of those which emerges from the mists of post-Roman Britain with a mention in the seventh- or eighth-century Tribal Hidage, levied at seven thousand hides like Essex and Sussex. Its probable geographical extent has been linked by historian Nick Higham with both the medieval diocese of Worcester and the British *civitate* of the Dobunni. Higham 1995, 156.

632, certainly, Penda was in alliance with Cadwallon of Gwynedd, attempting to take on the might of Edwin and succeeding at *Hæthfelth* on the eastern border of Mercia. These campaigns can only have enhanced Penda's credentials as a warlord and, although ten years later his brother Eowa's death is recorded as that of a king, it is hard to say that Penda, by then, was not either his co-ruler or superior. Bede records that his career was one of mixed fortunes, which is not that helpful but indicates that his rise to greatness did not follow a straight path.[156] It has been suggested that during Oswald's reign Eowa was in effect a Bernician puppet, or client king, in Mercia, just as Penda seems to have acted as a protégé of Gwynedd during Cadwallon's reign.[157] Above all, Penda emerges from the pages of Bede as a strenuous defender of heathenism and an indomitable leader of warbands: bold, resolute and dauntless. Bede had previously admitted his admiration for another great pagan warlord, Æthelfrith. He seems to have acknowledged the virtue of consistency, reserving his greatest disapprobation for either apostate English kings or, worse, those who were British Christians.

Penda's first interaction with Oswald may have been the murder of Edwin's son Osfrith, who had sought his protection after his father's death at *Hæthfelth*. Penda was acting as a subordinate, not an equal, as Rædwald's musings over whether to allow Æthelfrith to murder Edwin while the young prince was under his protection makes obvious. If this parallel murder was an attempt by Penda to politically outflank his brother Eowa, it seems not to have succeeded; but his ambition is as clear as Oswald's. He, like Oswald, arranged a marriage alliance with Wessex, although in his case it was the union of his sister with King Cenwalh, Cynegisl's son and successor. Cenwalh later repudiated her and was expelled by Penda. At some unspecified date Penda took on the kings of East Anglia and defeated them; but from the start it was to Northumbria, and to Oswald, that Penda looked as targets to beat back the tide of Christianity; to assert first his independence and then his superiority over the lines of the Idings and Yffings.

Oswald was not a passive observer of Penda's career. His alliance with the *Gewisse* demonstrates the lengths, literally, to which he would go to side-step Mercian ambitions. There have been various suggestions over the years that a cluster of Os-names in the Hwiccian genealogies of the seventh century might reflect an attempt by Oswald to plant a dynasty there, with a similar purpose to his alliance with the *Gewisse*. Perhaps this is where Oswald's otherwise unmentioned younger brothers went. The jury is out on that... so far.

Oswald must have had one eye on Mercia throughout his reign; he seems to have planned a pre-emptive strike on it in 642; but it was not his only or even his main territorial or martial preoccupation. His cultural and political background was wholly northern, and although the historical evidence for his activities beyond Northumbria is precious thin, there is little doubt that he was active in pursuing political ambitions there.

The northern, specifically Ionan interest in Oswald, his brother Oswiu and the fortunes of the kingdom of Northumbria is shown by a number of entries in the Irish Annals from 635 onwards. These are our principal source for Oswald's northern activities but they are both sparse and infuriatingly vague. His Dál Riatan patron, Domnall Brecc, suffered a series of reverses in the 630s and 640s which mirror a long-term decline in the fortunes of the Scots. The Battle of Magh Rath, dated to 637, saw an alliance between Brecc and Congal Cáech of the Dál n'Araide attempt to defeat Domnall mac Áedo of the Cenél Conaill. Magh Rath is located at Moira in County Down and the campaign can be seen as part of a long-running turf war over influence and tribute on the Irish mainland, which had been maintained by the kings of Dál Riata since the Treaty of Druim Cett in about 575. Congal

Cáech, who probably called in a marker from his kindred across the water in Argyll, was killed. Most historians believe that the result of the campaign was a disastrous loss of control for Brecc over former Dál Riatan territories in Ulster. Given the reciprocal obligations between northern kings it is possible, likely even, that Oswald fought on Brecc's behalf, or that he sent a warband in support. If so, his involvement did not make it into the annals.

At some time during the three years after Magh Rath in 637, a confusing variety of Irish annals record the defeat of Brecc's kindred at a place called Glen Mairson, probably on the Scottish mainland, followed by a siege of *Etin*, which must be Edinburgh. Bernician involvement in these campaigns again seems likely, especially given the historic northern interests of the Bernician kings in defending and expanding their territories as far as the River Forth. If Oswald was busy fighting a *congregatio* of southern English in those years (and again, the Annals do not agree on a precise date), then it was probably his younger brother Oswiu who led the Northumbrian warbands in the lands of Gododdin. Who the enemy were is another matter; but there is a clue in the events of 642, when Domnall Brecc died, slain at a place called *Srath Caruin* or Strathcarron, which must lie on the Carron River in the upper Forth Valley near Falkirk. The Annals of Ulster record that his conqueror was Hoan, king of the Britons.

What are we to make of this flurry of military activity? It seems to have been precipitated by Domnall Brecc's defeat at Magh Rath in 637, which tilted the balance of power on both sides of the Irish Sea. Hoan, more properly Eugein, appears as a king of the Strathclyde Britons in a stanza about his defeat in 642 of Dyfnwal Frych—that is, Domnall Brecc, in *Y Gododdin*...

> I beheld the array from the highland of Adowyn,
> And the sacrifice brought down to the omen fire;*

---

* Thought to be a reference to Anglo-Saxon offerings to their battle gods.

I saw what was usual, a continual running towards the town,
And the men of Nwython inflicting sharp wounds;
I saw warriors in complete order approaching with a shout,
And the head of Dyvnwal Vrych by ravens devoured.[158]

That a verse about the war between Strathclyde and Dál Riata found its way into the heroic poetry of the men of *Eidyn* (Edinburgh) is no great surprise. Eugein was very probably in alliance with the king of *Eidyn* in opposition to the combined warbands of Dál Riata and Bernicia. Oswald was duly repaying his obligations to his host and sponsor and pursuing his own northern ambitions by fighting against Britons. It was no more than his father had done before him. Whether the siege—*obsesio* as the Annals of Ulster describe it—of the Castle Rock at Edinburgh was successful is not recorded. All we can say for sure is that with the death of Brecc an era of Dál Riatan hegemony ended; that Oswald by implication lost a powerful northern ally; and that the battle between Britons and Lloegr for control of central Scotland continued through to the end of the century, with mixed results. Oswald may have been able to style himself overlord of North Britain and may have now regarded Dál Riata as a tribute kingdom.* Strathclyde and Gododdin may also by the end of Oswald's reign have submitted to him. There is no evidence that he suffered personal military defeat in any of these campaigns. Bede, then, in describing Oswald's unprecedented influence over most of the other kingdoms of Britain, was doing him no more than justice. The military luck he seemed to possess, reinforced by the potent *virtus* of Colm Cille, had carried him very far in a very short time.

---

* I have avoided reference to the term *Bretwalda*, which first appears in the Anglo-Saxon Chronicle nearly two hundred years after Oswald's day, in the entry for 829. Oswald is one of those kings listed, but it is a word loaded with connotations and there is no sound evidence that seventh-century kings used it of themselves. Bede wrote a list of those kings who possessed some sort of overlordship, which the Chronicle compiler used; but to equate this with *Bretwalda* is inappropriate.

Oswald's years as king were busy. His intense military, political and diplomatic activity mirrors the first decade of Edwin's rule and, probably, of Æthelfrith before him. One wonders, though, what sort of kingship this made for? How did kings in an almost permanent state of war plan for statehood, if indeed they had an idea of statehood? Edwin was able, after securing his borders, seeing off the competition and generating the wealth which came from territorial expansion, to consider more stately aspects of kingship. He had time to think about maintaining the highways; about the social and political aspects of religious conversion. Even so, he did not create a state that was capable of surviving him. There is no sense that he envisioned his church as an arm of state control, of economic and social stability. He did not found towns or trading settlements, even if he possessed a list of what his subject territories owed him; he did not even, as his father-in-law Æthelberht had, commission a set of written law-codes to define the rights and responsibilities of Northumbrians. His kingship, like those before him, was founded on customary right and on what had always been. There is no hint of what we would understand as a civil service except, perhaps, those enigmatic officers whose job it was to ensure that a woman with a newborn child might traverse his lands in safety or quench their thirst by the roadside.* And we do not know who they were, apart from Bede's allusive reference. That is a concept of security, of the king's peace. Edwin had heard of the sorts of governance which existed in Rome and in Frankish Gaul—his bishop, Paulinus, was Roman; his wife a product of Kent and Gaul—but he had not seen or experienced it, unless we count the construction of the Yeavering grandstand as an embodiment of the idea of

---

* EH II.16. Bede cites the story of the woman and newborn child as a proverbial saying; in the same place he records that Edwin cared so much for the good of his people that he 'caused stakes to be set up and bronze drinking cups hung from them' so that travellers might slake their thirst.

state function. There is a vague idea of Romanitas, a picture perhaps of the civic institutions of Rome that Paulinus had known. But this is not really evidence of statehood.

It is worth reiterating that Oswald, despite his Bernician pagan heritage, was Irish in upbringing and outlook, Irish Christian in education. Was his ambition to construct the foundations of a Christian state, or was he actually more pagan in mentality than Bede would have us believe? Was kingship just a life-interest, as land-holding was, as it had been for his very heathen father? What sort of a king was Oswald? What sort of king would he have made if he had lived longer?

To begin at the beginning, we see in the careers of Ida, Ælle and Cerdic, the legendary founders of royal Anglo-Saxon dynasties, little more than the leaders of warbands. To call them kings is to flatter them. Bede allows such men no more than the term *duces*. The equally obscure Arthur was, according to the Nennian account, a *dux bellorum*, leader in battle, a probable military rank of the late Empire.[159] This idea, of a people choosing or appointing a *dux* purely for the duration of a military campaign, is very much in line with the ancestral Germanic tradition of the 'leader in time of war', who stood down in peacetime—in theory at least. By the seventh century this concept was defunct: war or peace, the king was the king. But a king might emerge from among a group of competing warband leaders who claimed eligibility by birth: Penda appears first as the leader of a warband and Bede withholds the title king until later in his career.

Then there was the tribal chief, the senior aristocrat from the senior clan who combined ideas of tribal divinity with the function of war leader. Gildas's five British tyrants appear as tribal chiefs, based in fortified strongholds, often hillforts, with hereditary rights to eligibility: the sons of tribal chiefs, if Irish, were *rigdomna* or kingworthy; in the English kingdoms they were athelings. Æthelfrith fits the bill of tribal chief par excellence, as do

Rædwald, Áedán mac Gabráin, Domnall Brecc and Cadwallon—and so, for that matter, does Oswald. In their cases the title king is, as it were, a courtesy but even Bede was sometimes unsure in his use of the term.[160] Their sons might succeed—would be eligible to succeed—but their successor would be chosen by acclamation among the senior nobility of what amounted to the kingdom. That term is also loaded. As is evident from the Tribal Hidage, kingdoms came in all sizes, from the bijou three hundred-hide Gifla and Færpinga (unlocated but somewhere in the Midlands) on the scale of Rutland or Flintshire, to the more or less coherent kingdoms of Kent, East Anglia, Deira and Bernicia. Kings came in commensurate shapes and sizes which reflected the lands over which they held sway. To compare Æthelberht of Kent or Æthelfrith of Northumbria with the unnamed and unknown chief of the Gifla is not to compare like with like.

The overlord, the wielder of Bede's *imperium*, was the king who was able to subdue, conquer or otherwise render tributary lands beyond his ancestral homeland. Æthelfrith became overlord of, first, Deira, then his own Bernicia, then probably Rheged, East Anglia, Mercia and Lindsey. Edwin exercised similar imperium as, with extended authority, did Oswald. But overlordship was not an extension of kingship; it was not a higher form of authority, only wider; and overlordship vaporised as instantly as kingship on the death of its wielder. It could not be inherited.

Only later in the seventh century, in the persons of Oswiu of Northumbria and Ine of Wessex do we see individuals who might, just might, be called heads of state. Only under those kings was there a concept of statehood and of kingdom that we might recognise: one that survived the death of the person of the king. The extent to which Oswald envisioned such a state and had ambitions to achieve it is a moot point.

Historians long ago recognised that in both Britain and Ireland there existed other shades of kingship. In Bede's *principes*, *præfecti* and *duces* there are minor grades of English authority below the office of king (*rex;* plural *reges*). In Ireland it was rather the other way around: there were hundreds of kings, over whom authority might be exercised by high-kings and kings of all-Ireland. In Northumbria a rash of underkings pockmarks Bede's Ecclesiastical History from the reign of King Oswiu onwards. Most of these are junior members of the ruling dynasty acting as deputies and/or rivals in Deira. I have already speculated that Edwin's cousin Osric might have fulfilled this role in Bernicia during Edwin's reign and been able to both discharge the duties of a tributary king and enjoy the benefits of lordship over a significant territory. Penda's son Peada is described by Bede as *princeps*—prince, a sub-king who might expect to succeed his father, just like Oswiu's sons Alhfrith and Ælfwine.[161] Elsewhere Bede uses a variety of terms to denote what are later called *ealdormen*, really deputies, drawn from the most senior ranks of the nobility and, perhaps, from collateral lines of the ruling dynasty.

Towards the end of the seventh century a minor dynasty of such men appears in the far north of the Northumbrian territory in the persons of Beornæth (described as a *sub-regulus* by Eddius), Berht (whom Bede calls *duce*), Berhtred (whom he calls *dux regius*) and Berhtfrith (*princeps* or *præfatus*) of Dunbar, who seem to succeed one another as the king's men between Bernicia and the Forth. Berhtfrith is described by Eddius Stephanus, the biographer of St Wilfrid, as 'a chief man, next in rank to the king'.[162] Those five 'kings' recorded by the Anglo-Saxon Chronicle, whom Edwin slew in Wessex in 626 after the abortive attempt on his life, ruled under Cwichelm and must, in reality, have been *præfecti* even if they were of royal stock. In East Anglia, in Mercia, in Kent and elsewhere, kingship was occasionally shared by competing members of the same or rival dynasties until such time as one died or was ousted by the other. In Northumbria in the seventh century the lines were relatively clear. Those sub-kings or exiled athelings who threatened the authority of the king were dispatched and the resulting regal stability is one reason for the success of the Northumbrians as wielders of imperium over their rivals for the bulk of that century. Six kings managed to rule all the Northumbrians between 600 and 700: none was displaced by a *sub-regulus*; none (unless one counts Æthelfrith) was killed by an internal rival; and none of the four athelings known to have served as *sub-reguli* in the seventh century—Œthelwald, Oswine, Alhfrith and Ælfwine—ever succeeded their fathers in the overlordship of Northumbria.

By the time that English kings were being Christianised in the first half of the seventh century their rights and obligations were beginning to crystallise. A law code, written for Æthelberht of Kent, survives to indicate some of these; others can be inferred from the pages of Bede and other contemporary sources. If leaders were no longer kings solely in time of war, territorial protection and expansion remained the first items in their job descriptions. They must make war on their enemies and protect their people from external attack. With those responsibilities went the right and requirement to raise armies, define borders by treaty or earthwork, negotiate alliances and marry usefully; to collect tribute from the defeated and subjugated; to propagate heirs for the ruling dynasty. Kings chose their *principes* and *præfecti*, their *duces* and reeves. In the mead hall they feasted, shared treasure and gave gifts of rings and swords, ensuring that lines of patronage remained dynamic. Kings were also repositories of the animistic pride and fortune of their people, the embodiments of the Germanic and British gods of war and weather, fertility and luck. They were lawgivers and judges, the inspirers of poets, the patrons of metalsmiths and builders. They must conspicuously consume the surplus of the land and at the same time ensure the wellbeing of those who claimed them as their lord by sharing their wealth.

Although they did not yet exercise fiscal control over trade

—there was really no such thing as a town in seventh-century Britain, and no functioning coinage—they do seem to have controlled some of the goods which entered their kingdoms: salt, for example, luxury items like wine and olive oil, and the fur of the pine marten.[163] The locations of opportunistic, or at least intermittent, beach markets and fairs close to centres of royal power shows that kings were interested in trade and traders; but they can have been only dimly aware of the potential for trade as a sustainable source of revenue in a coinless realm.

The kings who were able to fulfil all these functions and who stayed alive for more than ten years or so must, in some sense, have contributed to the long-term success of their kingdoms. The absorption of smaller polities into greater ones, which marks the second half of the sixth century and much of the seventh, is the story of those kings whose success in war was matched by skill in maintaining good relations with their nobility and nurturing the agricultural potential on which basic economic wealth was founded—or at least not ruining it. But was the latter an accidental by-product of the former? Did kings have any idea what an agricultural economy meant, except in terms of their consumption of its surplus? The answer is that they must have had some idea, because there was a relationship between the fertility of the land and that of the warrior elite whose sons must be strong and plentiful, sufficient to man their warbands. And more than that, the success of the harvest was intimately connected with the 'luck' of the person of the king. Measuring the extent to which they were willing or able to affect that economy in any practical sense is a more difficult question.

Kings' rights and responsibilities were customary, an accretion of precedent and myth, of main force and military might. The kingdoms from which the earliest Anglo-Saxon states emerged have an appearance of fragility. So much was vested in the person of the king that his death brought the kingdom to its knees. And yet, there was a robustness to the institutions and political economies of the seventh-century kingdoms that allowed kings of sufficient maturity, vision and longevity to forge the makings of something more. Oswald inherited a kingdom ravaged by a year of apostasy, anarchy and rapine; and yet, within a year of his victory at Heavenfield he was acknowledged as overlord of most of Britain south of the Forth; had established a new church on lands which he was able to gift because he, or someone in Bernicia, knew what and where they were. That could not have happened had the economic and social bases of the kingdoms of Bernicia and Deira been dismantled by Cadwallon. The robustness of the machinery of kingship allowed it to recover rapidly from terrible reverses. That robustness was a function of how land was held, managed and administered. Its essence was the institution called the *scir*, or shire.

XI

Holy shires

Hærfest hreðeadegost,
hæleðum bringeð, gæres wæstmas

Harvest time is most prosperous,
it brings men the year's crops

BRACING ONESELF AGAINST
a winter gale coming out of the north-west, with the
ramparts of the Iron Age hillfort of Old Bewick at one's back and
the huge vista of the Cheviot Hills spread out across the horizon
it is hard to see, beneath the bleak magnificence of these snow-
fields, how Northumberland has ever been hospitable to human
life. The chiselled outlines of blank fields, skeletal trees and empty
skies offer little hope of bounty. You have to wait until after
the spring equinox, at the end of the Anglo-Saxon *Hreðmonað*
(*Hreða* was the name of a rather obscure goddess), when the days
become longer than nights. Now the northern lands catch up
with those far to the south. For six months they will enjoy more
sunlight and plants take immediate advantage of the lengthening
days to accelerate their growth until, in September, they ripen in
time for harvest.

Sit, later in the year, with a picnic lunch at Old Bewick, where
the medieval monks of Eglingham used to bring their bees in
the summer to feast on the pollen of purple heather, and take in
the same view. Meadow flowers abound, insects buzz, buzzards

hover on thermals rising from the vale. The land is alive. Clouds still scud towards you across the hills, seemingly only just above head-height, hurrying on towards the North Sea; a few linger over the dome of Cheviot itself at a shade under two thousand seven hundred feet. Nearer, the entrance to the ancient shire fastness of *Bromic* is unmistakable, guarded by the mouth of the Breamish gorge at Ingram and the rocky fortress of Brough Law which, in its heyday around the first century BC, boasted walls fifteen feet high of pink pyroclastic rock which glowed like a beacon at sunrise.

On the green hills tiny white dots show that the ubiquitous flocks of black-face Cheviot sheep are out on their high pastures. Saint Cuthbert, born in these parts in 634, the year of Heavenfield, experienced a vision of an angel while taking his turn watching the sheep and would have been entirely at home with the scene. On one occasion, when he was far away from home and needed shelter for the night, he came across a shepherd's dilapidated shieling and, pulling straw from the roof for his horse, was blessed with the gift of half a loaf and a piece of meat, still warm, which fell into his hands from the rafters. Even then, this was a bounteous land.

In the middle distance the hills give on to rolling meadows and arable fields of wheat and barley, dotted with fox coverts and the glint of sun off twisting blue–black becks. This is a rich, fertile landscape, well mannered and crisply maintained by the great landed estates which still own most of it: the Percys of Alnwick, the Greys of Chillingham, the Lilburn estate and others. There is little woodland except on the steep sides of sinuous denes, for the soil is too good to waste on growing trees. The earth is easily cultivated without the need for a heavy plough; the land is well drained and, if anything, there is not quite enough rainfall for the present-day farmer's liking.

Overlooked by the Cheviot foothills and by the sandstone

scarp on which Old Bewick perches is the line of the Devil's Causeway. Originally built by the Romans to link Corbridge with the sheltered harbour at Berwick-upon-Tweed, lengths of it have variously been replaced or overlain by the A697 Coldstream road and by the so-called Corn Road of the eighteenth century, which transported Northumberland's harvest to the coast at Alnmouth for export to London. In a land whose natural warp runs east–west along its rivers from sea to hills, the Roman road and the sea itself linked north and south so that Bernicia was a joined-up land, a geographical whole. But there were other ancient routes through this landscape and some of them can, with care, be reconstructed. One of the most important linked the ancestral seat of the kings at Bamburgh with the tribal holy mountain and cult centre at Yeavering. I imagine Oswald and his court making that journey of twenty miles or so towards the end of April because May Day, or Beltane in the British calendar, seems to have been the date when cattle renders from subject kingdoms were collected.[164] Cattle, probably horses too, were brought from across the north of Britain to be scrutinised and counted; no doubt more than a few were slaughtered for feasting. It was part conspicuous display of wealth, part rodeo, an opportunity for men to judge flesh and wrangling skills. Horses were prized above all things by kings, whose pride in weaponry and horseplay were key to their status as charismatic warrior leaders. Cattle were the principal measure of earthly wealth in a world where crops were necessary, but hardly romantic; their cultivation was menial, plebeian. At Yeavering the infrastructure for such ceremonial taxation was present in the great palisaded enclosure, a corral enclosing nearly three acres. The cowhands and wranglers of America's heroic western cattle country would have felt perfectly at home here. Perhaps the famous grandstand hosted part of a ceremony of oath-swearing, cattle-counting and submission—no finer natural stage for such pomp can be imagined.

The modern pilgrim on wheels must cross the rivers, meadows, plains and fells which separate fortress from palace along a series of small roads which seem to cut across the grain of the land, intersecting with the A1 and the London to Edinburgh North-Eastern Railway, the A697 trunk road and the line of the Devils' Causeway. Here and there you encounter a sharp right-angle bend that shows that the route has had to adapt to the new shape of the land imposed by agricultural enclosure acts a thousand years after Oswald's day. On the ground, on foot, a more probable route for the royal progress can be traced in footpaths, bridleways and fords, which follow a more natural trail, using rather than abusing the topography. One startlingly beautiful clear day in November 2011 I set out with my son Jack to trace that route.

From the foot of the indomitable crag on which Bamburgh Castle sits, the trail lay west and south for about two miles to the bank of the Waren Burn just before it empties into the tidal flats of Budle Bay. This was a busy landscape: Bamburgh was not just a fortress but a township; there were many steadings nearby and the proliferation of early English place-names in this part of Bernicia suggests widespread, if perhaps not very efficient, cultivation. The Waren Burn formed the southern boundary of the early Lindisfarne estates and the north-western edge of the *scir*, or royal shire, of Bamburgh. At the foot of the hill called Spindlestone Haughs, on which sits an early defended enclosure, the path is diverted to the south and follows the burn along its right bank through open, rolling farmland towards the tiny village of Lucker, past the site of a British Christian cist burial, across the high-speed electric rail line and over the modern road. The hamlet is now part of the parish of Adderstone-with-Lucker but it must originally have been its own parish, with the burn as the compound boundary of township, parish and shire. The path continues to trace the wavy line of the burn as far as

Warenford, whose location rather speaks for itself (*waren* seems to be derived from the Brythonic word for the alder tree). One must cross the river here to avoid steeper, boggier ground to the west, and shadow the burn on its north side for a mile or so, past the empty gatehouse of the Twizell estate, beneath the roaring traffic of the A1 in a bespoke but unappealing concrete tunnel and then through beech and hazel woodland to the site of an old sawmill at Twizell. Twizell is an ancient name for a fork in a river and here, where the Waren emerges from a steep-sided dene, it is joined by Cocklaw Burn. It is a place to pause and engage the sense of a place that may have lost much of its significance but can have changed physically hardly at all in fourteen hundred years.

Crossing this second ford, the path takes advantage of a gently sloping natural ridge as it emerges from woods on to open moorland pasture, avoiding higher ground to north and south and hugging the contours of rough upland pasture until it descends into the village of Chatton. At their highest point the sandstone fells reach over a thousand feet. The Iron Age hillfort of Ros Castle dominates the ridge and the vale to the west, but nowhere on the trail from Bamburgh climbs to more than half that height. From the point of view of the traveller on foot, in a waggon or on horseback it is perfectly adapted to be passable in all seasons. Looking at the first-edition six-inch Ordnance Survey map gives one a strong idea of continuity in this landscape, for this long-used route, now a series of apparently disconnected footpaths whose whole significance can only be understood by walking it, is overlooked by settlements and burial cairns from the Bronze Age onwards. It is a landscape layered with meaning and significance, peopled by the ghosts of ancestors, where the plaintive wail of the curlew and chattering squawk of the partridge must have brought to the minds of Bernicians the voices of lost spirits. The waterfall called Roughtin Linn, an aptly applied Brythonic name meaning 'roaring pool', must have been a refreshment spot for generation after generation of travellers plying this same route: salters, shepherds, robbers, kings' couriers and royal baggage trains alike. Their footsteps have long faded but they would still recognise every fold in the hillside, every line of the Cheviot massif in the misty blue distance, standing out like a whaleback and often, in late autumn, wearing a fresh crown of icing-sugar snow.

At Chatton, horse and waggon alike must have crossed the wide bed of the Till, the defining river of north Northumberland, which drains the east side of the Cheviots into the Milfield Basin and thence discharges into the Tweed. At any ford, each one a natural choke-point and a time for tension but also for breaking the monotony of the journey, the party must have slowed. Reluctant animals had to be coerced, recalcitrant wheels needed a shoulder's encouragement; regal bottoms must occasionally have had to dismount. Scouts must have gone on ahead, impatient retainers cursed and nervously watched the skyline. A flash flood might have held up progress for a night or two so that leather tents, equipment, firewood and supplies would have to be disgorged from the baggage train. All in all it must have resembled something of a circus, but one so fatalistically inured to the fortunes of the road and the seasons that one suspects not much would have fazed the protagonists. For the local inhabitants it was a chance to gawp at the great, perhaps to ingratiate oneself, often to be co-opted into temporary service.

A mile or so west of Chatton the trail made a crossroads with the Devil's Causeway and one imagines a staging post here with fodder for horses and food and ale for those on the king's—and later the church's—business. This, perhaps, was a more salubrious place to make the night's stop, although a mounted party travelling at decent speed and unencumbered by the trappings of a royal entourage could certainly expect to accomplish the Bamburgh–Yeavering journey in a single day and would press on. The keeper of the *mansio* here would have been a *cæpman*, the origin of the surname Chapman. He was both hotelier and trader, purveyor of news as well as victuals and supplies; he may even have been officially a king's man, such was the importance of maintaining the establishment with its potentially crucial role in intelligence gathering and in the summoning of the king's host.

The Bernician kings' progress towards Yeavering encounters no more than gentle slopes after Chatton but must make one more crossing of a significant river, perhaps at Haugh Head two miles south of the town of Wooler where five parish boundaries intersect close by a ford across the Harthope Burn. Immediately to the south, tucked into a sharp bend in the main road, is Surrey House, a wonderfully enigmatic, down-at-heel, pantiled ginger-bread farmhouse which has stood on the site since at least 1513 when the Earl of Surrey used it as his headquarters before the Battle of Flodden Field. Beyond the ford the trail keeps to the higher ground between Wooler Water and the Cheviot foot-hills, avoiding the flood-prone east bank, skirting the site of the present bridge at Wooler before turning west into the mouth of Glendale, in sight of Yeavering Bell, the 'holy' mountain.

A similar journey must often have been made by Aidan in Oswald's reign and afterwards. Bede implies that he had his own cell and church built at Yeavering, as well as other royal estates, as a base for preaching among the more remote communities and certainly as a means of ensuring that the fragile shoots of the Ionan mission were not allowed to die for lack of encourage-ment.[165] The provision of a cell, perhaps a circular building not unlike an Iron Age roundhouse in plan, allowed Aidan to asso-ciate himself with royal power and yet dissociate himself from its excesses. Irish bishop-missionaries were nothing if not acutely aware of the ironies of their position. Oddly enough, Brian Hope-Taylor identified the distinct traces of a circular house build-ing at Yeavering, some twenty-three feet in diameter, built into the defunct remains of what must have a been a sort of grand kitchen designed to prepare for great pagan feasting ceremonies (Building D3). Was Aidan more inclined than Augustine to heed Pope Gregory's softly-softly approach? Was this his modest cell?

Bede's portrayal of seventh-century kingship and the early years of the Ionan mission is intensely personal, event-driven and providential. The Ecclesiastical History is, after all, a story of how good kings prospered under the guidance of holy men and bad kings were punished by the divine hand sub-contracting to human agents. Modern historians are more interested in the things that Bede does not reveal, or what he actively conceals; archaeologists like to reconcile his portrait with that provided by excavation and the surviving evidence of the landscape—those parts of the past which, fundamentally, we can say we share with Bede and his kings and clerics. It is not enough, though, to follow Oswald and Aidan through their landscape, to imagine peasants working in the fields and accept, as Bede did, that there was a natural order to these things. We must try to understand how it all worked. If there was order, on what was it based, and how long had it been that way? This was, after all, a very different land from the one ruled over by the Roman emperors. The Britain of the seventh century, unlike the kingdoms of the Franks in Merovingian Gaul, had no functioning towns or civil service, no professional judiciary, no standing armies; no coinage or exchequer. And, what is more, there was no-one alive in the seventh century who could have said what life had been like under the lost race of giants—not even Bede, who knew more than anyone else about the centuries of the legions.

The lands north of Hadrian's Wall had always been peripheral to the Empire, even during the brief period in the second century when the Antonine Wall lassoed and temporarily enclosed them. That is not to say that the British between Forth and Tyne were left unchanged by Romanitas. Roman interests and influence spread far beyond their frontiers and, contrariwise, the peoples on the outer edge of the Empire took an intense interest in what went on inside. There is evidence, for example, that in the second century AD the Britons of the Breamish Valley were cultivating grain for the armies of Rome; and they seem to have done rather well out of it, because they built substantial villages of some architectural pretension, including the remarkable caput at Greaves Ash, and they cultivated huge tracts of fertile volcanic slopes in the foothills above Ingram.[166] In five summers of excavating in this landscape I came to a position of deep respect for these entrepreneurial, adaptable, tough and bold native peoples.

The tribes beyond the frontier, particularly the Votadini (the same Gododdin whose disastrous hung-over onslaught on Catterick was celebrated in epic Early Welsh verse) seem to have enjoyed, if that is the right word, a client relationship with the Romans as a buffer state between citizen and Pict. The Roman road system, strategically linking forts and signal stations, created a web of fast communications far into what is now Scotland. If the Romans failed to permanently conquer these lands it was probably not because they couldn't but because the game was not worth the candle. Their mineral prospectors knew where the most northerly exploitable ores were and decided that nothing beyond the frontier of Hadrian was worth their permanent attention.

From the third century onwards the predations of Scots, Irish and Picts forced periodic reinforcement of the Hadrianic wall, increasingly garrisoned with commanders and then whole war-bands recruited from the famously skilled warrior elites of the unconquered tribes north of the Rhine. German names, German gods, German warriors and their guttural language were all familiar to the Roman Britons of *Bryneich*. Even after the so-called Barbarian Conspiracy of AD 367, when a concerted and organised attack on the frontier by the northern tribes and Saxons acting in cahoots with the Wall garrisons led to widespread destruction, civil chaos and brutal repression, Rome had sufficient resources to re-impose military order in the North. Indeed, the theme of the period between 370 and 410 is the use of Britain as a platform for military usurpers to stake their claims to the western half of the fragmenting Empire.

There is emerging evidence that several of the Wall forts survived to function in some form during the fifth century. At Birdoswald, at Housesteads and Vindolanda, at Arbeia in South Shields and elsewhere excavation has revealed the footprints of timber structures erected over the remains of stone barracks and storage barns, along with tentative evidence for fifth-century Christianity and a mixture of 'British' and 'Germanic' artefacts. It is here, perhaps, that we see the traces of a transition from the bureaucratic, regimented and centralised imperial army system towards the local governance and mead halls of the earliest English kingdoms. Tony Wilmott, excavator of Birdoswald, and Brian Roberts, the historical geographer, see in the adaptation of the Wall forts and in the civil organisation which began to emerge along the frontier a clue to its evolution.[167] Suppose that at some point in the early fifth century, when we hear disturbing rumours that the British have been given permission to look to their own defences, the pay waggons carrying the soldiers' salaries—the same pay waggons which had proved so attractive to the Irish, Picts and Scots—no longer found their way to Britain. It was not that the Empire took no interest in Britannia: her natural resources, both above and below ground, were just as valuable as they always had been. It is no coincidence that the most lasting permanent border structure of the Western Empire was built just a few miles beyond the most northerly state-controlled lead mines in Britain, in Weardale and Allendale. But the late fourth-century Empire no longer had the unity or the means to exert influence over Britain or to pay for her defence. Governance devolved to the *civitas* capitals, the ancient tribal centres whose great families had embraced Romanitas for good or ill.

Along the Wall garrison commanders of the *limitanei*, the frontier troops, faced with the unattractive prospect of unpaid troops taking matters into their own hands, were forced to extract renders from the areas around their forts and to organise the fort hinterlands as economic units of production—they possessed, after all, both legal and military rights of control over the native population. Brian Roberts believes that the pattern of townships which later developed along the line of Hadrian's Wall—and it is a salutary fact that only in two places does the Wall itself form a later civic or parochial boundary—directly reflects the geography of these hinterlands. Along the mid-Tyne zone between Haydon Bridge and Newburn we find townships straddling the Wall with significant names: Walbottle, Heddon-on-the-Wall, Portgate and the village of Wall itself, not very far from Heavenfield. These townships may preserve units of render or taxation with surviving forts at their cores. It is not hard to envisage an emerging pattern of small economic units organically developing from ancient geographical topographies and new political realities, gradually coalescing into more formalised polities at a scale suitable to a post-Roman world. That is to say, the new Britain was not imperial, nor even regional, but local. The irony of this new reality is that the dying Roman frontier might have given rise to a new, post-imperial political core-land, the country of the mountain passes: *Bryneich*, Bernicia. The garrisons themselves had shrunk from their greatest strength in the early Empire. Rob Collins estimates that they ranged from one hundred and fifty men up to perhaps five hundred at the largest forts—still substantial in the context of North Britain.[168]

When historians look at the institutions and boundaries that are fossilised in later documents such as tax rolls, charters and monastic donations, they see that this new world reflected both ancient tribal custom and much that was new and foreign. The more successful leaders were able to extend their zones of control over several townships, sufficient that they could support an entourage in their hall and reward the service of warriors fighting in their warband. In return for renders the local big man offered protection from the predations of others. Institutionally it is not very different from the organised crime cartels which grew up in the United States during the Great Depression of the 1930s or, for that matter, as Stuart Laycock argues, the post-Soviet Balkans.[169] One man's tax collector is another's racketeer. Command is devolved and inherited along family lines; by and by a dynasty emerges, to be legitimised by claims of descent from mythical beings. In the case of the Bernician kings, in a land where the military commanders were predominantly German, the forebear of choice was Woden. In parts of Britain where Germanic warbands played no significant role in the organisation of defence, one sees dynasties claiming to descend from the late Roman general cum usurper Magnus Maximus.* Where there were no military garrisons we can infer that government and taxation devolved locally from *civitas* capitals down to individual landowners. If British landowners thought it politic to marry their daughters to handsome young warriors from Angeln, bringing a few of their young, manly comrades with them from their last posting, who can blame them? As a means of securing their land and its future it seems only rational.

If the economic basis of leadership in the fifth and sixth centuries was a unit later termed the township, it equates to what Bede, using Latin, called the *vill*. Its central place, the hall (and the hall may equally be a barn) to which food renders and services were owed, became synonymous with the *vill*, so that Gefrin, for example, was the central place of a township also called Gefrin,

---

* Harleian MS 3859 gives Maxim Guletic as progenitor of the line of Dyfed; Jesus College MS 20 gives Maxen as progenitor claimed by the kings of Glywysing. In effect, Maximus functions at the head of the genealogy as a mythological tribal god of war.

or Yeavering in English. As larger economic and military polities evolved, one *vill* among many became the focus for renders from other *vills*. This is the apparent origin of the royal *vill* or *villa regia* so often mentioned by Bede. Gefrin was not only the central place of the *vill* of the same name; it also emerged as the royal *vill* of the shire of Gefrin which consisted of a number of *vills*—in the region of a dozen—which were required to support the grander pretensions of those local governors/warlords who would lay claim eventually to the title of king.

Thanks to the work of Colm O'Brien and others in teasing out the many complexities of medieval historical documents, we can now describe a large proportion of the shire structure of Northumberland—effectively Bernicia—in the centuries before the Norman Conquest. Bamburghshire is one of the largest and the earliest attested of these. It is the shire seemingly given as dower to Æthelfrith's wife Bebba as early as the 580s and may have formed the core land of the Iding dynasty from which Ida's sons were able to expand their territorial control in the second half of the sixth century. A shire was sufficient to support a warband leader of Ida's status. His sons and grandsons having more expansionist pretensions, the nature of kingship similarly evolved so that as renders came to shire centres, kings now had to travel between shires in order to consume the fruits of their authority. And that is one reason why Oswald was required to make the journey from Bamburgh to Yeavering and thence to his other royal estates, month on month, year on year. Brian Hope-Taylor, Yeavering's excavator, saw the acquisition of this ancestral tribal seat as an annexation by the Idings, recently established at Bamburgh, of a native British royal institution. Forty years later, it is still hard to argue with him.

By extraordinary luck Bede gives us an unintended clue to the duration and economic significance of such visits. In describing Paulinus's visit to Yeavering in 627 to baptise the apparently enthusiastic populace of Bernicia, he relates that the bishop stayed with King Edwin and Queen Æthelburh for thirty-six days, which were spent dipping pagan heads in the cleansing waters of the River Glen.[170] Perhaps this coincided with Beltane,* when the king would be there to oversee the tributes of his vassals and perhaps give his blessing to betrothals and petty alliances.

The critical detail is the thirty-six-day length of the visit. In this number O'Brien sees a neat division not of months but of tenths of a year. This has strong echoes in the early law codes and in the later tithes of the church and it now seems plausible to suggest that the basic unit of economic render in the Early Medieval period (perhaps also in the late Roman period) was a ten per cent tax on agricultural surplus. If kings took a tenth render of the produce of a royal shire and stayed there for just over a month, it stood to reason that they must have been able to exact such renders from at least ten estates over a year. There might be several complications to this neat model, not least because it is hard to see the royal entourage traipsing the length of the kingdom through the depths of winter. This may explain why some royal shires—Bamburgh is the prime example—were larger than others, to cater for the extra needs of a prolonged overwintering.

What goods and services were rendered to kings, and how did the system work in detail? For Bernicia, in particular early seventh-century Bernicia, we have little direct evidence. The best early material is the law code of Ine, King of Wessex between 688 and 726. His code only survives as an addendum to that of King Alfred in the late ninth century, so it has to be treated with caution; but we can see in Ine's dooms (laws) some idea of the measure of control which late seventh-century kings wished or

---

* A 'Celtic' quarter-day festival held on the first day of May, or the day before, best known from its Irish name. The Brythonic version was *Calan Mai* and the *Mai* element may be reflected in the name of the tax called *metreth*, a form of British cattle tribute traditionally rendered on or about May Day.

tried to impose on their territories. Ine expected that an estate of ten hides would render:

10 vats of honey
300 loaves
12 ambers [probably something like a bushel—8 gallons] of Welsh ale
30 ambers of clear ale
2 full-grown cows or 10 wethers (castrated rams)
10 geese
20 hens
10 cheeses
A full amber of butter
5 salmon
20 pounds of fodder
100 eels[171]

A small estate looking forward to the visit of its lord had to keep back from its surplus sufficient to meet appetites on this scale. A king's entourage would consume these victuals in very short order, so we must suppose that a royal estate was much larger than the ten hides offered by Ine as an exemplar. It must be able to provide something like thirty-six days' consumption for a *gesith's* establishment; and by extension we can say that the food render might represent something like a tenth of the annual agricultural production of an estate of that size. So, what can be said about the hide, the unit of economy on which Ine's lawyers made their calculation? It is a term fraught with problems, if for no other reason than that it meant various things at different times and in different places to various people. Bede uses the Latin term *familiarum* to denote this unit of landholding, with a clear implication of size. Iona, he says, is only five hides in extent; the islands of Anglesey and Man, conquered by Edwin, were respectively nine hundred and sixty and three hundred hides in extent.[172] A generation of historians, working back from medieval documents, came to believe that the hide equated to about a hundred and twenty acres. But this is not really satisfactory, certainly not for the seventh century. More modern opinion would rather see the hide as a unit of render—in other words, not the size of a holding but its economic and agricultural potential so that more fertile, cultivated parts of the land could be rendered at a higher hidage than the same area in a poorer part of the land.[173]

The Tribal Hidage, the list of tributary kingdoms possibly produced by Paulinus for King Edwin in the late 620s, shows that the hide could be used as a measure of tribute to be exacted, sometimes punitively as in the case of the rapacious demand made on Wessex of a hundred thousand hides. At the most local level a single-hide estate might support a very small community or, as Bede's term *familiarum* implies, a single family. Hild, grand-niece of King Edwin and illustrious abbess of Whitby, began her holy career with an estate of a single hide on which she survived for a year with a small group of companions.[174] In that sense, the single hide is no more than a unit of subsistence. The smallest kingdoms listed in the Hidage—East Wixna or Sweordora (unlocated but probably in the fenlands south and west of the Wash) for example—were assessed at a paltry three hundred hides, like the Isle of Man. Ine's list of the render expected from a ten-hide estate suggests that this was the sort of holding which would be required to support a *gesith* or thegn who, having fought in the king's host, would need sufficient land to marry and support his martial, social and economic needs. Might a ten-hide estate be equated with the render from a small *vill*?

The best clue comes, again, from Bede when he describes the gift of lands by King Oswiu to found monasteries in the late 650s.* The donation consisted of twelve estates, six in Bernicia and six in Deira, each of ten hides. If the basic geographical logic of the township/*vill* is reasonably consistent, then these estates are *vills*, perhaps on the small side but *vills* nevertheless and identifiable to

---

* EH III.24; see also Chapter XVI.

contemporaries by their estate centres, which became monastic establishments under an abbot or abbess. In effect, Oswiu was alienating his right to extract render from these estates to support twelve communities of monks and nuns.* The communities would, in addition to consuming the customary renders of these estates—that is to say, a tenth of their surplus—be exempt from the military duties a *gesith* would owe from the same estate. Moreover, they would hold those rights and exemptions in perpetuity.

There is, here, an implicit acknowledgement of the existence of peasants or small tenant farmers, tied to the land, whose lives, because they were taken for granted by the *gesith* or monastic classes, lie beneath the radar of history. Their labour produced the surplus that supported a warrior class and, subsequently, a non-fighting class of monks, abbots and abbesses. We suspect from later sources that the range of obligations from a holding to its lord was not confined to agricultural surplus and military service. *Drengs*, who form a sort of middle class in early British law and in Northumbrian tax accounts as late as the thirteenth century, were responsible for services like truncage (the hauling of timber to the estate centre) and probably also for bridge maintenance, for supplying labour to work the lord's own fields and perhaps for ship-building. There were marriage taxes (*merchet*) and inheritance dues (*heriot*), which seem also to have been customarily imposed on those whose privilege it was to hold land for a life-interest. Underlying these dues and services is a concept of the cow or, more probably the ox, as a primary unit of wealth, almost a unit of currency in the absence of coin.

By the end of the seventh century we detect, in the laws of Ine, attempts not just to render was what owed to the king but

---

* It is arguable whether kings gave away portions of royal estates or whether, even in Oswiu's day, they were careful only to alienate second-rate or under-developed lands, perhaps those which had been without a lord for some time.

also to assert social control and impose administrative and fiscal order. A man who holds twenty hides, for example, shall sow twelve hides under cultivation; if a *ceorl* buys a beast and finds a blemish in it within thirty days he shall send it back to its former owner; if anyone finds swine intruding on his wood pasture he may seek compensation; and so on. There are monetary fines for infringements against these laws and historians see in such penalties not just an attempt at legal consistency but also a means of gathering income via fines. That kings were beginning to understand landscape in terms of the potential for exploiting resources is also evident in penalties for cutting down large trees, for failing to fence cultivated land properly, for infringing shared rights to common land. But this concept was still in its infancy in the year 700. A large proportion of the seventy-six caputs in Ine's Laws deal with issues at the heart of tribal society: individual rights and responsibilities and attempts to limit feuding over civil and criminal disputes; fewer are concerned with the church's role in ordering society and with agriculture; just one deals with regulating the activities of traders.

In Oswald's day, fifty years earlier, there is almost no evidence of royal interference at such a minute level. It is debatable how far the church acquisition of *bocland*—that is, land held in perpetuity—was a factor in this move towards fiscal and administrative royal control. Under Oswald's brother Oswiu and Oswiu's sons Ecgfrith and Aldfrith the expansion of royal interest in administration appears to coincide with the strengthening of the economic and social role of the church, not to mention its wealth. Kings may have learned more from their clerics than just a new moral code. If so, Oswald's apparently ingenuous gift of estates to ensure the security and longevity of Aidan's mission set a profound historic precedent, the implications of which he can only dimly have realised but which were, by Bede's day, matters of profound concern.

Gefrinshire, assuming it to be a royal estate in the seventh century, can be estimated to have been assessed for hidage purposes sufficient to provide thirty-six days' supplies for the royal entourage; unfortunately that does not mean that we can say how many loaves, cheeses, eggs or wethers that might equate to. We need to look more closely at the contemporary landscape to catch a glimpse of the workings of the shires. The wholly exceptional Yeavering complex aside, only two archaeological sites in Bernicia which might count as the centres of estates have been identified; and only one of these has been excavated. At Sprouston, on the south bank of the River Tweed a little to the east of Kelso, a substantial crop-mark site revealed by aerial photography shows what looks like the site of a township, complete with halls, barns, cemetery and field systems: the physical manifestation of the establishment of a senior royal companion of the seventh century.* A dozen or so miles to the east, tucked into the fertile terrace between the rivers Glen and Till in the Milfield Basin, a similar-looking site at Thirlings was excavated in the 1970s and early 1980s by Roger Miket and Colm O'Brien, revealing a detailed plan of the domestic arrangements of either Oswald's warrior elite or, perhaps, of the more modest *dreng*.[175]

Thirlings sits in a landscape crowded with the remains of prehistoric monuments: henges, pit alignments, standing stones and much more as yet undetected, which testify both to its long-term attractions for settlement and to the ritual associations of river, glen and mountain so obviously meaningful to the Bernician kings at Yeavering a couple of miles to the south-west. At the heart of the settlement was a hall-type building, modest by Yeavering standards, thirty or so feet long, built of round posts a foot in

* Smith 1991; and see Chapter XVIII.

diameter set in a trench and infilled with wall panels set with vertical planks. This hall stood within an oval fenced enclosure—fenced, presumably, both to keep stock out and to provide the privacy which was such an intangible but precious commodity to the Early Medieval elite. There is no real defensive component to the site, any more than there is at Yeavering or Sprouston: these settlements flourished in an orderly land. This hall and its enclosure were replaced by a bigger building in a larger rectangular fenced enclosure. This is the so-called Thirlings 'A' hall which has been reconstructed at Bede's World in Jarrow. It is an open-plan building with a single hearth, a longitudinally ridged roof and perhaps room for a sleeping platform. To the modern visitor it is no more than a humble cottage, if attractively honest and robust.

On three sides externally the subsoil was pockmarked with pits and posts, the paltry remains of all sorts of domestic installations whose functions can be inferred from other, less damaged sites around the country: posts and frames for drying, curing, stretching, workbenches and jigs for securing work in progress; pole lathes and shaving horses, hurdles and, lest we forget them, the evidences of children's play.

The use of timber in-the-round in some of the buildings shows a lack of architectural pretension compared to those constructed in Yeavering's prime in which the timbers were larger, much larger, and squared off; it also shows that the *vill* of Thirlings had access to woodland where there was a plentiful supply of trees, probably oak, in the order of forty to fifty years old. The Yeavering builders were able to commission the felling of much larger trees, perhaps a hundred years old; we might see here in subtle reflection the reach of the more modest thegnly hand as opposed to the royal fist, whose truncage renders commanded more extensive, more mature woodlands. But there are larger, grander buildings at Thirlings which show distinct similarities, albeit on a smaller scale, to the grand halls at Yeavering; the fashion for squared posts and great thick planks was eventually shared at both sites.

It is tempting to see in the variation of style, size and technique in these buildings a chronological succession, a manifestation of larger and more pretentious halls being consecutively constructed at Thirlings, which might show the influence of the Yeavering architects and builders and the increasing economic wealth of its proprietors. Building C, to the south of the enclosed halls, was in the order of fifty feet long, comparable in size to the smaller buildings at Yeavering. It had had a porch added at its west end and at the east end what looked like a small square annexe may have been a stairwell intended to give access to an upper floor, perhaps a set of private apartments or an agricultural loft: the walls had been reinforced, like those at the royal estate, with external buttresses. This is the apparent apogee, the grand design of the Thirlings estate and on a standard model ought to have been the latest building on the site.

Unfortunately for this convenient thesis, the radiocarbon dates do not support it. Timbers from all the hall-type structures at Thirlings were dated and their range, from perhaps the beginning of the sixth century to the first quarter of the seventh, does not appear to reflect progress from simple, small and primitive to large and sophisticated. Given the limits of radiocarbon dating techniques the excavators allowed for the possibility that all the buildings on the site were in use at the same time, roughly coinciding with the major structural phases at Yeavering. But there are two distinct alignments of buildings here: post-built, smaller buildings on a north–south alignment while the halls are broadly constructed east–west; this might be functional or an aspect of change in ownership.* There is also a much wider range of construction techniques than we see at Yeavering. I must say,

---

* Colm O'Brien tells me he thinks the alignments are in fact down to topography, with the north–south aligned buildings edging a rise on which the main complex stands.

though, that I can easily envisage a span of a hundred years here during which thegnly fortunes waxed and waned with those of the region and its leaders. Whether its inhabitants believed themselves to be British or Anglian, whether they cared either way, we will never know. Just as frustrating, archaeology is only now beginning to recover material evidence in this part of the North for the smaller hamlets and dispersed farms which must have supported the elite.

In all six halls were constructed at Thirlings, along with many other rectangular post-built structures which must have fulfilled a variety of functions for storage, grain-processing, weaving and overwintering of animals. Some of the halls may have stood at the same time, forming a substantial complex; the earliest may have been adapted for use as barns or accommodation for functionaries and guests. The architectural quality might vary along with the size and neatness of the timbers used, either chronologically or following economic and social fortunes; eventually they were all dismantled and, like Yeavering, the site was probably abandoned later in the seventh century.

Because the contemporary ground-level of the settlement at Thirlings had been truncated by weathering and the plough, no floor levels were recovered; finds were few and, in keeping with many other sites in the region, unrevealing: the odd iron knife, a few beads, some loom-weights. The building sequence, which in plan offers so much potential for tracing the fortunes of a thegnly estate complex, did not ultimately offer the stratigraphic detail which such a sequence needs. If the site at Sprouston is ever excavated, one has to hope that it will yield a few more secrets.

Until three or four years ago there was another conspicuous gap in the archaeological evidence for the mechanism of the early estates: there were no industrial or craft sites to match the stupendous metalworking, weaponry and art which we know to have been accessed by the Bernician kings; there were no peasants or artisans. That missing site has now been found after a rescue excavation in advance of quarrying was carried out under the direction of Clive Waddington.* Conveniently, Lanton lies a mile or so to the north-west of Yeavering, just across the symbolic and physical divide of the River Glen. Here, revealed by mechanical stripping of the topsoil and then excavated by hand, were the remains long sought by archaeologists of cart sheds and weaving huts, of metal-working shops, of the manufacture of polychrome glass beads and, glory of glories, contemporary pottery. Pottery is the stock-in-trade of archaeologists but is rarely recovered from Early Medieval sites in the North. We are not sure why: a combination of acid soils consuming sherds of ceramics hand-made and fired at low temperatures, a very small pottery industry and perhaps other unrecognised factors such as fastidious curation.† But at Lanton Quarry the remains of more than forty vessels were recovered. Here, then, is evidence for those industries the Bernician kings required to maintain their prestige, status and power: the material trappings of kingship. Here the royal paraphernalia of sword and knife, of bronze cauldron and whetstone, of drinking horn, draughtsboard and marten-fur mantle were crafted almost within sight of the great royal palace where such wonders were displayed and distributed while the king feasted with his nobles and planned his summer campaigns. It was not for another fifty years, until the reign of Aldfrith, probably the first literate ruler of the Northumbrians, that books as objects

---

* Waddington 2010; and at New Bewick Colm O'Brien and Tim Gates recovered the plan of a sunken-featured building belonging to a putative Early Medieval village: Gates and O'Brien 1988.

† Pottery is malleable and as a folk-art form it is sensitive to cultural change; often it is possible to date its production; when fired hard it is almost indestructible. It also breaks easily and is often discarded, so in most periods it is abundant. Its paucity on Early Medieval sites makes it hard to date. Its absence could be explained by its relatively high value in the period; if people took much more care of their pots, or recycled and mended them, perhaps keeping sherds as heirlooms, then pottery is less likely to have found its way into archaeological deposits.

became the treasured possessions of kings. From then until now, even philistine rulers like to have beautiful books around them. It makes them feel cultured, intelligent. More importantly, perhaps, we see in the more modest domestic structures at Lanton, and at New Bewick to the south-east, as we do at West Heslerton in the Vale of Pickering and on many other sites in South and East England, the evidence for what one might patronisingly call the ordinary folk: the unfree and the slaves who were tied to their land and whose comfort must come either from basking in the reflected glow of regal power or, if they were lucky, a tiny share of a silver dish and a morsel of sweetmeat from the royal table.

It has often been asked whether these people—the architect/builders, the smiths, the weavers, the peasants of the field—were British or Anglo-Saxon. In a sense it does not matter; it probably did not matter to them in any modern nationalistic sense. There has been an irresistible temptation for archaeologists to see in the variety and form of Early Medieval burials a distinction between 'native' and 'Germanic'; to see in the English language, in personal and place-names an indigenous underclass bossed by an invading elite; to see the culture of the Britons wiped from the pages of history by a pervasive foreign immigration. Gildas and Bede are equally responsible for much of that narrative and our experience of the modern world affords us some sympathy for that view. But it doesn't really stand up. The nationalist antipathy between Celt and Saxon has been overplayed, even if in some respects it must have existed and been traded upon from time to time, especially by those, like Bede, who had axes to grind. The institutions of early Northumbria, particularly of Bernicia, were a hybrid form with strong roots in ancient British custom, even if they owed some of their idiosyncrasies to the catastrophe of imperial meltdown. The population, if one wants to play the ethnicity card, were similarly hybrid but with a very strong genetic

1. ABOVE Bamburgh Castle, ancestral seat of the Idings, an indomitable fortress on Northumberland's wave-torn North Sea coast. Oswald's incorrupt right arm was brought here after his death in battle.

2. RIGHT Almost nothing remains of the seventh-century fortress at Bamburgh, except the site of Oswald's gate, a 'hollowed entrance ascending in a wonderful manner by steps', and the rock-cut well preserved in the keep.

3. RIGHT The medieval Abbey of Iona, visited annually by many thousands of tourists, is much reconstructed. But its setting, within the original Columban vallum, still gives a fine sense of place and isolation.

4. ABOVE Two hundred years after Oswald, his name, and those of Edwin and Oswiu, are included in the Anglo-Saxon Chronicle as those of kings who exercised imperium over all Britain: the so-called Bretwaldas.

5. BELOW The Franks casket, an eighth-century Northumbrian carved whalebone box decorated with scenes of Christian and pagan mythology. The siege it depicts is one of the very few surviving representations of the nature of warfare in this period.

6. BOTTOM A magnificent bronze hanging bowl retrieved from the Sutton Hoo ship-burial, near Woodbridge in Suffolk, decorated with distinctly British enamelled escutcheons. Could it have been a gift from King Edwin of Northumbria to his sponsor, King Rædwald of East Anglia?

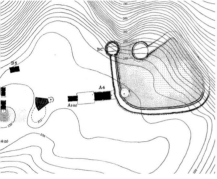

7. **TOP** Yeavering Bell, near the River Glen in north Northumberland: the 'holy mountain' of the Bernicians and their British forebears. Below the Iron Age hillfort on its twin summits lies the 'whaleback' plateau on which the Anglo-Saxon palace of Yeavering was built.

8. **ABOVE LEFT** Brian Hope-Taylor's plan of the palace of Yeavering in King Edwin's day, showing the great cattle corral, mead hall, feasting area and the unique grandstand. The royal township never had need of defences.

9. **ABOVE** The gilded Anglo-Saxon artefact known as the Finglesham buckle, depicting a spear-wielding, horned helmet-wearing Woden. The Anglo-Saxon god and his British counterparts draw on ancient animistic representations of a mythic warrior who embodies the tribal luck-in-war of the Anglo-Saxon kings.

10. **LEFT** At Heavenfield on Hadrian's Wall, in 634, Oswald raised a cross the night before his battle with Cadwallon, in a perhaps conscious echo of the Emperor Constantine some three hundred years earlier at the Battle of the Milvian Bridge.

11. LEFT A crude but evocative carving from Maryport, on the coast of Cumbria, of a spear-wielding, naked, horned God. Perhaps representing the British battle deity Belatucadros, it is a potent reminder of the more virile and bellicose aspects of Early Medieval kingship.

12. RIGHT Oswald remains the archetype of the chivalrous knight beloved of medievalists and of the pre-Raphaelite painters: Ford Madox Brown's portrayal (1864–6) of King Oswald and Aidan, first bishop of Lindisfarne, is mere fancy—Aidan was not the sort to kneel to any earthly king.

13. BELOW Lindisfarne's medieval priory and the unmistakeable outline of its castle. Beneath these monuments lie the remains of Aidan's first monastery and the fortress besieged by British forces in the 580s.

14. ABOVE A view of Bede's World in Jarrow, showing the reconstruction of the hall at Thirlings. The walls are of hazel wattle and daub, the roof of thatch. It gives a strong sense of the pleasures and privations of Early Medieval life.

15. LEFT A plan of Thirlings Manor, an Anglo-Saxon site in north Northumberland. The excavation here shows how a *dreng* of Oswald's day must have laid out his hall and farm, part of whose surplus he must render to a great lord, or to the king.

16. RIGHT A holy well dedicated to Oswald has been incorporated into a garden on the appropriately named Maserfield Road in Oswestry, Shropshire, close to where Oswald met his bloody end in battle with Penda's Mercians in 642.

17. RIGHT The crypt at Hexham is all that remains of the marvellous stone church built by Wilfrid in about 674. From here Wilfrid spread the cult of Oswald.

18. BELOW This strip of gold with a Latin inscription, part of the 'Staffordshire hoard' discovered in 2009, belonged to a Christian warrior. Archaeologists have considered the possibility that the hoard is a remnant of the treasure surrendered—around the year 650—by Oswiu of Northumbria to Penda of Mercia to prevent further devastation of Bernicia by Mercia or its British allies.

19. BOTTOM Nothing remains above ground of the abbey at Whitby where the council of 664 determined the fate of the Irish church in England; excavations have shown that an Anglian town once stood on the headland.

20. ABOVE The opening of Cuthbert's tomb in 698, as depicted in a twelfth-century illuminated miniature. After eleven years buried in the church at Lindisfarne, Cuthbert was exhumed and found to be miraculously incorrupt: the start of a great legend and enduring cult.

21. ABOVE LEFT The Cuthbert Gospel: the oldest surviving English book, in its original seventh-century binding—a subtle but exquisite masterpiece.

22. LEFT The opening page of St Mark's Gospel, from the Lindisfarne Gospels, perhaps the most famous of all Early Medieval books. Produced on Holy Island around the year 700, the Lindisfarne Gospels are a touchstone of Northumbrian pride today, as they have always been.

23. **LEFT** A head relic of Oswald created in Germany in the twelfth century, when his cult was widespread on the Continent, tapped into the ancient superstition of the 'luck in the head'.

24. **BELOW LEFT** A seventh-century coin from Kent shows a mail-shirted warrior with a bird on his arm, with a cross at his side, standing in what might be a ship or a dish. Is this an early depiction of Oswald the saint?

25. **BOTTOM LEFT** A seventeenth-century silver *Kreuzer* from Zug in Switzerland shows how long the cult of Oswald survived in Continental Europe.

26. **BELOW** A stained-glass window from the church of St John Lee, near Heavenfield, where Oswald raised his cross, captures the moment when the returning prince invoked the spirit of Colm Cille in his quest for victory over Cadwallon.

bias towards indigenous Britons and a balancing bias towards Germanic language and mythology.

The patronage of Anglian warlords ensured the supremacy of a cultural elite; the strength of indigenous institutions, landscapes and territories ensured their survival. Kings mostly bore Germanic names and claimed descent from Germanic gods; but what of the supposed founders of Wessex, those kings with names like Cerdic and Cædwalla which sound much more Welsh than English? What of the marriages between British princesses and English athelings? What of Anglo-British alliances like that of Penda and Cadwallon? Even Bede, who hardly likes to admit it, was very much au fait with British place-names and customs; he may, even, have spoken some Brythonic. And how did Rædwald, that archetypal heathen Anglian king, acquire the stunning bronze hanging bowl decorated with very British-looking escutcheons with which he was buried, if not from his protégé Edwin whose own, probably 'British' smiths at Lanton could manufacture such glories?

Like the hybrid tradition of the seventh-century church which forged British, Irish and Continental traditions into a unique monastic and literary culture, we ought really to see Northumbria, and perhaps the bulk of England, as a blend of sophisticated, self-confident native institution and people with an invigorating German self-consciousness and vision of which the Idings are perhaps epitomes. If the underclasses of the seventh century were tied to their land, so were their ancestors. Most of the population in most of the settlements in most of Britain stayed where they were in the centuries after the Imperial administration withdrew or was ejected. If Gildas's fleeing Britons are real, they are the upper crust of nobility, those with horses and servants and enough portable wealth to survive exile in Brittany, the land over the sea which they made their own. In the archaeological record of the Early Medieval period the invisibility of many of the natives may have much to do with an inability to observe, particularly to date, the continuity of 'native' settlements into the sixth century and beyond. But, however tempting it is to ask if Oswald's pole-axed skull is British or German by virtue of its DNA, the more complex reality of life in Early Medieval Northumbria is much more interesting.

XII

OH BROTHER,
WHERE ART THOU?

Daroð sceal on handa, gar golde fah

*The javelin in the hand,
the gold-glittering spear*

T̲H̲E̲ ̲D̲E̲S̲T̲I̲N̲Y̲ ̲O̲F̲ ̲T̲H̲E̲ ̲E̲A̲R̲L̲Y̲
Medieval king, pagan or Christian, was to die on the field of battle. The greatest warriors were charismatic and dauntless, unencumbered by doubt or tactical nicety, falling on their prey with such impetuosity that the enemy, committing the smallest mistake, might never recover. Oswald was battle-hardened, a commander of repute, skilled and resourceful and at the height of his powers. He was able to draw on the forces of great numbers of elite warriors: the companions of his exile; the *gesiths* of Bernicia, Deira and many other lands; of aspiring athelings, young-bloods and many a campaign veteran. And yet the fate of his father, uncle and cousins was his too. For Bede, his death in battle sealed Oswald's reputation as the 'most Christian king', the first and greatest royal martyr.* It pre-figured his extraordinary post-mortem career and epitomised the life and death of the best sort of king: martial with his enemies, generous to his warriors and to the church; humble in the company of God's appointed priests and munificent with his people.

---

* EH III.9 He is *Christianissimus rex Norðanhymbrorum*. Bede, perhaps significantly, never uses the word martyr of him.

Oswald's internal policies focused on the success of the Ionan mission and on the mechanics of royal patronage; externally he was an expansionist, as were so many of his contemporaries. Followers must be rewarded; a king must win glory: wars must be fought and treasure taken. His near neighbours were either subjected by conquest or they submitted. Further afield he forged alliances aimed at limiting the power of Mercia, the most obvious threat to Northumbrian supremacy. The fatal campaign of 642 seems to have been planned as a pre-emptive strike against an alliance between Penda of Mercia and King Cynddylan of Powys. The culminating battle of the campaign was fought at *Maserfelth* on 5 August 642. We cannot be sure of the circumstances of the battle or the events that led to it. What is certain is that Oswald was cut down by the enemy, perhaps by Penda himself; that Penda's brother Eowa was also killed; and that the field of battle was held by the Mercians and Welsh. Bede adds some telling details of his own regarding Oswald's last minutes.

> It is also a tradition which has become proverbial, that he died with a prayer on his lips. When he was beset by the weapons of his enemies and saw that he was about to perish he prayed for the souls of his army. So the proverb runs, 'May God have mercy on their souls, as Oswald said when he fell to the earth.'[176]

Bede goes on to say that 'the king who slew him ordered his head and hands to be severed from his body and hung on stakes.' The defeat, then, was absolute: the army of Oswald utterly destroyed. His earthly 'luck', the luck of the pagan Anglo-Saxon kings, which was such a crucial and yet intangible element of kingship, had finally and irrevocably run out. His *comitates*, the close companions and veterans who had accompanied him into exile and in his triumphant return, must surely have perished with him. There was no-one left to guard his physical honour in death, to attempt retrieval of his body from the blood-soaked battlefield. If his passing marked the beginning of the next chapter in

Oswald's career as saint and martyr, the disastrous reversal of fortunes at *Maserfelth* spelled potential disaster for Bernicia and the Idings; it might also have spelled disaster for the Ionan mission to Lindisfarne, whose tender shoots had been protected by *their* king. It was in the natural order of things that Bernicia's subject kingdoms should now regard themselves as free of all tributary obligations. Would Deira reassert its independence? Would rivals fight for the throne? For the next thirteen years Penda was the Dragon of the Island, the supreme warlord of English Britain. It was left in the hands of Oswald's brother Oswiu, eight years his junior, to ensure that Bernicia survived to fight another day.

The circumstances of Oswald's fatal campaign against Penda have been the subject of much spilled ink over the years. All judgements hinge on the identification of *Maserfelth* and any number of suggestions have been made to provide a definitive location. On the face of it, there is only one reasonable candidate. Since at least the twelfth century Oswestry, the otherwise unpretentious market town that nestles against the Welsh mountains a mile or so east of Offa's Dyke between the rivers Severn and Dee, has been claimed as the place of Oswald's death. The obvious derivation of the name from Oswald's tree or cross—a reference to the wooden stake on which his severed head was impaled—is matched by the Welsh form *Croesoswald*. There is a church here dedicated to Saint Oswald which may well predate the Norman Conquest. There is also a holy well with the same dedication. Why, then, doubt Oswestry as the site of Oswald's martyrdom?

The problem lies firstly with the fact that Oswestry lies in the historic kingdom of the Wrocansætan, well outside core Mercian territory, hard against the foothills of the Welsh mountains: what on earth was Oswald doing there? What, for that matter, was Penda doing there?* The second issue that niggles historians is

* Wrocansætan: the name is known from the Tribal Hidage and derives from the Roman *civitas* capital *Virconum Cornoviorum*, now the village of Wroxeter in Shropshire.

that neither *Maserfelth*, nor its Brythonic equivalent *Cocboi* or *Maes Cogwy*, variously cited in the Nennian *Historia Brittonum*, the Welsh Annals and several later Welsh poems, has survived. This has allowed both place-name specialists—and place-name studies, where only fools and angels dare to tread, are best left to specialists—and historians of the period to suggest alternatives. There is a Makerfield (Romano-British *Coccium*) in Lancashire; and it has been argued that Oswestry, which does not appear in the Domesday Survey of 1086, was invented to appropriate a late cult of Oswald. Others have suggested that a site in Lindsey, along the road system where so many other battles were fought in this period and where the cult of Oswald saw a great flowering in the late seventh century, would better fit the known geopolitics of Oswald's reign. This is special pleading, though.*

I see no good reason to doubt Oswestry as the site where either Oswald's body parts were displayed or where he died— not necessarily the same thing. The battlefield must, I think, be near by. *Maserfelth* and *Maes Cogwy* both mean 'border-field', which suits Oswestry. There are precedents for Bernician kings waging campaigns in the region (Æthelfrith at Chester in 616; Edwin on Anglesey in the 620s); and Oswald had a perfectly reasonable motive for a pre-emptive strike against Penda's growing power-base. Historians have, I think, generally neglected a likely Bernician interest in this part of the world. In the heart of modern Cheshire, some miles to the north-east of Oswestry and close to the zone of Æthelfrith's campaign of 616/17, are the famous brine springs at Nantwich, Middlewich and Northwich, all of which were developed as settlements by the Roman state and jealously protected right through the Middle Ages. The Nennian list of The Wonders of Britain seems to refer to the Cheshire springs 'from which salt is boiled, wherewith various foods can

---

* A comprehensive and credible review of the case for and against Oswestry is outlined in Clare Stancliffe's paper 'Where was Oswald killed?'; Stancliffe 1995b.

be salted; they are not near the sea but rise from the ground.'*
Early Medieval kings took a keen interest in salt and regarded it
as a royal perquisite. Was Oswald protecting what he saw as interests of the Bernician crown from attempts by Powys and Mercia
to take control of them? Or was he trying to muscle in on an
operation in which Powys and Mercia wished to retain a duopoly
interest?[177] And had his father set a precedent when he fought at
Chester? There is, as it happens, a striking cluster of apparently
early dedications to Oswald in this area. It includes churches
at Chester itself; at Brereton, Lower Peover and Winwick in
Cheshire.[178] Are these the faint echoes of statements of loyalty
to Northumbrian kings or examples of its patronage protecting
areas of interest?

There is another clue that historians have generally failed to
exploit. Bede says that the 'great battle' in which Oswald fell was
fought at 'a place called in the English tongue *Maserfelth*'.[179]
Bede often gives Anglo-Brythonic translations; but only rarely
does he imply that the place was known primarily by a Brythonic
name, for which he offers a translation more familiar to his readers. *Maes Cogwy* was, it seems, a place referred to mainly by its
British name. It was probably, therefore, in or close to a British
kingdom, which allows it to be placed reasonably on the western
edge of Mercia where it marched with Powys.

If we accept Oswestry, or somewhere very near it, as the site
of *Maserfelth* and of Oswald's martyrdom and many subsequent
miracles, a plausible reconstruction of his last campaign can be
attempted. Penda is the key. He first appears in a notice of 626 in
the Anglo-Saxon Chronicle, when he supposedly becomes king
of the Mercians. In 628 he fights against Cynegisl and Cwichelm,
father and son kings of the *Gewisse*, at Cirencester. All three survive and an 'agreement' is made; perhaps borders are negotiated,

---

* *HB* 68. Bede, in his general introduction to Britain's geography and resources, also
mentions salt springs: EH I.I.

hostages exchanged, treasure and tribute surrendered. But we cannot say who emerged the stronger. Penda, we gather, is ambitious, if not yet powerful. Four years after the Cirencester standoff, he makes common cause, perhaps as a junior partner, with Cadwallon of Gwynedd in the assault on Edwin at *Hæthfelth*. Cadwallon it is who installs himself in Northumbria while Penda returns to Mercia with his prize, Edwin's son Eadfrith. Bede does not yet allow him the title 'king' but calls him an 'energetic member of the royal house': *dux*, perhaps, not *rex*. In 642 he fights with and kills Oswald as *Rege Merciorum*; two years later Cenwalh of Wessex (Oswald's brother-in-law), having married Penda's sister, repudiates her and is expelled by Penda. At an unknown date in the following few years he is at war with East Anglia, to whose court Cenwalh has fled, and then a series of devastating campaigns takes him into the heart of Bernicia.

Penda's brother Eowa seems, for much of this time, to have been the senior member of the family—he, after all, was the great-great-grandfather of the celebrated eighth-century Mercian king Offa. He is cited by both the *Historia Brittonum* and the Welsh Annals as a victim of the conflict at *Maserfelth* and the Mercian historian Nicholas Brooks has argued that he fought on Oswald's side. If this is true, we must envisage Oswald's foray into Mercia as a campaign in support of a tribute king against his chief rival, and brother, the rising star Penda; it is Penda's survival and later dealings with Bernicia which tempt us into thinking he was the senior Mercian in 642. The location of the final battle in the campaign suggests that Penda and his ally King Cynddylan of Powys were massing a force on the Mercian border for an all-out assault on Eowa in the Mercian heartlands.* August is late in the year to begin a campaign, so I envisage a period of a month, or two

* Cynddylan is not mentioned by Bede or the Nennian sources but Stancliffe (1995b) argues persuasively that later poetic traditions of Powys which do mention him can be trusted.

months, of manoeuvre and stand-off. Oswald either marched his army across the Pennines through the old kingdom of Elmet to Chester, as his father had probably done; or south to Doncaster and then south-west to join Eowa at Lichfield, all along Roman roads. Were there also contingents from the south: from Hwicce, where some historians believe Oswald had installed Bernician athelings as a client dynasty; or from Wessex, on whose support Oswald ought to have been able to count?

Either Oswald underestimated the strength of the enemy or he was outwitted by strategy and local knowledge; very possibly the British/Mercian force drew him towards the mountains in a false pursuit: even the greatest warrior is vulnerable far from home and on the enemy's own patch. An alternative, that Oswald was duped by Eowa into falling into a trap of his brother's setting, cannot be discounted. Victory, when it came, perhaps against exhausted troops low on supplies, was overwhelming. In his moment of heathen triumph, Penda dragged Oswald's body from the field so that the remnants of his army should not be able to take it home for burial, dismembered him and displayed his limbs and head as trophies, a ritual heathen sacrifice to Woden, the Hanging God and deity of battle. The greatest of earthly warriors had been brought down by a new power in the land. After fourteen years of campaigning, Penda had with one stroke dispatched both his rival for the kingship of Mercia and the Christian overlord of Britain.

The enormity of Penda's insult to Oswald's body cannot really be appreciated in a Christian context; after all, his slaughter by a pagan ensured that Oswald was revered as a pre-eminent martyr. His holy life and glorious death ensured that he was 'translated to the heavenly kingdom'.[180] Once the Christian soul has left it, the body is so much flesh and bone, its burial according to rite more a matter of courtesy and hygiene than celestial qualification. It is true that the place of burial mattered to early saints and their followers: shrines became immensely important sources of healing and inspiration, as places for prayer and the gathering of pilgrims (and traders). To that extent, depriving Oswald of an earthly burial in his own land among his own people was a punitive act. But to grasp the more visceral tribal and heathen meanings of Penda's treatment of his enemy one has to turn to the Beowulf poem, and to the famous resting place of King Rædwald.

Beowulf, at the end of a life of heroism and gift-giving, fought one last battle against a dragon who had been terrorising the kingdom of the Geats following the theft of a golden cup from the dragon's lair by a slave. When he fell at last, fatally wounded, his body was guarded by a faithful warrior and kinsman, Wiglaf, while a bier was prepared for him to be carried in ceremony to the place of his funeral. From the site of his mortal combat with the great worm an 'untold profusion of twisted gold was loaded onto a wagon, and the warrior prince borne hoary-headed' to a place high on a headland that seafarers might see it from afar. Beowulf's people brought great quantities of wood from all around: *Geata leode ad on eorðan unwaclicne, helmum behongen...*

> The Geat race then reared up for him
> a funeral pyre. It was not a petty mound,
> but shining mail-coats and shields of war
> and helmets hung upon it as he had desired.
> Then the heroes, lamenting, laid out in the middle
> their great chief, their cherished lord.
> On top of the mound the men then kindled
> the biggest of funeral fires. Black wood-smoke
> arose from the blaze, and the roaring of flames
> mingled with weeping...[181]

Laments are sung for Beowulf; an enclosure is built around the remains of the pyre; a great barrow is constructed over and in its chamber treasures are placed torques and jewels, 'wealth in the earth's keeping' where no mortal man may use them again. We have a very fair idea of how such a mound would look from the Sutton Hoo excavation. It is true that the East Anglian king was buried in a ship; but in every other way the mix of personal, royal and military trappings recovered from Mound I proves that the Beowulf account reflects actual pagan reality, not mere poetic fancy.

> Then the warriors rode around the barrow,
> twelve of them in all, athelings' sons.
> They recited a dirge to declare their grief,
> spoke of the man, mourned their king...

> This was the manner of the mourning of the men of the Geats,
> sharers in the feast, at the fall of their lord:
> they said he was of all the world's kings
> the gentlest of men, and the most gracious,
> the kindest to his people, the keenest for fame.[182]

Oswald and his people were deprived of the obsequies befitting a great warrior king. The conspicuous consumption of the funeral feast, the placing of treasure and weapons beyond gift or use so evident in the Sutton Hoo ship burial and in pagan Anglo-Saxon burials by the thousand, were essential components of death for the warrior king, as they were for fulfilment of his earthly life. Penda would allow no such end for Oswald or the Bernicians who mourned him. And the Idings were not just robbed of their farewells and mourning rituals, the necessary components of social bonding in the Early Medieval kingdom; they failed to retain possession of the body of their dead king.

Timeline: AD 632 to 642

ABBREVIATIONS

EH—Bede's Ecclesiastical History
HB—Nennius: *Historia Brittonum*
ASC—Anglo-Saxon Chronicle
AU—Annals of Ulster
ATig—Annals of Tigernach

Names of battles are shown in **bold**

632 Edwin is killed at the **Battle of *Hæthfelth*/Meicen** on 12 October by Cadwallon of Gwynedd and Penda of Mercia (ASC 'E' recension). Edwin's son Osfrith also killed; the other, Eadfrith, flees to or is taken prisoner by Penda and is later killed in Mercia.

 —James the Deacon remains in Northumberland, probably living near Catterick, and survives until the Synod of Whitby in 664.

 —Death of Mohammed the prophet at Medina, at the age of sixty-three.

633 Fursey arrives from Athlone to establish see at Cnobheresburg (?Burgh Castle), granted by Sigeberht of East Anglia.

633–4 Northumbria collapses into constituent kingdoms; reverts to paganism under Eanfrith (son of Æthelfrith) and Osric (cousin of Edwin); Osric besieges British in an *oppidum municipium* and is defeated and killed by Cadwallon. Cadwallon lays waste to Northumbria.

634 Eanfrith sues for peace with Cadwallon in Bernicia and is murdered with his companions.

 —Oswald returns from exile to claim Northumbrian kingdom, with ?brother Oswiu and a retinue including Dál Riatan and Ionan warriors. He defeats and kills King Cadwallon at the **Battle of Denisesburn** after raising his cross at Heavenfield.

 —Possible birth date of Cuthbert somewhere near the Tweed Valley, of noble parents.

—Wilfrid born, also of a noble Anglian family.

—Possible date of marriage of Oswiu to Rhieinmelth, grand-daughter of Urien of Rheged (*HB*).

—Birinus, possibly a graduate of a Columban monastery, preaches to the West Saxons (ASC).

635   Oswald sends for Aidan, an Irish monk/bishop from the Scottish island of Iona, to convert Northumbria to Celtic Christianity. Aidan establishes monastery on the island of Lindisfarne and becomes the first bishop of Lindisfarne. Foundation of monasteries at Melrose, Hartlepool and Coldingham follows.

—?**Battle between Mercia and East Anglia**: Penda defeats Egric and Sigeberht. Sigeberht, having abdicated to join the church, is dragged from a monastery to lead army; fights with a stick (could be as late as 643) and is killed.

—Probable date of Oswald's marriage to ?Cyniburh, daughter of Cynegisl, king of Wessex.

—(or 636) Oswald is present at King Cynegisl's baptism into the Roman church.

—A great snowfall kills many in Ulster (AU).

—Possible date of birth of Alhfrith, son of Oswiu; or Alhflæd, their daughter.

636   Cwichelm baptised at Dorchester-on-Thames (*ASC*); and dies.

—Probable date of birth of Œthelwald to Oswald and Cyniburh.

637   **Battle of Magh Rath in Ireland**; defeat of Domnall Brecc's allies inc. Congall Ceach of the Dál nAraide. Dál Riata effectively cedes rights over Ulster.

—Congregation of the Saxons against Oswald (ATig) (or 639 AU).

—?Penda enlarges Mercia to include East Anglia; slays two East Anglian kings. Dál Riata now probably tribute to Northumbria. Bernician and Deiran warriors may fight in the battle (Moisl 1983).

638   **Battle at Glenn Mureson** (AU; 640 in ATig); Domnall Brecc is defeated by the Strathclyde Britons.

—**Siege of Edinburgh** (*obsesio Etin*: AU; 640 in ATig)—by Oswald or Oswiu?

639   Death of Dagobert I.

—Bishop Birinus baptises Cuthred, son of King Cwichelm of Wessex, at Dorchester;

—?**Battle of Oswald**, king of the Saxons (AU) against a southern confederation.

640   King Eadbald of Kent dies; succeeded by Eorconberht (to 664).

641?   Northumbrians, possibly under Oswiu, defeat kingdom of Manau having besieged *Din Eidyn* in previous campaigns. In concert with Domnall Brecc's efforts against Britons?

642   Campaign against Mercia by Oswald drives Penda into Wales? Oswald is killed in the **Battle of *Maserfelth*** on 5 August (probably close to Oswestry) fighting against Penda of Mercia and possibly Welsh allies of Gwynedd. He is cut up and his head displayed on a pole at Oswestry/*Croesoswald*.

—Oswald is succeeded by his brother Oswiu in Bernicia and by Oswine (son of Osric; a cousin of Edwin) in Deira.

—Cynegisl of Wessex dies; succeeded by Cenwalh (a pagan: to 673). He marries a sister of Penda but repudiates her. Cenwalh is driven out of Wessex by Penda and seeks refuge with King Anna of East Anglia. Regains the throne in 648.

—Cuthbert given over to foster parents at *Hruringaham*.

—Domnall Brecc dies at hands of Owain mac Beli of Strathclyde in **Battle of *Strath Cairuin*** (Strathcarron).

XIII

MIRACLES WILL
HAPPEN

Wudu sceal on
foldan blædum blowan

*A wood shall bear blossoms
and fruit on the earth*

OSWALD'S CINEMATIC LAST

stand gave almost immediate rise to a popular cult cen-
tred on the supposed site of his martyrdom. His fame in life
endured and surpassed death in a manner fitting for his short but
dazzling career as a Christian warrior and tribal chief. The bodies of Bernician kings belonged in the sacral ground of Yeavering
beneath the holy mountain of Glendale, or by the sea beneath
the ramparts of Bamburgh. But now, the king who had spent
so much of his life as an exiled freelance was also to be alienated
from his homeland in death.

It is hard to say how the battlefield might have looked in the
months after the slaughter of *Maserfelth*. Some bodies would
have been retrieved by camp followers and relatives; those of
the Bernician army might have been subject to abuse or mutila-
tion or fed to dogs. The dead of the Mercian and British hosts
were perhaps cremated on a great pyre, a mound raised over their
ashes just as his companions had raised a mound over Beowulf's
remains; or they might have been interred in mass graves like the
victims of Æthelfrith's Chester campaign a generation earlier.

Valuable metalwork will have been stripped from enemy warriors: the lion's share, the gold and silver, great swords and finest fittings, would become part of Penda's and Cynddylan's own treasure hoards, winners' booty to be recycled or hidden, buried in a field to tease archaeologists. Survivors took trophies: weapons, naturally, but probably also more gruesome souvenirs. If Penda took Oswald's head and arms, he would not have been the only warrior to carry off such trophies. Whether the impaled remains were left on the battlefield or taken to a fortress belonging to Penda we cannot say. In the ensuing months carrion feeders stripped the remaining corpses, leaving white bones to bleach in the sun. The blood-soaked ground recovered in a year or two. Potassium-loving plants grew there to mark the spot. The grass grew a darker shade of green.

We do not know if Oswald's brother Oswiu fought with him at *Maserfelth*; it is, I think, very unlikely. In truth, we do not know what sort of relations these two brothers enjoyed. Oswiu is not mentioned at all by Bede until after the disaster on the borders of Powys, so we can only guess that he was part of the Heavenfield campaign and others fought against the North Britons during Oswald's reign. What we do know is that he brought up Oswald's infant son Œthelwald, probably at his own court and that, a year after Oswald's death at *Maserfelth*, he 'came thither with an army' and took Oswald's remains away with him.[183] Oswald's head—with its gaping sword-slash wound—was given to the community on Lindisfarne and buried in the church there; his hands and arms were encased in a shrine, suitably made from silver, and interred in the fortress at Bamburgh, probably below the church dedicated to Saint Peter, now ruinous, which may have had an early crypt. Here they became, Bede tells us, objects of great veneration. As Aidan had predicted, they remained 'incorrupt' up until the time of Bede.

Oswiu's expedition deep into Mercian territory was

undertaken at great risk. He cannot realistically have hoped to confront and beat the combined armies of Mercia and Powys, given the devastation wrought on the Bernician host. More likely he led a raid, probably relying entirely on mounted warriors. That he succeeded argues for a degree of bravura and derring-do on his part. It also implies that his brother's head and upper limbs, assuming they were identifiable (the whole thing has a rather grisly feel to it), were of sufficient value for the risks to be worth the reward. One imagines that the journey back must have been pretty hairy too, with all the forces at Penda's disposal out to catch him. So why bother?

There is a clannish element in his motivation, of the 'nobody insults my brother's body' sort; blood is and was, after all, thicker than water, and in tribal societies such insults are neither taken lightly nor forgotten. Blood feud was a constant source of conflict and interest in the Early Medieval period. Penda's possession and humiliation of the great warrior's body was a stain on Bernician pride. It was a challenge to both the Bernician *folc* and, more particularly, the dead king's brother and successor. There is also something of the ancient Norse idea of dividing the sacral luck of the king on death into shares, each of which imparted some of that luck to those who possessed it. In keeping the arms and hands Oswiu was ensuring that some of his brother's luck passed to him; in donating the king's head to Lindisfarne he was aiming to ensure the continuing success of Aidan's mission. Christian as he was, Aidan would not have been in any doubt of the potency of that gift and the continuing promise of patronage and *virtus* which came with it.

This hovers between Christian sentiment and tribal totemism: Oswald's martyrdom and his earthly reputation seem very rapidly to have become something of a popular cult. The talismanic value of his body parts was huge and they belonged, in as equal parts as they could be, in Aidan's church at Lindisfarne and the king's own stronghold at Bamburgh: our king; our kin; our body; our magic. Conscious, perhaps, of Aidan's prediction that Oswald's right arm would never wither and conscious, too, of its martial reputation, Oswiu built for it a subterranean trophy cabinet in which it would play no small part in the creation of a mythology for the Anglo-Saxon kings of the Northumbrians. He had precedent to inform him, if nothing else: Edwin's head had been brought to York after the battle of *Hæthfelth* and Oswald ensured that the church was restored so that it might be housed properly.

It was not long before Oswald's magic began to rub off: literally. Within a 'short time' of his death strange events began to occur which shed light not only on Oswald's stellar reputation but also on the virtuous powers of corporeal magic at first, second and third hand, in the imagination of the Early Medieval mind—almost impossible, in fact, for the twenty-first century mind to comprehend (only rock stars seem to inspire such postmortem devotion now: Jim Morrison in Paris, Jimi Hendrix, Michael Jackson, Elvis...). The king was dead: long live his relics and anything they might have touched. Oswald, in death, was about to embark on a journey more remarkable even than his life. He was to become one of the most widely revered saints of medieval Europe, from Iona to Salzburg.

When a certain traveller (we do not know his name) was passing the site of the king's martyrdom on horseback 'not long after' Oswald's death, he may have been aware of the general vicinity of battle, but otherwise supposedly saw nothing untoward. His horse, Bede says, suddenly tired, bent its head to the earth and began to foam at the mouth. It fell to the ground and the rider, believing it to be in its death throes, dismounted and stood by, unsure what to do. The horse continued to writhe until, as popular legend had it, it rolled over the spot where the Bernician king had breathed his last. The horse's pain began to ease and after a while it rolled over and got to its feet, apparently so unharmed by its ordeal that it began to graze greedily on the grass...

> When the rider, who was an intelligent man, saw this, he realised that there must be some special sanctity associated with the place in which the horse was cured. He put up a sign to mark the site, shortly afterwards mounted his horse, and reached the inn where he intended to lodge. On his arrival, he found a girl there, niece of the patron, who had long suffered from paralysis. When he heard the members of the household lamenting the girl's grievous infirmity, he told them of the place where his horse had been cured. Why need I say more?[184]

Why indeed? Having been carried in a cart to the site marked by the horseman, the girl was laid down and fell asleep; and on waking found that she could walk home in perfect health. It is easy for the twenty-first-century cynic to see in this episode a great deal of wishful thinking and the power of suggestion tacked on to a predisposition to see the miraculous in chance—or even contrived—events. In the Early Medieval period the miraculous was a universally accepted fact of everyday life. It would have come as a surprise to no-one that so renowned a warrior, so virtuous a king should bring luck in death as he had to his people in life. What is perhaps more significant for the historian is Bede's tacit admission that this earliest manifestation of a cult of Oswald was a popular one: its origins had nothing to do with a church or monastery. Not only that, but the early recipients of the saint's favour were not necessarily all of noble blood. The first, indeed, was no monk or wandering pilgrim but a horse, one of the supreme symbols of heathen kingship; its owner was a secular aristocrat.

Whatever spin Bede might have wished to impart, he was bound to reveal that sick men and beasts were being healed at this spot right up to his own day: so much so that...

> people have often taken soil from the place where his body fell to the ground, have put it in water, and by its use have brought great relief to the sick. This custom became very popular and gradually so much earth was removed that a hole was made, as deep as a man's height.[185]

If the fully developed English and Continental cult of Oswald was to see its full flourishing in churches and monasteries endowed with great gifts of land, books and the saintly king's relics, its origins lay deep in the primal superstitions of the countryside and the pagan heart of early kingship. The head and arms were retrieved by his brother and taken as totemic trophies; the homeopathic virtues of the death-site were appropriated by local folk who cared perhaps a little for Oswald's Christian virtues but, it seems, far more for the pagan virility conferred on him by right and by descent from a great chieftain; power and virtue are not always easy to tell apart.

It is not so easy either to see Oswald's Ionan and Bernician *geist* finding much favour with the local population unless, as the historian James Campbell suggested in a highly perceptive volume of essays in the 1980s, there were British Christians in that region—as there almost certainly were in Northumbria.[186] The possibility, in fact, that the origins of the popular cult which grew up at Oswestry were British is strengthened by Bede's account of another miracle at the site of his death. A Briton, he says...

> was travelling near that place where the battle had been fought, when he noticed that a certain patch of ground was greener and more beautiful than the rest of the field. He very wisely conjectured that the only cause for the unusual greenness of that part must be that some man holier than the rest of the army had perished there. So he took some of the soil with him wrapped up in a cloth, thinking that it might prove useful, as was indeed to happen, as a cure for sick persons.[187]

There is plenty to intrigue here. First, Bede is clear that the man was a Briton. Did he have a British source for this story, or was the Britishness of the witness an essential element of the popular tale—an exotic detail? Next, the greenness of the grass suggests to any archaeologist worth his or her salt one of two things: a greater depth of soil than the surrounding area which, during summer, would retain moisture and therefore appear greener and more lush, or 'beautiful'; or greater soil fertility produced by high levels of potassium (blood and bonemeal) or nitrogen. The archaeologist begins to ask what sorts of impacts might produce such features, and the thought of a burial pit comes to mind. Perhaps this was a mass grave? Strictly speaking, there should have been nothing corporeal of King Oswald to bury.

The second element is equally interesting: the Briton concluded that someone holier than the rest of the army had been slain there. This indicates strongly, if Bede was doing justice to his sources and not over-cooking them, that the Briton was well aware that this was a famous battle site. If so, it might be very natural for him to conclude that the holy person in question was Oswald, a fellow Christian and renowned warrior for Christ—even if, in other respects, he was an enemy of the British. Did the Christians of the Marches believe, rightly or wrongly, that Oswald had come to their lands to fight for their souls and rights of conscience? If so, how did they square that with Oswald's defeat of his at least nominally fellow-Christian Cadwallon of Gwynedd? Dare we suggest that the conflict between Eowa and his brother Penda was that between a Christian and a pagan?

There is something more. The fact that it was the soil, presumably soaked in holy and very royal blood, which retained magical properties (like the food and silver dish gifted by the royal right hand; like the head and arms) echoes very ancient associations of supernatural transmission by touch in both pagan British and Germanic traditions and in Continental Roman Christian practice. Victricius, the late fourth-century bishop of Rouen, declared that the power of saints was such that it passed into even fragments of their bodies, each fragment 'linked by a bond to the whole stretch of eternity'.[188] It was not such a great leap in the Early Medieval imagination to allow that cloth, water and soil might take on these properties by touch in a homeopathic hierarchy of value which extended beyond secondary contact to tertiary association and beyond. The very earliest Irish saints' tombs, slabs erected playing-card fashion as tents over the holy resting place, had holes cut in them so that pilgrims might take a handful of dust from the sanctified soil. There were those in the church who believed in the inviolability of the corporeal relic; but there were also those who accepted practically, if not morally, the imperative of distributing the virtue of the saints among the faithful—and perhaps unfaithful.

There is a story, preserved in the anonymous Life of Gregory the Great, which makes it absolutely clear that the power and credibility of secondary relics had already become a matter of surpassing interest to the church in Rome. Some men came to Rome 'from Western parts' seeking relics for their master. Pope Gregory, knowing the potency of such items and eager to disseminate their power, consecrated some relics of the various holy martyrs, placed them in separate boxes and sealed them with the papal seal so that they might be carried back to the master.

> On their return journey, while they were resting by the wayside as men do, it occurred to their leader that he had done foolishly in not finding out what he was taking back to his master. So he broke the impressions of the seals and found nothing inside the boxes except some dirty pieces of cloth. Thereupon they returned to the man of God, saying that if such rags came to their master, they were more likely to be condemned to death than to be received with any thanks.

Gregory, so we are told, was patient with the men and asked them to pray to God for a sign that the relics were authentic. He then took a knife and made an incision into one of the cloths, whereupon it bled.

> He said to them, 'Do you not know that at the consecration of the Body and Blood of Christ, when the relics are placed on His holy altar as an offering to sanctify them, the blood of the saints to whom each relic belongs always enters into the cloth just as if it had been soaked in blood?'[189]

Not only does the striking eucharistic element in the story show just how the early church developed a logic for the power of corporeal relics; it also reveals how attractive such logic was to those of heathen sympathies who were only too easily impressed, as these doubters were, by the efficacy of sympathetic magic.

The Briton who took the bag of soil from what he supposed to be the spot where Oswald died found lodgings that night in a village where the locals were enjoying a feast. If he was a Briton we might infer that he was not freeborn and perhaps not noble but that he was known to the villagers. Was this a British village and therefore welcoming to Britons as of right? Was the man a well-known traveller on an errand for a great lord (someone like the men in King Ine's British cadre of couriers), in which case one imagines him bearing some mark of his rank: a horse, perhaps; a penannular brooch of recognised 'Celtic' style and value; a patterned cloak or a dispatch satchel? The hall in question does not seem to have been a hostel like that visited by the horseman of the first miracle; it was a private house or hall full of guests or dependents. The occasion could be one of the quarter-day feasts. It is on such occasions that the historian heartily wishes for more detail from Bede. At any rate, the man was received by the owners of the house and began to eat and drink with the rest of the company. That he conspicuously hung his precious bag of soil upon a wall-post is hard to credit: did the other guests not think it odd? Did they not question him about it? Perhaps they were preoccupied...

> They lingered long over their feasting and tippling, while a great fire burned in the midst of the dwelling. It happened that the sparks flew up into the roof which was made of wattles and thatched with hay, so that it suddenly burst into flames.[190]

Bede's readers would have been only too familiar with the horror of a hall catching fire. At Yeavering and elsewhere there is plenty of archaeological evidence, if one needs it, to testify to the potential impermanence of even a well-built structure. There is just enough detail here for us to infer that the hall was in an area of agricultural abundance; not a hill village where the thatch would have been of turf or heather, but belonging to an arable landscape. This, in fact, must have been the sort of hall excavated at Thirlings and elsewhere; not so very different from the great hall where Edwin's thegn described the short and brutal life of man, only on a more modest scale: the *vill* of an estate. The Briton, along with all the guests...

> fled outside in terror and confusion, quite unable to save the burning house which was on the point of destruction. So the whole house was burned down with the single exception that the post on which the soil hung, enclosed in its bag, remained whole and untouched by the fire. Those who saw it were greatly amazed by this miracle. After careful inquiries they discovered that the soil had been taken from the very place where Oswald's blood had been spilt.[191]

So far in Bede's list of miracles—a small sample, he assures us, of those he has heard—there is nothing that requires the receivers of Oswald's favour to have been Christian. It is too easy to make the assumption that the Briton must have been a Christian and that the locals of Wrocansæte must have been pagan. In fact it is probably better to allow that Oswald's 'luck' was equally impressive in the minds of all those who were touched by it—Christian or pagan. But whatever spin Bede might put on these events—and he swiftly restores Oswald to a Christian context after these two tales—there is no evidence that the church took institutional possession of the growing Oswald cult until much later in the century when formalised cult centres began to emerge in Bernicia and, more improbably, Lindsey and Sussex. At Oswestry various sites of interest were preserved in memory until a church was built there, but we cannot date its foundation at all closely and there is even some doubt that it was founded before the Norman Conquest. As the historian Catherine Cubitt has pointed out, there is a distinct division between the monastic, institutional cults of Anglo-Saxon England and the popular, local and, for want of a better word, peasant cults which thrived under their own impetus.[192] Such cults involve animals being cured, increases in crop yields, thriving trees and upwelling springs. These are rural, low-born interests; and what is more, they bear strong associations with animist beliefs that spirits were to be found in the mineral, organic, life-giving elements of the natural world. Oswald, almost uniquely, attracted a cult following from the rural poor and secular nobility, from royal dynasts and from monastic enthusiasts of his pious example.

Either Bede did not have more information on the development of the cult at *Maserfelth* or, more likely, he chose to avoid mention of it in his Ecclesiastical History because of the very evident and disturbing pagan associations popular legend suggested. Many stories were told which portray Oswald in a much less Christian light than Bede would have been comfortable with. Of these, the only one given much credence by most historians is that cited by Reginald of Durham in his *Vita Sancti Oswaldi* of the twelfth century.* Reginald was, to say the least, less dispassionate than Bede. Much of his Life of Oswald is derivative of the monk of Jarrow; his detailed descriptions of Oswald and of incidents in the king's life are either ludicrous or too similar to hagiographic convention to be taken very seriously. If there are stories in his account which came from credible sources they are hard to identify. But Reginald's story of Oswiu's raid to retrieve the remains of his brother carries immediate conviction, partly because it is hard to see it as part of hagiographic orthodoxy. It is utterly pagan in feel and appears to be derived from an independent source to which Reginald had access.

* Regrettably there is as yet no proper English translation of the *Vita Sancti Oswaldi*, the Latin text of which is to be found in Arnold 1885.

Oswiu was supposedly searching the battlefield for the remains of his brother. One imagines that there was more than one stake on which a head or arm was impaled as a gift to the battle-god Woden. A year after the slaughter, recognition of the fraternal arms, no doubt stripped of their armour and adornments, might well have posed a problem, even to his brother and even if they were, as Bede says, improbably incorrupt. But a great bird came to Oswiu's aid, picking the dead king's right arm from its stake and carrying it to a nearby ash tree. The tree was thereafter resistant to decay and later became the site of a church. The bird dropped the arm and where it fell a spring rose from the ground; this too became a holy site, perhaps the very well preserved by Oswestry Council in a sunken garden off the appropriately named Maserfield Road. From here Oswiu recovered the arm and, finding one to match, made off with them and the head. It is a gruesome scene to imagine. The importance of the story lies in the identification of the 'great bird of the crow family' as described by Reginald, with the Raven, the traditional companion in war of the god Woden; and of the tree as an ash—Yggdrasil, the Norse tree of life and death, where Odin hanged himself in sacrifice. Yggdrasil was supposed to connect the heavens and the earthly world of man with a subterranean well whence many rivers sprang. This is potent stuff, and the story is unlikely to have been made up by any Christian monk. The tale, together with the circumstantial evidence of Bede's two battlefield miracles, make me suspicious that the site of the church and well, that is to say the place where Oswald's remains were impaled and which became Oswestry, cannot quite be the same place as the battlefield. I think Penda took his trophies and displayed them at some site of significance at a distance from the site of the battle; just how far away it is useless to speculate. But I think the association between battlefield and impalement must be reasonably close, since by Reginald's day they had merged into one site with a new name:

Oswald's Tree. It might just as well have been named Yggdrasil.

The site of Oswald's death and the fate of his corporeal remains seem, then, to have appealed to both Christian and pagan, Briton and Anglian, at a fundamental level of superstition and belief. It is perhaps overly obvious to say that in Oswald, pagan and Christian, British and Germanic, sacral and temporal were fused as in no other king of the Early Medieval period. But here is the essence of his fascination for historians, just as the potent combination of elements proved so enduring in Britain and the Continent for more than five hundred years after his death. Oswald was Woden-sprung, like his famous heathen father. He was a great warrior with a famed right arm which delivered death to his enemies and luck and wealth (the Old English words *eadig* and *sædig* are interchangeable) to his people.[193] He was a conqueror of conquerors; he was graced with the favour of both Woden, the battle-god of the Anglo-Saxons, and that of the king of Heaven—perhaps also with the horned and spear-wielding chutzpah of the northern British war god Belatucadros, the 'bright, shining one'. He sponsored the baptism of kings and the establishment of dioceses. He brought victory, glory and honour as well as booty and gifts to his warrior-companions. He shared his luck and riches with the poor of his fatherland and with the church whose lands were his endowments. Faced with his own end he prayed for the souls of those who fought with him. In death his corporeal luck was transmitted to whomever possessed or had come into contact with his remains; his Christian virtue and healing power could be transferred by touch and employed by the virtuous. He appealed to the tribal, totemic king-worshippers of his Bernician homeland and to the rural lay people of distant lands. He had been blessed with the favour and endorsement of a great house of Irish monasticism and in turn had been rewarded with earthly success in battle and conquest.

For Bede he was most holy and victorious, the paradigm of

Christian kingship and a striking example to those contemporaries of Bede who did not share all, or any, of his virtues; for everyone else he was a cult figure whose magic could be vicariously enjoyed and celebrated. His death could be seen as both a sacrifice for the continued luck of his people and as martyrdom in the cause of the nascent church.

Ownership of the Oswald cult did not remain just in lay or low-born hands. With such a saint available to them, Oswald became an early focus for the entrepreneurs of the cult of royal saints. What surprises historians is that it should have taken so long for the church to appropriate this most valuable martyr. It was not until thirty years after Oswald's death that the popular cult was identified with an ecclesiastical institution. It did not do so where one might expect such a cult to flourish: at Lindisfarne, which he had founded and where his head was buried. Aidan's community either did not wish to attract the attention and crowds which overt veneration of Oswald's relics would bring; or they were uncomfortable with the pagan overtones of the head cult, well known in both Ireland and Britain.

The Bernician home of the Oswald cult was Heavenfield, where he had raised his cross the night before battle. Bede tells us that the brethren of the church at Hexham made a pilgrimage to there every year on the day before the anniversary of his death on 5 August. Recently, Bede says, a church had been built there, and the present unprepossessing building is probably on the same site. But as I have suggested, the actual site of the cross may have been in the ruins of the Roman mile turret known as 25b which seems to lie at the centre of an enclosure of unknown date but suggestive size and shape. We know the date of the foundation at Hexham: 673, very probably the year in which Bede was born. It was built by that most controversial figure Wilfrid, scourge of unorthodox practices and of the Irish church and champion of all things Roman and splendid; but also a man most active in seeking the patronage and approbation of kings. The annual pilgrimage is probably to be dated no earlier than that time, although there is every reason to suppose that some sort of local cult of the cross site was already developing, much as it was at Oswestry and, perhaps, while Oswald was still alive.

Bede knew of miracles which had occurred there and he cites one which was experienced by a man still living in his own day. Bothelm, a monk of the church at Hexham, had broken his arm in a fall on ice. Suffering terrible pain from the fracture, he asked one of the brothers, whom he knew was to visit the site of the cross, to bring him back a fragment of the wood. Perhaps reluctant to take a chip from the holy monument which was already subject to the depradations of souvenir hunters, the brother retrieved a piece of moss which grew on it. Bothelm placed the moss in his bosom and went to bed, and at midnight awoke feeling something cold close to his side; reaching for it, he realised that his arm and hand were as sound as if he had never been injured.

Bothelm was not the only holy man interested in possessing fragments of wood associated with Oswald. Willibrord, renowned Continental missionary of the later seventh and early eighth centuries and pupil of Wilfrid, somehow on his travels acquired a fragment of the stake on which Oswald's head had been impaled. Where and how this valuable treasure came into his possession, we cannot say; but we might infer that it was given him by Wilfrid. Willibrord placed the splinter in water and used the resulting drink to heal a sick scholar in Ireland, where Oswald's fame had naturally enough been spread by his connections with Iona and by monks who returned to Ireland from Lindisfarne. The scholar had led a less than perfect life and, having fallen victim to a plague, was on the point of death. He begged Willibrord to help him, evidently having heard that the monk possessed relics of the saintly king. When the stake-infused drink cured him, he turned to the Lord and became a missionary. It is a story firmly belonging to the conventions of hagiography. Willibrord was in Frisia when he told this story to Wilfrid and Wilfrid's companion Acca, later bishop of Hexham and close friend of Bede; this must have been in the 690s, fifty years after *Maserfelth*. If he did in fact have a piece of the stake, it must have been curated as a relic from that time and perhaps passed through several sets of hands.

Acca, who related this miracle-story to Bede at third hand, told him of another Oswald miracle from an apparently even more improbable location. A monastery had been founded at Selsey in the kingdom of the South Saxons in the first half of the 680s, among a people previously untouched by the conversion. Some years after its founding it was, like many other parts of the island, struck by a virulent plague. Among the victims was a young Saxon, a recent convert, who in his febrile state was visited by a vision of St Peter. The boy had been left alone while the rest of the monastic community observed a three-day fast in the hope that God would deliver the surviving monks from the ravages of the disease. The apostle brought the boy good news—up to a point. He, the boy, was shortly to be released from earthly pain and taken to Heaven. The rest of the monastic community were to be restored to health. These favours, the boy was to tell his abbot, Eappa, were granted at the intercession of King Oswald because that very day was the anniversary of his death. The abbot went to check in the monastic calendar and found that this was indeed the case. And true to the apostle's word, the boy died but all the other monks at Selsey were spared.

> Many who heard of the vision were wonderfully encouraged to pray to the divine mercy in times of adversity and to submit to the wholesome remedy of fasting. From that time, not only in this monastery but in many other places, the heavenly birthday of this king and soldier of Christ began to be observed yearly by the celebration of masses.[194]

Historians have long recognised in this anecdote, often repeated by Acca, the deliberate establishment in a monastic community of a saint's cult. The monastic calendar was developing as a means of observing saints' days and it is highly likely that this particular calendar was brought to Selsey by its founder. And what these three anecdotes, of Heavenfield, of Willibrord and Selsey, have in common is Wilfrid. He it was who, exiled from Northumbria by King Ecgfrith in 681, initiated the mission to the South Saxons which resulted in his founding of Selsey. He was the teacher and mentor of Willibrord. He was probably the entrepreneur behind the establishment of an annual pilgrimage to the site of the cross at Heavenfield and he was almost certainly behind the otherwise unlikely veneration of Oswald at Selsey some time in the 680s. His motives remain to be considered; but there seems little doubt that he was an active promoter of Oswald, perhaps initially as a protector for the foundation at Hexham.

Wilfrid was not Oswald's only influential post-mortem patron. In the decade in which Selsey was established as a cult centre for Oswald, a Lincolnshire monastery, Bardney, was founded by King Æthelred and Queen Osthryth of Mercia with some very significant relics of the royal saint. The monks of Bardney, apparently harbouring ill-will towards the memory of a king who had conquered their kingdom in the days of their fathers, refused to allow the royal couple to bring Oswald's remains there. How they were persuaded otherwise is a matter for later consideration.* What is significant is the fact that this king and queen were in possession of Oswald's body parts. Assuming these to be the actual torso and legs of the martyred hero (and naturally one harbours doubts about this), one is curious to know where they had been during the previous forty years; how they were identified; and how they came into the hands of the Mercian ruling house. The crucial detail in Bede's account of the miracles which occurred at Bardney, overcoming the monks' initial resistance

* See Chapter XVIII.

to the deposition of Oswald's relics there, is the presence of his banner of purple and gold (the two royal colours). Bede's description of this banner, which he tells us was hung over Oswald's tomb at Bardney, lies behind the otherwise obscure origins of the present-day flag of Northumbria, much cherished by its inhabitants. Its importance, if we accept that this was Oswald's battle standard at *Maserfelth*, is that it provides a clue to the parallel history of his remains: a provenance, if you will. We suppose that the head and arms were removed from the field of battle as macabre trophies and taken, probably, to the place now called Oswestry (or perhaps the nearby stronghold and hillfort at Old Oswestry), where they were displayed before being retrieved by Oswiu a year later. Oswiu could be certain that they were his brother's remains because of the ominous act of the large bird in plucking the arm from its stake and carrying it to the ash tree; the head, one infers, could still be identified facially. But how could the rest of the body be identified on the battlefield? It must surely be the case that the headless and armless corpse was wrapped in the king's own battle standard at the time and removed to a place where it was stored. Why? And by whom?

If Penda's son Æthelred was in possession of these remains after about 679 when Bardney was founded, it is possible that Penda himself ordered that the body be kept; he would surely have been interested in keeping Oswald's battle standard as a trophy. Equally, some enterprising local might have scavenged them as trophies and later gifted them (for a price?) to Penda or his son. There is a third possibility, that the relics might have come into the personal possession of the queen; for Queen Osthryth was the daughter of King Oswiu of Bernicia, whose raid in 643 might also have resulted in his obtaining the standard, torso and legs. Oswald was her uncle.

Oswald's death precipitated a new crisis in Northumbria. His brother Oswiu was recognised as his successor in both Bernicia and Deira by right of having the same inheritance: Æthelfrith andAcha. There is, however, some evidence* that in Deira he was not accepted as readily as Oswald had been. Like his predecessors he must establish his fitness to rule by his deeds as a warrior and politician. Oswald's legacy, which placed Bernicia at the head of all the English kingdoms and others besides; which had established an institutional Christian church with missionary and economic functions; which might conceivably lead to the unification of many of the kingdoms under a northern imperium, must now be tested by the rules of its day. Was Northumbria to be forged into a truly united kingdom? Were the Christian political treaties which the subject kingdoms of the English had embraced (willingly or unwillingly) to have a meaningful future in creating a culture of responsible and civilised kingship? Would Oswiu repudiate the church, or would he realise its potential for creating a political entity which we might recognise as a state? Would the new power in the land, his brother's slayer Penda, strike him down before he could establish himself?

---

* See p.262; he placed a Deiran prince, Oswine, there as sub-king and was most particular to ensure that his powers of patronage were spread evenly throughout the two kingdoms.

XIV

FAMILY AFFAIRS

Cyning sceal rice healdan

*A king shall guard
his kingdom*

OSWIU BEGAN HIS REIGN
in a position of weakness: the bulk of the Northumbrian army had been destroyed at *Maserfelth* and the living potency of Oswald's Bernician imperium died with its king. Besides, Oswald's *gesiths* had owed him the personal loyalty of a warrior to his lord; Oswiu, in defending his brother's legacy, must start afresh. Many of the estates whence Oswald had drawn his fighting elite were now lordless, unable to render the new king the services of warriors who were dead, and whose sons were infant. The Bernician host was insufficient to defend the fatherland. There was a literal vacuum of operational power, of regional political function. Executive control at shire level must have devolved to the reeves, those intermediaries between king and estate; noble families whose lord was dead and who could not provide a son of fighting age to take his place in the king's host might have been displaced from their homes by those who could. Competition for the new king's patronage in the shocking aftermath of Oswald's death must have been fierce: old rivalries revived among the northern nobility; opportunities for fortune and favour seized. Beyond

the borders of Bernicia and Deira, Picts and Strathclyde Britons, lords of Rheged, Powys and Gwynedd would meet in their great halls and contemplate one last chance for the *Gwyr y Gogledd*, the Men of the old North, to rise against the Saxon.

Penda was the immediate external danger. During the first thirteen years of Oswiu's reign he was able to mount periodic raids into Northumbrian territory from Mercia and these were so successful that at one stage even Bamburgh was under threat of capture and destruction. Oswiu must have attracted his own warband during his years in Irish exile and, probably, during campaigns in the North on behalf of his brother; but in the autumn of 642 he was in no position to take on the new power in the land in open battle. He must bide his time, defend his shrunken kingdom and use his political skills to forge effective alliances. He may have lacked the extraordinary charisma of his martyred brother but the Oswiu who emerges from the pages of Bede is an astute, canny, ruthless politician of great sophistication. He was the first, the only, Northumbrian king of the seventh century to die in his bed. He deployed his talents to great effect, securing not only the legacy of Oswald, but his own considerable achievement in constructing the first great English state.

Even at the beginning Oswiu was not without friends. He could rely on a core constituency in Bernicia by virtue of his reputation as a warrior and his birthright. His loyalty to the Irish mission on Lindisfarne is striking, and was fulsomely reciprocated. In the first year of his reign, having retrieved Oswald's remains from British territory far to the west and south, he gave the dead king's head to be buried in the cemetery on Lindisfarne. It was perhaps an uncomfortable gesture for the community to receive, but they cannot have been insensible to what seems to modern sensibilities an odd sort of compliment. The luck in the head, as it has been termed, was a manifest symbol of royal and divine favour: it bestowed protection, literal and psychological.[195] In return,

Oswiu won support for the series of dynastic policies which he implemented almost immediately.

Like Oswald before him Oswiu was aware that a son born before accession was not regarded as entirely legitimate.[196] That was probably why Oswald had waited to marry until after his return to Northumbria. Oswiu already had three children. One, born out of wedlock to the Irish princess Fina would later play his own part in the Bernician succession, although not without opposition. With Rhieinmelth, his British consort, Oswiu had a son, Alhfrith, and a daughter, Alhflæd, neither more than seven or eight years old at his accession when Oswiu himself was still a young man of thirty. By judicious marriage he might advance both the legitimacy of his offspring and his political ambitions. He seems to have felt most vulnerable in his relations with Deira, whose *gesiths* were loath to accept him as king by right. A Deiran cousin would fit the bill perfectly.

In choosing a bride who was not just a princess of Kent but also the daughter of his dead uncle Edwin, Oswiu hoped to kill two birds with one stone. Little can he have realised what he was letting himself in for; but this was no impetuous fling on his part. Oswiu was enough of an Ionan protégé to seek the legitimacy which might be conferred by his bishop. These were delicate issues for the church. Oswiu was married; his queen and children were known to the Lindisfarne community, their near neighbours on the Northumbrian coast. Bede tells us nothing explicit about such awkward arrangements; it did not suit his narrative. But from small fragments of historical evidence we might piece together the train of events which led to the installation of a new queen.

The ninth-century Durham *Liber Vitae* is a sort of medieval visitor's book, recording gifts to the community of St Cuthbert. Its core belongs to a set of records probably kept on Lindisfarne from the earliest days of the community and maintained, with many additions and modifications, not to say fictions, until it attained its final form in the Middle Ages. In many respects it is not trustworthy: the first king cited in its list of donors was Edwin, dead before the community's foundation; but the first queen cited as a donor is unlikely to be such a retrospective insertion. She is *Rægumeld*, an anglicised spelling of Rhieinmelth. My reading of this entry is that, with the connivance of Bishop Aidan, Oswiu's queen was 'retired' into the hands of the Lindisfarne community with a suitably generous donation on her behalf. The donation possibly consisted of part of her dower lands, perhaps one of the Northumbrian estates listed in the earliest possessions of Lindisfarne in Islandshire or along the River Tweed; but more probably some form of moveable wealth, such as treasure, or perhaps books. Where she actually lived out her days can only be a matter of speculation; she would not have been allowed to live on the holy island itself. But her children both survived and were maintained by Oswiu's court until the complex rivalries of the 660s led to a family feud.

That Aidan was complicit in Oswiu's plans can be inferred not just from the possible fate of the queen but in the events surrounding the installation of Oswiu's new consort. Oswiu's ambassador to his prospective wife at Canterbury, where the fortunes of the Augustinian mission had revived with the accession of a Christian king, Eorconberht, was a priest named Utta. Eorconberht was, according to Bede, the first king to order that all the pagan shrines in his kingdom be destroyed. At the Kentish court his cousin Eanflæd, daughter of Edwin and grand-daughter of Æthelberht, was living after returning from the exile imposed by her cousin Oswald after Heavenfield. She must be fetched:

> Utta intended to travel to Kent by land but to return with the maiden by sea; so he went to Bishop Aidan and begged him to pray to the Lord for himself and those who were to make the long journey with him. Aidan blessed them, commended them to the Lord, and gave them some holy oil...[197]

The point of telling this story, set up as a retrospective on the great bishop's virtuous life, was to show the power of Aidan's blessing, for in due course on the return journey a storm blew up fit to sink the vessel in which the precious party was returning; but Utta poured the holy oil on the turbulent waters of the North Sea and all was miraculously well. The back-story here is slightly more subtle: through Utta, Oswiu sought and won the approbation of his principal holy man for the mission to Kent. It mattered to Oswiu and his constituents, and it will have mattered to the king and princess of Kent. Aidan's blessing was not just provident: it was essential. Eanflæd's willing or unwilling career as queen of the Bernicians began, then, in auspicious circumstances just as her life had: she was baptised by Paulinus at Easter shortly after her father, Edwin, was delivered from the assassin's blade and she from her mother's womb. At a stroke Oswiu secured a suitable Christian wife of impeccable breeding and political value; soothed any worries which the church might have had concerning the dispatch of his previous queen; and, moreover, succeeded in reforging the old alliance between the Idings and the Yffings so that he might be recognised as king of all the peoples north of the Humber.

In due course, Oswiu's offspring with his cousin Eanflæd might hope to succeed to both Bernicia and Deira. For the time being he did not feel secure enough south of the Tyne to impose direct rule there. His son Alhfrith was too young to deputise, as was his nephew, Oswald's son Œthelwald. Oswiu chose to rule Deira through a *sub-regulus*, the last prince of the Yffings: Oswine, the son of that Osric who had apostatised, taken on the army of Cadwallon in the year of the interregnum and been killed for his trouble. We cannot say what sort of a man Osric was; he had played a weak hand and lost; he is no more than a footnote to the seventh century. Of Oswine we can say much more because he was a favourite of Bede, of Aidan, of his own people and also, to begin with, of Oswiu.

> Oswine was tall and handsome, pleasant of speech, courteous in manner, and bountiful to nobles and commons alike; so it came about that he was beloved by all because of the royal dignity which showed itself in his character, his appearance and his actions; and noblemen from almost every kingdom flocked to serve him as retainers.

To a politician like Oswiu this early portrait of the chivalrous Prince Hal might reveal a double edge: it might suggest that Oswine was in the business of recruiting a warband sufficient to challenge the authority of his over-king. Only time would tell. To churchmen like Aidan and Bede it was his virtue which both impressed and concerned them; for he was that rare, almost unique beast, a humble king. His great piety attracted the favour of Aidan; perhaps as a young man he had been educated on Lindisfarne under the bishop's protection. It is significant that, the Deirans having no bishop of their own, their principal ecclesiastical lord was the royal holy man of the Bernicians. Oswine, in recognition of this relationship, gave Aidan a fine horse, that symbol of kingly favour and rank. Aidan, despising the sort of dignity and comfort which such trappings conferred, gave it away to a beggar. Bede loved that sort of story and gave it special emphasis as an admonition to the kings and bishops of his own day who inevitably suffered by comparison. Oswine was horrified; probably insulted. Meeting Aidan at dinner the Deiran prince upbraided the Irish bishop, saying that he could have given any old nag to the holy man if he was going to be so free with his gifts. Aidan's well-honed response was to ask the king if he regarded the son of a mare as dearer to him than the son of God? Oswine took this admonition and thought deeply about it. Later, returning from a hunting expedition and warming himself in the hall by a great fire surrounded by his thegns, the priest's words struck him with such force that he unbuckled his sword and threw himself at the bishop's feet:

'Never from henceforth,' he said, 'will I speak of this again nor will I form any opinion as to what money of mine or how much of it you should give to the sons of God.' When the bishop saw this he was greatly alarmed; he got up immmediately and raised the king to his feet... The king, in accordance with the bishop's entreaties and commands, recovered his spirits, but the bishop, on the other hand, grew sadder and sadder and at last began to shed tears. Thereupon a priest asked him in his native tongue, which the king and his thegns did not understand, why he was weeping, and Aidan answered, 'I know that the king will not live long; for I never before saw a humble king.'[198]

Humble he may have been; humility would not prevent Oswine from fulfilling his own tribal destiny and the prophecy of the admiring Aidan by raising an army against Oswiu. His rebellion, seven years in the fomenting, took place against a complex backdrop of church consolidation and external threat.

Throughout the later 640s and into the next decade Penda was able to attack his neighbours with impunity, driving Cenwalh from Wessex, raiding East Anglia and seemingly able at will to carry his warbands deep into Northumbrian territory. At no point before 650, however, did either Penda or Oswiu feel able to mount open war on the other. It was a period of retrenchment and desultory campaigning of the sort familiar in tribal Europe after the death of a great warrior king. Lindisfarne, at least, was preserved from attack: there was no loot to be had there, it being such a modest establishment.

It is easy to think of Aidan's small community on his tidal island, supported by a number of estates, constituting the entirety of the early Northumbrian church. If there are times in the seventh century when notices of new foundations reach us, mostly we can only say that by a certain date such and such a monastery must have been founded. But it is worth asking how many churches and monasteries there were at the end of Oswald's reign. His patronage of Aidan and Bernician membership of the Ionan paruchia were secured by Oswiu; but how far had that mission spread in the eight years since Heavenfield?

We may confidently say that at least six other churches existed in Northumbria, although there are likely to have been many more lost to history. The king had his own churches at Bamburgh and at Yeavering; perhaps also at other royal estates. There had been a church at a Deiran *villa regia*, Campodonum, in Edwin's day, which was destroyed by Cadwallon but rebuilt by later kings—perhaps by Oswine. Paulinus's church at York still stood—it was sufficiently established to receive Edwin's head after his death at *Hæthfelth*—and Oswald ensured its completion. There has, we know, been a minster church on that site ever since. Bishop Aidan founded at least one, probably several more, satellites of Lindisfarne in the years after Oswald's death. The only one we can identify, thanks to a Bedan anecdote, lay on the north side of the River Wear where Aidan gave Hild, great niece of Edwin, a single hide of land on which to found a monastery.* Another lay perhaps upstream from the mouth of the River Tyne just east of Jarrow at a place called *Donemutha*. This may be the place where, in his childhood, Saint Cuthbert had prayed for a party of monks who were in danger of being swept out to sea on a raft of timber they had collected.[199] Then there is that obscure, enigmatic congregation which survived all the depredations of war and strife, somewhere close to Catterick, ministered to by James the Deacon throughout the reigns of Oswald and Oswiu. I have already suggested that there may have been an abortive monastic foundation at Heavenfield.

Melrose, the community which Cuthbert was to join as a young boy, was certainly in existence by the end of the 640s; most historians accept the possibility that there was an active British Christian community here which survived from the end of

* EH IV.23 The location of this tiny monastery is unknown; there was a settlement existing at Chester le Street (*Kuncacæster*) on the River Wear in this period; the later Wearmouth monastery lay further downstream opposite modern Sunderland.

the Roman period in northern Northumbria; so it may not have been the only one receiving young nobles like Cuthbert. There were British churches in the Pennines too, later to be purged and taken over by Wilfrid. Of the other possible early foundations we might cite that at Ebchester, the small Roman fort on the south side of Durham's Derwent Valley, whose monastery was named after Æbbe, the uterine sister of Oswald and Oswiu.* She later established a more remote community on the sea-pounded rocky coast north of Berwick at a place now known as St Abb's Head. I think it possible that her foundation at Ebchester—by no means the only early monastery to be located on a Roman military site— may have served as the retirement home for her sisters-in-law Cyniburh, the widow of Oswald, and Rhieinmelth, the discarded spouse of Oswiu. What conversations might those three royal women have had, protected from the inconstant political fates of the world of men: a daughter of Acha and sister of Oswald, brought up in the shadow of Iona at the centre of the Christian world; a princess of Wessex, cast off from her culture and family; and perhaps the last royal princess of Rheged, that legendary British court of faded grandeur and poetic legend?

We know also from Bede that Aidan's Irish monks—and scores, if not hundreds more came from Ireland in the decades after Heavenfield—felt a missionary obligation to preach to the poor and to the widely dispersed communities of the North. No doubt solitary monks, fulfilling their desire for *peregrinatio*, the wandering exile for Christ, built themselves modest cells in the hills and valleys of Northumbria; but none has recognisably survived.

* Bede's prose Life of Saint Cuthbert (*PLC* X) uses the term *uterina* of her. This can mean either that Bede believed Æbbe to share the same mother, Acha, as Oswald and Oswiu but not the same father; or possibly that she was Oswald's twin. Much debate has failed to achieve a consensus on the father; if not Æthelfrith, then whom? Perhaps she was born posthumously in about 617; might that distinguish her as having, in Bede's eyes, no father? Alternatively Acha could have had an otherwise unknown first husband, but this is most unlikely.

There is a ring of what look like Early Medieval cells inside a pre-historic enclosure on Ingram Hill in the Breamish Valley, on land once owned by Lindisfarne; were there pioneering monks here in the seventh century? Others may have formed small communities in equally remote places, invisible to the archaeological record except by some chance survival of a Christian artefact.* There must have been many other foundations, either those whose names we know but which are unlocated or those time has forgotten, which did not survive. Others might be inferred from enigmatic structures on sites identified through excavation or from the air: there is a good candidate at Sprouston on the River Tweed, probably lying within a Lindisfarne estate but belonging to a secular lord. There was, as yet, nothing remotely like the parochial system which was to emerge in the eighth century and which has framed the English territorial and ecclesiastical landscape ever since. When that system did emerge it was rooted firmly in political and economic bedrock: on the shires and *vills* on which food and military renders were imposed. The parochial system was, in fact, an extension of these; the tithe, which first appears under a law of Æthelwulf, father of Alfred the Great, was a fiscal formalising of the ten per cent render.

What we can say with certainty is that under Oswiu, and in particular under the influence of Queen Eanflæd, there was an explosion of monastic endowments across Northumbria from the mid-650s onwards. This second wave of foundations, all in imitation of the Irish model established so brilliantly at Lindisfarne, would hard-wire political reality to the spiritual revolution brought about by the Ionan mission and, inadvertently or otherwise, forge

---

* During an antiquarian picnic expedition along the Breamish Valley in June 1861 a small silver cross with an Alpha and Omega on one side and the inscription AGLA or ACGA on the other was produced by a farmer at Hartside; it has not been seen since, but it may have belonged to a monk of Hexham whose bishop, in Bede's day, was Acca. *Proceedings of the Berwickshire Naturalists Field Club* 1862, Anniversary Address, page 242.

a new political culture in Anglo-Saxon England: the beginnings of the modern idea of statehood. While the inward-looking, conservative, diocesan rump of the Augustinian mission survived but achieved little more than survival in Kent, Oswiu, on the back of his brother's divine inspiration, conceived a church at the social and economic heart of his kingdom: a spiritual imperium to go with that wrought by the sword. The backdrop to this extraordinary new relationship between church and state, king and cleric, is all too familiar: dynastic rivalry and foreign invasion.

Northumbria's neighbours to the north and south saw the death of Oswald as a chance to test the resilience of the new king's forces. The Annals of Tigernach note a battle between Oswiu and 'the Britons' (Picts? Welsh?) under the year 643; perhaps this records his raid to retrieve his brother's head and arms; it may also preserve the notice of a raid on his northern borders. We cannot date the first of Penda's incursions against Oswiu; there were probably several campaigning seasons during which Penda exercised his army's appetite for fighting, looting and spoliation. His own insatiable desire for battle does not appear to have extended to the idea of conquest or territorial acquisition. He may have contented himself with the idea of affirming his control against internal opposition over the lands that he considered 'Mercian'.

The earliest sure reference to external depredations comes not from Nennius or Bede but in the Anonymous Life of Saint Cuthbert, written around the year 700. As a young man of about seventeen the future holy man joined the community at Melrose in Roxburghshire (now Scottish Borders); but before that he had fulfilled his obligation to serve his earthly king in Oswiu's army: 'when dwelling in camp with the army, in the face of the enemy, and having only meagre rations, he yet lived abundantly all the time and was strengthened by divine aid...'[200] His hagiographer does not say against whom he was fighting, but it must have been about 649 or 650, for he gave himself up to monastic life in 651.

About this time, tensions between Oswiu and his Deiran sub-king Oswine erupted into civil war and Penda embarked on a series of devastating raids deep into Northumbrian territory, perhaps knowingly exploiting internal tensions. We know too little of the broader picture in the North to be able to say which came first, or who exploited the timing of the other. Oswiu may have been threatened from both north and south and in such circumstances the opportunity to strike against him may have appealed to enemy and ally alike. There is no record before the mid-650s of Oswiu and Penda meeting face to face in battle. Penda's attack was part, it seems, of a concerted campaign of devastation which included a siege of the tribal fortress at Bamburgh. Even then Bamburgh must have presented a formidable face to anyone rash enough to try to take it. To the west, to landward, it appears like a giant natural rampart: an indomitable fist rising from and against the sea. Its access to a harbour and the well that provides it with fresh water meant that any Mercian attempt at a siege was futile. Penda decided to try to burn it, and so he had his army dismantle all the surrounding dwellings (peasant houses and workshops serving the royal court, I wonder?) and make with their timber an immense bonfire. Bede's description of the heaps of beams, rafters, wattle walls and thatching which the army raised against the cliff is one of the most telling in our early sources; but the assault was patently doomed. Penda can only have hoped for a lucky spark to strike the buildings of the fortress beyond its palisade; perhaps in impotent fury he lost his cool. Was he specifically intent on getting at Oswald's incorrupt right arm, his trophy from *Maserfelth*?

We do not know who was inside; one suspects that the king was away campaigning elsewhere. In any case, Bede tells us that it was Aidan, now in his last years and living a secluded life on Inner Farne, who saw the flames high above the fortress and feared that the city might be lost—and all his work with it. He raised his eyes and hands to Heaven and prayed for salvation from this pagan evil. As if in answer, 'the winds veered away from the city and carried the flames in the direction of those who kindled them.'[201] Hoist, as it were, by their own petard, the enemy retreated, realising that Bamburgh was divinely protected. Geographers might reasonably see in this narrative the quite natural evening shift from an offshore to an onshore breeze. No contemporary churchman would have seen it in any other light than the intercession of the one true God, of Christian virtue overcoming pagan impiety, with unbaptised natives thinking perhaps of intervention by the god of storms þunor (the Old English version of 'Thor'). It would also not have been lost on the bishop, his king and their people that both Lindisfarne and Bamburgh were protected by the magic of Oswald's head and incorrupt right arm.

Bede had more trouble dealing with Oswine's rebellion: here were two worthy Christian kings in conflict over earthly territories. Oswine, humble though he may have been, harboured ambitions to cast off the yoke of Bernician domination over his people. No reminder that Oswiu was as well qualified to rule over Deira as his brother had been by right of their maternal descent, no marriage to a princess of Deira, had reconciled Oswine—and perhaps his constituents—to Oswiu's rule. It is not worth speculating further on the dynamics of such personal politics. The fact is that Oswine raised an army against Oswiu in the summer of 651. The size of his warband was no match for that of the Bernician king, we are told; in this Bedan detail is a hint that perhaps Oswine timed his rebellion to coincide with Penda's attack, hoping that Oswiu had his hands full elsewhere. We might even speculate on a Mercian–Deiran alliance. If that is the case, it was hopelessly mismanaged: Oswiu was ready for him, and in such overwhelming numbers that Oswine decided to disband his army rather than risk annihilation, seeking temporary refuge while he considered his limited options.

The geography of these events is fascinating. Oswine assembled his army at *Wilfaresdun*. There is no consensus on the exact location of this otherwise unknown settlement, but Bede offers us unusual precision when he tells us that it was about ten miles north-west of *Catræth*, the ancient Roman town which guards the Great North Road and a critical eastern entry point to the Pennine kingdoms. This places the action close to that modern traveller's signpost to the North, Scotch Corner, where the A1 meets the westbound A66. Scotch Corner may be named after the Scot's Dyke, a still partly visible massive ditch and bank built either side of Gilling Beck to prevent, it would seem, an advance by the old Roman route across the Pennines. It is a truism that a dyke looks both ways; so one must be careful not to assume which side was intended to be defended. Nevertheless, the modern village of Whashton, a good candidate for Bede's *Wilfaresdun*, lies two miles to the west of Scot's Dyke on a promontory overlooking Gilling Beck; the dyke separates it from the royal *vill* of *Catræth* and the Great North Road. Whatever period the dyke belongs to—and consensus is that it is Early Medieval in date, perhaps part of the Swaledale earthwork system—Oswine might have exploited it as a defensive redoubt against Oswiu. Whether or not this is the right interpretation, the denouement of the rebellion took place in Deira. Oswiu had not been waiting at home for a knock on the door.

The end was ignominious in the extreme. Oswine, with a single companion named Tondhere, took refuge in the nearby house of a supposedly faithful *gesith* called Hunwold, in sight of the dyke at the *vill* then called Gilling (now Gilling West). Hunwold betrayed Oswine to the king, who sent a thegn called Æthelwine to kill him. The date was 20 August 651. It is now, at a moment regarded by Bede as a foul stain on the Christian kingship of Oswiu, that we first detect the decisive intervention of his queen, Eanflæd. Possibly she had already attempted to broker a deal between her second cousin Oswine and her husband. If so, she had been unsuccessful. Her allegiance to the Deiran cause must both have given her personal pain and raised marital tensions. But she was no wallflower: Eanflæd had been brought up in the courts of Kent and Frankia, where politics were a messy and pragmatic business. Eanflæd asked the king to give land at Gilling for the construction of a monastery where the souls of both kings, victim and murderer, would be prayed for, in expiation of his crime.[202] Significantly, the first abbot of the foundation was the priest Trumhere, a kinsman of both Eanflæd and Oswine. In one sense this is a transmission of the pagan law of blood-price, or *wergild*, into a Christian context: a payment to compensate the victim's family, to atone, and more specifically to prevent a blood feud, that bane of medieval society.

In Eanflæd's 'request' we also see the inception of a trend for male and female lines of Northumbrian royalty to compete for the disposal of royal lands to the church as a tool of political influence, with family members being placed strategically to maintain and develop dynastic interests. In its maturity this trend became a policy which embraced the acquisition of holy relics—such as those of Oswald, Edwin and their like—to enhance the dignity of the foundation and attract more gifts to enrich it; it became greedy for land and prestige and eventually its success would attract the wrong sort to the holy endeavour. By Bede's day the practice had got out of hand—disastrously so. But in its infancy it was a brilliant conception; and it seems to have been Eanflæd's idea.

Aidan cannot have approved Oswiu's treatment of the Deiran sub-king. What his reaction was we cannot say because he did not long survive the atheling. Bede tells us that his death came just twelve days after Oswine's; long enough to have heard the news: perhaps it broke his heart. But he seems to have been ill for some time. His last days were spent not on Inner Farne or at

the halls at Yeavering were. The original was burned down. It had a western annexe, but only as an addition to its rebuilding after the first fire. There is the nice possibility that the annexe was constructed over the place where Aidan died, to sanctify it within the house of God. This church also burned down, but this time it was not replaced; by this phase of the township there were far fewer buildings. So it may be that Bede's second rebuild is unhistorical; or the third church was built elsewhere in the Yeavering complex— perhaps as building C4 a little to the north-west; or the township in question was not Yeavering but another 'not far away' from Bamburgh. I believe Yeavering to be a convincing candidate.

Aidan's legacy is profound. Without his shining qualities of determination, humility, moral authority and patient exhortation it is doubtful if Oswald's ambitions for a Christian Northumbria would have come to fruition. He played an absolutely key role in educating the sons of Æthelfrith in the duties of Christian kings and retaining the spiritual essence of the Irish church in its English incarnation. There was something, even, of the shaman in Aidan, as there had been in Colm Cille: these high-born Irishmen were bred to wield a certain sort of tribal, semi-divine power. They possessed immense charisma; their words bore more than spiritual weight. They did not consider themselves inferior to any below God; certainly not to their secular lords. They were capable of healing and cursing, of influencing by prophecy and of conferring powers on those whom they favoured. Bede knew that this had been a special generation and, identifying himself so fervently with its virtues, he bitterly regretted its passing.

Oswiu's continued patronage of Lindisfarne as the mother-house of the Northumbrian church, and as part of the Ionan *paruchia*, remained firm—at least for the time being. Aidan was succeeded first by an Ionan priest, Finan (a relative of the king: he was a kinsman of Fina, the Irish princess who bore Oswiu's first child); then by another, Colman. The Northumbrian church

connection

did not, indeed it could not, yet produce its own great holy men. But many of Northumbria's noble youths, perhaps the second sons of the king's *gesiths*, were being attracted in numbers to the monastic life and would graduate as a famous generation of English monks, priests and bishops. The missionary and ascetic zeal of the Ionan mission was not easily dissipated. For thirteen years after Oswine's death, Aidan and his successors were able to marry the spiritual values of Iona with those Columban political ambitions which Oswiu well understood. He could not achieve the fruition of his policies until he had decisively ended the threat posed by Penda. He was not yet in a position to do so; but with the threat of Deiran rebellion staunched by Oswine's dispatch he was able to extend his reach towards the southern kingdoms and began to draw the Mercian fire. And in Oswine's place he chose a deputy to rule over the Deirans: Œthelwald, son of Oswald. By 651 the atheling was probably sixteen years old, sufficient to begin recruiting his own warband and build a court suitable to his rank. His birthright ought to ensure both his and the Deirans' loyalty to Oswiu—in theory, at least.

PROMISES, PROMISES

Cyning sceal on healle
beagas dælan

*The king in his hall
shares out rings*

IT COMES AS SOMETHING

of a surprise to hear from Bede that Penda, the pre-
eminent heathen warlord of the mid-seventh century, tolerated
the preaching of Christianity in Mercia. He did not despise
Christians, we hear: only hypocrites.[203] That is to say, he reserved
his contempt for those kings who, having converted, failed to
practise what they preached. Bede was trying to set the stage for
the conversion of the Mercians and Middle Angles and, given
what he had previously said of Penda, he had some explaining to
do. The context was, broadly, the acceptance of the faith by several Anglo-Saxon kingdoms in the early 650s and specifically the
conversion of Penda's son Peada. Bede revealed something of his
own prejudices here as well as trying to unknot the complexities
of a rash of diplomatic initiatives in which sometimes Oswiu and
sometimes his son Alhfrith took the lead.

Bede, writing with the benefit of hindsight in the 730s, identified three strands of Christianity active in the first decades of
the English conversion. His bias against British Christians is
blatant and uncompromising. They were not just wrong; they

were wicked.* Not only had they failed to step into line after the Augustinian mission; they had wilfully refused to obey the instruction of the Papacy and, worse, they had neglected their holy duty to assist in the conversion of the heathen English. Their kings, Cadwallon in particular, had made war on the Christian English of Northumbria. Even their own priests (and Bede is flagrant in his partisan use of Gildas's sixth-century rantings) believed they had lost God's favour as a result of their impiety, infidelity and rapine. Perhaps Penda felt the same way about his contemporaries in Powys, Gwynedd and beyond. One of Bede's difficulties was that, in traducing British Christians and tarring them all with same brush, he found it difficult to discuss those British Christians in English territories who had kept the faith alive against all odds; and so they have effectively been written out of the Bedan narrative. The history of the Borders churches, with which Bede must have been familiar, is passed over; so too are the probable British origins of one or two of his heroes: Cuthbert, for example.

Bede was slightly less uncomfortable with the Irish question. The Irish, he believed, were wrong, stubbornly so, in their reluctance to accept the orthodoxy of the (true) Catholic church of which he, Bede, was such an ardent disciple. But the Ionan mission which Oswald had fostered provided an exemplar of ascetic virtue for which Bede could not hide his admiration, and many of his contemporaries suffered by comparison. Most of the missionary conversions of the southern English had, in the first instance, been undertaken by Irish monks or those Englishmen whom they had trained. The Augustinian church had perfomed very little missionary work: it was diocesan, essentially urban, and its English mission was to restore the system of bishoprics which ministered to the existing faithful (however many of them there

* I am most grateful to students of the North East Centre for Lifelong Learning for many discussions on this subject, which clarified some of these arguments—in particular to Alan Hinton.

still were) by converting, or reconverting, their kings.

Bede, too, despised hypocrites. He gave heathen warriors like Penda and Æthelfrith comparatively sympathetic treatment: they possessed the virtues of their faults; they were God's instruments of retribution. The Christian life must be one of virtue, humility, generosity and forgiveness, as exemplified by Aidan. Those very rare kings who lived up to the divine responsibilities of their office (Oswald, Oswine) were constant reminders of the failings of others, especially Bede's contemporaries. God had not granted dispensation to kings to break His rules; those who, like Oswiu, committed terrible crimes, must pay. Even so, Bede was sufficiently Anglo-Saxon in his outlook to accept the necessity of a just war, or one fought in defence of the fatherland.

From the dynastic muddle of the early 650s Bede tried to draw his providential message; it was by no means straightforward. Alhfrith was Oswiu's son by Rhieinmelth; half-Briton, he had been born before Oswiu's succession and might therefore be regarded as ineligible to succeed; he had a sister, Alhflæd, of marriageable age. Oswiu's second marriage, to Eanflæd, had by now produced their first and his third son, Ecgfrith. He was too young to be a direct threat to anyone, but his birth must have underlined for Alhfrith the long-term weakness of his own position. There was also Oswald's son Œthelwald to consider: he was absolutely eligible to succeed his uncle and bore the genetic stamp of his illustrious father. He had replaced Oswine as sub-king of Deira in about 651, but whether this was Oswiu's initiative or his own independent challenge, is unclear. To these three Northumbrian athelings one must add Talorcan, king of the Picts. He was the son of Eanfrith, the half-brother of Oswald and Oswiu who had briefly ruled Bernicia before Oswald; succeeding to the Pictish throne in about 653 Talorcan might claim right of succession over at least Bernicia. Here are the makings of a particularly knotty and melodramatic Dark Age soap opera.

Like all the best soap operas this Shakespearean epic-in-the-making involved intermarriage between two great houses engaged in bitter conflict. Alhfrith married Penda's daughter Cyneburh and his sister Alhflæd married Penda's son Peada. Historians have often tried to read into this double alliance a sort of share-price index: was Oswiu's gifting of his daughter a sign of his weakness, hoping to stave off further Mercian attacks; or was it the other way round, with Penda hoping for a peaceful alliance so he could consolidate his rule at home? Were both kings more afraid of their own sons than their traditional enemies, or were they all just playing their hands expediently without a long-term plan, waiting to see how the dice fell? Well, the clues are there to be read. Bede places the initiative with Peada, whose father had installed him as sub-king of the Middle Angles (broadly modern Leicestershire and Northamptonshire). Bede says that Peada directly asked Oswiu for his daughter, and we might read into this the act of a prince asserting independence from his father by making a powerful ally. Oswiu, in time-honoured fashion, required that Peada become a Christian. Peada accepted these terms with the apparent enthusiastic support of Alhfrith, his recently acquired brother-in-law and evident friend. It all seems very clubby, although it is hard to imagine that the parental in-laws, Penda and Cynewise, were on the guest-list.

What lends this flurry of betrothals high political significance is that Peada received baptism from Bishop Finan of Lindisfarne in a grand ceremony accompanied by *ealdormen* and *gesiths* and their servants at one of Oswiu's principal royal estates: a place which Bede called *Ad Muram*.[204] Infuriatingly we do not know what Bede means by this 'At-the-Wall', despite the attempts of many generations of historians to pin it down. He tells us that the place was so called 'because it stands close to the wall which the Romans once built across the island of Britain', and that 'it is about twelve miles from the east coast'. We have modern villages called Wall, Walbottle, Wallsend and so on which fit the first part; but none of these is twelve miles from the sea. Walbottle has most often been suggested as a candidate for *Ad Muram* (Old English *botl* denotes a settlement); another is Newburn, a known *villa regia* and crucially the lowest fording point across the River Tyne. But twelve walking or rowing miles from the east coast at Tynemouth would bring a traveller to *Pons Aelius*, the site of a Roman bridge across the River Tyne and later the city of Newcastle. On the south side of the bridge an early monastery was built at Gateshead (*Ad Capra*: the goat place); the north side would be the natural focus for a *villa regia*; Hadrian's Wall certainly passes close by, and the natural pairing of monastic establishments on opposite sides of a river makes logistical sense. However, the archaeological evidence for an important early Anglo-Saxon settlement beneath the Norman keep at Newcastle is not as yet convincing. Nor do we know what state the *Pons Aelius* was in during the seventh century; there has always been a ferry crossing here but, if we knew that the bridge was still functioning, that would strengthen Newcastle's case as a place of more than passing importance.[205]

Either way, Bede is referring to a significant location on the southern flank of Bernicia. It is made more significant by another baptism which took place there at 'about the same time', to use Bede's unhelpful phrase.[206] The conversion of King Sigeberht of Essex *Ad Muram* 'at the instance of King Oswiu', together with that of Peada, begins to look like a concerted attempt to outflank Penda politically by extending Oswiu's military and spiritual imperium over Penda's eastern neighbours. Penda's response was predictable. Within a year of these events he had invaded East Anglia and killed its Christian king Anna at the Battle of Bulcamp. Anna had been responsible for the conversion and restoration of another of Penda's enemies, Cenwalh of Wessex, and had recently annexed the lands around Ely; his strategically crucial position on

Penda's east flank made him an obvious target for the Mercian king to strike.

Now Penda unleashed his full fury against Oswiu. The details of this campaign are frustratingly few. The Nennian account is back-to-front, and obviously so; reconstructed, it should go something like this:

> The kings of the British... had gone forth with King Penda in his campaign to the city called Iudeu... Then Oswiu delivered all the riches that he had in the city into the hands of Penda, and Penda distributed them to the kings of the British, that is the 'Distribution of Iudeu'.[207]

Bede's more polished version does not substantially contradict this bald account of a great Northern 'congregation' against the Northumbrians:

> About this time King Oswiu was exposed to the savage and insupportable attacks of Penda... Oswiu was at last forced to promise him an incalculable and incredible store of royal treasures and gifts as the price of peace, on condition that Penda would return home and cease to devastate, or rather utterly destroy, the kingdoms under his rule.*

The critical issue is the identification of Iudeu, which Bede does not mention in the context of this narrative but which he does identify in a much earlier, general account of the geography of Britain.[208] In describing the Forth–Clyde isthmus he says that the Picts and the Irish were separated by two long arms of the sea. Halfway along the eastern branch (the Firth of Forth) was the city of *Giudi*. This is patently the same as the Nennian *Iudeu*. Historians have traditionally identified the city—that is to say, a fortress—with Stirling, on the grounds that it had natural defences and was so often the site of later conflicts. If Penda was able to drive Oswiu's forces all the way up to the Forth then Bernicia was in dire straits. But there are other ways of reading

* EH III.24; Colgrave and Mynors 1969, 291. There is a slight hint in Bede's language (*innumera et maiora quam credi*) that he is quoting directly from a poetic, perhaps British, source.

these accounts. Neither states that Penda besieged Oswiu in *Urbs Giudi*, so we might infer an alliance at-a-distance between Penda and, say, the Picts and Britons of Strathclyde, which would suit the general political situation of the mid-seventh century. The incalculable riches handed over as tribute to prevent further devastation must have come from Oswiu's treasury, accumulated from tributes exacted from the Picts and other nations during his reign; it seems that by the terms of the alliance the treasure was distributed between Penda's British allies and himself. The tribute did not end there: Bede says that Ecgfrith, Oswiu's young son by Eanflæd, was given as hostage into the care of Penda's queen, Cynewise. This set the seal on what was evidently supposed to be a treaty to end the conflict and render Bernicia, if not Deira, subject to Mercian imperium. The balance of power had shifted decisively; except that one of the parties did not see things that way.

A Northumbrian reverse on the edge of Pictland, at the hands of Penda's British allies and perhaps involving Oswiu's kinsman King Talorcan, would have been seen by the British (and their historians) as a great triumph and by Oswiu as one of those fortunes of war. Since the summer of 2009 archaeologists have naturally contemplated the possibility that the Staffordshire hoard is a share of this great treasure carried back to Mercia by Penda's men or his British allies; if so, they were rather careless with it. The jury is, as yet, out on that: the 650s would be at the earliest end of the possible date-range of its dumping. What we can say is that Oswiu, humiliated as he was, did not suffer catastrophic defeat; for at the end of 655, perhaps the same year as the 'Distribution of Iudeu', perhaps a year after, he was able to bring Penda to a final, decisive battle on his own terms in territory much closer to home.

Bede's account of the campaign of 655, which ended deep into the winter months in the south of the region of *Loidis* (modern Leeds) raises a number of awkward questions. He says that Penda refused to accept Oswiu's great treasure 'for he was determined to destroy and exterminate the whole people from the greatest to the least'.[209] The British sources surviving in the Nennian account suggest strongly that the treasure was handed over; how to reconcile these opposites? I think the acquisition of Ecgfrith as a hostage is decisive in showing that the deal was in fact done: vast quantities of treasure were handed over along with the even more precious legitimate son of the Northumbrian king. Subsequent to the summer campaign, which historians agree must have ranged all the way from the southern borders of Northumbria to the Forth and which led to a punitive treaty, someone broke faith. Either Penda continued to raid—on his way home?—or, having paid him off, Oswiu decided that he did not, in retrospect, like the terms. I think the former is more likely, because Oswiu, by breaching his tributary terms, would have risked his son being executed. He might conceivably have taken that risk but it is hard to see him being forgiven by his all-too-active queen.

Where the great ancient road known as the Roman Ridge between Castleford and Doncaster (now the A639) crosses the River Went (or *Winwæd*) at Thorpe Audlin, it is prone to periodic flooding. Time out of mind north–south traffic has been squeezed between the Humber-head wetlands and the lower slopes of the Pennines; any further to the east and the road would have been too frequently impassable: it must have been an engineer's nightmare. Wherever the road between Corbridge in Northumberland and Lincoln, a hundred and sixty miles to the south-east, crosses a river there is a risk of flooding; and armies moving along it from the Roman period onwards were vulnerable to the strategic flaws of fords and bridges: they are choke points where a pursuing host can catch its prey. Likewise, they can act as points of defence along a line of retreat. Between Corbridge and Lincoln at least seven battles were fought in the seventh century along the line of this road; probably there were many more unrecorded. The battle on the River *Winwæd* was as important as any.

We cannot say for sure how Oswiu and a small Northumbrian force came to meet Penda's great army here in the middle of December. Bede's providential version has it that Oswiu, hearing that Penda refused to accept peace, bound himself with an oath: 'If the heathen foe will not accept our gifts, let us offer them to him who will, even the Lord our God.' He promised that if God granted him victory he would give his baby daughter Ælfflæd and twelve small estates to the church. It turns out to have been one of the more significant oaths in British history. In this spirit, says Bede, Oswiu entered the fight with his tiny army.

Penda's forces were considerable. He boasted the banners of no fewer than thirty legions, according to Bede. This must mean that he had thirty warbands under their own commanders at his disposal: many of these were *duces regii*, *ealdormen* and sub-kings from the provinces under Mercian control; but there were also kings of tributary nations. They included British chiefs such as Cadafael, son of Cadwallon of Gwynedd, and perhaps contingents from further north. They included Æthelhere, king of the East Angles. They also included Oswald's son Œthelwald, king of Deira, who seems in extremis to have nailed his colours not to the mast of his uncle's standard but—treacherously—to that of his seemingly more powerful Mercian neighbour. The *Winwæd* was, indeed, right on the border between his territory and Mercia. One might legitimately also ask who was not present? Peada, son of Penda, king of Middle Anglia and son-in-law of Oswiu, was not; or if he was, he did not fight on his father's side: few who did lived to tell the tale.

Penda's army, then, was large and powerful by Early Medieval standards: in the several thousands and full of senior, experienced commanders. Long after the end of a campaigning season in which he had been bested and humiliated—perhaps in fury that Penda had broken the terms of their agreement; perhaps at the behest of his queen (had she laid the proverbial sword in his lap?)

whose young son lay in Mercian hands; perhaps on the tail of Penda's victorious and crapulous return home after a year of rampage—Oswiu struck south along Ermine Street hoping to catch his enemy by surprise. He does not seem to have been able to call on many allies, which suggests that his plan had not been long in gestation. Did Œthelwald play a role in the time and place of battle? Did he give Penda intelligence of the attack; or was he playing both sides? We cannot say; but when it came to battle Oswald's son did rather less than justice to his father's reputation and, having apparently been in the vanguard of Penda's army, drew his forces aside to await the outcome 'in a place of safety'.[210]

Penda's army must, I think, have been positioned on the north side of a river which, according to Bede, was swollen by heavy rains. Their line of retreat, if indeed they were retreating or merely unsuspecting of attack, was cut off. The Nennian source, in describing Cadafael's night-time defection in the hours before the battle, has been taken as a hint by some that Oswiu, like his brother before him, launched the decisive attack at dawn in the Irish tradition. It would explain the ensuing chaos. The Mercians and their allies were driven back into the waters of the swollen river; there was no escape. Hundreds, both warriors and their chiefs, were cut down or drowned in the flooded river, encumbered by booty, weaponry and soaking clothes. So disastrous was the battle for the Mercian alliance that few if any of the thirty commanders survived. In the case of the East Anglian king, his entire host was slaughtered. Many more drowned in flight than were destroyed by the sword in battle, according to Bede's bald but telling account. The last great heathen king of the Anglo-Saxons was cut down with all his followers and Oswiu, as improbably as his brother, had pulled off a brilliant victory, one with profound consequences. Once again, the luck of the Idings had held.

The immediate consequence was to elevate King Oswiu from the status of a lone wolf in the forest to the sword-wielding

Christian imperium which Oswald had enjoyed and which, it must have seemed for so long, would be denied his brother. Oswald's legacy as a hybrid Christian-warrior king, patron of the Irish church and of other Christian kings, was finally assured. In his hour of need Oswiu had, like Edwin before him, made a Faustian pact. Under the eye of his queen he would now repay those promises and more. Once again the efficacy of prayer before battle in the name of the Columban vision of political Christian kingship had been proven. The last great champion of heathenism was dead. And, what is more, Oswiu's prodigal son Ecgfrith was restored to him.

Early Medieval kings were not much more prone to sentiment than tyrants of any other period. They ruled by expedient in an expedient world. Their political decisions were made, by and large, on the sort of criteria familiar to observers of modern politics. Political histories tend to consist of the repayment, when in power, of pledges made on the way up. Presidents, prime ministers, dare one say archbishops and popes, media barons and bankers all face the dilemmas posed by a system of patronage whose rules are as unchanging as human nature. What one pays to whom over how long is a nicety of the game. Selling one's soul to the Devil is a trope with a long pedigree.

Those aspiring men and women who find themselves without what eighteenth-century naval officers called 'interest'—that is, influence or access to sympathetic patrons with influence—tend to have to make bolder pledges than those who can count on surer support. The exiled tribal prince is a perfect type for the hero lacking 'interest', in a weak position, possessing little to bargain with except hope. Edwin, Oswald, Oswiu and many another before and since (one thinks offhand of Elizabeth Tudor in the 1550s; of Churchill in 1939; of Lenin in Zurich; or Bonaparte in 1799 and again in 1815) must, like Caesar, cast their die, cross their Rubicon and see what befalls.

Edwin had promised Paulinus that if he regained his kingdom he would convert to Christianity. He delayed the fulfilment of that promise for many years until he had wrung more out of it. Edwin, once king, was in a strong negotiating position: he was able to make an informed political decision which weighed very carefully the pros and cons of taking his people from the familiar, if whimsical, homeland of the Germanic pantheon of capricious gods into the promised land of a single, omnipotent being. This God promised life after death to a people addicted to augury and sympathetic magic and deeply sceptical of phenomena they could not witness themselves. In return, He required adherence to a code of conduct not entirely at odds with the heathen mind but much more demanding: more demanding because the code had a purely rational logic behind it. It was this rationality, more than the promise of everlasting life, which attracted a new generation of canny tyrants, who saw its potential as a civilising political tool.

Oswald and his younger brother are special cases not only because, having been converted during impressionable youth in an atmosphere of extreme spiritual and political potency, they were proper 'believers'; but also because their hybrid upbringing imbued them with a strong sense of the potential for rational kingship. Their teachers—Ségéne, Aidan, the monks of Colm Cille's spiritual kingdom-on-earth—were clever, learned men, intellectuals who could and did argue a case with passion and reason. If heathen kingship was about the embodiment of tribal luck in the person of the king, heathen practice was about raising the odds and predicting the success of a venture, whether it was the harvest, childbirth or the outcome of a battle. The death of the king voided all bets. Christian missionaries attempted to show kings that by implementing the teachings of Christ they ensured themselves and their earthly kingdoms a life beyond the mortal. The lessons taught by Aidan to his Bernician protégés were intended to instruct them in how to be good kings; to show that even if they fell from perfection they could expiate their sins; that effect followed cause; that intention affected outcome; that the luck of a Christian people would survive the earthly passing of a king; that their prayers after death could ensure his everlasting rule with God in Heaven and the continuation of their tribal fortunes.

Their Germanic heritage and the patronage of the kings of Dál Riata taught the Bernician princes much about tribal models of kingship, its potency and vulnerabilities. Here were two young men of shining parts, in whose upbringing huge energies were invested, with the chance to see kingship, and by extension statehood, as a project with potential in the longer term. Their sort of kingship must survive the death of the person of the king. Oswald's sacrifice in battle was in real terms made for the benefit of the grander project: the foundation of a Christian, rational state. We cannot say that Oswald was explicitly aware of his place in this grand scheme; he more than any other was forced into expediency; but his mentors were and so, it seems, was his brother.

In the aftermath of the triumph at the *Winwæd* Oswiu must, before he could fulfil the promises made before battle, deal with practicalities. Œthelwald was removed from the throne of Deira and replaced by Oswiu's battle-lieutenant Alhfrith, whose marriage to Penda's daughter qualified him for guardianship of the southern flank of Northumbria. We do not know what happened to Oswald's perfidious son; there is a suggestion that he retired to a monastic foundation at Kirkdale on the southern edge of the North York Moors;* more likely he paid for his treachery with summary execution. Here was one atheling who, seeing his place in the pecking order diminish year by year, scion by scion,

---

* In the nineteenth century an engraved tomb-slab at St Gregory's Minster, Kirkdale, is supposed to have read *Cyninge Æthelwald*; modern archaeologists are generally sceptical. Wood 2008.

had made a pact with the wrong devil. Peada, Oswiu's son-in-law, who had not followed Penda into battle, was rewarded by his confirmation as king of the Southern Mercians, those peoples living to the south-east of the River Trent. Bede reports that he did not enjoy the fruits of his kingdom for long; it was said that his wife, Oswiu's daughter Alhflæd, treacherously had him murdered a year later. Here is the tip of a political iceberg whose below-the-surface machinations are beyond our ken, if not our imaginations.

Oswiu's youngest daughter (Ælfflæd was just over a year old) was given to the church as a sort of virgin sacrifice (as her mother had been) and twelve small estates, of ten hides each, were offered for the foundation of monasteries. Oswiu's increasing political sophistication is shown very clearly in his dispositions. Six of the estates were located in Bernicia, six in Deira, in a conscious attempt to join two kingdoms and two separate peoples into one. Unification was a project which had been attempted by several predecessors and which had not survived any of them. Oswiu's deliberately even-handed gift was intended to aid permanent unity and, once again, one detects the hand of his queen, Eanflæd. But there is more to be wrung from the bare facts of these monastic foundations. We know what sort of gift ten hides amounted to because the Laws of King Ine prescribed the food render expected from an estate of that size (see Chapter XI). Bede says that the ten-hide estate was 'small'. Oswiu was not giving away a substantial portion of the lands from which he could exact services and renders: his 'tenth' was enough to supply a modest family establishment and no more. The modest family now being installed on each of these twelve modest estates was to be one serving the king by its prayers instead of its arms. Its abbots (or abbesses) would be *gesiths* for Christ. The means Bede describes as being provided for monks 'to wage heavenly warfare and to pray with unceasing devotion that the race might win eternal peace'[211] included a site on which to build a permanent establishment and the loaves, honey, geese, ale, butter, hens and fodder which came from its dependent hamlets and small farms.

Where were these monasteries? Might their locations offer more tangible clues to Oswiu's thinking in alienating this land? Was the land his personally to give away or did these foundations take place on lands lacking a lord because of warfare or other strife—of which there had been much? We know the sites of just two of them, both in Deira. Reading between Bede's lines we infer that one was located at *Heruteu* (Hartlepool), the other at *Streanæshealh* (traditionally identified as Whitby, although there have always been doubts). Both lie on the coast at good harbours of strategic importance; the latter was probably the site of a Roman signal station. On the model of Lindisfarne we might suggest that this second tranche of donations was a direct instrument of royal power, with each lying close to a *villa regia,* as Lindisfarne did to Bamburgh. In this way the king and queen, on their peripatetic progress, might always be close to a monastery in whose prayers they were obliged to be prominent. Sponsors, after all, want a little something for their money. Other very early monasteries sited close to or within royal estates include those at Campodonum, Donemutha and Hexham. Furthermore, there are frequent associations between former Roman military establishments and early foundations which might be more than mere coincidence. I have a suspicion, and it is no more than that at present, that in inheriting at a remove some of the state functions of a defunct empire, Early Medieval kings might have identified, or been allowed to identify, prominent Roman military structures as being particularly in their gift, if not especially valuable except in terms of prestige. The rash of royal and early ecclesiastical sites along Hadrian's Wall would be compatible with such an idea. The historian Ian Wood believes that many of these early foundations must cluster along the Vale of Pickering and the

Lower Tyne Valley: an example of those 'cultural corelands' from which the Early Medieval kingdoms emerged in the sixth century.* This pattern is also echoed in Ireland, for example in the *Magh Tochair* of Donegal, and one sees hints of such a distribution in the British ecclesiastical centres of the Tweed Valley; so there were precedents from which the Idings might have derived inspiration. It has long been recognised that there is a more than coincidental similarity between the borders of some early kingdoms and the Anglo-Saxon dioceses which succeeded them; the shires of North Northumberland show plainly how secular ideas of territory were transferred to ecclesiastical usage.†

With this model in mind, Ian Wood suggests that of the twelve monasteries in this donation, we might add tentatively to Hartlepool and Whitby the early foundations at Gateshead, Bywell and Tynemouth (all on the Lower Tyne) and Stonegrave and Hovingham close to the Vale of Pickering.[212] All of these are plausibly situated on or near royal estates, and at the hearts of their respective kingdoms. The subliminal message concealed within Oswiu's repayment of his pledge is therefore one in which land was alienated from the royal portfolio and invested in a more subtle display of power: the patronage of initially small communities, whose abbots and abbesses were very likely of royal stock. This laid down a pattern for weaving extended networks of dynastic obligations among the Angles of the Northumbrian kingdoms. Here was a means of employing those client kin who were not eligible for the kingship but who might be in a position to lobby for rivals; of employing them in what must have appeared a harmless way as guardians of the collective spiritual memory and aspirations of the dynasty. Their permanence encouraged them to put down roots, to literally and figuratively stabilise the fateful,

* See p.95.
† Higham 1995: the putative boundary of the kingdom of the Hwicce and the Diocese of Worcester is a striking example; see p.191.

XVI

WOOD AND STONE

Ceastra beoð feorran gesyne,
orðanc enta geweorc

*Cities are seen from afar,
skilful work of giants*

BETWEEN THE LATER FOURTH
century and the time of Oswald no major stone structure
was built in Britain, so far as we know. There were no masons;
no specialist craftsmen who knew the secrets of lime mortar or
Roman concrete; there was no need for what one might call cor-
porate architecture, unless one includes defensive dykes intended
to keep armies at bay. Roman forts, town walls, aqueducts, roads,
baths and signal stations and maybe, just maybe, a Christian
stone church or two, still stood here and there, and there is
evidence that occasionally some of them were patched up. But
no new stone structures stood before Oswald's completion of
Paulinus's church at York in the late 630s; and forty years later
it was derelict. After that, nothing until Wilfrid had it repaired
and began construction of the abbeys at Ripon and Hexham after
670. Bridges, houses, churches—grandstands, even—from the
fifth to the mid-seventh centuries (and far beyond in royal and
domestic architecture) were conceived, designed and fashioned
in wood. A robust hall of hewn oak might stand for a hundred
years; most were abandoned, burned or remodelled long before
the material lifespan of the structure expired. It was an organic

world, adapted to changing fortunes and impermanence, to the rhythms of the seasons, to men's destinies and especially those of kings. The best wooden architecture, revealed by the excavations at Yeavering and later reflected in the design of illuminated manuscripts and high crosses, had pretensions to greatness as works of art and artifice. The poetic exuberance and joie de vivre of carved decoration celebrated the skills of a woodsman/metalsmith culture whose ideas of embellishment were inspired by the zoomorphia of brooches, shields and swords and more readily transmitted into the liquid potential of wood than stone. Only later in the seventh century did those skills return to Britain from the Continent. Until then common knowledge of Roman structural techniques was confined to wondrous contemplation of the works of giants.

When Finan came from Iona to succeed Aidan as bishop and abbot in 651, he...

> constructed a church on the island of Lindisfarne suitable for an episcopal see, building it after the Irish method, not of stone but of hewn oak, thatching it with reeds...[213]

Construction in stone was certainly known in Ireland—large numbers of early cells and shrines survive from this period—but the conceit that stone buildings reflected high status, dignity or grandeur did not belong in the Ionan tradition. It came from Rome. When Wilfrid commissioned the building of Hexham Abbey in the 670s his biographer overflowed with awe:

> My feeble tongue will not permit me to enlarge here upon the depth of the foundations in the earth, and its crypts of wonderfully dressed stone, and the manifold buildings above ground, supported by various columns and many side aisles, and adorned with walls of notable length and height, surrounded by various winding passages with spiral stairs leading up and down; for our holy bishop being taught by the Spirit of God, thought out how to construct these buildings; nor have we heard of any other house on this side of the Alps built on such a scale.[214]

Contrast Eddius's description of Hexham with Bede's of Lindisfarne a few years earlier:

> There were very few buildings there except for the church, in fact only those without which the life of the community was impossible. They had no money but only cattle; if they received money from the rich they promptly gave it to the poor; for they had no need to collect money or to provide dwellings for the reception of worldly and powerful men, since these only came to the church to pray and to hear the word of God. The king himself used to come, whenever opportunity allowed, with only five or six thegns, and when he had finished his prayers in the church he went away. If they happened to take a meal there, they were content with the simple daily fare of the brothers and asked for nothing more.[215]

In the physical transition from wood to stone, with its evident resonance for contemporaries, might be seen a metaphor for the conflicts and opportunities which Oswiu, Eanflæd and the Northumbrian church sought to manage in the ten years or so after the battle on the *Winwæd*. This decade has often been portrayed as one of crisis in the relations between kings and their priests, between an eccentric rural Irish church of pure asceticism and a worldly, orthodox Rome—not least because Bede painted it that way. It is also a little too easy to trace in the careers of two contemporary holy men, Cuthbert and Wilfrid, a personification of the crisis. Cuthbert, the Irish-trained English would-be hermit—simple in habits and needs, his relationship with his god deeply personal—stood squarely in the conservative tradition of Aidan and his successors. Wilfrid—charismatic, ambitious, Roman in taste and inclinations, diocesan in sympathies—was the orthodox reformer, scornful of what he saw as an uncanonical, reactionary tradition laughably out of date with the rest of the Catholic world. Hiding behind the rhetoric, as is so often the case with political change, lay the resolution of administrative incongruities that had become too awkward to ignore. Those involved at the blunt end saw conflict and crisis; those with a broader outlook saw an opportunity for progressive reform and harmony.

At the end of Oswald's reign in 642 there were half a dozen or so churches in Northumbria. The English part of Britain had about the same number of bishops. Rome's direct connection with the Anglo-Saxons was through Canterbury. Papal knowledge of the early Anglo-Saxon church was patchy: messengers travelled between Rome and its Atlantic outposts infrequently; information about the lands at the far end of the pilgrim route was almost always out of date. The Metropolitan Archbishop of Britain, Honorius, was the last of the original Augustinian mission. His successor, Deusdedit, would be the first native to hold the office.

Patronage and authority in the church were as diverse as its British, Irish and Roman cultural traditions. In Canterbury and its daughter sees authority was vested in the bishop according to a well-established Roman hierarchy. Monastic rule in the south was likely to vary with the person of the abbot and the traditions of the foundation, but abbots were subject to their bishops. The Irish church established by Oswald and Aidan at Lindisfarne had a very different notion of authority. In the monastery the abbot was supreme: he owed duty and allegiance to his patron and to his spiritual Lord, but to no other mortal; at Lindisfarne, as at Iona and many other Irish foundations, he was also the bishop so that diocesan functions, such as they were, were exercised by the paruchia of the mother church downwards to its dependencies. The British church looks as though it must have been something like that of Ireland: its Easter practices were certainly considered anachronistic by Augustine, although it seems that British bishops enjoyed primacy over the abbots of their monasteries. So long as there were few establishments these anomalies were either cherished as a form of diversity or overlooked. As the number of monastic houses and, we presume, lay churches began to multiply, so did the potential for inconsistency. Conflict, when it became a matter for state intervention, was almost bound to happen in Northumbria where, from the date of the foundation of Lindisfarne in 635, all three traditions existed side by side.

In the north of the kingdom British churches and British traditions seem to have predominated, judging by the surviving numbers of inscriptions, long-cist cemeteries, Eccles-type place-names and direct references to establishments such as *Mailros/* Melrose. Lindisfarne was founded south of the River Tweed bordering on this ecclesiastical province—deliberately so, perhaps. Such was Aidan's personal authority and such was the esteem and awe in which Colm Cille's Ionan *paruchia* was held that it seems British priests were content to belong in this sympathetic new order. But in any case Aidan was not a doctrinaire abbot and bishop; he came from a tradition in which the head of every foundation stood under God's judgement and no other; diversity was a matter of celebration in Irish tradition. He would probably have felt the same about James the Deacon, Paulinus's long-lived companion practising in his solitary church (of stone or wood, one wonders) near Catterick all those years. Did Aidan know of James? Did the latter visit his nominal bishop on Lindisfarne or did he unswervingly look south towards Canterbury and his Roman conscience?

Of the churches whose existence we can be sure of, we can also say that their patrons, that is to say those who had donated their land and owned the right to appoint their priests, were kings: Edwin, Oswald and Oswiu in Northumbria, Cynegisl in Wessex, Æthelberht in Kent and so on. Lindisfarne was as much Oswald's church as it was Colm Cille's. The land on which such establishments were founded came customarily with the obligation to render food and services to its owner, the king. Those services were not cancelled by the foundation of a church or monastery; they were commuted to prayer in perpetuity. After the death of the founding patron, his monks must continue to pray for his soul in payment for their freehold rights. If, as at Lindisfarne, the new king continued his patronage of the foundation, an interesting situation arose, as the Durham *Liber Vitae*, which lists the donors to Aidan's successors, implies. No new gifts of land and treasure to the community could, as it were, erase the founder's mark. Lindisfarne was the foundation of Oswald and always would be (despite a spurious later attempt to insert Edwin at the head of the list of patrons). It stood to reason that when later kings, their wives and collateral relations endowed the monastery anew, the efficacy of the monks' prayers for their patrons, old and new, must be diluted, so to speak. It equally stood to reason that kings and other wealthy members of the warrior elite should wish to demonstrate their Christian credentials by endowing new foundations in which their name headed the list of patrons. One cannot help thinking of the histories of great football clubs, with their chairmen's names emblazoned on shiny new stands which they have paid for, with the occasional successful manager or heroic striker sanctified by having his name replace that of a long-dead and partially forgotten donor on some part of the holy ground. Only the boldest (and richest) dare to provoke the wrath of the faithful by playing the ultimate trump card: razing the old stadium and raising a new one, with a single sponsoring name on it. The rules, rewards and risks of patronage and sanctity do not change much.

For Oswiu, it was not enough to continue his brother's patronage of Aidan at Lindisfarne. Oswine's murder was an opportunity to expiate his earthly sins and establish himself as the founding patron of a new monastery at Gilling. In anticipation of his victory over Penda and in thanks for the birth of his daughter, his munificence was cast twelvefold. None of these foundations would be as great as Lindisfarne, but in their profusion Oswiu and his queen ensured that their patronage was spread more equably among Northumbrians: so that the faith should be spread more widely, no doubt, but also so that the tangible and political value of their patronage should be distributed and demonstrated likewise. One great foundation had been enough for Oswald: one king, one great house, one relationship with a great holy man. With Oswiu's foundations, his relationships with abbots multiplied accordingly. But to whom were they to owe their ecclesiastical duty? And how were they to be controlled?

There was only one bishop of the Northumbrians, the ambition of Gregory and Paulinus to found a second metropolitan see at York having come unstuck in 632. After Aidan it was Finan and after Finan, who died in 661, it was another Ionan appointee, Colman. The bishops of Northumbria were by virtue of their Irish heritage and the founding patron, Oswald, also abbots of Lindisfarne. Even before the theatrical denouement of 664 at the Synod of Whitby there were tensions among Northumbria's senior churchmen, which show the potential flaws in this historic arrangement. This is demonstrated by the fortunes of a new community founded on the eastern edge of the Yorkshire Pennines at Ripon. Eata, its first abbot, had been a protégé of Aidan, trained in the Irish manner on Lindisfarne. By about 651 we find him in charge of the monastery at *Mailros*, or Melrose. It is possible that he was the founding abbot there but, as I have said, most historians now believe it was a pre-existing, British institution. In that case Aidan may have consciously deployed Eata there as a diplomatically safe, conciliatory deputy in an area of delicate British sensitivities. Several years later he moved to Ripon to found a new community there, taking the young Cuthbert with him as guest-master.[216] Perhaps the same motive applied: there were British Christian communities in the Pennines too. But this time there was a royal patron, the half-British Alhfrith, recently installed by his father Oswiu as sub-king over the Deirans. Oswiu had splashed his wealth in the foundation of those twelve ten-hide monasteries after the defeat of Penda; Alhfrith's friend, brother-in-law and fellow sub-king Peada had recently founded a

monastery at *Medehamstede* (Peterborough) with Oswiu's blessing. Alhfrith was keen to make his own mark on the ecclesiastical
map.

Ripon, regardless of Eata's personal loyalties to Lindisfarne
and Finan, was a long way from the mother-house and owing
its patronage to a collateral member of the ruling dynasty. How
might that play out? Aidan had received the unswerving loyalty of a former sub-king of Deira, the murdered Oswine, and
Alhfrith's relationship with Lindisfarne must initially have been
cordial, for Finan either gave Eata permission to leave Melrose or
was responsible for sending him there. But within three or four
years of his arrival at Ripon, Eata had been replaced:

> Meanwhile because the whole state of the world is frail and unstable as
> the sea when a sudden tempest arises, the aforesaid Abbot Eata with
> Cuthbert and other brethren whom he had brought with him was driven
> home, and the site of the monastery, which he had founded, was given to
> other monks to dwell in.[217]

More than replaced, then: he was expelled with all his companions. Here was an apparently open rift between the Deiran
church and the Bernician mother-house, precisely what Oswiu
had been trying to avoid. Not for the first time it brought into
serious question Oswiu's policy of setting up cadets of the royal
household as sub-kings. Oswine's murder had set an unfortunate precedent: Œthelwald had probably seen the shadow of
Alhfrith looming and made his ill-fated bid, jumping before he
was pushed; Alhfrith cannot but have seen himself in a similar
position, with Ecgfrith, Oswiu's young son by Eanflæd, coming
up on the rails. Was this a premeditated shot across the bows her-
alding a breach between father and son? Was Alhfrith testing the
murky waters preparatory to insurrection, or merely acting the
independent son to an overweening father? We are not privy; and
if Bede was, he does not say. What did that rift mean for ecclesiastical authority? How was Lindisfarne to react to the expulsion

of one of its favourite sons? What was Alhfrith's motive for this volte-face?

The beneficiary of the management coup at Ripon was Cuthbert's almost exact contemporary, Wilfrid. It is hard to like him: even his most ardent admirer and biographer Stephen* could not conceal Wilfrid's self-serving ruthlessness; but in his charismatic charm, self-belief, bloody-minded ambition and love of wealth, his relentless energetic pursuit of material and spiritual conquest, we are made acquainted with the most tangible and flawed human character of the age. Like Cuthbert he was born into a noble family, perhaps in Deira, in the year either side of Oswald's victory at Heavenfield. His father was a *gesith* with estates and connections at court. An argument with his stepmother (not the first or last in recorded history) prompted Wilfrid to leave home at fourteen and, on the recommendation of his father's friends, he was introduced to Queen Eanflæd. He was immediately noticed: clever, handsome and socially gifted, he found favour with the queen and when he declared his intention to devote his life to the church she gave him into the care of an elderly *gesith* called Cudda who, paralysed and tired of life at court, declared his intention to retire to Lindisfarne.

Under Aidan, then, in the last years of the bishop's life, Wilfrid was taught the rule of the Ionan monks. It was not enough: he dreamed of travelling to Rome. In about 652, after Aidan's death, he was given permission to leave Lindisfarne and the queen recommended him to her cousin Eorcenberht, king of Kent. We do not know how he travelled: in later decades, when the pilgrimage to Rome was almost a commonplace, there were a number of routes combining both land and sea. The coastal route was quicker; probably safer too. The land route offered the chance

---

* Stephen identifies himself in the preface to his *Life*; in EH IV.2 Bede referred to Wilfrid's singing master as 'Æddi, surnamed Stephen'. The assumption that the two are the same has led to a traditional ascription of the *Life* to Eddius Stephanus.

to visit shrines and churches of repute and make useful connections, but also to attract the attention of thieves and unfriendly
lords. Wilfrid stayed at Canterbury for a year before a suitable
travelling companion could be found for him; here he first read
the current orthodox version of St Jerome's translation of the
Psalms; he saw the workings and trappings of a more Continental
court and of the Augustinian church; he met Benedict Biscop, a
fellow Northumbrian who shared his ardent desire to see Rome
(Biscop made the journey no fewer than six times in his life) and
together they embarked on the pilgrims' trail through Frankia.
They will have taken passage from one of the Kentish ports such
as Sandwich or Sarre and probably sailed to Quentovic, the international port and trading settlement near the modern town of
Étaples on the River Canche in the Pas-de-Calais.

The route through France was designed according to taste,
as any tourist itinerary is. There were any number of churches
where a Latin-speaker might find hospitality; there were shrines
of great holy men like St Martin at Tours; there were the dangers
of the road and opportunities to see natural wonders. The Rhône
Valley became a well-trodden trail leading south through Lyons
to the Roman city of Arles, from where many pilgrims, dreading
the Alpine passes in winter, continued to the coast at Marseilles
and took passage by boat to Ostia and Rome (the journey on
which poetic pilgrim Percy Shelley would perish twelve hundred
years later).

At Lyons, the principal city of Gaul, full of architectural
splendours, pomp and dignity (as well as seedy court politics,
urban squalor and poverty) Wilfrid and Biscop parted; according to Eddius, Wilfrid found himself the protégé of Archbishop
Dalfinus* who wished to adopt him as his son and confer on him

---

* *VW* IV; this is a mistake on Eddius's part: Dalfinus was apparently the Count of
Lyons; his brother Annemundus was archbishop; Colgrave 1927, 153.

great estates and the hand of his daughter in marriage. Dalfinus was overwhelmed by Wilfrid's peaceful gentleness and saintly mind, we are told. However irritating the sycophantic tone of his partisan biographer, and in spite of history's negative judgement of his later career, Wilfrid's charisma, his immediate electric effect on those who met him, is unmistakeable.*

Dalfinus's flattery detained Wilfrid at Lyons for a year before he continued his journey to the holy city. In Rome Archdeacon Boniface, a papal counsellor, acted as his enthusiastic spiritual and canonical guide. Wilfrid assiduously visited the shrines of the martyrs, studied the books of the gospels and was taught the orthodox forms for the tonsure, the calculation of Easter and other ecclesiastical niceties. In the magnificent colonnaded basilica of Constantine, which contained the shrine of the founder of Christian Rome, the apostle Peter, he was blessed by Pope Eugene. During his months in the city Wilfrid saw many wonders and collected quantities of gifts and relics. On the return journey he was detained in Lyons for a further three years, taking the Roman tonsure, until Dalfinus was allegedly murdered by Queen Baldhild.†

Wilfrid finally returned to England at about the time that Eata was being given thirty or forty hides at Ripon to found his new monastery. On his appearance at the court of Northumbria Wilfrid, now in his mid-twenties, had the same effect on Alhfrith

---

* He reminds me of one other historical figure above all: the vain, death-or-glory genius Nelson whom men would follow into any adventure, whose presence almost literally and magically lit up every room into which he walked, if only his mood was right. There is an essential fragility in the type: it must be loved unconditionally, pampered, indulged. If it is nourished, it repays the devotion of its followers tenfold. Denied, it can turn very nasty indeed.

† Baldhild lived a remarkable life, having been born into a noble, possibly royal Anglo-Saxon family and sold into slavery in Gaul before becoming the wife of Clovis II. Under his successor Clotaire she retired to her monastery at Chelles and died in about 680. She almost certainly knew Hereswith, the sister of Saint Hild (see p.313), who also retired to Chelles after marriage into the East Anglian royal family.

as he had on so many others. He charmed, he wooed; he was adored. Alhfrith gave him a ten-hide estate on which to found his own monastery in the Roman manner. No-one has yet been able to identify the *Stanforda* which Eddius Stephanus identifies as the site of this new foundation (Stamford in Lincolnshire, Stamford Bridge near York and Stainforth in the Pennines have all been suggested). He rose quickly within the ranks of Alhfrith's retainers and in the king's estimation.

In Wilfrid's deposition of Eata from Ripon a year or two later in about 660, we are forced to read several narrative strands. There is Alhfrith's growing sense of self-confidence, his willingness to challenge his father's authority and perhaps his response to a Deiran constituency resentful of Bernician overlordship (both temporal and spiritual); his fear of a stepbrother growing in years and in potential threat (Ecgfrith was probably about fifteen in 660 and is thought to have married a year later). Alhfrith must also have been sensible to the growing number of kingdoms to the south whose churches were spiritually and politically allied to the Roman cause: in all senses, North and South met in Deira in the late 650s. Then there is Eanflæd's role at court. She was Roman in outlook, having been raised and educated in Frankia and at Canterbury. She must promote the interests of her sons (the last, Ælfwine, was born in about 661) and daughters, if necessary at the expense of her stepchildren. There is Wilfrid, her former protégé, now at Alhfrith's court, very much the bright young thing and thoroughly Roman and Frankish in outlook. In his patronage of Wilfrid it is possible to see an attempt by Alhfrith to advance his cause both by asserting independence from his Lindisfarne-affiliated father and by attaching himself to the Deiran party and the sensibilities of his stepmother. Would he, like Oswine and Œthelwald, over-play his hand?

Oswiu may have seen the Romanisation of his court and satellite as a moral threat; more likely he recognised it as a political challenge to be met and then exploited. He must already have been considering the administrative problems posed by the multiplication of monasteries, abbots and their reciprocal relations with the courts of Bernicia and Deira and the mother-house of Lindisfarne. He appears to have maintained his personal allegiance to Iona but he was far too canny and experienced a politician to allow sentiment to guide his strategy. He had not been deaf either to the wisdom of his Irish mentor Aidan or that of his worldly Gallo-Kentish wife.

Oswiu was the first Northumbrian king we know of who deployed sub-kings to rule Deira. Historians have often seen this as an aspect of his military and political weakness. I think it more likely that, just as he was willing to explore novel relations with the church as a means of political expression, so he was experimenting with political structures, realising that a more complex form of kingship was required to successfully manage his new imperium—probably, after Penda's destruction, the greatest in extent of any seventh-century king.

The world was changing, growing larger. It was not enough to conquer and subdue neighbouring kingdoms: one must consider their administration and the patronage of their nobility. Young men of noble blood had, for the first time, a choice of career either in the king's host or in the church. The church offered men with a diverse range of talents, with intellectual rather than martial zeal—men like Wilfrid and Cuthbert—a chance to forge careers which, dependent as they were on royal patronage, meant they must also exploit political opportunities as they arose. The admirable and unworldly spirituality of the Irish church might not sufficiently meet the new challenge. Oswiu and his brother had enjoyed intensely personal relations with Aidan and his successors and with their mentors on Iona. The abbot and bishop of Lindisfarne fulfilled a broad pastoral role but was able also to act as a personal chaplain and supernumerary advisor to the king (not unlike, in this respect, a tribal chief-priest: a Coifi). With the accretion of more numerous and larger estates came necessarily a managerial role equal to that of a great landowner. That role would lend them increasing power: Aidan's eventual successors, the prince-bishops of Durham, were potentates in their own right. Moreover, one thing above all separated the ranks of churchmen from their secular friends and lords: they could write. Edwin may have been the first king to exploit this magical talent, if it was he who commissioned Paulinus to draw up the Tribal Hidage. Did Oswiu also realise the administrative and legal potential of the written record? There is one small item of evidence that he did, in a remarkable entry in the Anglo-Saxon Chronicle where Oswiu's mark on written history is his signature, a simple cross that adorned the re-endowment of *Medehamstede* in 664.*

And then, there was the anomalous set of relations between the abbots of the new houses and their bishop. If Ripon was founded originally as a daughter-house of Lindisfarne—as, presumably, all the other new monasteries were—to whose rule did Wilfrid now submit? Oswiu, I think, did not require a direct challenge from his son to make him aware of the need to resolve these issues. But Wilfrid's overly large presence on the field of play may well have precipitated him towards decisive action. That, and the death in 661 of Lindisfarne's second abbot/bishop, Finan. His successor, Colman, was an Irishman of equally impeccable Ionan credentials and just as 'frugal and austere' as his predecessors.[218] Oswiu,

---

* Laud (E) version of the ASC *sub anno* 656; the re-endowment was sponsored by Penda's son King Wulfhere, brother of Peada, and confirmed by Oswiu in about 664. Other signatories, all of whom contributed a single + as their mark, included several kings, Cyneburh the wife of Alhfrith, Deusdedit the Archbishop of Canterbury, and the young abbot of Ripon, Wilfrid. This is one of the earliest accounts of a written charter of endowment, confirmed by a Papal Bull of Vitalian. It indicates that the church, at least, recognised the value of a king's signature and a written record of endowment as evidence of title deed.

Bede says, 'greatly loved' his new bishop; he may also have seen in his arrival the opportunity to embark on much-needed reform with a man who might, by virtue of his relative inexperience and recent arrival, be channelled in a progressive direction.

Bede would have us believe that the resolution of these difficulties was prompted by a more domestic, personal conflict. Eanflæd had come from Kent bringing Roman rituals and services and her own chaplain, Romanus. James the Deacon had been observing Roman practice in the observation of Easter and other ceremonies these thirty years. At Lindisfarne, Finan had had his own internal antagonist, another Irishman called Ronan who had spent time on the Continent and was now a fervent supporter of orthodox practice, much to Finan's very real irritation. With such tensions in the air, Bede tells a story of disharmony and dysfunction at the heart of the Northumbrian court:

> ... it is said that in these days it sometimes happened that Easter was celebrated twice in the same year, so that the king had finished the fast and was keeping Easter Sunday, while the queen and her people were still in Lent and observing Palm Sunday.[219]

There is no doubt that in Bede's day and for a hundred years before, the Irish method of calculating the date of Easter had been regarded as outdated and anomalous by Rome. Blood had been spilled after Augustine's disastrous meeting with the British bishops in 604; pressure had been applied; many southern Irish churches had submitted and been brought into line with papal orthodoxy as far back as the 630s when a delegation was sent from Ireland to Rome and returned in no doubt of what Catholic rectitude required. A letter survives, written by Cummian of Clonfert to Oswald's friend and mentor Ségéne, abbot of Iona, about the time that Oswald was returning to Bernicia to reclaim his patrimony. Begging the paruchia of Colm Cille to fall into line, he famously described the position of those he saw as bigoted reactionaries:

Can anything be more absurd than to say of our mother the church—
Rome errs, Jerusalem errs, Antioch errs, and the whole world errs, the
Irish and Britons alone are in the right?[220]

Iona held out for almost another century. For the church of
Colm Cille it was not so much that the precise method of calculation of Easter was doctrinally critical; it was a matter of the
independence of the Ionan paruchia from any outside attempt to
regulate its rule and observances; it was a matter of culture. The
arguments on both sides have such profound echoes for our contemporary relations with Europe and attempts to harmonise various political and economic practices across the Continent that it
is no wonder that the debate has held such fascination for historians. Easter was not the only issue, either. The form of monastic
tonsure and various other disciplinary matters touched sensitive
nerves on both sides; it came down to arguments about papal
authority and discipline and the desire to belong, or not belong,
to a united European vision. *Plus ça change...*

Bede's account of chaos at court is surely an exaggeration. The
king and queen had been married for twenty years and somehow
muddled along; they may have led comparatively separate lives
or been content to tolerate each other's personal tastes and loyalties, for all we know. Besides, as the historian Richard Abels has
pointed out, the number of years in which the difference in Easter
calculation might have affected the court in this way was very
small: in the twenty-two years after Oswiu's marriage to Eanflæd
in 643 Easter was celebrated on the same day by both Roman and
Irish reckonings no fewer than nineteen times.[221] Crisis? What
crisis?

The Bay of the Lighthouse

God sceal on heofenum,
dæda demend

*God is in heaven,
the judge of deeds*

WHITBY IS A BUSTLING AND atmospheric north Yorkshire fishing port variously inundated by black-coated, mascaraed Goths bearing well-thumbed copies of Bram Stoker's *Dracula*, ice-cream-licking daytrippers, folk musicians and the odd archaeologist on pilgrimage to the ruins of the famous abbey which stands defiant on the cliffs above the town like a Caspar David Friedrich painting: by turns eerie, wind-blasted and steeped in piously romantic mythology.

In 664, even as God's judgement was visited on His people by a virulent outbreak of what is suspected to have been bubonic plague, churchmen and women gathered here from all parts of the island and beyond to debate the Paschal controversy. The summer had begun portentously with an eclipse of the sun on May Day.[222] Despite various problems with Bede's identification of *Streanæshealh* most archaeologists and historians believe that Whitby is the place he meant and that his translation into Latin, *sinus fari*, can reasonably be interpreted as meaning 'the Bay of the Lighthouse'. The lighthouse in question has never been found, but it would fit well within the string of Roman signal stations which dotted the Yorkshire coast in the late fourth century after a great seaborne invasion of the British province by Picts, Scots and Saxons: the so-called Barbarian Conspiracy.

As an Early Medieval conference centre, Whitby was admirably placed. It has a fine, sheltered port accessible from anywhere along the east coast of Britain and from the ports of Northern Gaul. All along that coast or its navigable riverine arms lay important royal or ecclesiastical sites and, perhaps as importantly, it was familiar to the merchants of the North Sea littoral, that great trading basin which connected Britain economically, culturally and linguistically with the Low Countries, Scandinavia and the kingdom of the Franks. Between the Tees and the Humber are several candidates for early *wic* sites where coastal traders could beach their shallow-bottomed craft; indeed, a town which today looks rather cut off from the world was a perfectly central place in the mid-seventh century, with a harbour capable of accommodating substantial sea-going craft. Not for nothing were early monasteries—Iona, Derry, Lindisfarne, Whitby, Jarrow and Wearmouth, for example—sited on significant nodes in what the researcher Cowan Duff has termed the European Ecclesiastical Superhighway, linking the British Isles with Gaul, Rome, Byzantium and the Holy Land.[223] By the end of the seventh century churchmen and women were seasoned travellers, with reasons to travel and a network of safe, comfortable staging posts whose incumbents shared a common culture and the language of the Roman Empire. The communications revolution of our own times can hardly be more significant than this key element in the survival of the cultures of late antiquity.

That is not to say that the convening of a council here was not a major logistical undertaking. If Whitby was one of Oswiu's twelve ten-hide foundations then it could hardly have been expected to support the large numbers of delegates and their entourages who must have arrived in a steady stream during the late summer months of 664—very likely, did they but know it, bringing the deadly plague with them. The council was a royal initiative, and royal estates must therefore have been pressed into catering, transport and construction service even if the ecclesiastical participants might be content to spend some of their time in fasting: talking is hungry work. Summonses to the Council must have been sent out in good time, accommodation organised or built, stabling and fodder prepared and provided; the monastery's smiths and farriers must have worked double shifts unless the kings brought their own establishments with them.

The great gaunt ruins of the Benedictine abbey built in the thirteenth century on the headland at Whitby have almost nothing in common with the foundation credited to Edwin's great-niece Hild in the late 650s. She, the daughter of that Hereric who was murdered at the British court of Elmet during Edwin's reign, was baptised by Paulinus and after her great uncle's exile probably went to live with her sister Hereswith who had married into the royal family of East Anglia. Hild's formative spiritual education took place under Aidan at Lindisfarne during the Deiran rapprochement of Oswiu's reign, so that when the king invited her to found the monastery at Whitby her outlook was that of Rome overlain with Iona: her sympathies were Irish; her establishment is likely to have been modest and, in layout, similar to that at Lindisfarne. But she had already been abbess of both the unnamed monastery on the north bank of the River Wear and that on the headland at Hartlepool. *Streanæshealh* presented her with a chance to initiate an ideal community in both spirit and material form. If, as seems likely, she had much in common with her cousin and successor Queen Eanflæd we might see the inception, in this great gathering, of the idea of Whitby as the Deiran royal cult centre which it later became.

Two important campaigns of excavation on the headland have failed to show exactly where the heart of Hild's complex was. It must have been reasonably large because she was the head of both male and female communities here: Whitby, like Hartlepool, was a so-called double monastery under the rule of a single, female abbess. The complex of stone foundations revealed to the north of the medival abbey in the 1920s was not excavated with modern techniques and many of the records were lost.* What might have been the flimsy remains of the earlier monastery, made of wattle and daub, were thought by the original excavators to be no more than internal partitions in later stone buildings, and what survives of the site record does them no justice.[224] As in so many other cases, like Lindisfarne and Iona, the focus of Hild's monastery was probably overlain and largely obliterated by the later medieval complex so that its layout and form will probably never be elucidated. Was it, one wonders, of wood and wattle, or had the idea of stone buildings formed in the minds of its founding royal patron and his abbess?

Excavation of a substantial cemetery to the south of the medieval abbey in the 1990s has thrown up the intriguing possibility that Christian burials were taking place here long before Hild's foundation. Roman pottery was recovered from some of the burials and a very late or sub-Roman glass bead was also found in a grave. If, like Old Melrose, Whitby was the site of a former or existing British church, here is both a motive for its foundation, or re-foundation, and a twist to the orthodox account of the Council of Whitby. Bede portrays the dispute as being between the Ionan-inspired church of Lindisfarne and that of Rome and Canterbury but we know that the British church survived and even thrived in many places in the West and North. There may well have been

* Attempts by the distinguished archaeologists Dame Rosemary Cramp and my own teacher Philip Rahtz to reconstruct the evidence show that by the time of the first Viking raids on Northumbria around 800, Whitby must have been a substantial settlement. In fact, it had by then become the royal burial place of Northumbrian kings and queens, apparently taking on some of the tribal and dynastic functions of Yeavering.

British bishops in attendance at Whitby, unmentioned either by Bede or by Wilfrid's biographer Eddius Stephanus, because by their day the British church in Northumbria was irrelevant—or they wished it to be irrelevant. It is not hard to see where British sympathies might have lain.

Bede says that the Council was called jointly by Alhfrith and Oswiu to resolve the debate over the timing of Easter and other matters of orthodoxy; but even if that were substantially true, the political tensions of the preceding few years ensured that there were more expedient matters at stake. King Oswiu, Bede says, believed that nothing could be better than the practices and teachings of the Irish church, which he and his brother Oswald had been taught during their childhood on Iona; his natural sympathies lay with Colm Cille. Oswiu, then, had no personal aesthetic or spiritual dilemma on which he sought counsel, unless he genuinely sought Paschal peace in the royal bedchamber. If that was his only problem, the bedchamber is where that dispute would have remained and been resolved. For him this was probably not a matter of conscience: Northumbrian unity and the recognition of his imperium were at stake. On the other hand Alhfrith, influenced by Wilfrid and other Romanists, threatened by the looming presence of Ecgfrith and wishing to flex his Deiran muscles, looks as though he were seeking a showdown with his father and was prepared to stake all on the outcome of the debate over orthodoxy.

Both men had much to lose. In handing over the political debate to the church and in siting the Council in Deira, Oswiu looks, as so often beforehand, to have been playing a weak hand. If the Council under Alhfrith's and perhaps Eanflæd's influence resolved that the Northumbrian church should convert to orthodoxy it could not be seen as anything other than a defeat for Lindisfarne and for the king: it would fatally compromise his position. The primacy of Canterbury over Iona would be irrevocable. If Oswiu refused to convene the Council or accept its decision he would be isolated at a time when his southern imperium was beginning to be threatened by the emergence of Penda's son Wulfhere in Mercia. Wulfhere may have been converted under Oswiu's auspices, but he married a Kentish princess and politically he looked to the South for support.

Alhfrith, if he lost, would have to submit to his Bernician father and lose the precious independence he had been asserting, ultimately to be replaced by Ecgfrith as successor-in-waiting; or he must resort to open rebellion. The stakes, then, were high. But in jointly hosting the Council at Whitby, on Deiran soil but under the aegis of a Lindisfarne-trained Bernician protégé of Deiran royal stock, Oswiu was playing a subtle hand; not necessarily a weak one. We cannot, at this remove, tell whether the cards were marked, with senior clergy lined up behind their royal patrons and ready to vote according to a whip, or whether their intellectual or spiritual independence was in any way corruptible. Nor can we say what words of counsel Eanflæd might have offered her husband: did she attempt to persuade him of the virtues of the Roman cause or did she, as Anglo-Saxon heroic custom required, act as disinterested peacemaker and cup-bearer among members of the royal family?

In visualising the Council of Whitby as a game of political poker one might be giving the protagonists too much credit for forethought. Early Medieval kingship was mostly an expedient affair, with policy made on the hoof. My feeling is that Oswiu was sufficiently confident of himself that he could afford to let Alhfrith challenge him; even so, the timing of the events of 664 may have forced his hand and ensured that when the critical moves were made, he must improvise.

The Anglo-Saxon historian Richard Abels has argued persuasively that the death of Archbishop Deusdedit of Canterbury, who succumbed to the plague on 14 July, was the trigger that made imperative an immediate resolution of the question.[225] As overlord of the English kingdoms Oswiu naturally enough saw the appointment of a new archbishop as an extension of his royal patronage. The new metropolitan at Canterbury should be his nominee. If there were an alternative candidate proposed by the Roman party, then Bernicia's obdurate refusal to accept orthodoxy on Easter and other matters might weigh heavily against his choice with Pope Vitalian. Vitalian's predecessor, Eugene I, had recently been introduced to Alhfrith's enthusiastic young protégé Wilfrid; he must also have read in the correspondence of Pope Gregory that great man's vision for an English church. Here is Oswiu's first and most obvious political motive for falling into line with Roman convention, whatever his personal sympathies.

The cast assembled at Whitby in the late summer or autumn of 664 was both impressive and carefully chosen. There were two kings, representing Irish and Roman sympathies. This says much in itself: Oswiu did not intend to allow a voice to Wulfhere of Mercia, nor to the kings of Wessex, East Anglia or even Kent, in whose capital city the now-deceased archbishop had resided. Oswiu's message is that this was an internal Northumbrian issue even though, in attempting to nominate the next metropolitan of Canterbury and writing to Pope Vitalian—that is to say, having a literate churchman write to Pope Vitalian—Oswiu would portray himself as *Regi Saxonum*: king of all the English peoples.*

So: two kings. There were also three bishops: Colman, who in today's language would be described as a hard-liner on the Irish side; Cedd, bishop of the East Saxons and an alumnus of

---

* Oswiu's letter to Vitalian, taken to Rome by the unfortunate Wigheard who died soon after arrival, does not survive but Bede was able to quote verbatim from the Pope's reply (EH III.29). Assuming that Oswiu did not dictate his letter to Wilfrid, the conclusion must be that the letter was written either by Colman's immediate successor, Tuda or, more likely, by Eata after his succession to the abbacy of Lindisfarne. Alternatively, Oswiu might have waited until he had appointed a new bishop in Wilfrid's absence: Bishop Chad.

Lindisfarne; and Agilbert, a Gallic bishop who had held the see of Wessex and who was firmly of the Roman persuasion. He was the senior of a party that comprised his own priest Agatho, James the Deacon, Eanflæd's priest Romanus and Wilfrid, presumably accompanied by a party of his Ripon monks. Agilbert had a poor command of the English tongue and so Alhfrith's silver-tongued priest Wilfrid was asked to plead the Roman cause. On the Irish side were Hild, Colman, Cedd (who acted the part of disinterested translator) and a great many followers from both Whitby and Lindisfarne. Conspicuous absentees were Abbot Boisil of Melrose and Cuthbert; both had been struck down by the plague, from which Cuthbert (by the power of prayer), but not his mentor, recovered.[226] Nor does it seem as if Eata was present, but we do not know why.

There are immediate echoes here of a previous constitutional set-piece, Edwin's conversion debate of 626 in his great hall on the Yorkshire Wolds, some thirty miles to the south of Whitby. The timber hall, with its central hearth, its architecture of war and precedence and pagan royal divinity, would have made the perfect setting for Oswiu to pull off a similar tribal coup. But was there a hall at Whitby? Had Hild caused such a building to be constructed in her new monastery? It seems unlikely, given her ascetic leanings. In that case, one must envision either that there was a nearby *villa regia* with a suitable venue for debate (by no means impossible) or that the Council took place in much more humble, perhaps very crowded surroundings. I think it possible that, given the urgency lent to the Council by Deusdedit's death, Whitby might have been chosen precisely because it lay close to a *villa regia* which was habitually visited in the late summer or early autumn, so that the Council coincided with the gathering of its annual food render. Early Medieval life may have been miraculous but it was also pragmatic: people needed feeding and housing.

Bede implies that the debating chamber was crowded, with some delegates having to stand: however this first great council of the English church might be dressed, it has the ring of a tribal gathering, with the king at the centre sitting in judgement on those below him in his sacral role as law-giver.

> King Oswiu began by declaring that it was fitting that those who served one God should observe one rule of life and not differ in the celebration of the holy sacraments, seeing that they all hoped for one kingdom in heaven; they ought therefore to inquire as to which was the truer tradition and then all follow it together. He then ordered his bishop Colman to say first what were the customs which he followed and whence they originated.[227]

The meaning here is unequivocal: Oswiu would not allow the two traditions to continue side by side; there would be one church for the Northumbrian people (and, by implication, for the English over whom Oswiu enjoyed imperium). Bede's apparent verbatim quotations from Colman and Wilfrid during the debate that followed must be taken with a dose of seasoning. It was a rhetorical commonplace to reconstruct dialogue on the basis of what one thought ought to have been the case. But Bede was relying on eyewitness testimony, probably from several of those who had either been there as young men and women or who had heard many stories from their elders. No doubt there were contradictory recollections from Lindisfarne and Whitby, both of them monasteries where Bede had correspondents. As so often before, the historian felt the need to conflate varying accounts in order to provide a coherent narrative. In the case of Whitby, given Bede's own fundamentalist adherence to the Roman cause, it was necessary to show how the arguments of the Catholic party had convinced the king.

The debate became increasingly semantic, convoluted and bitterly personal; it must have continued among the churchmen and women perhaps over several days, if not weeks; how much of it took place in public before the two kings and their courts is hard to say. Against Colman's appeal to the traditions of his forefathers and the authority of saints John and Colm Cille, Wilfrid pursued a line similar to that of Cummian in the 630s, incredulous that the Irish believed themselves, and only themselves, to be right in the face of all the evidence. Bede gives him the following speech:

> The Easter we keep is the same as we have seen universally celebrated in Rome, where the apostles St Peter and St Paul lived, taught, suffered, and were buried. We also found it in use everywhere in Italy and Gaul when we travelled through these countries for the purposes of study and prayer. We learned that it was observed at one and the same time in Africa, Asia, Egypt, Greece, and throughout the entire world, wherever the Church of Christ is scattered, amid various nations and languages. The only exceptions are these men and their accomplices in obstinacy, I mean the Picts and the Britons, who in these, the two remotest islands of the Ocean, and only in some parts of them, foolishly attempt to fight against the whole world.[228]

The judgement attributed to Oswiu by Bede was a masterstroke of enlightened self-interest, delivered with a Da Vinci-esque smile of enigma, according to Eddius, which might be interpreted as one of either submission or triumph.[229] The coup de grâce was delivered after an admission by Colman that St Peter, on whose authority the Roman case had been made, had been granted the keys to the kingdom of Heaven.

> Thereupon the king concluded, 'Then, I tell you, since he is the doorkeeper I will not contradict him; but I intend to obey his commands in everything to the best of my knowledge and ability, otherwise when I come to the gates of the kingdom of heaven, there may be no-one to open them because the one who on your own showing holds the keys has turned his back on me.' When the king had spoken, all who were seated there or standing by, both high and low, signified their assent, gave up their imperfect rules, and readily accepted in their place those which they recognised to be better.[230]

Whatever spin Bede and Wilfrid's biographer might put on Oswiu's judgement and its benevolent reception, the result was a decisive unification of the English church. Oswiu, by apparently giving in to his son's pressure, had completely outflanked him, retaining his political supremacy, ingratiating himself with the Pope and deflecting Alhfrith's bid to isolate his father from the southern kingdoms. From a personal point of view the victory was bittersweet. Oswiu's patronage of the church founded by his brother was seemingly fatally compromised. Colman and a large contingent of the community at Lindisfarne refused to accept the verdict. Following the Synod, he would resign the bishopric of Lindisfarne and lead his followers on a new pilgrimage of isolation, first to Iona and then to the west coast of Ireland.

Oswiu, his political capital restored decisively, took the opportunity to undertake the reforms which he must have been contemplating for the best part of a decade. Colman having vacated Lindisfarne, the king determined to separate the monastic and episcopal functions of the Northumbrian church by appointing Tuda, an Irish-trained Romanist, as bishop for his people. His new see would be at York in the heart of Deira, maintaining both geographical and tribal distance between him and Lindisfarne and reviving, after sixty years, the original intention of Pope Gregory to give the North a see in the old Roman provincial capital. There is evidence from excavations at Fishergate in the 1980s that by the late seventh century York was minting coins and hosted a settlement of Frisian traders: did they follow and exploit the arrival of episcopal dignity, or was it, one wonders, the other way around?* The rump of Colman's community, whose loyalty to the king overcame their distaste for his reforms, was placed under Abbot Eata, Oswiu's long-time safe pair of hands and a candidate calculated to placate the Irish/British party in

---

* Kemp 1996; Kemp and others have argued that there were at least two distinct areas of activity in later seventh-century York: around the church, which was probably close to the current minster in the Roman principia; and on the east bank of the River Ouse at its confluence with the River Foss.

the Northumbrian church. Cuthbert, Wilfrid's humble contemporary, became his prior at Lindisfarne.

Oswiu's reform had important administrative implications, not often discussed by historians. By separating the offices of abbot and bishop, Oswiu ensured that in future the abbots of all the Northumbrian houses came under the authority of the bishop. There was, from now on, a hierarchy of precedence and discipline by which king appointed archbishop under whom bishops and then abbots owed their duty. No longer would Oswiu have to juggle an ever more complex web of abbatial patronage. Before Whitby it must have seemed as if his abbots, perhaps a score of them representing monasteries great and small, had begun to constitute a parallel order of *gesiths*, retaining whose personal loyalty could only become an increasing burden on royal patronage. Now their counsel, their management of lands and communities were organised under the quasi-judicial person of the bishop. The king, like all good leaders, had learned the art of delegation. If there is a moment in early English history when one can identify the emergence of the concept of a civil service, an idea of administrative statehood, surely this is it.

Oswiu was swift in deploying his enhanced political capital. A replacement must be found for the deceased archbishop, Deusdedit. Oswiu took counsel to ensure the right candidate was put forward. One is reminded forcibly here of a conversation that took place between Lord Palmerston and Talleyrand, respective foreign secretaries of Britain and France, in about 1830 when a suitably consensual candidate was being sought to become first king of the new Belgian state.

> PALMERSTON TO TALLEYRAND: Let us try and find someone... who... might satisfy everyone.
>
> TALLEYRAND TO PALMERSTON: I consider that everyone means you and us.[231]

In this case, *you* and *us* were Oswiu and the new king of Kent,

Egbert, whose consultation, as tributary ruler under Oswiu's imperium, was perhaps more by historical courtesy than political necessity. Egbert proposed Wigheard, a member of the community at Canterbury. The details of his career and the exact circumstances of his appointment are not clear; Bede himself gave more than one contradictory account. It is certain that he died shortly after his arrival in Rome for ordination by the Pope. What also seems likely, given that he was a member of Deusdedit's church, is that he was Egbert's personal choice. Oswiu might have been tempted to impose his own candidate but was probably content to go along with Egbert's nomination. What mattered was that he, Oswiu, was seen to have the appointment at least equally in his gift. If Pope Vitalian ordained his candidate, Oswiu might metaphorically wave a piece of paper at his people and claim the legitimacy of an unparalleled imperium papally sealed and stamped. Who could argue with that?

It seems that Alhfrith did, for after Whitby he is barely heard of again. Bede alludes to a rebellion without giving us any detail or explanation.* Oddly, Wilfrid's biographer, who took a closer interest than any in the young star's patron, also fails to tell us what his fate was. Bede's last mention of the Deiran sub-king is a record of him sending Wilfrid to Gaul to be consecrated bishop. Neither Bede nor Eddius seems to have been reliably informed about the precise sequence of events, but it seems that Oswiu's new bishop, Tuda, became a victim of the plague shortly after his appointment. Eddius tells us that an election took place after Whitby among the kings and the counsellors of the realm, which resulted in Wilfrid being elevated to the new see at York. This seems odd, given that Oswiu had apparently appointed Tuda to the bishopric. Do we have here the most compelling evidence for

---

* EH III.14. Alhfrith is listed as one of those who, like Œthelwald, attacked Oswiu during his reign.

Alhfrith's fate? Did he set Wilfrid up as a rival to Tuda even while Oswiu's new bishop was still alive? If he did, he was following in the steps of his unfortunate predecessors as Deiran sub-kings and over-reaching himself. We do not hear of him again.

Eddius's account of the journey to Gaul is predicated on Wilfrid's apparent assertion that since none of the existing bishops in the island of Britain was canonically sound, he must travel to Gaul to ensure the orthodoxy of his consecration. Richard Abels considers that there may be a more prescient motive: if Alhfrith rebelled against his father in the months after Whitby and was killed, Northumbria might have been a bit too hot for Wilfrid to stick around. Typically, Oswiu seized this political opportunity, while Wilfrid extended his stay in Gaul, to declare the see vacant and install a man of British–Irish sympathies in his place. The man he chose was Chad, brother of Cedd the bishop of the East Saxons and another former pupil of Aidan.* He was dispatched to Kent, probably in anticipation that he would be consecrated by Wigheard on his return from Rome with the pallium. Oswiu, it seems, had managed to have his cake and eat it.

Oswiu could not have known that Wigheard would die and that the Pope would not send a replacement until almost the end of the decade. By the time Wilfrid returned, having been consecrated as bishop by Agilbert and having survived an unwelcome adventure at the hands of pagan wreckers on the south coast, he no longer had a see, or a patron to argue his cause. He retired, with apparent good grace, to his abbacy at Ripon, although given his later record of bitter conflict with kings and archbishops I doubt if he was happy with his lot. I suggest that meanwhile, from about 665 until Oswiu's death, Ecgfrith was installed as sub-king

---

* There were four brothers; the other two were Cynibil and Cælin. After Whitby Cedd returned to Essex but before long came to his own foundation at Lastingham and died there of the plague. He was briefly succeeded by Chad before his elevation to the bishopric.

in Deira; in time Wilfrid would forge relations with a new patron.

Between the battle on the *Winwæd* in 655 and 670 there is no record of military conflict between Northumbria and the other English or British kingdoms. Æthelberht of Kent, perhaps by right of historical tradition and moral authority, had held imperium without winning a great battle or having to display his leadership in war on annual hostings. Oswiu first proved himself in battle and then showed equal courage, skill and ruthlessness in maintaining his imperium in the face of a wholly new set of kingly challenges. After 655 his battles were political, dynastic: Whitby was his greatest tactical victory, a companion-piece to the equally unlikely triumph of the *Winwæd*. In uniting and extending the spiritual and civil reach of the church, Oswiu established his credentials as the first of the great British state-builders. He succeeded where that other Romanophile, Edwin, had failed. He was the first of his line to die in his bed. Believing himself to have fulfilled his sacral obligations and having convinced himself of the unifying values of the Roman church, he intended, as Bede records, to end his days in Rome with Wilfrid as his companion in pilgrimage. He was, instead, interred at Whitby where his widow and daughter would become abbesses; his son and undisputed heir Ecgfrith became king of all the Northumbrians in his stead. Shortly before his death a new archbishop was installed at Canterbury: Theodore, the improbably elderly Greek-speaking monk from Asia Minor who would take church and state reform to a new level in an extraordinary twenty-year career.

Oswiu's political acumen and maturity are striking. Lacking his brother's stellar charisma and 'luck', he substituted martial and magical fortune with a carefully calculated combination of ruthless expediency, canny debate and a startlingly mature, even visionary conception of government. If Oswald fused the kingly roles of pagan and Christian divinity with the heroic virtues of Beowulf, Oswiu developed a model of kingship more recognisable to

Timeline: AD 642 to 671

ABBREVIATIONS
EH—Bede's Ecclesiastical History
HB—Nennius's *Historia Brittonum*
ASC—Anglo-Saxon Chronicle
AU—Annals of Ulster
ATig—Annals of Tigernach
PLC—Prose Life of Cuthbert
VW—Eddius Stephanus's *Vita Wilfridi*

Names of battles are shown in **bold**

642   Campaign against Mercia by Oswald drives Penda into Wales. Oswald is killed in the **Battle of *Maserfelth*** on 5 August fighting against Penda of Mercia and possibly Welsh allies of Gwynedd. He is cut up and his head displayed on a pole at Oswestry/*Croesoswald*.

           —Oswald is succeeded by his brother Oswiu in Bernicia and by Oswine (son of Osric: a cousin of Edwin) in Deira.

           —Cynegisl of Wessex dies; succeeded by Cenwalh (a pagan: to 673). He marries a sister of Penda but repudiates her.

           —Cuthbert given over to foster parents at *Hruringaham*.

           —Domnall Brecc dies at hands of Owain mac Beli of Strathclyde in **Battle of *Strath Cairuin*** (**Strathcarron**).

643   King Oswiu goes to Oswestry and fetches Oswald's remains; inters arms at Bamburgh in silver casket and gives head to Lindisfarne.

           —Record of a **battle between Oswiu and the Britons** (ATig).

           —Oswiu sends priest Utta for Eanflæd of Kent to be his wife. Miracle of the oil on stormy sea, by Aidan's blessing.

           —Miracles begin to be associated with the site of Oswald's death.

643–50? Periodic raids by Penda into Bernicia, as far as Lindisfarne.

           —Death of Sigeberht of East Anglia, dragged from monastery and forced to fight a **battle against the Mercians**, who kill him (possibly as early as 635) (EH III.18); death of Ecgric of East Anglia in same battle; succeeded by Anna.

644 Paulinus dies as bishop of Rochester; buried in St Andrew's, Rochester.

 —Kentishman Ithamar succeeds Paulinus as bishop.

645 Penda drives Cenwalh of Wessex into three-year exile among East Anglians; Cenwalh protected by King Anna of East Anglia.

 —Ecgfrith born to Oswiu and Eanflæd, daughter of King Edwin.

c.646 Foundation of monastery at Hartlepool (*Heruteu*) by Heiu, ordained by Aidan ?first abbess of English monastery. Heiu soon retires to a dwelling at *Kælcacæstir* (?Tadcaster) and is replaced by Hild (*c.*650), great niece of King Edwin (EH IV.23).

647 Former Queen Æthelburh dies at her monastery at Lyminge in Kent, site of a former Roman villa.

 —Possible date of foundation of monastery on north bank of River Wear (Chester-le-Street?) with Hild (aged thirty-three) as its first abbess.

648 Cenwalh regains throne of Wessex after exile in East Anglia.

 —?Start of civil war between Oswiu and Oswine.

649 Possible date of **attack on Northumbria as far as Bamburgh by Penda** and Mercian army 'during Aidan's episcopate' while he is living on Farne (could be as early as 644). Attempt to burn Bamburgh prevented by Aidan's prayers, which deflect the wind.

 —Wilfrid, aged sixteen, chooses to become a monk and is sent to Lindisfarne with Cudda, a paralysed former *gesith* and servant of Queen Eanflæd (*VW* 2).

650 **Mercian attack on East Anglia**: destruction of monastery at *Cnobheresburg* (Burgh Castle?); temporary expulsion of Anna to ?*Magonsæte*.

 —Probable date of Agilbert's installation as bishop of the West Saxons. ?Death of Birinus.

 —?Cuthbert serving in Oswiu's army 'in the face of the foe'.

651 Oswine disbands army but is betrayed by his *gesith* Tondhere at *Wilfaresdun* north-west of Catterick and murdered. Oswine is succeeded as Deiran sub-king by Œthelwald aged ?sixteen (to 655).

—St Aidan dies in the church at ?Yeavering on 13 August (EH III.17). He is buried in the cemetery at Lindisfarne and succeeded by Bishop Finan.

—Monasteries by now founded at Melrose, Coldingham, and ?Gilling West (by Eanflæd, in expiation for the murder of Oswine). Trumhere, a kinsman of Eanflæd and Oswine, is first abbot of Gilling.

—?Cuthbert becomes monk at Melrose under Abbot Boisil.

652 Some time after this Oswiu is forced to retreat as far as Stirling and sue for peace, with hostages including Ecgfrith.

—Wilfrid in Wessex, received by king after letter of introduction by Eanflæd.

—Probable date of marriage of Æthelthryth of East Anglia to Tondberht, chief of the Gyrvians or 'men of the fens' (dies 655).

—Finan builds church on Lindisfarne, of hewn oak thatched with reeds (EH III.25).

—Death of Ségéne, abbot of Iona (AU, ATig).

—?Wilfrid travels to Kent under the protection of Eanflæd's cousin King Eorcenberht to wait for suitable opportunity to travel to Rome; meets Benedict Baducing (Biscop); is exposed to current Roman version of Jerome's psalms.

653 ?Succession of Talorcan, son of Eanfrith, to kingdom of southern Picts.

—Peada of Mercia, Penda's son, marries Oswiu's daughter Alhflæd and is baptised *Ad Muram* by Finan; beginning of Irish mission to Middle Angles (roughly Leicestershire and Northamptonshire). Alhfrith is active in Peada's conversion.

—?Sigeberht *Sanctus* of East Angles baptised by Finan *Ad Muram* (Newcastle?).

—Oswiu's son Alhfrith (aged ?seventeen) probably marries Penda's daughter Cyneburh.

—?Sigeberht the Little dies in **Battle against Wessex**. Sigeberht the Good succeeds to kingdom of Essex.

—Cedd sent by Oswiu to found see in Essex at Bradwell on Sea (*Ythancaestir*) and Tilbury; he is consecrated as its first bishop by Finan on Lindisfarne.

—Archbishop Honorius dies (last living member of Gregorian mission). Succeeded by Deusdedit, first native-born archbishop (consecrated 655: to 664)

—Wilfrid (aged ?nineteen) and Benedict Biscop make journey from Northumbria to Rome; Wilfrid stays for a year in Lyons on his way, and is taken under the wing of Dalfinus, who offers Wilfrid land and his daughter.

654   Penda kills King Anna of East Anglia at **Battle of Bulcamp** in Suffolk.

—?Foundation of Lastingham for Œthelwald (so he can be buried there) in remote part of North York Moors, under Cedd's direction (EH III.23); must be before 655.

—**Battle of Strath Ethairt**: Talorcan defeats grandson of Áedán mac Gabráin (ATig).

—Birth of Ælfflæd, daughter of Oswiu and Eanflæd.

655   The 'distribution of Iudeu' and campaign against Oswiu by Penda on the ?Firth of Forth; Oswiu forced to give up a huge ransom (*HB* 65; EH III.24).

—Oswiu's son by Eanflæd, Ecgfrith, held hostage under Queen Cynewise of Mercia.

—**Battle of the River *Winwæd***, south of Leeds, probably at Thorpe Audlin where the River Went is crossed by Ermine Street. Penda, king of Mercia, and thirty chieftains (including Æthelhere, king of East Anglia) are killed. Œthelwald waits to see who will win. ?Oswiu kills him. Oswiu achieves dominance over Mercia. In thanks for victory Oswiu transfers one hundred and twenty hides to Lindisfarne control, for the establishment of twelve monasteries (this after an oath made in desperation at *Urbs Giudi*).

—Oswiu rules over Mercia until 658 (EH III.24).

—Oswiu subjects the Picts to his rule (EH III.24).

—With Peada, Oswiu founds *Medehamstede* (Peterborough) monastery.

—Oswiu transfers rule of Deira to his son Alhfrith aged ?seventeen.

—Wilfrid returns to Lyons after months in Rome and stays for three years with Dalfinus.

656   Peada murdered by treachery of Alhflæd.

657   Foundation of monastery at Whitby under Abbess Hilda; Ælfflæd is given into her hands.

—?Death of Talorcan, king of Picts and grandson of Æthelfrith and Bebba. Oswiu subjects the greater part of the Pictish race to English rule (EH III.24).

—Cumméne becomes abbot of Iona (to 669).

—Oswiu hands control of Southern Mercia, below the Trent, to Peada.

658   Count Dalfinus of Lyons is murdered on the orders of Queen Baldhild (former Anglo-Saxon slave and wife of Clovis II); Wilfrid returns from pilgrimage to Rome tonsured and with relics and gifts; granted ten hides of land at ?Stamford by Alhfrith, to whom he has been commended by Cenwalh of Wessex for his knowledge of Roman practices.

—Mercian rebellion by Immin, Eafa and Eadberht sets up Christian Wulfhere, son of Penda, as king of Mercia.

—Wulfhere makes Trumhere (formerly founding abbot at Gilling), kinsman of Eanflæd and Oswine, first bishop of Mercia.

659   ?Abbot Eata founds monastery at Ripon, with Cuthbert as guestmaster (PLC VII).

660   Wilfrid given Ripon with thirty hides (*VW* 8). Bede says Alhfrith gave him forty hides (EH III.25). Wilfrid expels community of Eata including Cuthbert (PLC VIII) after dispute over Roman/Irish forms.

—?Ecgfrith marries Æthelthryth (later Ætheldreda or Audrey) of East Anglia, daughter of King Anna.

—Cumméne, abbot of Iona, visits Ireland to tour the Iona paruchia (ATig).

661   ?Ælfwine, son of Oswiu and Eanflæd and brother of Ecgfrith, is born.

—Penda's son Wulfhere ravages Ashdown at heart of kingdom of Wessex. New West Saxon see established in Winchester around this time.

—Death of Bishop Finan of Lindisfarne; succeeded by Colman.

—Death of King Sigeberht the Good of Essex; succeeded by Swithelm, son of Seaxbald; baptised by Cedd.

663   Wilfrid ordained priest by Agilbert (Gaulish) of Dorchester-on-Thames (bishop of Wessex 648–60).

664   Re-endowment of *Medehamstede* (Peterborough) by Wulfhere with Oswiu and other kings as co-sponsors, witnessed by Archbishop Deusdedit; all sign with a + mark.

—Plague (after July comet); Archbishop Deusdedit dies. King Eorconberht of Kent dies, succeeded by Ecgbert I (673). Cuthbert struck down by plague; recovers.

—Cedd dies of plague at Lastingham.

—Boisil dies of plague at Melrose.

—Council of Whitby (*Streanæshealh*). Hosted by Hild, abbess of Whitby. Delegates include Agilbert, Colman, Wilfrid, Oswiu, Alhfrith, James the Deacon and Romanus. King Oswiu convenes synod to determine which church to follow: Iona or Rome. Decides in favour of Rome.

—Bishop Colman abdicates from Lindisfarne and is replaced by Eata as abbot, not as bishop; Colman founds monasteries at Inishbofin and Mayo.

—Tuda is chosen as new bishop of Northumbria with his see at York; he dies of the plague

—Wilfrid elected as bishop of Northumberland at York.

—Cuthbert becomes prior of Lindisfarne.

—?Alhfrith dies this year or soon after. Possibly succeeded as sub-king of Deira by Ecgfrith.

—Wigheard sent by King Egbert of Kent and Oswiu with a letter to Rome to have a new archbishop appointed. Wigheard dies in Rome.

—King Sighere of Essex apostasises after plague; begins to rebuild temples and idols (EH II.30).

665   Wilfrid consecrated bishop of York; but by ?Agilbert in Gaul, not at York (perhaps because of lack of qualified Roman-style bishops in England after plague); stays in Gaul and influence wanes temporarily. Returns to Ripon and rules there for two to three years. English Christian kingdoms in a state of crisis until arrival of Theodore.

—Benedict Biscop arrives in Lérins and stays for two years at the monastery.

666   Chad (Ceadda) is appointed bishop of York by Oswiu in Wilfrid's absence.

669   Arrival of Archbishop Theodore of Tarsus in England with his monk Hadrian, and accompanied by Benedict Biscop; Theodore undertakes a tour of the Christian states to bring them into line with apostolic doctrine and discipline.

—Wilfrid restored to see of Northumbria.

—Chad returns to Lastingham as abbot, but is then sent to Mercia as its bishop under Wulfhere. He is granted land at Lichfield to establish see.

—Benedict Biscop becomes abbot of St Peter and St Paul monastery in Canterbury.

—Death of Cumméne, abbot of Iona; succeeded by Failbe.

670/1   King Oswiu dies of natural causes at fifty-eight years of age. Succeeded by Ecgfrith, his first son by Eanflæd

—Wilfrid expels monks from Ripon and builds a stone church, probably financed by the plunder of British churches in the Pennines.

—Wilfrid tries to extort land from Ecgfrith in return for persuading Queen Æthelthryth to consummate her marriage with Ecgfrith. She remains a virgin.

—Eight-year-old Ælfwine, Oswiu's youngest son, is sub-king of Deira until 679.

—Queen Eanflæd retires to Whitby Abbey.

XVIII
Habeas corpus

Is seo forðgesceaft
digol and dyrne; drihten ana wat

*Our future fate is dark and hidden;
only the Lord knows*

AIDAN'S BODY HAD LAIN IN
the holy soil of Lindisfarne for thirteen years when
Colman decided that he could not in conscience live with the
judgement of the Council at Whitby. Bede says that he...

> left Britain and took with him all the Irish whom he had gathered
> together on the island of Lindisfarne. He also took about thirty men
> of English race, both companies having been instructed in the duties of
> monastic life. Leaving some of the brothers in the church at Lindisfarne,
> he went first to the Island of Iona, from which he had been sent to preach
> the word to the English. From there he went on to a small island some
> distance off the west coast of Ireland, called in Irish Inisboufinde, the
> island of the white heifer.[232]

One has some sympathy for Colman, who must have believed
himself personally betrayed by his patron King Oswiu. That dis-
may was shared on the island of Colm Cille, whose community
would not accept Roman orthodoxy for another two generations.
Colman now sought a new Lindisfarne and chose Inishbofin,
some three miles off the coast of Connemara, County Galway.
This foundation is remarkable for the insight it gives us into the

hundreds or thousands of such enterprises dating to the sixth and seventh centuries in the British Isles. The site of Colman's monastery has never been excavated but is still visible on Inishbofin's fertile east plain: it lies by a stream fed by a freshwater lough and just a few hundred yards from a sheltered sandy beach. It seems to have survived into the tenth century but the community there left no records. Fortunately, Bede was well informed about its history under Colman:

> When he reached this island, he built a monastery and placed in it monks whom he had brought from both nations. But they could not agree together because the Irish, in summer time when the harvest had to be gathered in, left the monastery and wandered about, scattering into various places with which they were familiar; then when winter came, they returned and expected to have a share in the things which the English had provided. Colman sought to put an end to this dispute and at last, having travelled about far and near, he found a place suitable for building a monastery on the Irish mainland called in the Irish tongue *Mag éo*.*

Here, then, were cultural tensions between different nationalities based not on the ecclesiastical rule they followed but on deeper, more ancient traditions, which were domestically incompatible. The source for this story was Mayo which, by Bede's day, was a famous seat of learning and known across Europe as Mayo of the Saxons: twenty-eight acres in extent with generous estates and home to hundreds of monks, many of them exiles or pilgrims from England. Bede's correspondents gave him the following illuminating details of Colman's acquisition of the site:

> He bought a small part of the land from the chief to whom it belonged, on condition that the monks who settled there were to pray to the Lord for him as he had provided them with the land. A monastery was forthwith built with the help of the chief and all the neighbours and in it he placed the English monks, leaving the Irishmen on the island.[233]

* EH IV.4; Colgrave and Mynors 1969, 347. *Mag éo*, the plain of the yew trees; that is, Mayo. The Annals of Ulster record Colman's arrival at *Inis Bó Finne* under the year 668.

Here is testimony to the process by which great landowners, the Irish equivalent of *gesiths*, came to follow their kings in patronising the church; they were probably known by the term *érenach*, or *coarb*. Such lay patrons became a prominent feature of Irish foundations just as, by Bede's day, they were in Northumbria. Nowhere could there be a clearer statement of the mutual incentives for holy men and their patrons in setting up communities; and underlying it is the desire for legitimisation, stability and the dignity and luck which a great bishop of the paruchia of Colm Cille could confer on a warrior elite. At the heart of the matter is control of the agricultural potential of land, the labour and management to exploit it, and the benefits such capital investment could bring for both parties.

Indivisible from the legitimacy and sanctity of such pioneering missions was a need for a God-given, some might say magical or superstitious, talisman. And when Bede tells us that, on his departure from Lindisfarne, Colman 'took with him some of the bones of the reverend father Aidan', leaving 'some in the church over which he had presided, directing that they should be interred in the sanctuary', we are offered a clue to the process by which such magical virtue was transferred from one site to another.[234] The Annals of Ulster record, in noting Colman's arrival on Inishbofin in 668, that he brought with him the relics of saints; no doubt some of these were, in turn, taken on to seed the fortunes of *Mag éo*.

From the earliest days of the Christian church shrines had been erected over the relics of martyrs and special holy men and women; many of these shrines developed into monastic or episcopal establishments and some of them, in turn, became centres of urban revival. Xanten* in Germany (Saint Viktor) and Tours in France (Saint Martin) are the classic type-sites: both developed

---

* Xanten: the name derives from the Latin *Ad Sanctum*, the place of the shrine.

around the extramural cemeteries of important Roman towns. England's primary martyr was Saint Alban, whose shrine on the hill above the Roman town of Verulamium has been a place of pilgrimage since the third century; many other foundations attest the potency of corporeal remains and the sites of miraculous events or martyrdom. In Ireland an impressive array of structures evolved to house the relics of the saints. Slab shrines, which look like stone playing cards propping each other up tent-like, were provided with holes through which pilgrims and cure-seekers could reach in to touch saintly dust; house-shrines were constructed to mimic the cells where holy men had prayed; altars and *leachta** were built to contain the bones of founding saints; and the tombs of lay patrons, too, became foci for veneration. The portability of human remains after ritual exhumation, washing and encasing in a suitable vessel was to become a stock-in-trade of monastic and church expansion across Europe during the Early Medieval period. Of the posthumous heroes of this missionary import–export business, none is more luminous than Oswald.

There was, surely, a punitive element in Colman taking possession of Lindisfarne's precious relics. His sense of rejection by Oswiu and, perhaps, his own failure to argue more effectively at Whitby were unendurably bitter blows. Likewise, the holy island's primacy in the English mission was doubly damaged by the setting up of a new metropolitan see at York and by the physical loss of its founder's bones; Lindisfarne would have to find a new and potent patron saint, while the paruchia of Colm Cille invested its energies in a new project. At York, where Paulinus's church had been completed by Oswald and then rebuilt after decades of neglect by Wilfrid, King Edwin's head was the principal relic. It had been retrieved from the battlefield at *Hæthfelth* in

---

* *Leachta*: rectangular drystone settings containing the bones or other relics of holy men and women; very often simple stone crosses were set in them as memorials. See Thomas 1971.

632 and it is reasonable to see, in the re-establishment of the episcopal seat at York, the arrival of a Frisian trading colony and the
possible repair of some of the city walls, an attempt to replicate
the development of a Tours or Xanten by late-seventh-century
Northumbrian kings.

Corporeal remains were a very real commodity to be invested
on behalf of a community or a tribal elite. There is more than a
hint of animism here. In the late Bronze Age landscape of Northumbria, as elsewhere, the remains of ancestors were interred
beneath barrows and cairns to propitiate the spirits, to bless and
fertilise the land and, in a sense, to claim it for the kin. The bones
of the saints were deployed in similar fashion, as symbols of the
luck and virtue of a founder or community; as elements of a ritual
of fertility. The presence of the relics of a saint was of great value:
as a magical protection; as luck; as title deed and seal of legitimacy; above all, perhaps, to attract pilgrims and future patronage, which were the means of economic and social success among
increasingly competitive monastic and church communities.

Edwin's head at York in Deira and Oswald's at Lindisfarne in
Bernicia: a dilemma of totemic loyalty for the Northumbrian people? Perhaps; but more likely a reflection of the political reality
that the Anglian peoples of the North were not to be united by
mere administrative reform or royal persuasion. Under Oswiu's
successor Ecgfrith the inherent tensions in northern dynastic
affairs did not resolve themselves. Competition between Deiran
and Bernician saints erupted into what amounted to ecclesiastical
civil war. In death, as in life, Oswald and Edwin played the parts
of heroes on opposite sides.

The arrival of Archbishop Theodore at Canterbury in May 669
filled the void in ecclesiastical authority which had threatened the
fragile stability of the English church since Whitby; more than
filled the void. Theodore, immediately wielding the authority
vested in him by the Pope and effectively authorised by Oswiu's

acceptance of papal jurisdiction, ordered Chad to surrender the see of York to Wilfrid.* The sixty-seven-year-old Greek-speaking monk had been chosen well. In a twenty-one-year incumbency he set about re-organising the dioceses of Britain and implementing a set of canonical rules which survive substantially as the foundations of the Church in England. He took a hard line with kings and bishops who challenged his authority in ecclesiastical politics; and with his monk Hadrian he also established a brilliant school at Canterbury, ushering in an era of outstanding scholarship.

After Oswiu's death in 670 or 671 Ecgfrith, now about twenty-five years old, acceded the throne and installed his young brother Ælfwine, aged just ten, in Deira. If Oswiu had allowed Deiran sub-kings to become too powerful, his son would not, apparently, make the same mistake: Ælfwine was no more than a figurative royal presence: Northumbria was to be ruled as a single kingdom (although I have a suspicion that Ecgfrith's mother Eanflæd might have acted as regent in the southern kingdom). We know nothing of the inauguration rituals involved; we can only assume Ecgfrith's universal acclamation by the nobility of Northumbria—there were, after all, no other legitimate candidates if we accept that Alhfrith had been disposed of after Whitby.

If, as I believe, Ecgfrith had been sub-king of Deira between Whitby and his father's death, the new king may already have enjoyed a close friendship with his bishop, Wilfrid. Wilfrid now set about exploiting this relationship to reflect the dignity proper to a Roman bishop of all the Northumbrians. If Wilfrid had done little more than see to the repairs of Paulinus's and Oswald's church at York, at Ripon he masterminded an altogether grander project, constructing a basilica with crypt (the latter of which survives more or less intact), dressed stone, aisles and columns. This was a building fit for a Roman bishop.

* Chad, having returned to Lastingham, was offered the see of Mercia and Lindsey under King Wulfhere and established his see at Lichfield.

Afterwards, when the building had been finished, he invited to the day of its dedication the two most Christian kings and brothers, Ecgfrith and Ælfwine, together with the abbots, the reeves and the sub-kings; dignitaries of every kind gathered together... Then, when the sermon was over, the kings started upon a great feast lasting for three days and three nights, rejoicing amid all their people...*

Northumbria had seen nothing like this before; not only was the architecture more imposing than any existing building in the kingdom; its altar was adorned with cloth of purple and gold. Wilfrid also commissioned the production of a set of gospels written in gold on parchment of purple. The gospels were encased in gold studded with jewels. This splendid occasion was more than just a dedication ceremony. Wilfrid took the opportunity to record before these witnesses the possessions Ecgfrith and his father had given over to the community at Ripon—including, intriguingly, many churches in the Pennines that had been 'deserted' by British clergy.† It was an oral equivalent of the document known as the *Historia de Sancto Cuthberto*, which recorded gifts made to Lindisfarne, establishing legal title over those possessions. It was also a challenge to the dignity of the kings. Wilfrid's economic pulling-power was such that he could bring masons and glaziers, scribes and jewellers from Frankia to embellish his temple. Two generations earlier Edwin had fulfilled the dual role of divine ruler and chief priest of his people; Paulinus had been, in the first place, no more than his wife's priest. Now, bishops might

---

* *VW* XVII; Colgrave 1927, 37. If Ælfwine was already sub-king of Deira, the other sub-kings mentioned must have come from tributary kingdoms: Rheged, perhaps? Lindsey? Lothian?

† *VW* XVII; the churches were in the districts of Ribble and Yeadon, Dent and Catlow, far into the Pennines. It is impossible to say for how long they had been abandoned, or whether Wilfrid had expelled their priests, but the detail suggests that there had been an active British church in the Pennine kingdoms of Elmet and probably Rheged within recent memory. What the churches would have looked like physically is a matter of speculation; could they be archaeologically distinguished from domestic structures?

compete with kings in magnificence, if not yet wealth or power. How would Ecgfrith and his successors respond?

This new relationship between king and bishop, which Oswiu had anticipated in theoretical terms but not in the overwhelming physical person of Wilfrid, began to play out almost immediately: there was a crisis in the royal court. Ecgfrith had been married at the age of about sixteen to a princess of East Anglia, Æthelthryth,* the daughter of King Anna. She was at least ten years Ecgfrith's senior and had already been married to a prince of the fenlands of South Gyrwe (one of the small fenland kingdoms in the area around Ely, south of the Wash) called Tondberht; the marriage was childless. After his death she was given to Ecgfrith at a time when an alliance between Oswiu and her uncle King Æthelwold was a political necessity in the face of Mercian pressure on the East Midlands. She was a most reluctant bride. Not only had she taken a vow of chastity during her first marriage; she continued virgin during her marriage to Ecgfrith. Not unnaturally, one might ask why Ecgfrith married her if the union was unlikely to produce an heir?

Now that Ecgfrith was king, producing a legitimate male heir became a matter of urgency. The queen was intransigent. Wilfrid, in whom she found a friend and confidante, was asked by the king to intervene—this is according to Bede who asked Wilfrid in person for his account of the situation.[235] It seems that the king was so desperate, as it were, to achieve nuptial and procreative consummation that he offered Wilfrid estates and money if he could persuade the queen to fulfil her wifely duties. The mind boggles; it doesn't say much for the royal couple's relationship. But in this matter, for once, Wilfrid's arguments and charm were deployed in vain. In about 672 the marriage was dissolved; Æthelthryth retired first to the abbey of Oswald's sister Æbbe at Coldingham

---

* Also known as Ætheldreda and St Audrey.

on the Berwickshire coast and then to the Isle of Ely, where she founded a monastery on her own original dower lands. In death, as in life, she was unsullied: upon her exhumation by the nuns at Ely her body was found to be incorrupt.*

Ecgfrith was free to marry again. His new consort was Iurminburh, of whom we know almost nothing; her background is completely obscure, although the name is suspiciously Kentish, even Frankish; her unnamed sister married a king of Wessex. Wilfrid initially did rather better out of his failed diplomacy than he could have expected. Æthelthryth left him substantial estates along the Tyne Valley and at Hexham, in 673, he created an abbey complex even more stupendous than that at Ripon. But in the new queen he found, or made, a determined enemy.

Eddius Stephanus, Wilfrid's biographer and the English church's first singing master, made great play of tying the fortunes of his precious bishop to those of the kingdom and, in particular, the king and queen. In his first few years on the throne, Ecgfrith, like all Northumbrian kings before him, was required to prove his military might and the superiority of the Northumbrians in battle. There was, first, an invasion from the North, from Pictland. Ecgfrith raised a body of horsemen and counter-attacked with the support of a sub-king, Beornæth.† The Northumbrian host...

> slew an enormous number of the people, filling two rivers with corpses so that, marvellous to relate, the slayers, passing over the rivers dry foot, pursued and slew the crowd of fugitives; the tribes were reduced to slavery and remained subject under the yoke of captivity until the time when the king was slain.[236]

Shortly after this campaign Wulfhere, king of Mercia, apparently

---

* See p.357 for a discussion of incorruption.

† *VW* XIX; Beornæth is the first recorded member of a line of Northern sub-kings who may have had a principal stronghold at Dunbar. See Chapter X. There has been much debate about whether the horsemen in question were an actual cavalry unit, fighting on horseback, or whether they rode to battle and dismounted. See Cessford 1993, Hooper 1993 and Higham 1991.

at the head of an allied army of the southern English, attacked Northumbria and was repelled. Both Eddius and the author of the *Historia de Sancto Cuthberto* recorded that Ecgfrith's army was very small. Wilfrid seems to have accompanied the king. We are not given the site of any battle in this campaign (somewhere along the Great North Road between Lincoln and Catterick seems highly probable); all we know is that shortly afterwards Wulfhere died; one is tempted to think that the campaign was rather half-hearted, but it does seem to have resulted in the temporary annexation of Lindsey by Ecgfrith. Eddius's motive in describing the two 'invasions' is perfectly clear. He wanted to show that while the king and his consort were supporters of Wilfrid they enjoyed success; when they turned against him God saw to it that their luck ran out.

The rift must have begun before the Mercian invasion; either Wilfrid had got wind that Theodore wished to reform the diocesan structure of the English church and divide Northumbria into smaller sees; or, as Eddius would have his readers believe,

> Ecgfrith's queen, named Iurminburh, was at that time tortured with envy owing to the persuasions of the devil... This sorceress shot poisoned arrows of speech from her quiver into the heart of the king... She eloquently described to him all the temporal glories of Saint Wilfrid, his riches, the number of his monasteries, the greatness of his buildings, his countless army of followers arrayed in royal vestments and arms.[237]

Whatever underlying personal tensions there may have been, and there is little doubt that throughout his life he attracted such critical attention, Wilfrid had somehow lost the king's favour. Ecgfrith's victory over Mercia had been accomplished with...

> ...the aid of Saint Wilfrid, who was with him, but especially through the prayers of Saint Cuthbert, who was absent. After this battle King Ecgfrith gave Carham and whatever pertains to it to Cuthbert and held him in the highest veneration as long as he lived...*

* *HSC* 7; South 2002, 49. Carham lies on the south bank of the River Tweed some

The message to Wilfrid was unmistakeable: Bernician Lindisfarne was to receive a gift of land in celebration and thanks for the victory against Mercia; Deiran Ripon was not. Cuthbert, now prior of Lindisfarne, increasingly revered by his contemporaries and very much the gentle ascetic, had replaced Wilfrid in the royal favour. But for archaeologists and historical geographers there is more to this brief passage than meets the eye. The key phrase here is *et quicquid ad eam pertinet*: 'whatever pertains to it'. Elsewhere in the *Historia de Sancto Cuthberto* we find *cum suis appendiciis*: 'with its dependencies'. Here we have a small but highly significant clue to the way in which land was held and donated in the seventh century. Names like Carham (and later Warkworth, Jedburgh and others mentioned in the *Historia*) are those of *vills* or townships; that is to say, territorial units whose dependent settlements owed them food renders and services. In other words, these are the component parts of shire estates, being alienated by royal gift into the hands of the great monasteries.

Shires generally seem to have comprised units of either six or twelve *vills* adjacent to one another and forming contiguous territorial units.* In the later Middle Ages Carham formed the core of a parish which extended on both sides of the River Tweed and seems to have encompassed the territory of former British churches on the north side of the basin at Eccles. Whatever pertained to Carham in 675 looks as though it were at least a half-sized estate consisting of about six *vills* or townships. There may, at some point, have been a shire of Carham, which would have abutted Gefrinshire (Yeavering), Yetholmshire (Kirk Yetholm) and Norhamshire (Norham), the last of which was also certainly

ten miles north-west of Yeavering.

* South 2002, 125–6. One of the most remarkable developments in landscape studies in the last thirty years has been the recognition that the boundaries of many of these units remain substantially unchanged in Northumbria and elsewhere in England, Wales, parts of Scotland and Ireland.

a possession of Lindisfarne. Carham, significantly, is less than three miles from Sprouston, the major Anglian township on the Tweed identified by aerial photography in the 1970s and which is also thought to have British origins.* If, as archaeologists believe, it was abandoned in the late seventh century, there may be a case for arguing that, as a lordless estate, its donation with Carham was an attempt to revive its economy under monastic management: better it had an economy whose surplus went to God than no economy at all. The extra responsibility seems to have been too much for Cuthbert: within a year of this donation he had retired to his cell on Inner Farne, building walls so high that he might see nothing but sky, and suffer no other earthly distraction to interfere with his contemplation of God.

King Oswiu had set a precedent for donating land to monasteries in thanks for victory (and their prayers) after the battle on the *Winwæd* but he had been careful to distribute his patronage widely and equally among his two kingdoms; Ecgfrith, in continuing the tradition, was taking sides. If royal patrons were to become partisan, the inevitable response from ecclesiastical entrepreneurs was to compete more vigorously for their favours. It was not just ambitious abbots like Wilfrid who entered this competition. Queens Eanflæd and Æthelthryth had been prepared to use their powers of patronage to favour their own ecclesiastical causes and now royal women began to see how they might use the same mechanism to promote dynastic interests. The benefits of ties between churches and their patrons were mutual: churches and monasteries attracted wealth, which could be used to promote the careers of collateral members of the family. For royal women there were multiple opportunities. Their sisters, daughters, nieces could enjoy the fruits of their endowments; more significantly, ecclesiastical communities and their abbots or abbesses

---

* Smith 1991 and see Chapter XIII.

could and would lobby for the promotion of their patrons as candidates for kingship or other high office. In the paruchia of Colm Cille there had been a synergy between ecclesiastical and political ambitions: several of Colm Cille's descendants became abbots on Iona. The royal families of the English kingdoms were also quick to exploit these opportunities and many of Wilfrid's monasteries would be bequeathed by him to his relatives: here he is playing the English equivalent of the Irish érenach, but wise heads foresaw the political risks involved and it worried them.

A year after Ecgfrith's victory against Mercia, Wulfhere was succeeded as king by his brother Æthelred, whose queen was Osthryth, Ecgfrith's sister. In 675 the royal couple founded a monastery at Bardney in Lindsey on the edge of the fens east of Lincoln. Very little is known of the circumstances of its foundation—the first abbot was probably a member of the former ruling dynasty of Lindsey. There was a strategic element in its location in a territory formerly regarded as part of Northumbria and the royal couple were keen to invest the new abbey with a significant relic.

> There is a famous monastery in the kingdom of Lindsey called Bardney, which was greatly loved, venerated and enriched by the queen and her husband Æthelred and in which she wished to place her uncle's bones.*

The bones in question were those of Oswald; that is, what was left of him. I suggested in Chapter XIII that the clue to the whereabouts of these bones during the previous forty years lies in the fact that they had been wrapped in Oswald's purple and gold battle standard. Now this immensely valuable capital asset was to be spent on endowing their monastery. The receipt of such relics was a matter of immense prestige for the monks of Bardney; at least, it ought to have been...

---

* EH III.11; Colgrave and Mynors 1969, 247. *Beardaneu* was the original form of Bardney.

The carriage on which the bones were borne reached the monastery toward evening. But the inmates did not receive them gladly. They knew that Oswald was a saint but, nevertheless, because he belonged to another kingdom and had once conquered them, they pursued him even when dead with their former hatred. So it came about that the bones remained outside all night with only a large tent erected over the carriage in which the bones rested.[238]

Here is a tantalising glimpse of the sort of ceremonial which must have been witnessed, probably with less pomp, by the monks at Lindisfarne when Oswald's head arrived. The cynic might ask why the king and queen had not thought to ask the monks if their gift would be welcome. The insult caused by rejection of such a noble gift must have stung.* The monks of Bardney, then, not to mention whoever had been placed in charge of the precious relics, were in an invidious position. Time for a miracle.

But a sign from heaven revealed to them how reverently the relics should have been received by all the faithful. All through the night a column of light stretched from the carriage right up to heaven and was visible in almost every part of the kingdom of Lindsey. In the morning, the brothers in the monastery who had refused the relics of God's beloved saint the day before, now began to pray earnestly that the relics might be lodged with them. The bones were washed, laid in a shrine constructed for the purpose, and placed in the church with fitting honours.[239]

Many miracles were subsequently associated with Oswald's relics and with the soil on which the water from the washing of his bones fell. A visiting abbess from another Lindsey monastery begged some of this soil from the queen and, taking it home wrapped in a cloth inside a casket, used it to cure a convulsive man possessed by the devil. A boy with a recurrent fever, perhaps malaria, was cured when he sat by Oswald's tomb.

---

* In the eighteenth century ships of the Royal Navy, when arriving at a neutral port, would be sure to send a boat in under the command of a lieutenant to check that the navy's gun salute would be returned appropriately; the dignity of the flag could not be exposed to any breach of protocol in that way.

Oswald's fame was spread far and wide not just by physical association with his relics but also because of the enthusiasm with which stories about him were told throughout the Christian kingdoms, especially where new missionaries were preaching to prospective or recent converts. His heroism in battle, his links with the famous island of Iona and with Aidan, his personal qualities and the undeniable effect of his relics made for a persuasive package. His was a 'good' story. His luck, transferred miraculously in death from his spirit to his corporeal remains and anything with which they came into contact, seemed to rub off, literally and figuratively.

Oddly enough, the development of the cult of Oswald in Bernicia and Deira was slow, and late. Perhaps for obvious reasons Oswiu and Eanflæd did not promote the dead martyr; after all, who would not be discomfited by comparison with such an exemplary dead brother? In Ecgfrith's day a cult centre did develop at Whitby, and was heavily invested in by the women of the royal household; but it did not embrace Oswald. Oswiu was buried there and his widow retired to the abbey under the care of the great Hild. When Hild died in 680 she was succeeded as abbess jointly by Eanflæd and her daughter Ælfflæd, sister of Osthryth of Mercia and of Ecgfrith.[240] Ecgfrith's queens were excluded from this coterie. We cannot be sure where Iurminburh ended her days; she certainly took the veil after Ecgfrith's death, as Eddius records[241] and was listed among the patrons of Lindisfarne in the Durham *Liber Vitae*. Like Ecgfrith's first queen, she failed to produce an heir. Ecgfrith, it seemed, did not possess the family's lucky genes.

That Whitby was Deiran in its loyalties is confirmed by the arrival there in the early 680s of King Edwin's bones in circumstances which suggest an attempt to replicate Oswald's installation at Bardney and found a cult. In the anonymous Whitby Life of Gregory, which is a flagrant propagandist hagiography of the pope behind the Augustinian mission, Edwin is understandably promoted as rightful heir to that mission—after all, Eanflæd was his daughter, Ecgfrith and Ælfflæd his grandchildren; one of them almost certainly commissioned, perhaps even wrote, the Life. After his death on the field of battle in 632 Edwin's head had been taken to York and placed in the church built by Paulinus and recently restored by Wilfrid.

> Now there was a certain brother of our race named Trimma who exercised the office of priest in a monastery of the South English, in the days of their king Æthelred, while Eanflæd was still living and in the monastic life... A certain man appeared in a dream to the priest and said to him, 'Go to a place that I will tell you of, in the district known as *Hæthfelth*, where King Edwin was killed. You must remove his bones from there and take them to *Streanæshealh*.'[242]

The priest, understandably, was confused and sceptical. Where was he to look? He was to go to a certain village in Lindsey and ask a certain *ceorl* (the anonymous hagiographer had forgotten the names) who would show Trimma where to look. Trimma decided that there was some trickery here and tried to ignore the man in his dream; but the man persisted, whipping and rebuking him. Quite what lies behind this story is not clear: a monk's vision in a state of trance? The scourging is not an uncommon part of such tales; Colm Cille was forced to ordain Áedán mac Gabráin after refusing a visionary urging and then being scourged. In the end Trimma set off on what must have seemed a futile quest:

> he quickly went off to find this *ceorl* and, on making enquiries, soon found him according to the directions given him. He questioned the *ceorl* closely and learned by certain marks, which the man explained clearly, where he ought to look for the king's relics. As soon as he got the information, he went at once to the place which had been pointed out to him, but on his first dig he did not find what he was looking for; however, after digging more carefully a second time, as often happens, he found the treasure he desired and brought it with him to our monastery. And now the holy bones are honourably buried in the church...[243]

As the first authenticated archaeological excavation in the British Isles, this story has its own fascination. It raises any number of questions about who sanctioned Trimma's quest—Eanflæd must be the prime suspect—and how the intelligence was gathered. And then, how did this certain *ceorl* know where Edwin's bones were buried? Were they on his farm? It all seems a bit like *Treasure Island*; and yet, there is a real event underpinning the story. Its political significance as a component in the deliberate and planned elevation of Whitby to the principal cult site of the Deiran (and by implication Northumbrian) royal family is unmistakeable, as is the parallel down-grading of Lindisfarne/Bamburgh and Bardney.

It is ironic that Wilfrid, the principal opponent of Ionan Christianity and instigator of the triumph of the Roman orthodox church, should also ultimately be a prime instrument in the development of the cult of Oswald. His episcopal elevation had not compensated for the loss of his royal patron Æthelthryth and the hostility of Iurminburh. The queen's implacable opposition prompted Ecgfrith, in 678, to call Archbishop Theodore to Northumberland on the pretext, real or constructed, that Wilfrid's see was too big to minister effectively to its people. Theodore had probably seen this coming and was amenable. Wilfrid's power was effectively unchallenged in the North and his huge see was ripe for reform. King and Archbishop agreed that Northumbria would in future be divided into four dioceses, with sees at York, Hexham, Lindisfarne and, eventually, Abercorn on the Firth of Forth. Wilfrid would lose three-quarters of the ecclesiastical domain over which he had ruled—but not without a fight.

Wilfrid determined to travel to Rome to seek redress from the Pope and left Ecgfrith with a threat of divine retribution, just as Augustine had threatened the British bishops in 604: 'On this day twelvemonth you who now laugh at my condemnation through malice, shall then weep bitterly over your own confusion.'[244] He may have intended this to convey his confidence that in a year he would return with a papal bull supporting his case to wave in their faces. His hagiographer Eddius naturally enough in retrospect saw in it a prophecy which, in the fullness of time, came true: within a year Ecgfrith's young brother Ælfwine lay dead, killed by the Mercian king Æthelred in battle on the River Trent. There seems to have been no decisive victory here, for in the aftermath of battle Archbishop Theodore managed to broker a treaty in which Ecgfrith relinquished the right to avenge his brother in return for compensation; Lindsey remained in Mercian hands and, for the immediate future, the boundary of the two kingdoms was stabilised on the River Humber.

Wilfrid returned from Rome a year later, having pleaded his case in terms immodest enough to make the most sympathetic modern reader cringe with embarrassment; but successfully, and brandishing his bull. The king (and queen) were unmoved. Papal interference in matters reserved for royal prerogative and sanctioned by the metropolitan in Canterbury was not negotiable especially if, as Eddius records, the king believed Wilfrid to have purchased his bull.[245] Wilfrid was imprisoned, then given into the hands of a reeve called Osfrith in the royal borough of *Broninis* to cool his heels while he decided whether to accept the king's offer of a reduced bishopric and a renunciation of the papal bull.[246] As added insult, Queen Iurminburh took possession of a box of his most precious relics and carried them with her at all times, even into her chariot when she was abroad.

We do not know the location of *Broninis* but an island fortress in Bernicia is likely (the *inis* suffix means island, as it does in Irish and Welsh) and a case has been made to identify it with the hill on which the castle stands on Lindisfarne;[247] Osfrith, judging by his name, might be a collateral member of the Iding dynasty. Ecgfrith's policy towards Wilfrid was not entirely successful. The dispossessed holy man cured the reeve's wife of a palsy after which the reeve asked the king to release him; so Ecgfrith sent Wilfrid to Dunbar, where a reeve called Tydlin, evidently made of sterner stuff, had fewer scruples. But here, the fetters made to shackle the former bishop would not fit: they were found variously to be too big or too small. To a contemporary this is not as daft as it sounds: Bede makes reference to a man who was suspected of possessing 'loosing spells' in a story about the warrior called Imma who survived the Battle of the River Trent in 679 and whose fetters similarly kept falling off him. That Wilfrid was capable of pulling off such a feat, or inducing the idea that such loosing spells were in his power, should not surprise.[248] But Wilfrid had more tricks up his sleeve, it seems...

> Meanwhile the king and queen, who had been making their progress with worldly pomp and daily rejoicings and feasts, through cities, fortresses, and villages, came upon a certain occasion to a nunnery called Coldingham, over which presided a very holy and discreet abbess called Æbbe, the sister of King Oswiu. At this place the queen became possessed with a devil that same night, and like Pilate's wife was so plagued and scourged that she scarcely expected to live till day.[249]

Æbbe, now elderly but in full possession of her faculties and the immense moral authority which her experience and birthright entitled her to wield, went to her nephew the king and, explicitly linking the queen's illness to Wilfrid's imprisonment, begged him to liberate his prisoner and restore Wilfrid's reliquary. The king acquiesced; Wilfrid was freed into exile and the queen recovered. This sounds like a direct diplomatic intervention on Æbbe's part, playing the role of the wise aunt to perfection. Might there be a causal link between this intervention and Wilfrid's establishment of the cult of Oswald in Sussex in the next two or three years?* Was this the fulfilment of a promise to venerate Æbbe's brother's holy name as a repayment for her help in his hour of desperation?

* See Chapter XIII.

INCORRUPT

Meotod ana wat hwyder
seo sawul sceal syððan hweorfan

*Only the Ruler knows whither
the soul shall turn then*

IN THE FIRST YEARS OF THE

twelfth century, during the decades-long construction of Durham's stupendous Romanesque cathedral, one of its monks wrote a history of his community from the earliest times.

> This holy church derives its original, both as regards its possessions and its religion, from the most fervent faith of Oswald, that most illustrious king of the Northumbrians, and a most precious martyr; for, to the praise of God, it preserves within the safe custody of our shrine, with inviolate care, those most sacred relics, worthy of all veneration, the incorrupt body of the most holy father, Cuthbert, and the adorable head of that king and martyr, Oswald.[250]

On 29 August 1104 the relics of St Cuthbert and King Oswald were translated* from the White Church on Durham's peninsula into a bespoke shrine below the floor of the eastern apse of the new cathedral. The relics were famous both for their wonderful preservation during an epic journey through time and space and for the miracles which so often attended them. No less a

---

* Translation is the act of disinterring human remains and placing them in an aboveground container.

temporal lord than William I of Normandy had been reduced to fever and ignominious retreat when he challenged Cuthbert's potent magic. Even so, sceptics asked themselves if the saint's legendary incorruptibility in life and death would stand the test of contemporary scrutiny. An anonymous monk, writing some years later, recalled that...

> Some, founding their opinion on vain conjectures, dreamt that long before this our time his body has been removed to some other place by some secret act of violence, but that his grave, although it can no longer boast of its precious treasure, is not deprived of the glory of his virtues; but, in proof of its old possessor, is resplendent with frequent miracles, even at the present time. Others admitted that the sacral remains are still here, but, that the frame of a human body should remain undissolved during the revolutions of so many ages, they said was more than the laws of nature allow of...[251]

The temptation to take this opportunity to look inside Cuthbert's sacred coffin was overwhelming; the dilemma almost unbearable. Would the curious be punished for their impiety? Would they be disappointed, and risk the relics losing their healing powers and protective virtues for the Durham community? The stakes were high: the value of these holy bones was incomparable; on their history the edifice of the palatine bishopric of medieval Durham, almost a kingdom within a kingdom, rested. The ceremony was anticipated with excitement and trepidation:

> ...the day of the approaching translation being made known far and wide, there was a great flocking to Durham from every side. Men of all ranks, ages and professions, the secular and the spiritual, all hastened to be present.[252]

After much deliberation and soul-searching the brethren resolved to examine the contents of the chest in which the supposed relics were contained. In truth, the monks of Durham had reason to believe that their saint's body might yet be incorrupt. For had he not been exhumed some years after his death in 687 and found in a marvellous state of preservation as proof that, in death as in life, he was untainted?

Cuthbert, prior of Lindisfarne, later reluctant bishop to King Ecgfrith and finally a solitary hermit in his tiny sanctuary on Inner Farne, was brought back to Lindisfarne after his death. There he was washed and wrapped in cloth, robed in his priestly garments, wrapped once more in a waxed shroud and interred in a stone sepulchre at the right hand of the altar in the church.

> After eleven years, through the prompting and instruction of the Holy Spirit, after a council had been held by the elders and licence had been given by the holy Bishop Eadberht, the most faithful men of the whole congregation decided to raise the relics of the bones of the holy Bishop Cuthbert from his sepulchre. And, on first opening the sepulchre, they found a thing marvellous to relate, namely that the whole body was as undecayed as when they had buried it eleven years before.[253]

It was as if Cuthbert were still alive, wrote his anonymous biographer. The limbs were still supple when the body was lifted from its grave; the vestments and shrouds appeared in perfect condition and when the monks unwound the headcloth they found the saint's head had 'kept all the beauty of its first whiteness'.[254]

Bede, moved to verse, made the connection between Lindisfarne's spiritual primacy in England, Cuthbert's unblemished career and the evidence of the body:

> Blest home! how great a guest shines in this place,
> Free from all stain, where joy and glory blend!
> With ease, Omnipotent, his blest remains,
> Thou bidst corruption's gnawing tooth to spare...[255]

There were precedents for the veneration of an incorrupt saint. Oswald's right arm, preserved a few miles to the south of Lindisfarne in the church at Bamburgh, had never withered, as a sign of God's favour after the king had given his feast and the silver dish on which it was served to the poor. Aidan had intervened directly to ensure that the ceremonial importance of the king's munificence should not go unmarked. An idea that the incorruptible corpse was a reflection of earthly virtue and post-mortem godly favour was not new. No less an authority than Paul, writing to the Corinthians in the very earliest years of what became the Christian era, had established the precedent:

> Behold, I shew you a mystery.
> We shall not all sleep, but we shall all be changed,
> in a moment, in the twinkling of an eye, at the last trump
> for the trumpet shall sound, and the dead shall be raised
> incorruptible, and we shall be changed.
> For this corruptible must put on incorruption,
> and this mortal must put on immortality.[256]

It seems that the monks of Lindisfarne had some idea that their saint might be found incorrupt—why, otherwise, decide to raise him from his interment? It is tempting to look for either a Continental or insular instance which might have been the immediate inspiration either for the disinterment or the vocabulary used by the anonymous monk in describing Cuthbert's lustrous whiteness.* In about 650 Saint Fursa, the Irish monk who had converted the East Anglians, died and was left unburied for a month before his interment, with no signs of putrefaction.[257] His body was translated four years later, still incorrupt. In 695, just two years before Cuthbert's exhumation, the body of Queen Æthelthryth, Ecgfrith's reluctant first wife, had been disinterred by her sister at Ely and found to be incorrupt after sixteen years, proof of her virtuous and virginal life.[258] An eyewitness to that exhumation, the doctor who had treated her for a tumour, confirmed to the astonishment of the congregation that the scar of his operation had healed. Æthelthryth was re-buried in a stone

---

* Colm O'Brien has hunted for parallels in the New Testament and elsewhere; so far the search for the hagiographer's direct source has been unsuccessful. I am most grateful to Colm for several discussions on this intriguing aspect of the incorruption narrative.

sarcophagus, recovered from the cemetery of the Roman town of *Grantacæstir*, modern Cambridge. As it happens she was not the first in her family to be favoured: in about 664 Æthelburh, her sister, had died as abbess of the monastery of Faremoutiers-en-Brie (to the east of Paris). After seven years the monks of that community decided to bring her bones into their new church:

> On opening her sepulchre they found her body as untouched by decay as it had also been immune from the corruption of earthly desires. They washed it again, clothed it in other garments, and translated it to the church...[259]

We cannot say if Fursa or some other unrecorded saint set a fashion for incorruption in the late seventh century. There was, though, an established procedure for disinterring the bones of holy men and women and raising them to a more prominent place in a church to ensure that they received due respect and that the miracles of healing which they were expected to perform might somehow be more effective. This idea of translation is so ancient that looking for direct precedent is superfluous: as a practice it probably goes back to the sky burials of animist pastoralists.* We are left with the possibility that the Lindisfarne community felt compelled (by the Holy Spirit according to the anonymous author; by Cuthbert himself according to Bede) to bring his presence more intimately into the lives of those who missed him; that having exhumed him they felt a natural, if gruesome, curiosity to look on his face once more; that having found the body incorrupt it was immediately taken by them as a mark of the most special divine favour. Given the monks' very likely knowledge of the corporeal fates of Æthelthryth and her sister, not to mention fellow-Irishman Fursa, we may suspect a predisposition to expect,

---

* I have excavated Bronze Age burial monuments in the Cheviot Hills where collected remnants of such excarnation rituals—that is, when the body is exposed on a scaffold to be scavenged by birds—have been very carefully curated in a wholly non-Christian context.

perhaps to contrive, a form of incorruption.

Recent advances in forensic archaeology make it possible to postulate that Cuthbert's body may have been less decomposed than one might expect from the normal processes of putrefaction and autolysis (biological self-consumption). Thirty years ago there was very little literature or research on the decay of human remains, despite the frequency with which excavators encountered them. That situation changed dramatically with the development of the science of taphonomy (from the Greek: it means, literally, the law of burial), after the excavation of an eighteenth- and nineteenth-century crypt at Spitalfields in the East End of London between 1984 and 1986, and with the belated collaboration of archaeologists with criminal investigators which led to the establishment of forensic archaeology as an applied discipline in its own right.[260]

From the crypt of Nicholas Hawksmoor's baroque masterpiece of Christ Church with All Saints, Spitalfields in the shadow of the City of London came more than nine hundred deceased humans, many of whom had been interred in wooden coffins sealed inside lead caskets. It was effectively a giant, if macabre, laboratory. Bodies were recovered in every conceivable state of preservation. It took a certain sort of dispassionate character to deal with it all, month after month underground in the odd surroundings of a busy East London neighbourhood with a fruit and vegetable market just across the way.

In extreme cases soft tissue preservation included brain matter, adipocere (an unpleasant chalky wax derived from fat), skin and muscle tissue. Other bodies were found desiccated. In these, the liquids from internal organs and soft tissue had been absorbed by coffin wood and the sawdust with which coffins were often packed to prevent unseemly bumping and rattling during funeral processions; the lead seals had broken so that moisture had been able to drain away; and the coffin had been kept in a stable environment in which cool, dry air was able to circulate. The result was that clothing, skin and tendons were preserved.

The condition of a striking number of corpses found in the Spitalfields crypt calls to mind the anonymous hagiographer's description of Cuthbert's exhumed body. The critical conditions here were isolation from the normal burial environment of damp soil, worms, insects and so on; a protective lead coffin and shroud; and a combination of natural processes in which chemical mummification had taken place. The stability of the burial environment ensured the absence of further decay. In these individuals facial features were recognisable; post-mortem stubble on male bodies gave an appearance more of dissolute slumber than death and the sort of lustrous whiteness observed by Cuthbert's exhumers after a mere eleven years of interment can easily be imagined.

That such processes might have occurred in an Early Medieval context is confirmed by the excavation in 1981 of a vault beneath St Bees Priory in Cumbria. Here, interred in a punctured lead coffin dating to about 1290, a corpse was exhumed by archaeologist Deirdre O'Sullivan and subjected to modern post-mortem examination.[261] This showed that chemical changes had occurred in body fats after death, protected from external decay processes by the lead coffin and by a wax shroud; these had formed fatty acids which crystallised, dehydrated and acidified the corpse, preventing further bacterial decay. Rob Janaway, the forensic archaeologist who was present at many of the Spitalfields disinterments, believes that lead ions, released when lead interacts with the organic acids present in a human corpse, may have an inhibiting effect on the micro-organisms associated with decay.[262]

It is possible that the monks of Lindisfarne had attempted some form of embalming during the original preparation of Cuthbert's body in anticipation of his later elevation. There are references to the use of myrrh and aloes as embalming agents in Bede's commentary on the Song of Songs.[263] But forensic science does not require this to have happened: clean, cool, dry conditions—and Lindisfarne, it must be remembered, has very sandy, well-drained soils—together with some form of protective covering such as waxed shroud and lead or stone sarcophagus, will suffice. The possibility that Cuthbert was first buried in a coffin made of lead—the same material in which his church at Lindisfarne was clad by Bishop Eadberht within a few years of Cuthbert's death—is a very real one and would explain perfectly the state of his disinterred body in 698.[264] The lead—many tons of it—can only have been procured from a major Roman site, and Corbridge or Whitley Castle are the most obvious candidates. If the church at Lindisfarne was sheathed in lead, there surely must have been sufficient to provide a lead coffin for Cuthbert. One would very much like to know if his predecessors, the two East Anglian abbesses and Fursa, had been clad similarly; Roman burial in lead coffins is known in several hundred instances. There is also the case of the late Roman form of interment known as a gypsum burial, in which there seems to have been an attempt to preserve corpses using the desiccating properties of this anhydrous mineral: there are instances at Poundbury in Dorset and, perhaps more significantly, at York.[265]

Cuthbert had not wanted to be returned to Lindisfarne; had feared his presence might be a sort of circus attraction or distraction (he was right). Even he could not have anticipated the tribulations to which his fragile body was to be subjected over the next thousand and more years. Almost a hundred years after his translation, Lindisfarne was subject to the first mainland raid on Britain by those Scandinavian raiders who came to be called Vikings...

Anglo-Saxon Chronicle sub anno 793
In this year terrible portents appeared in Northumbria, and miserably afflicted the inhabitants: these were exceptional flashes of lightning, and fiery dragons were seen flying in the air. And soon followed a great famine;

and after that in the same year the harrying of the heathen miserably destroyed God's church in Lindisfarne island by rapine and slaughter.[266]

A contemporary, the great Northumbrian scholar Alcuin, conveyed the appalling shock felt by Northumbrians when he wrote to King Æthelred:

> ...never before has such terror appeared in Britain as we have now suffered from a pagan race, nor was it thought that such an inroad from the sea could be made. Behold, the church of St. Cuthbert spattered with the blood of the priests of God, despoiled of all its ornaments; a place more venerable than all in Britain is given as a prey to pagan peoples.[267]

In another letter, this time one of sympathy and consternation to the bishop of Lindisfarne, he wrote:

> ...the distress of your suffering fills me daily with deep grief, when heathens desecrated God's sanctuaries, and poured the blood of saints within the compass of the altar, destroyed the house of our hope, trampled the bodies of saints in God's temple like animal dung in the street. What can we say except weep with you in our hearts before the altar of Christ and say, 'Spare thy people O Lord and give not thine heritage to the Gentiles lest heathens should say, "Where is the God of the Christians?"'
>
> What security is there for the churches of Britain if St Cuthbert with so great a throng of saints will not defend his own? Either this is the beginning of greater grief or the sins of those who live there have brought it upon themselves. This indeed has not happened by chance; it is a sign...[268]

Somehow the community at Lindisfarne held out for another eighty years, by which time a Danish army had settled in England and overwintered as far north as the River Tyne. Many treasures belonging to the monastery were destroyed or looted; many monks were killed. The island community once sheltered by the military might of the Bernician kings in their fortress at Bamburgh was vulnerable to further attack from land and sea. Cuthbert's and Oswald's relics must be protected. The twelfth-century English chronicler Symeon of Durham wrote:

Raising, then, the holy and uncorrupt body of the father, they placed beside it in the same shrine (as we find it mentioned in old books) the relics of the saints; that is to say, the head of Oswald the king and martyr, beloved of God, which had formerly been buried in the cemetery of the same church, and a part of the bones of St Aidan... Having collected these relics, they fled before the barbarians, and abandoned that noble pile, the mother church of the nation of the Bernicians...*

What 'old books' Symeon was referring to we do not know. There is more than one version of the legendary travels of the monks and their precious shrine. An alternative narrative provided by the *Historia de Sancto Cuthberto* suggests that the relics were removed in the 840s and taken to Norham, on the banks of the River Tweed; Symeon dates the abandonment of Lindisfarne to 875, the year of Halfdan the Dane's attack on Northumbria.[269] At one point it seems as though an attempt was made to remove some of the relics to Ireland (an attempt prevented by divine intervention and a storm).[270] Eventually the monks settled at Chester le Street, the site of a Roman fort, *Kuncacæster*, on the Great North Road between Durham and Gateshead. For almost a hundred years this became the seat of the bishops of Bernicia until their final removal to Durham, where a succession of churches was built to house the relics and provide for the community of Cuthbert until the construction of the cathedral began in 1093. Throughout this period the potency of the relics of Cuthbert, Aidan and Oswald was maintained, enhanced by miracles of healing and prophecy and by donations to the community. The relics contained in the shrine embodied not just the virtue and God-given power of the ancient kings of Bernicia but something of the ancestral luck of the Northumbrian race. It is difficult for a sceptical and cynical twenty-first-century secular society to fully grasp

* Symeon, *Libellus de Exordio XXI*; Stevenson 1993, 655–6. Reference to 'part' of the bones of St Aidan reflects the author's reading of Bede's account of Colman taking Aidan's relics with him to Mayo after Whitby in 664.

the power and importance of such objects and the places associated with them unless one turns to face Mecca, or Jerusalem. This is powerful magic. Even into the sixteenth century, immediately prior to the Protestant Reformation in England, the Earl of Surrey felt obliged to divert from his march against the Scots at Flodden Field to pick up Cuthbert's banner from Durham: that is, to ask for the blessing of the saint and carry his totemic standard into battle.

The opening of the shrine in 1104 was, then, a matter of political and symbolic significance in establishing the bona fides of the new cathedral and reinforcing its tangible links with a glorious but now quite mythical past. This was a test and a rite intended to transcend the overt Norman iconography of Durham's French bishops and their historically antipathetic behaviour towards the monks of the community of St Cuthbert; to soothe native sensitivities.

When, in the last days of August 1104, the shrine in which Cuthbert's relics lay was opened 'aided by instruments of iron', the monks found 'a chest covered on all sides with hides'.[271] This, we infer, was the casing fabricated to hold the original relics on their travels from Lindisfarne. Within this chest was the coffin now on display in Durham Cathedral and regarded as the earliest surviving decorated carved wooden object from England. Its simple knife-cut iconography of gospels and saints is perfectly in tune with the aesthetics of Lindisfarne in Cuthbert's day. There is no serious doubt that this was the 'light chest' described by Bede and made to receive the exhumed remains of the saint in 698. Inside, beneath the lid, was a sort of tray resting on horizontal bars with a metal ring at either end by which it could be lifted out. On the tray, near the head, lay the tiny, exquisite book now known as the Stonyhurst Gospel or Cuthbert Gospel—the only complete Early Medieval book from England still in its original binding. It did not belong to Cuthbert but was probably placed in the coffin soon after his translation; it is regarded as contemporary with the more famous Lindisfarne Gospels, produced within a few years of 700. It is one of the most important historic and artistic artefacts of Early Medieval England. In spring 2012 it was purchased jointly for the British Library and Durham Cathedral and University.

Much has been written about these relics. The artefacts accompanying the saint included his ivory comb, his portable wood and silver altar, a Eucharistic paten and chalice; sacramental cloths and vestments of Byzantine silk. Suffice it to say that on removing the shelf the monks found Cuthbert inside, accompanied by an odour of the 'sweetest fragrancy' and in 'a perfect state' with the bones of the other saints packed around him.[272] Almost overwhelmed with fear and emotion, the monks proceeded to investigate. The anonymous monk's account, and a later version written by Reginald of Durham, have an almost forensic quality about them; the archaeologist could hardly wish for more detail. When the monks had summoned the courage to touch the contents of the coffin, they were able to remove Cuthbert's wrapped remains intact. Reginald adds an important observation: that the base of the coffin, where the relics of the saints had been compressed against the shrouds in which they were wrapped, 'was blackened by the closely packed dust of their putrefaction'.[273] This suggests that the container had not been substantially disturbed since the original translation; Cuthbert's body had decayed further after its reburial, but it had done so in situ. This is entirely consistent with a single translation from the original (whether lead or wood or stone) into the light coffin in which the remains were to embark on their remarkable travels.

Of all the corporeal relics the coffin had contained—Cuthbert, parts of Aidan, bones of several bishops of Lindisfarne and of the Venerable Bede—Oswald's head alone was replaced when the coffin was reburied; the others were relocated elsewhere in the cathedral. This begs the question of how the monks knew which was the head of the royal martyr. Since 1104 Cuthbert's shrine has been opened three times. In 1538 Henry VIII's commissioners destroyed many of the shrines in the cathedral, exhumed the coffin of Saint Cuthbert and examined it for signs of incorruption before replacing it in the tomb. In 1827 the relics were examined in detail and Canon Raine found that the skull was now in 'an imperfect state'.[274] The tomb was reopened for the last time by Canon Greenwell, the indefatigable antiquary, in 1899. This time the fragments of skull were examined in detail and photographed. When reconstructed, the skull Greenwell saw showed clear signs that its owner had been felled by a blow from an edged weapon, which produced a gaping three-finger-wide slash across the front of the skull. This is a wound of battle, or of execution. It cannot belong to any of the saints whom we suppose to have accompanied Cuthbert on his post-mortem journeys. It may be the most intimate possible evidence for Oswald's fatal encounter with Penda. If we can say that Oswiu picked the right skull off the right stake at *Maserfelth*, there is reason to believe that this skull is the same one. If further testimony for the credibility of the relics as a group is required, it comes in the form of the superb pectoral cross, missed by the monks in 1104 and by the commissioners in 1538 and only retrieved during Raine's even more intimate examination in 1827. Made of gold inset with garnets, it was found deeply buried in the earliest wrappings of the saint's body and had been suspended around Cuthbert's neck by a gold-twisted silk cord. Its seventh-century provenance is unchallenged.

The histories of Oswald's other body parts—right and left arms, hands, torso and legs—are almost equally compelling; and almost equally telling in illuminating Oswald's extraordinary potency throughout the medieval period across England and parts of Europe. There was only ever one Cuthbert, but the story of King Oswald's bones is vastly complicated by their multiplicity: at least five medieval churches, including Durham Cathedral, claimed to possess his head; there are several claims for arms and any number of unspecified 'relics'. The Bardney tomb, graced not only by a substantial proportion of Oswald's body but also by continuing royal patronage and the presence of the martyred king's battle standard, was further adorned with precious gifts and embellishments by no less a king than Offa, the late-eighth-century Mercian contemporary of Charlemagne.[275] That Mercian royal interest in propagating Oswald's cult continued into the tenth century. Under Æthelflæd, so-called Lady of the Mercians, queen of Mercia and daughter of Alfred the Great, several churches dedicated to Oswald seem to have been founded and in 909 she may have been personally responsible for the removal of his tomb from Bardney to a new monastic church at Gloucester: she is one of the earliest, best-attested and most regal of a long line of body-snatchers.[276]

A more mundane fate met the precious right arm, encased in its silver reliquary at Bamburgh and interred in the crypt of St Peter's church by Oswiu. Around 1055 a monk called Vynegot stole it and took it to Peterborough. According to the chronicler Hugo Candidus, Peterborough also managed to acquire one of Oswald's ribs and 'some of the ground on which he was killed'.[277] For the propagators of the cult of Oswald the division of his body was manna from heaven. Almost anyone could claim ownership of an Oswald relic—and they did.

Fragments of the stake on which he was impaled had spread to Ireland and to Frisia by the early part of the eighth century. The royal monastery of Chelles, near Paris, was given an unspecified relic of Oswald, probably by Charlemagne, towards the end of that century. The most spectacular reliquary of all belongs to the church dedicated to him at Hildesheim in Germany. Made in the 1180s of gold and silver and containing a textile bag with most of a skull, minus the lower jaw, the lid of the octagonal reliquary is in the form of a dome with a finely worked gold head on top, wearing a crown set with precious stones and enamel.[278] By 1300 another Oswald skull was being claimed by the church at Schaffhausen in Switzerland; and another, perhaps originally residing at Zeddam, now belongs to the Rijksmuseum *Catharijneconvent Utrecht* in the Netherlands. A relic-list from Willibrord's early foundation at Echternach in Luxembourg claimed to possess yet another Oswald skull.

A comprehensive DNA testing programme on all the claimed Oswald corporeal relics would be a fascinating project. It would inevitably in some senses devalue many, if not all of the relics; and to worry about whether they are 'real' or not is also in a way to miss the nature of the medieval faith in relics and the vast industry it spawned. But for the twenty-first-century archaeologist the fascination in the results would match that of the monks of Durham, tremulously unwrapping the bindings of their saints in the candlelit majesty of a great cathedral.

Oswald's continuing fame outside the original and early centres of his cult can partly be attributed to the multiplication and wide dissemination of his relics at a time when Irish, Northumbrian and Mercian monks were proselytising among the unconverted peoples of northern Europe. Royal women, too, are notable for their enthusiasm in propagating his virtues. The first of these was related to Athelstan (895–939), grandson of Alfred the Great and the first king who might truly lay claim to the title *Rex Anglorum*: king of all England. His identification with Oswald as the first great Christian English king (conveniently forgetting Edwin), is easily understood by association. His half-sister Edith married Otto the Great of Saxony and, as it were, took Oswald with her.* Another part of the appeal lies in his status as the first great martyr of the English and the hybrid

* An extensive study of three of these royal women has been made by Dagmar Ó Riain-Raedel 1995.

Christian/pagan divinity embodied in his 'luck'.

Not every cult centre possessed relics of Oswald: Wilfrid's foundation at Selsey in Sussex was based on no more than Wilfrid's entrepreneurial zeal and the presence of a calendar that listed Oswald's feast day, 5 August, as a major festival. Such calendars were spread widely across Europe, and very many of them kept Oswald's name alive, through Germany and Switzerland, Austria and beyond. One must also credit Bede, whose apparently late conversion to the virtues of Oswald ensured his presence at the heart of the Ecclesiastical History, one of the most widely copied and widely read texts in Early Medieval Europe.* Bede's and Oswald's fates were tied literally and figuratively together, for Bede's relics were added to those of Oswald and Cuthbert after his death in 735. It was an irony not lost on Bede that Oswald's earthly imperium continued to expand within the Christian realms long after his death in battle.

There is another archaeology of Oswald, more shadowy, which allows us to detect on the fringes of credibility something of the effect his mythology continued to have on later generations. To begin with, a number of medieval holy wells appear to be associated with the more pagan elements of the early Oswald cult. The first suggestion of an association with a well is Reginald's admittedly late story of the right arm that fell from the ash tree whither it had been brought by the raven-like bird.† Other Oswald wells are to be found at Elvet, a short walk across the River Wear from the cathedral at Durham and a possibly early cult site for Oswald; Winwick and Warton in the pre-1974 county of Lancashire (and possibly on the southern border of Northumberland in the late seventh century); Astbury in Cheshire, Kirkoswald in

---

* Bede's prototype for the chronology of the Ecclesiastical History, his *Chronica Maiora* of 725, gives almost all credit for the conversion of the Angles to Edwin. Thacker 1995, 112.

† See Chapter XIII.

what used to be Cumberland, Grasmere and Burneside in old Westmoreland.* Close to the site of Turret 25b at Heavenfield is a spring, used by the excavators of the turret in the 1950s, called the White Well. The locations of most of these wells in areas of very late Germanic settlement or control tends to reinforce the idea that the earliest cult of Oswald was a popular British idea: as Alan Thacker has pointed out, pre-Christian native cults often associated springs with the veneration of head-relics.[279] The prefix 'white' at Heavenfield suggests, naturally enough, an association with Oswald's Irish *nom de guerre*, *Lamnguin*: Whiteblade. A possible early church dedication to Oswald at Whittingehame in East Lothian suggests another possible *Lamnguin* association.[280] There is much more research to be done on the association of 'white' names with elements of the Oswald cult.

There is an intriguing series of coins, belonging perhaps to the early part of the eighth century, which have been discussed by, among others, Michelle Ziegler.[281] This is the so-called K-series of early Anglo-Saxon silver pennies, or *sceattas*, which have been found in the south and east of England and which for the most part are housed in the Fitzwilliam Museum, Cambridge. The obverse has an image of a king drinking from a cup or chalice, sometimes with a cross above it. The reverse shows a warrior with long hair and apparently clad in mail. In his right hand is a long cross whose stem reaches the ground; on his left hand perches a bird. The king is standing in what could be interpreted as a ship or dish. Below the left hand with the bird is a T-shape. The temptation to associate the bird with Oswald's raven and the possible dish with the silver platter that he gave to the poor is very strong. At such an early date the only mints in the south-east of England were London and Canterbury; if these coins were minted at the latter, it might be argued that the figure on the reverse with the

* Thacker 1995, 102.

bird is Augustine, although he had no particular association with birds. If it is Oswald we have to ask, why Kent? Oswald had no clear connection with that kingdom, whose Northumbrian connections are confined to Edwin and the Deiran royal line of the Yffings; for a while his young cousins were sheltered there. Sussex, which might be expected to trade on its Oswald associations, did not have a mint so early.

The only coinage with indisputable Oswald iconography comes not from England but from Switzerland. At Zug, in the early seventeenth century, a series was minted which has Oswald with sceptre and raven on the obverse and the imperial German twin-headed eagle on the other. This can be explained by the presence in Zug/Schaffhausen of an Oswald head cult, probably originally founded in the late eleventh century by Judith, wife of Tostig, the deposed Earl of Northumbria who invaded northern England with the help of a Norwegian army but was slain by his brother Harold II at the Battle of Stamford Bridge in 1066 (three weeks before the latter was himself defeated and killed at Hastings).

Church dedications to Oswald offer equally problematic associations, mainly because the earliest recordings of such dedications often occur in a post-Conquest setting; there are very few which can be absolutely asserted to belong to the eighth century. The only example that can be confidently placed so early is that of the church at *Scythlescæster*.[282] Symeon, probably drawing on a lost Northumbrian chronicle, records the death in 788 of King Ælfwald of Northumbria at an unidentified site on Hadrian's Wall. The king was taken for burial at Hexham, where the Northumbrian cult of Oswald was at its strongest, and a church, dedicated to him, was built at the site of the battle. *Scythlescæster* has not been identified: Chesters, not far to the west of Heavenfield, is one possibility; the Roman fort at Birdoswald, which shows signs of occupation after the end of the fourth century, is another obvious candidate.

The many other Oswald church dedications, more than fifty of them in the North of England, have been the subject of detailed study.[283] They are problematic in the sense that identifying early dedications, when records often do not antedate the Domesday Survey of 1086, is virtually impossible without the sort of historical note provided by the Ælfwald story; the large numbers of Oswald dedications which may date to the high medieval period does, of course, reflect his continuing popularity in the English consciousness. Even so, it is striking that they are concentrated not in Bernicia, as one might expect, but across a broad belt in the north Midlands (that is to say, in Mercia) and Yorkshire/Lancashire. This must reflect the interest taken by Mercian kings and queens in Oswald's cult status—an attempt, perhaps, to appropriate it from its populist origins and to associate themselves with Oswald's post-mortem and overtly royal powers of patronage. The paucity of Oswald dedications in his Bernician heartland probably reflects the desire of the Lindisfarne community in the eighth century to promote Cuthbert, a less ambivalent figure and one whose complete corporeal relics they hung on to tenaciously throughout the following centuries.

Oswald's vigorous promotion in the decades and centuries after his death shows that his spiritual patronage was as effective as his lordship had been in life. Whatever the complex psychological reasons for attaching personal success in health and fortune to the veneration of the relics or memory of a dead royal martyr, it seems that Oswald's luck did not run out on the battlefield at *Maserfelth*: his presence, potency and charisma were still being felt hundreds of years after his passing, reinforced by Bede, Alcuin and other chroniclers and by the preservation and multiplication of the physical properties of those virtues. Kings, peasants, monks sought to associate themselves with Oswald, to belong in some sense to the empire of his glorious legend. As the embodiment of the luck of first his own people, the Bernicians, and later the English as a whole; as a talisman to kings and as a tap root into a more animistic British past, Oswald succeeded as no other early saint, except perhaps Cuthbert, was able. Famously generous, brilliant in battle, a fighter against all odds and winner of Christian glory in death against a great enemy, Oswald was the first quintessential English hero. Not until the early nineteenth century, perhaps, did England acquire an equally potent replacement in that self-invented, charismatic and fatally brilliant warrior-martyr and secular saint, Horatio Nelson.

XX

MEN OF LETTERS

A sceal snotor hycgean ymb
þysse worulde gewinn

*The wise man must always consider
this world's conflicts*

WITH THE RULE OF OSWALD'S
nephew Ecgfrith it must have seemed that the luck of
the Idings was finally running out. Married twice to virgin
queens, he failed to produce an heir. Impetuous military campaigns led to disastrous defeat for the armies of Northumbria and
to his death in a Scottish glen at the hands of the Picts in 685. The
savaging of his host at Nechtansmere seems to have been com-
memorated in stone in a great carving at Aberlemno in Angus,
which survives as a memorial to his folly; later historians see in
this year the beginning of a permanent decline.* Never again
would a Northumbrian king wield imperium over the larger part
of Britain. Fifty years later, with the death of its pre-eminent
chronicler Bede, Northumbria's continuous narrative history is
virtually discontinued for three hundred years.

Even before Ecgfrith's untimely death in battle at the age
of about forty his failure to produce a legitimate son caused

---

* Nechtansmere has usually been identified with Dunnichen in Angus; but the Early
Medieval historian Alex Woolf has recently argued convincingly for the merits of
Dunachton, further to the north and west on the shore of Loch Insh. Woolf 2006.

consternation among the Bernician nobility and in the mother-house of her church. Unwillingly called to the bishopric of Lindisfarne in 685, Cuthbert's wish to retire to the privacy of Inner Farne in his last years was thwarted by the burdens of his unwonted office. His value as a man of great humility and wisdom drew him reluctantly into the debate over the succession. It also shows us that half a century after Aidan's arrival, church and monarchy had become twin facets of a complex state. In a story calculated to illustrate Cuthbert's visionary talents and his political identification with the Idings, Bede relates how Ecgfrith's sister, Ælfflæd, sent for Cuthbert to consult with her...

> He went on board a ship with the brethren and came to the island which lies at the mouth of the river Coquet from which it receives its name. It is famous for its companies of monks, and it was here that the same abbess asked him to meet her. Having got into conversation with him, suddenly, in the midst of their talk, she fell at his feet and adjured him by the terrible awe-inspiring name of the King of heaven and of His angels, that he would tell her how long Ecgfrith her brother would live and rule over the kingdom of the English. 'For I know,' she said, 'that through the spirit of prophecy in which you abound, you can also tell me this, if you wish.'[284]

Anyone acquainted with the political narratives of the period recognises in this request a prompt by a senior member of the ruling dynasty for a holy man of paramount reputation to nominate or 'ordain' a successor to the throne of Northumbria. Here again we see how women of the royal family could be prominent in the machinery of dynastic patronage: Ælfflæd was attempting to arrange the endorsement of a successor to her childless brother. Cuthbert's reluctance to be drawn into such a discussion is understandable: he had spent much of his career as a monk trying to avoid the worldly affairs of kings. But he was not quite as ingenuous as Bede liked to paint him. On being more or less forced to accept the bishopric by Ecgfrith, shortly after his meeting with Ælfflæd, he extracted a heavy price in expanding Lindisfarne's property portfolio with large estates. Later we find him warning Queen Iurminburh to flee after a prescient vision of Ecgfrith's death. And it must not be forgotten that as a youth he had fought in the king's army. He had a distaste for matters of secular society and state, but he was not naïve. He, like the king's sister, knew the potential consequences of a vacant throne for both the fortunes of the Idings—the patron founders and protectors of Lindisfarne—and for the future of the whole kingdom. For him there was only one choice.

> After a short time he said: 'Do not say that these are lacking; for he will have a successor whom you will embrace with as much sisterly affection as if he were Ecgfrith himself.' She answered: 'I beseech you, tell me where he is.' He said: 'You see how this great and spacious sea abounds in islands? It is easy for God to provide from any of these a man to place over the kingdom of the English.' So she understood that he was speaking of Aldfrith, who was said to be the son of Ecgfrith's father, and was then in exile among the islands of the Irish, for the study of letters.[285]

Aldfrith, returning to Bernicia in 685 even as Ecgfrith's body was being carried by his *comitates* not to Bamburgh but to Iona for burial, would be England's first literate king, a sign of the extent to which Christian culture had penetrated Northumbrian society.[286] And he was not just literate: he was a scholar of high repute whom some historians have suggested was responsible for setting down in words two of Anglo-Saxon England's greatest poems, *Beowulf* and *Widsith*.[287] Bede tells us that Aldfrith 'ably restored the shattered state of the kingdom, although within narrower bounds'.[288] As part of this restoration he expanded the use of coinage introduced on a very small scale by his brother under whom, for the first time, there is evidence of an attempt to stimulate trade by developing an emporium at Jarrow.[289] We cannot yet say if it was as a result of frequent journeys between Britain, Ireland and the Continent by clerics seeking enlightenment, relics, books and craftsmen that stimulated kings' interest in international trade in the eighth century; but we must suspect it.

The island alluded to by Cuthbert during his interview with

Ælfflæd was Iona. Aldfrith was studying in the monastery of Colm Cille when he received the news that Ecgfrith had died; here also he became friends with Adomnán, Colm Cille's hagiographer and successor as abbot. Aldfrith was not the only highly literate traveller to pass through the hands of the Iona community: Aldhelm, the most learned man of his time before Bede and author of a number of serious religious works, who had studied at the Canterbury school founded by Theodore and his monk Hadrian, may have met Aldfrith on Iona; they corresponded as friends in later years. Perhaps the most exotic of visitors in Adomnán's day was the Gaulish bishop Arculf who, attempting to return home to Gaul from an extended journey to the Holy Land, was blown off course and duly found himself in the Inner Hebrides. Adomnán made good use of his luck in persuading Arculf to let him compile from his anecdotes a book on the holy places, including plans of important buildings. Adomnán later took a copy of this book, known by its Latin title *De Locis Sanctis*, to Northumbria and presented it to his friend King Aldfrith. Bede was privileged to be able to read and then abridge it for a wider audience.

Aldfrith, whose Irish name was *Flann Fina* by association with his mother, was a character more in sympathy with Aidan and, perhaps, Oswald than he was with his bellicose brother Ecgfrith. He was no warrior. Bede, who regarded him as illegitimate, nevertheless admired his learning; but, as an unashamed devotee of the more martially inclined of his ancestors, perhaps regretted that Aldfrith did not embark on wars of conquest or seek to extend the frontiers of Northumbria to their former bounds. Nevertheless, Aldfrith presided over a kingdom of astonishing and lasting creativity: the era of the Lindisfarne Gospels and the near-complete Bible manuscript known as the *Codex Amiatinus*; of the Stonyhurst Gospel; of the marvellous monastery at Jarrow in which Bede was to live and die; of the gaunt but affecting architecture of the church at Escomb in County Durham, which is the most complete surviving monument of its day; of the great stone crosses at Ruthwell and Bewcastle. Not least of that kingdom's achievements was to produce Bede himself, a giant of Early Medieval scholarship whose list of works covers every branch of learning and whose erudition was and is staggering. His books are not just marvels of scholarship but evidence of a sort of early industrial revolution, which required animal husbandry and processing on a dramatic scale to produce thousands of sheets of perfect vellum; inks and paints for writing and illumination; leather for bindings; glass for windows. The noise of the copyists in the scriptorium there, reading out loud as they wrote, must have sounded to the contemporary ear like a swarm of bees.

Take Bede alone and here is a fitting legacy for the luck and achievements of the Idings, not just in fashioning the first Anglo-Saxon state sufficiently robust to survive the deaths of its kings but in forging a hybrid culture of Angle and Scot, Briton and Irish, whose exuberance and craft, sophistication and heroic scale is an enduring linguistic, architectural and literary monument.

And yet… and yet did not Oswald Iding sow a wind that his descendants in the eighth century would reap as a whirlwind; which would almost overwhelm medieval kings from Richard I ('the Lionheart') to Henry VIII and very nearly shake the edifice of the English polity to its foundations? Did no-one see it coming in the trickle of monastic donations made to the humble Irish monks by Oswald and his clever brother? The answer is yes: at least one man tested the wind and saw the storm coming, even if he did not see it coming from the sea.

In 734, exactly one hundred years after Heavenfield, Bede wrote a letter to his friend the bishop of York—a letter that survives. Egbert was no ordinary bishop, but a cousin of King Ceolwulf, brother of a future Northumbrian king, Eadberht, and an early teacher of Alcuin. Bede, too infirm, as he says, to make the visit to York to see his friend, was writing within a year of his own death; probably conscious of it. In part we are reading the nostalgic admonitions of an old man who sees, or believes, that the church of his day is a shadow of what it was in the glorious days of the seventh century under those kings whose lives are so subtly drawn by Bede himself. In these days, he wrote...

> it is reported of some bishops that they have no men of true religion or self-control around them, but instead are surrounded by those who give themselves up to laughter, jokes, storytelling, eating, drinking and other seductions of the soft life...[290]

In part it is a complaint written to a fellow-cleric whose brother is the king—and, therefore, there is something of an open, public appeal for reform and for the continuation of God's (and Oswald's and Aidan's) work in converting and ministering to the Northumbrian people...

> because the places in the diocese under your authority are so far apart that it would take you more than the whole year on your own to go through them all and preach the word of God in every hamlet and field, it is clearly essential that you appoint others to help you in your holy work; thus, priests should be ordained and teachers established who may preach the word of God...[291]
>
> For we have heard, and it is indeed well-known, that there are many of the villages and hamlets of our people located in inaccessible mountains or in dense forests, where a bishop has never been seen in the course of many years...[292]

Bede wants more bishops: he is demanding diocesan reform from the one man who, with the king, can achieve it; and Bede is probably the one cleric in the kingdom with sufficient intellectual authority to make such a demand. His hope for the fulfilment of Gregory's original plan for twelve Northumbrian sees would never happen; but in the year of his death the archbishop's pallium, which had been promised to Paulinus more than a hundred years before, was finally sent.

The letter to Egbert is also absolutely striking in what it reveals about the state of the English church in Bede's day, as if the lid of discretion he applied to his contemporaries in the Ecclesiastical History has, in semi-private, been lifted. It is our primary source for understanding what had become of the legacy of the conversion. Since the death of Aldfrith in 705 it had evidently been the practice of kings to alienate more and more lands to the church in return not just for political support but also for even more venal reasons; in response, a whole generation of young men, it seemed, had turned away from the traditional ways of the *folc*. In the penultimate chapter of the Ecclesiastical History, Bede had hinted at his intense discomfort:

> In these favourable times of peace and prosperity, many of the Northumbrian race, both noble and simple, have laid aside their weapons and taken the tonsure, preferring that they and their children should take monastic vows rather than train themselves in the art of war. What the result will be, a later generation will discover.[293]

Bede had a pretty shrewd idea, and he used his letter to Egbert to reinforce his message unambiguously. There are many monasteries, he says, which do not deserve the name, having nothing of real monastic life about them.

> Such places which are, in the common phrase 'useless to God and man', because they neither serve God by following a regular monastic life nor provide soldiers and helpers for the secular powers who might defend our people from the barbarians, are both numerous and large.[294]

Bede's fears were twofold: he saw the end of religion and the loss of the Northumbrians' ability to defend the homeland:

> It is shocking to say how many places that go by the name of monasteries have been taken under the control of men who have no knowledge of true monastic life, with the result that there is nowhere that sons of the nobles or retired soldiers can take possession of.[295]

The social contract on which Northumbrian tribal society was based had been ruptured. Since time immemorial, and probably long before the arrival of the Idings, it had been based on the gift of land for a life-interest in return for military service and food renders. Those renders and services supported a royal military elite whose function in representing their people was to protect the land, display prestige and conquer weaker territories. The character of the political and economic geography of Britain was predicated on land-holdings defined and bounded as units of render held for a life-interest, the hides, to a hierarchy of central places: *vill* and *villa regia*. The commutation of these renders to prayer, which formed the principal ecclesiastical contract enabling the settlement of monks in religious communities to serve the needs of the faithful and pray for the founding patron or donor, removed such lands from the portfolio of the king; removed them in perpetuity. In return for the extraction of such lands from their natural cycle of life-interest transfers, the church brought stability, capital investment and agricultural and economic progress, along with the everlasting salvation of the founding patron. Oswald did not foresee the wholesale transfer of lands to any *gesith* who wished to avoid what was in effect the national service. In plain, modern terms this was a tax dodge fashioned by *faux* conscientious objectors. Oswiu had not seen it in his modest donation of twelve ten-hide estates; neither Ecgfrith nor Aldfrith had over-indulged in their purchase of prayer and legitimacy. But their successors did. While there were now many young men of fighting age who had no prospect of being able to acquire land, marry, raise children and live a virtuous secular life...

> There are others, laymen who have no love for the monastic life nor for military service, who commit a graver crime by giving money to the kings and obtaining land under the pretext of building monasteries, in which they can give freer reign to their libidinous tastes; these lands they have assigned to them in hereditary right through written royal edicts... thus they have gained unjust rights over fields and villages, free from both divine and legal obligations...[296]

How had this come about? In the first place, it was the *reductio ad absurdum* of the practice we begin to see under Oswiu and Eanflæd: the use of monastic donations as a tool of political and familial patronage. In Alhfrith's hijacking of the Ripon donation; in Eanflæd's Gilling intervention after the death of Oswine, those roots were sown. Not until the death of Aldfrith, apparently, was this policy so heedlessly followed that kings began to alienate lands in bulk and without regard for the implications. Aldfrith's son, Osred, was only eight when he succeeded in 705. In such vulnerable times it is not surprising that the Idings' capital assets should be sold in exchange for the support of the military elite. But that land could not easily be recovered to the royal portfolio; and the effect on the land itself, on its bonded and semi-bonded *drengs*, *ceorls* and serfs, can only be imagined. It is possible that *gesiths* now holding hereditary rights in the *vills* were incentivised to develop the economic potential of their lands; we cannot say. If that was the case, the kings had in any case surrendered their right to tax it; they had not yet developed a means of doing so. In the eighth century, in Mercia, powerful kings began to experiment with ways in which they could bring back some of the landed surplus into the royal fisc; and by the time the shires and townships of Northumbria emerge into the historical record in the twelfth and thirteenth centuries a complex range of services, dues and obligations had been reimposed on land. But the Northumbrian state was never able to enjoy imperium over the other kingdoms again. It could not afford to.

That there had been licentiousness and a relaxation of the monastic rule during the century between Heavenfield and Bede's letter to Egbert is hardly surprising—at least on a small scale. With the expansion of the church some dilution of the quality of its guardians—and they had been men and women of outstanding virtue and capabilities—is no revelation. The monastery of Oswald's sister Æbbe at Coldingham on the Berwickshire coast had, even during the founding abbess's life, attracted criticism for alleged debauchery of which Æbbe herself was, apparently, unaware. God punished that community by burning it down.[297] And who could blame a generation of young men who, dazzled by the artistic brilliance and dignity of the great monasteries at Jarrow, Hexham, Whitby and Lindisfarne, thought that career a better bet than yomping with the king's host when there were in reality not many new lands to conquer. Behind this lack of opportunity for martial glory, for treasure and the rewards suitable to a young *gesith's* rank lies, ironically, the motivation for young, unmarried men from Scandinavia sailing over the sea to look for opportunities—and treasure—at the end of the century. In the unprotected monasteries of Northumbria, which must have seemed like the eighth-century equivalent of a turkey shoot, they saw rich pickings. The monasteries were unprotected because the church, or what pretended to be the church, owned all the land with which earlier kings had been able to sustain their armies. In 793, with the first raid on Northumberland's vulnerable coastal monasteries by Viking pirates, the whirlwind descended.

One is tempted to see in the career of that turbulent priest Wilfrid a portent of things to come. Often in conflict with his sponsoring kings, a great lover of wealth and its trappings, jealous of his possessions and, at his death, perhaps the richest man in Europe, Wilfrid was only too well aware of the potential for the church to use its capital assets in trading blows with secular powers; but no-one, not even his harshest critics, would claim that Wilfrid was in any sense a fake, a secular lord masquerading as a monk to avoid military duty. His monastic foundations were grand, especially by comparison to the modest intentions of Aidan and Cuthbert, and most of them were passed down to collateral members of his family; but they were real.

The process of alienation which Bede described in apocalyptic terms can be observed at a more subtle level in the *Historia de Sancto Cuthberto*, that ancient record of the lands given to

Lindisfarne from its founding by Oswald in 635.

Historians have tended to concentrate on what the *Historia* tells us about land-holding, and rightly so. But the document also reveals the variety of ways in which monastic entrepreneurs could acquire sometimes very large tracts of land.

The island of Lindisfarne was first given to Aidan to establish a monastery from which to convert the Northumbrians, in imitation of that built by Colm Cille on Iona in about 565. Oswiu had made his first donation at Gilling in expiation of his crime in murdering Oswine. A few years after this, in 655, he made his famous donation of twelve ten-hide estates to fulfil a promise made in anticipation of his victory against Penda. Donations as thanks for victory are a recurrent theme in the *Historia*.

Ecgfrith gave more land to Lindisfarne after Cuthbert 'raised a boy from the dead'; and then there is that curious donation of Carham after the victory against King Wulfhere of Mercia in 674, even though Wilfrid, and not Cuthbert, had accompanied the king into battle.[298] His prayers, at a distance, had been sufficient to earn an earthly reward. The fifth entry in the *Historia* records that after Cuthbert reluctantly agreed to become bishop of Hexham, then Lindisfarne, in about 684, Cuthbert (meaning the community of Lindisfarne) was given lands in York, at Crayke a few miles to the north of York, and at Carlisle. Ecgfrith's motives in granting these lands are a matter of speculation, but in part it must have been payment for Cuthbert's agreement to be bishop and, therefore, for Cuthbert's political and spiritual support for Ecgfrith and his immediate family.

After this there is a break in the sequence of donations to Lindisfarne until 737, when Ceolwulf, the king to whom Bede dedicated his Ecclesiastical History, abdicated, took the tonsure and retired to the holy island 'with great treasure'.[299] More than a hundred years after that king's death Bishop Ecgred supposedly translated his bones and those of Cuthbert (and Oswald) to a new see at Norham on the River Tweed and 'rewarded' the community with two *vills*; such, perhaps, was the value of those relics. The same bishop built more churches at Gainford and elsewhere on the River Tees, and gave those lands to Lindisfarne also. The motives for some of these donations are obscure, but they were surely made in the expectation of spiritual, political or material return and they must stand for the otherwise unrecorded but apparently large numbers of *vills* which were alienated by Osred and his successors for naked profit or short-term political interest.

King Osberht, who was king of Northumbria in the middle of the ninth century, attempted to seize back two *vills* from the control of St Cuthbert's community, presumably marking a point where kings realised the need to recycle some of these lost lands. Much good it did him; he died within a year. Well before Bede's death, it is clear, land—and the renders and services which could be extracted from it—had become a commodity to be traded for all sorts of benefits and motives, both high and low. Monasteries found that they needed cash, or its equivalent, to build and restore churches (how, one wonders, did Cuthbert's successor at Lindisfarne purchase enough lead to clad the church there?); to buy books and the relics of saints so that their establishments might reflect and enhance their reputations and influence.

Kings must also have needed cash to replace lost opportunities for winning booty, for lost tribute from subject kingdoms, and to support their peripatetic progress through a decreasing number of royal estates. In parallel, the alienation of royal lands to the secular nobility diminished both the pool of land that could be used to support the military elite, and the pool of young unmarried males from whom that elite was recruited. The process, gradual or not, was sufficiently noticeable to set off alarms in the mind of Northumbria's historian. It is comprehensible; that does not make it anything but reckless.

It would take the singular military, moral and diplomatic

skills of Alfred the Great towards the end of the ninth century to impose a replacement set of obligations on the people of England so that they might organise resistance to the Danish armies of Halfdan, Guthrum and Ivar the Boneless. Even Alfred's determination to carry out monastic reform was insufficient to save Northumbria's once-great houses. Melrose was destroyed in a raid by Kenneth MacAlpin in 839; Lindisfarne was abandoned in 875; Hexham Abbey was burned to the ground in the same year; Monkwearmouth and Bede's Jarrow were deserted at about the same time and not re-founded for two hundred years; Ripon lasted until 948 before being razed. By the time William I embarked on his genocidal rampage through Northumbria in 1069–70 there were almost no functioning monasteries in the land which had given rise to such a golden age of art, culture and spirituality. Only the tiny band of monks who still devotedly carried their saints' relics around with them in a fragile wooden coffin, who clung tenaciously to the memory of what they had owned and been, kept the spark of Oswald's and Cuthbert's legacy alight and kindled its revival at Durham.

Under later English kings the over-riding need to provide opportunities for young, unmarried members of a new military elite to gain glory and fighting experience would lead to an extraordinary age of crusades and of military expansionism. That fundamentalist cause would follow a familiar pattern of purity and self-denial, community spirit and pious zeal followed by cynicism and degrading licentiousness (and more tax evasion) so graphically traced in the history of the Knights Templar. Periodically kings would try to bring land that had been carelessly alienated back into the royal portfolio. Henry VIII's policy of recycling it all in a single (or double) tranche of dispossessions led to a new religion and a new phenomenon called the middle class; it saved the Tudor monarchy from bankruptcy, even if that policy is implicated in the outbreak of civil wars in the 1640s.

The age of imperialism and capital that followed did not materially change the nature of the game. In the 1820s, during the near-revolutionary atmosphere of the Reform crisis in Britain, the prime minister, none other than the Duke of Wellington, argued that democracy was a dangerous thing: had not the patronage system worked sufficiently to win the long wars against France? He was right: Britain was able to field a large number of exceptionally gifted military, and especially naval, commanders who had been promoted through a system which Oswald and Oswiu—and for that matter Colm Cille—would have recognised. That it retained power and influence in the hands of a social and economic elite is not in doubt; that it was anti-democratic is perfectly true. That it worked in the invention of a new British imperium—and an idea of God-given greatness, which can be directly traced to Bede and thence to Oswald—is demonstrable. It was not in the interests of the great and powerful to promote the careers of cowards and incompetents; their performance reflected on the judgement of the patron. And so the military elites of the seventh century and eighteenth and nineteenth centuries were just that. They comprised the best of the best, picked, trained and encouraged by their patrons and supported on landed estates sufficient for them to avoid the shattering boredom, poverty and ignorance of the labourers in the fields. The rules of patronage have not changed; probably will not change.

Who bears the blame for the alienation of Northumbrian lands into the wrong hands, if not the kings who granted them? Who appointed the abbots and bishops who failed their communities? The rules of patronage which bound king, church and land in an eternal knot still apply; sometimes they are broken. Promise, reward and legitimacy retain their potential to create heroes and villains: the currency may have changed a little, the sums still work out the same.

Did Oswald see it all coming? I think not.

Timeline: AD 672 to 735

672 King Drust expelled from Pictland. Ecgfrith crushes Pictish uprising with the help of Beornheth of Dunbar. Bruide mac Beli succeeds to Pictish kingdom.

—Ecgfrith's Queen Æthelthryth becomes a nun at Ely; Wilfrid thus loses his principal royal patron.

—Synod of Hertford: Theodore begins process of dividing Britain into dioceses.

—First documented reference to the people of *Nordanhymbrorum* (EH IV.5).

—Bishop Chad dies.

673 Foundation of Hexham Abbey by Wilfrid on estate given by ex-Queen Æthelthryth.

—King Egbert of Kent dies; succeeded by his brother Hlothere (685).

—Ecgfrith marries Iurminburh of ?Kent or Frankia.

—Bede born on land owned by soon-to-be founded Wearmouth monastery.

—Cenwalh, king of Wessex dies; his widow Seaxburh attempts to take control but fails.

674 King Wulfhere of Mercia invades Northumbria and is repelled. Lindsey annexed by Ecgfrith, later recovered by Æthelred of Mercia in 678–9. Northumbria now too big for one bishop: dispute with Wilfrid?

—Ecgfrith grants estate at Carham to Cuthbert of Lindisfarne (not Wilfrid) in thanks.

—Wearmouth monastery founded by Benedict Biscop on land given by Ecgfrith.

675   King Wulfhere of Mercia dies. Succeeded by his brother Æthelred.

—Foundation of Bardney monastery by Æthelred of Mercia and Osthryth, daughter of Oswiu. Endowed with Oswald's trunk and legs.

—?Foundation of monastery at Abingdon under King Cenwalh of Wessex, possibly at *villa regia*; possibly a double monastery.

—Death of Colman on Inishbofin, County Galway.

676   Cuthbert retires to Inner Farne to contemplate.

—King Æthelred of Mercia attacks and subdues Kent.

—A comet appears, wrongly dated by Bede to 678 (EH IV.12).

678   Archbishop Theodore visits Northumberland at Ecgfrith's request. Sends the Picts (at Abercorn) Bishop Trumwine, a friend of Bede's. Divides see into four (Lindisfarne–Bernicia, York–Deira, Lindsey and later Abercorn) and curtails Wilfrid's power.

—Wilfrid expelled (Bede EH V.24); travels to Rome to seek intervention from the pope; prophesies doom to Ecgfrith.

679   **Battle of the River Trent**: Ecgfrith's younger brother Ælfwine is killed but battle is indecisive. Archbishop Theodore oversees peace treaty between Mercia and Northumbria (to include recovery of Lindsey).

—Death of Æthelthryth (Etheldreda) at Ely.

—Benedict Biscop makes fifth and final journey to Rome.

679–?82   Probable date of Arculf's pilgrimage to the Holy Land and, on his attempted return, his arrival by 'accident' at Iona where he is interrogated by Adomnán.

680   Abbess Hild dies at Whitby (burial place unknown). Eanflæd becomes abbess of Whitby jointly with her daughter Ælfflæd.

—Wilfrid returns from Rome brandishing a papal missive. Ecgfrith dismisses it. Wilfrid is imprisoned in *Broninis* (unknown), finally at Dunbar.

—Bede enters Wearmouth monastery aged between five and seven.

—Abercorn established with Northumbrian bishop on the Forth.

—Synod of Hatfield.

—Possible date for translation of Edwin to *Streanæshealh* (cf Ian Wood 2008).

681   Wilfrid is released into exile in Mercia after the queen falls ill. In Sussex he converts the pagan Saxons, who abjure paganism because of a three-year drought. Rain falls on the day of their baptism (EH IV.13).

—Probable date of foundation of Selsey Abbey and before 685 establishment of cult of St Oswald there.

—Jarrow monastery founded (see 685) by Benedict Biscop on land granted by Ecgfrith; first abbot is Ceolfrith.

683   Death of Æbbe, abbess of Coldingham and uterine sister of Oswald (aged ?seventy-five).

—Death of apostate Sighere of Essex; succeeded by Christian brother Sebbi.

684   Ecgfrith dispatches pre-emptive force to invade Ireland (in pursuit of Aldfrith?) against advice of church (including Cuthbert).

—Cuthbert visits Ælfflæd, sister of Ecgfrith, at Coquet Island; discusses succession.

—Synod of Twyford (?Whittingham) where Theodore and Ecgfrith persuade a reluctant Cuthbert to become bishop of Hexham, which he swaps with Eata for Lindisfarne (in the following spring). Lindisfarne is given substantial estates at York, Carlisle and Crayke.

685   Cuthbert consecrated at York; visits Carlisle with Iurminburh and has vision of Ecgfrith's death.

—Monastery dedicated at Jarrow on 9th Kalends of May (23 April) by Ecgfrith.

—Ecgfrith launches pre-emptive strike on Northern Picts.

—Army (including Beornheth of Dunbar and King Ecgfrith) is slaughtered 20 May at Battle of Nechtansmere (Dunnichen or Dunachton); called *Linn Garan* in *HB*.

—King Aldfrith (Ecgfrith's half-brother) succeeds, probably under the influence of Cuthbert on Lindisfarne; Aldfrith may be on Iona at the time of Cuthbert's prophecy.

—Ecgfrith is taken to Iona to be buried (possibly; Jarrow believes he should have been taken *there*). All Northumbrian conquests north of Forth and Solway are lost. Rheged is retained.

—It rains blood; milk and butter turned into blood (ASC).

—Cuthbert and Eata swap roles: Cuthbert returns to Lindisfarne and Eata to Hexham as bishop.

686   Wilfrid restored to see at York with lands at Ripon and Hexham, probably after reconciliation with Theodore.

—Adomnán of Iona visits Northumbria, esp. Jarrow. Adomnán gives Aldfrith a copy of the *De Locis Sanctis* dictated to him by Arculf.

—Plague.

—Cuthbert again retires to the solitude of Inner Farne.

—Raid on Kent by Cædwalla of Wessex; installs brother Mul on Kent throne. Takes control of Wessex, South Saxons, Surrey, Jutes and all Wessex; conquers Isle of Wight; kills opposition royals.

—Death of Eata, bishop of Hexham and former abbot of Melrose, Ripon and Lindisfarne.

687   Death of Cuthbert; dispute between Wilfrid and Lindisfarne monks; they are purged.

—Mul of Kent burned to death.

688   Ine succeeds to throne of Wessex until 726.

—Cædwalla voluntarily abdicates and goes to Rome to be baptised (influenced by Wilfrid while in Sussex?).

689   Cædwalla of Wessex dies in Rome, possibly as result of injuries received in conquest of Wight.

690   Archbishop Theodore dies; buried at Canterbury in monastery of St Augustine.

—Benedict Biscop dies aged sixty-two.

691   Wilfrid expelled by Aldfrith.

692   Mercia reconquers Lichfield.

—Wilfrid is in exile in Mercia, founding monasteries at Oundle, Brixworth etc.

—Acca becomes abbot of Hexham.

693   Death of Bruide mac Beli.

695   Æthelthryth disinterred by sister, Seaxburh, and found to be incorrupt.

c.697   Aldfrith marries Cuthburh (sister of King Ine of Wessex); son Osred is born.

—Osthryth, wife of Æthelred of Mercia, murdered by the Mercians.

698   Beorht of Dunbar, at head of Northumbrian host, is killed by the Picts.

—Cuthbert's coffin at Lindisfarne is translated and his body found to be incorrupt. It is placed in a decorated wooden casket. Bishop Eadberht is buried beneath Cuthbert in his original sarcophagus. The Lindisfarne Gospels may have been completed by this date.

*c.*700   Anonymous Life of St Cuthbert written by a monk of Lindisfarne. Possible date for production at Wearmouth–Jarrow of the *Codex Amiatinus*, oldest known surviving copy of Jerome's Vulgate Bible.

702   Wilfrid called to account at church council at Austerfield, West Yorks. Archbishop Berhtwald excommunicates him. Wilfrid sets off for Rome again, aged sixty-nine, with Acca.

*c.*703   Bede completes *De temporibus*; Wilfrid and Acca visit Willibrord in Frisia on their way to Rome; hear stories of Oswald's cult there, and his relics.

704   Death of Aldfrith at Driffield. Eadwulf (unknown parentage) usurps kingdom of Northumbria. Tries to expel Wilfrid.

—Death of Adomnán of Iona; succeeded by Conamail.

—Æthelred of Mercia (reigns from 675) abdicates and retires to become abbot of Bardney monastery in Lincs.

705   **Siege of Bamburgh**. Osred (aged eight, son of Aldfrith) succeeds to kingdom of Northumbria; protected by Wilfrid and Berhtfrith of Dunbar who raises the siege: Eadwulf is exiled.

—Synod of Nidd: Wilfrid restored to his lands at Hexham and Ripon. Wilfrid retires to Oundle in Mercia; intervention of Ælfflæd suggests Aldfrith wishes Osric to succeed.

708   Bede accused of heresy over his calculation of the ages of the world; refutes with finely calculated riposte; is antagonised by Wilfrid.

709   Wilfrid dies at the age of seventy-five. Leaves monasteries and portable wealth to close relatives.

711   Berhtfrith of Dunbar attacks Picts in revenge for the deaths of his father and grandfather, at a **Battle in Manau** between Stirling and Linlithgow.

714   Probable date of death of Ælfflæd, sister of Ecgfrith.

716   Iona capitulates and agrees to follow Roman rule. AU note the expulsion of Ionan communities across Druim Alban by Nechtan of the Picts.

—King Osred is killed in a plot by his kinsmen. Kingdom briefly usurped by Eadwulf. Succeeded by Coenred.

—Abbot Ceolfrith of Jarrow retires and sets out on pilgrimage to Rome.

—Bede's verse Life of St Cuthbert.

—Æthelbald succeeds to the Mercian throne (to 757). He refers to himself in charters as *Rex britanniae*.

717   Eadwulf's death in ?Dál Riatan exile reported in Irish Annals.

—Archbishop Nothelm returns to Canterbury from Rome with papal annals relating to the conversion of England; communicates with Bede.

718   Osric succeeds to kingdom of Northumbria.

721   Bede's prose Life of St Cuthbert.

*c.*725   Bede writes *De temporum ratione* (Concerning the organisation of time).

729   Osric dies; Ceolwulf succeeds to kingdom of Northumbria. King Nechtan of the Picts is driven from his kingdom.

731   King Ceolwulf imprisoned in a coup; is forced to enter monastery at Lindisfarne. Gives significant endowments to the monastery. Recovers kingdom.

—Bede completes Ecclesiastical History of the English People. Effective end of contemporary Northumbrian history.

734   Bede's Letter to Archbishop Egbert of York (brother of King Eadberht) on spurious monasteries etc.

735   Death of Bede. ?Alcuin of York is born.

—Nothelm moves from being archpriest at St Paul's in London to archbishopric of Canterbury. ?Appointed by Æthelbald of Mercia.

Appendices

APPENDIX A

⌘

The Bernician
king-list problem

THE GENEALOGIES of the early Bernician kings have never really added up to the satisfaction of historians: there are too many contradictions between and among the scanty sources. The convenient explanation is that the sources are unreliable or unhistorical, messed up either by scribal error, carelessness or wilful deceit for dynastic ends. Here, I propose a simple re-reading of the sources, doing no injustice to any of them, which allows trust to be placed in the succession and broad dating of the Bernician king-lists.

The genealogy of Oswald's father Æthelfrith, and that of his forbears, is suspect because in copying it from an original Mercian source the British historian known as Nennius seems to have been unsure of himself.[300] Nennius's Bernician king-list has it that *Ealdric genuit Ælfret. Ipse est Ædlferd Flesaur:* 'Ealdric begat Ælfred; that is Æthelfrith the Twister.'* It is not very helpful. We might read it to mean that Ealdric, that is Æthelric, bore a son named Ælfred, whose *nom de guerre* was Æthelfrith; but it doesn't convince. The original source behind the fragments

---

* *HB* 57. The ascription of the work known as the *Historia Brittonum* to the cleric Nennius has been convincingly challenged; my use of his name is more for convenience than academic rectitude.

Nennius put together has become garbled, as if a line is missing; more likely there were two sons, Ælfred and Æthelfrith. We know that Æthelfrith had another brother, Theobald, mentioned by Bede; and elsewhere in *HB* 61 Nennius implies that there was another, Ecgulf. My best guess is that Æthelric had four sons, because Ælfred turns up independently in an Irish Annal.* If it didn't matter, we might chalk the problem up to the 'don't know, can't tell' column with which Early Medieval genealogies are littered. But it does matter, because the only chance to create a narrative outline for the period between Ida's legendary arrival at Bamburgh and Æthelfrith's unification of Deira and Bernicia in about 604 depends on whether, or how far, the Bernician king-list can be trusted.

A date for Æthelfrith's birth can only be estimated by guessing his age at accession to the kingship. The *Historia Brittonum* allows him twenty-four years as king, the last twelve of which he was king of both Bernicia and Deira. Early Medievalists concur that Æthelfrith became king around 592–3. At what age? There is almost no point speculating: anywhere from twenty to forty, maybe younger, maybe a bit older. Historians like to put brackets around such things: 'he must have been at least such and such when he took the throne' or, 'he couldn't have lived that long'. Learned articles are full of such statements. The fact is, we don't know. If he was sixty when he died that would give a birth date of 557, which is not unreasonable; but he could just as easily have been seventy, or fifty. Think of Archbishop Theodore reaching England at the age of sixty-seven and holding office for more than twenty years after that.

Æthelfrith had a British wife before Acha. Nennius has it that he gave his first wife (he specifically uses the word wife, not queen, so I suspect that at the time Æthelfrith was not yet king),

* See Chapter IV, p.65.

whose name was Bebba, the fort of *Dinguoaroy* and that it was re-
named after her: *Bebbanburgh* or Bamburgh. This sounds a little
like the chronicler guessed her name from the name of the royal
fortress; but otherwise this marriage is credible. *Dinguoaroy*, like
Flesaur, is Brythonic: the native language of the Britons from
which Welsh, Cornish and Breton were starting to develop in this
period. It contains elements which might mean something like
the 'fort of the theatre or assembly-place': intriguing in itself.[301]
Bamburgh, then, had been a British fortress before the English
had it; and this is more or less confirmed by excavations in the
castle. If Æthelfrith 'gave' it to his wife, it implies that as part of
a marriage settlement he gave her the estate, or Early Medieval
shire, of Bamburgh for her dower. That would explain why it
came to be re-named after her. It would have been a generous
gift indeed, for Bamburghshire as we understand it was a large,
fertile and productive landholding.*

Whatever the truth about Æthelfrith's first wife, she only bore
him one son we know of: Eanfrith. That Eanfrith ended up an
exile among the Picts suggests that Bebba, or whatever her real
name was, had Pictish blood. If so, it is evidence that the kings
of Bernicia who preceded Æthelfrith sought an alliance between
themselves and the Picts and so married him to one of their princesses. That the dower seems to have been so generous might
imply that Æthelfrith had early expectations of becoming king
of Bernicia and that the alliance was regarded as of the highest
importance. I suggest that an alliance with the Picts was designed
to isolate the kingdom that lay between them: Gododdin.

This is tricky stuff. What seems clear is that when Ida, the
dynastic founder, came to Bernicia in the middle of the sixth century he was able to do little more than cling to a beach-head; that
the beach-head was Bamburgh/*Dinguoaroy*; that he must have

---

* See Chapter IX; it is possible that at this early date Bamburghshire was much smaller
than it later became.

seized the fort and held it against a concerted British campaign to oust him. In his sons' day the English warbands gradually extended their reach and power to control the whole of the kingdom of Bernicia, formerly the British *Bryneich*: probably the lands between Tyne and Tweed. Æthelfrith ultimately emerged as the beneficiary of this dynastic sacrifice, no doubt bloody and arduous. He was the only grandson of Ida to rule the Northumbrians.

The detail of this campaign is infuriatingly précised by Nennius's account:

> Four kings fought against them [the sons of Ida], Urien, and Rydderch Hen, and Gwallawg and Morcant. Theodoric fought vigorously against Urien and his sons. During that time, sometimes the enemy, sometimes the Cymry [Britons] were victorious, and Urien blockaded them for three days and three nights in the island of Metcaud [Lindisfarne]. But during this campaign Urien was assassinated on the instigation of Morcant, from jealousy, because his military skill and generalship surpassed that of all the other kings.[302]

This narrative, perhaps derived ultimately from a poem, tells of a grand coalition of British warlords who, fearing the rising threat of the English of *Dinguoaroy*, set out to destroy them, to drive them back into the sea whence they came. The location of the siege is significant. *Metcaud*, the British name for the tidal island of Lindisfarne, lies a few miles to the north and in plain view of Bamburgh Rock. The Idings, then, were involved in a last-ditch defence of their core territory, in imminent danger of being wiped from the pages of history.

Who were these four British kings? Urien can be identified as the Lord of Rheged, the Solwegian kingdom which seems to have included Galloway, Cumbria and parts of the northern Pennines. Rydderch Hen was king of the Britons of Strathclyde; Gwallawg is identified in other genealogies as the father of Ceretic, king of Elmet. Elmet, which survives even today in place-names like Barwick-in-Elmet, was a Pennine kingdom roughly equating to the bulk of West Yorkshire. Its boundaries may have extended as far east as the wetlands at the head of the River Humber, in which case it separated the northern English of Bernicia and Deira from their southern counterparts in Mercia and Lindsey. Morcant, of whom we know virtually nothing apart from his presence in this assault, can be inferred to have represented the northern British: the kings of Gododdin who ruled the area around the Forth from their fortresses on Castle Rock, Edinburgh, and Traprain Law in East Lothian. All the British kingdoms of the period were Christian, at least nominally. They could, therefore, portray themselves as fighting a holy war against the heathen English.

Nennius's all too brief account of what seems to have been a lengthy campaign ranging across much of the North-east implies that the final showdown, the siege of Lindisfarne, was raised by an act of betrayal that passed into British infamy. Since Theodoric is named as the defender and raiser of the Siege of Lindisfarne, he ought to have been king of Bernicia at the time. But the numbers do not add up. Nennius offers us a detailed sequence of early Bernician kings:

Ida reigned 12 years
Adda reigned 8 years,
Æthelric reigned 4 years,
Theodoric reigned 7 years,
Freodwald reigned 6 years,
Hussa reigned 7 years.*

This takes us to the supposed start of Æthelfrith's twenty-four-year reign which, given his death in 616/17, gives us an end-date for the list of 592–3. Taking this chronology at face value gives dates for Theodoric, and therefore of the Lindisfarne campaign, of 571–8. But Nennius adds a confusing yet superficially convincing

---

* Adda, Æthelric and Theodoric were Ida's sons; Freodwald and Hussa are not cited in the genealogy as his sons so they may have been nephews or other collateral members of Ida's family—his brothers, even.

detail: that in Freodwald's reign, which in this sequence ought to be between 578 and 585, the Kentishmen received baptism from the mission of Augustine.[303] Now the date of this mission is one of the half-dozen or so dates in English history that every school child used to know: 597. We cannot have our cake and eat it.

The problem arises from Bede back-calculating Ida's reign from his first sure regnal date: Æthelfrith's death in 617.* The Northern History has it that he reigned twelve years in Bernicia and twelve in Deira and twenty-four in both. This has nearly always been read to mean that he reigned twenty-four years in Bernicia (i.e. from 592/3) and annexed Deira in 603/4, thereafter uniting the two kingdoms. This interpretation requires that the detail about Augustine's mission is an error, a pretty big one as these things go: at least twelve and perhaps eighteen years. Not impossible, but it needs some explaining. It means that Ida's seizure of Bamburgh is dated to 547, which most historians agree is too early; it also means that the Anglo-Saxon Chronicle entry for 588, which records Æthelric (Æthelfrith's father) gaining possession of Deira on Ælle's death and ruling there for five years, creates an anomaly, especially since his rule over the Bernicians is placed before 571. That is some comeback. And then, it leaves Deira without a king between Æthelric dying in 592/3, and Æthelfrith who is supposed to annexe it twelve years later. It will not do.

There are two general approaches to such dating problems. One, very reasonably, is to accept that they cannot be resolved.†

---

* Bede was using a list almost identical to the Nennian genealogy and included in material known as the Moore Memoranda because it was appended to the so-called Moore manuscript copy of Bede's Ecclesiastical History (Cambridge, *University Library*, Kk. 5. 16); neither includes any of the Nennian glosses.

† Warnings on the potential manipulations of these genealogies are well heeded, for example Dumville 1977 and Kirby 1963; but there is no prima facie reason to reject this section of the Anglian genealogies out of hand. Its alternative versions vary only slightly and the original on which all these lists was based cannot be later than about 737.

The second obliges the historian to suppose an error, or series of errors, which can take many forms. Scribal mistakes, such as miscopying xvii for xxvii when using Latin numerals for dates, are common in annal entries. Errors of omission are easy to envisage too, such as missing a name off a list; and so on, right up to the deliberate falsifying of ancestors and dates to suit topical political motives. The rule of thumb must always be to prefer the scenario that posits the fewest errors; otherwise, historians can more or less make up any solution which suits them. Simplest is best: time to sharpen Occam's razor.

The straightest and, it seems to me, most elegant solution to the problem of dating the early Bernician kings is to invert the standard interpretation and postulate that Æthelfrith ruled for twenty-four years in Deira, the last twelve of them in Bernicia. This is perfectly reasonable as far as Nennius goes: the line 'Æthelfrith reigned twelve years in Bernicia and another twelve in Deira'[304] can comfortably be read this way. That the Anglo-Saxon Chronicle 'E' entry for 593 records him becoming king of 'Northumbria' simply reflects the traditional interpretation of the Nennian king-list, possibly influenced by Bede. He was almost certainly not king of a united Northumbria so early. The assumption that he was first king in Bernicia has remained unchallenged, so far as I know, but that is all it is: an assumption. There is no reason I can think of to maintain it as a rock of Bernician studies.

What follows from this realignment? Æthelfrith becomes king of Deira in 592/3, when the Chronicle says his father's reign there ended. So far so good. He becomes king of Bernicia in 603/4, the year in which we know he won a famous battle against the Dál Riatans. There is no problem there either, so far as raw chronology goes; in fact, it turns out to work rather well (see my discussion of the Battle of Degsastan in Chapter II).

The dates for the reigns of the Idings would then work out as follows, give or take a year or two in each case and inserting the one year allotted by the Moore Memoranda[305] to Glappa:

Ida	560–71
Glappa	571–2
Adda	572–80
Æthelric	580–4 (in Bernicia); 588–92/3 in Deira
Theodoric	584–91
Freodwald	591–7
Hussa	597–603/4

This sequence would place Theodoric's reign and, therefore, the siege of Lindisfarne in the mid-580s, which most historians would accept as feasible; and it allows Freodwald to be reigning, just, when Augustine's Christian mission arrived in Kent. In fact, the incidence of Freodwald's death in that year would make it more memorable, more likely to attract a note in an Easter table.

That Æthelric should depart the kingdom of Bernicia in around 584 and become king of Deira four years later is much more plausible than the great comeback implied by the accepted chronology and provides, I suggest, the context and backdrop for the final British catastrophe. If he was driven out, or took refuge, at the time of the first of a series of British assaults leading up to the siege of Lindisfarne, Theodoric's assumption of the kingship after successfully seeing off the threat makes sense.

One might propose the following scenario: after four years of Æthelric's kingship of Bernicia a confederacy of British warbands drives him out and in the ensuing long-running war his brother Theodoric is forced into a last-ditch stand on Lindisfarne somewhere between 584 and 588, which is successfully relieved by the betrayal and death of the British overlord Urien. Æthelric or his very warlike son Æthelfrith (aged what: twenty?) take advantage of the weakness of Rheged by capturing their fortress and palace at *Catræth* and win renown by the successful defeat of the Gododdin warband there (in 585–8?) commanding a combined Deiran/Bernician force and ending for ever the threat posed by the spears of Rheged. From this position of strength, in 588 Æthelric, perhaps with the aid of his son, deposes King Ælle by political or physical means and assumes the kingship of Deira. Æthelfrith succeeds him in Deira in 592/3, during the Bernician reign of Freodwald.

This chronology provides the simplest and least contradictory solution to the problems posed by the Nennian king-list and gives us a plausible scenario for Æthelfrith's early career. It remains to consider the circumstances of his marriage and gift of Bamburgh to Bebba. If the alternative chronology I propose is close to the truth, Æthelfrith must marry and gift Bamburgh to his British wife during his father's reign in Bernicia: 580–4. Eanfrith, the son born of this marriage, would then be about thirty-four at the death of his father and fifty at the death of Edwin. Presumably, after his father's fall Æthelfrith and his wife lose possession or control of Bamburgh and by the time Æthelfrith regains control over the North in the name of the Idings some twenty years later she is dead or otherwise disposed of so that he is free to marry Acha.

APPENDIX B

##

The genealogies
of the kings

IN ONE HUNDRED and eighty years from 560 to 740, the kings of Northumbria graduate from legendary forefathers Ida of Bernicia and Ælle of Deira to men, contemporaries of Bede, whose lives can be described in some detail. Royal families are always interested in their legitimacy: then and now they wish it to be known that they either spring from gods—Woden in the case of the pagan Anglo-Saxons—or are divinely appointed; and the *Dei Gratia* minted on to our coins today ultimately derives from the first Christian anointing of a Dál Riatan king by Colm Cille in the sixth century.

Bede tells us that there were 'those who compute the dates of kings', a cadre of heralds who recited pedigrees at feasts, weddings and anointings. The genealogies compiled here are reconstructed from references in Bede and the Anglo-Saxon Chronicle and the northern king-lists preserved in the *Historia Brittonum*. Some of the minor figures and their relations have to be inferred; it is not always certain which child belongs to which queen, for example. But the Germanic habit of alliterative naming of children is a help: Æthelfrith seems to have had one son, Eanfrith, by his British wife Bebba; the others, by Acha, all begin with 'O's and so we infer that they are 'uterine' brothers.

Æthelfrith's line dominated the seventh century, which makes things relatively simple until the death of Osred in 716, after which other collateral lines of Idings, descended from Æthelfrith's uncles, re-emerge from obscurity leaving us little hope of reconstructing their genealogies in detail. But these diagrams carry a health warning. After Æthelfrith dates are pretty certain: Bede had access to king-lists kept by the 'computers' and knowing the lengths of kings' reigns he worked backwards from his own time; but when it comes to Ida and his sons, historians from the Venerable Bede onwards have been hard pressed to rationalise some of the contradictions which emerge from a number of sources. This is partly because, until Bede's day, dates were calculated in regnal years—that is, such and such happened in the tenth year of the reign of so and so. It was Bede who popularised the dating of events, including the accessions of kings, from the incarnation: *anno domini*. See Appendix A for more information.

Here I have attempted to rationalise the competing genealogies to produce a scheme that reduces the guesswork to a minimum; but the health warning stands. Even so, it is a significant and fascinating fact that most of the genealogies of the English kingdoms have start dates in the middle of the sixth century. This must reflect some sort of political reality; it may also reflect the credibility of the computations as first written down in the seventh century by Christian clerics, eager to play their crucial role in the legitimisation of their sponsoring kings.

What one might be seeing is the great-grandparental dynastic founder being, as it were, cast in stone by a new breed of computers: those who did not merely remember, but wrote down what they remembered.

KEYS TO THE GENEALOGIES OF THE KINGS

The seventh-century Deiran royal house

Names in capital letters denote kings of Deira or Bernicia in their own right (not sub-kings).

Italics denote males.

Names in grey boxes are those of kings who ruled both Bernicia and Deira, or princesses who married kings elsewhere.

Names in boxes with double outlines denote royal women who became abbesses.

The seventh- and early eighth-century Bernician royal house

Names in capital letters denote kings of Deira or Bernicia in their own right (not sub-kings).

Underlined names are those of male scions who became sub-kings of Deira.

Italics denote males.

Names in grey boxes are those of kings who ruled both Bernicia and Deira, or princesses who married kings elsewhere.

Names in boxes with double outlines denote royal women who became abbesses.

The early Anglo-Saxon kings of Northumbria

Names in capital letters denote kings of Deira or Bernicia in their own right (not sub-kings)

Italics denote males

Names in grey boxes are those of kings who ruled both Bernicia and Deira, or princesses who married kings elsewhere

THE SEVENTH-CENTURY
DEIRAN ROYAL HOUSE

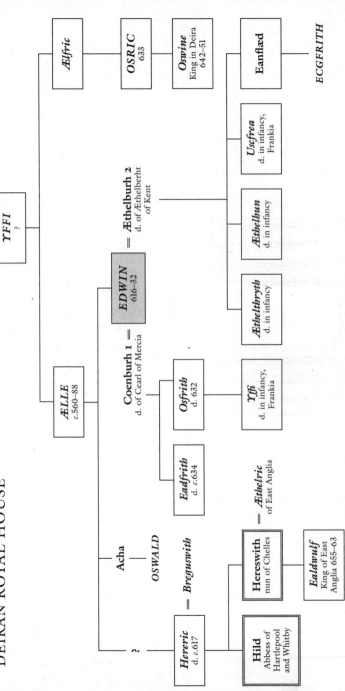

THE SEVENTH- AND EARLY EIGHTH-CENTURY
BERNICIAN ROYAL HOUSE

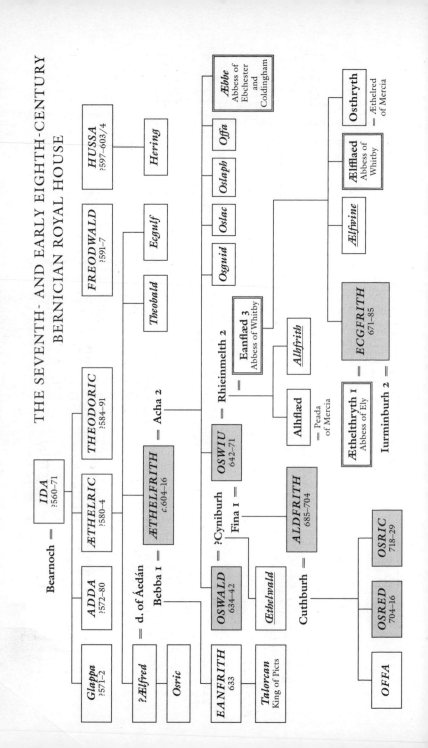

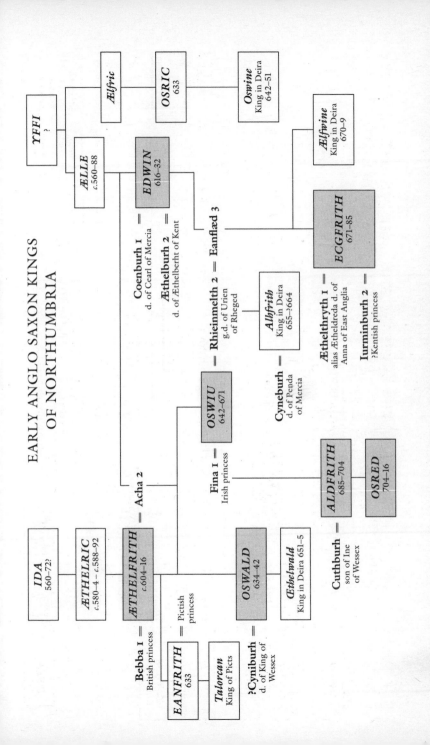

EARLY ANGLO SAXON KINGS
OF NORTHUMBRIA

瑠

A note on
the languages of
seventh-century
Britain

READERS of Early Medieval histories can be forgiven for feeling confused by the variations in names, spellings and terminologies used by historians and archaeologists. There are good reasons for this confusion: as the contemporary Northumbrian historian, the Venerable Bede, tells us, there were several languages in use in his day in Britain. He spoke both Latin and what we tend to call Anglo-Saxon or Old English—the language of the *Beowulf* poet. Bede probably also knew something of the language we call Brythonic (linguists sometimes use the term Old Welsh or Primitive Welsh): this was the language of the Britons before and during the Roman period. The Irish and Scots both spoke Old Gaelic, the forerunner of the modern languages spoken in Ireland and the Western Isles and Highlands of Scotland. A fifth language, Pictish, was spoken by the majority of the tribes in what is now Scotland; but we know virtually nothing of it, save that it belonged to the same language group as Brythonic.

Problems arise through translation and copying. Bede wrote (and thought) in Latin. When he named a place or person or a thing in another language, he either rendered it in Latin or he transliterated; either way, his spelling is his own because Brythonic and Gaelic were not primarily written languages and

Anglo-Saxon, if written at all in his day, was primarily written in the runic alphabet. The same goes for the British historian known as Nennius who, in the early ninth century, was compiling a series of documents of Brythonic origin from 'a heap' of material which he had found belonging to the previous several centuries: he too rationalised names and places. Later scribes sometimes mis-copied or 'modernised' archaic spellings. To add a further layer of complication, all the languages extant in Britain in this time, with perhaps the exception of Latin (stabilised in its written and spoken forms by the church) were changing; and changing fast. With care, linguists can reconstruct earlier spellings and pronunciations, but the overall result is that historians of the eighteenth century onwards have been rather inconsistent in the way that they cite names, having drawn them from so many variant sources. The only consolation I can offer is that I have tried to be consistent in the spellings I have used. So Æthelfrith, King Oswald's father, is given the Anglo-Saxon diphthong, which gives the first syllable the sound of 'a' as in 'hat'. Oswald (who thankfully is always spelled that way even if he probably heard a 'v' rather than a 'w') had a brother whose name is variously spelled Oswiu or Oswy; a sister called either Æbbe (I am sticking with my diphthongs) or Ebba or even Abb; and an uncle who might be Eadwine or Edwin. But if the spellings are problematic, the names themselves are clear: the 'Os' element beloved of many early kings means God; Oswald's name means 'God's rule'— rather appropriate. Æthelfrith means 'noble peace'—perhaps less appropriate for a thunderous warlord.

Place-names are notoriously difficult to interpret. Very often a name has changed out of recognition from its original; the Anglo-Saxon ear hears sounds very differently from the British ear; a Latin ear equally so. The classic example, taught to all undergraduate archaeology students as a cautionary tale, is that of York. To the British it was probably *Eborakon*, or *Caer Ebrauc*,

GLOSSARY OF
USEFUL WORDS

atheling. This name, often mistaken to mean prince, or heir, conferred the right to be considered for the kingship. It was a reflection of eligibility by birth, rather than right.

bocland, laenland. Before Oswald, and the reappearance of the church in England, almost all property was held 'of the king'. He rewarded service in his household or army with the right to enjoy the fruits of agricultural surplus of an estate suitable to the rank of the *gesith* or *dreng* (q.v.) concerned. The estate came with not only a known boundary and settlement site but also with the unfree farmers and serfs who lived on it. When the head of the household died the estate was returned to the king's portfolio, to be distributed again to the next generation. It seems probable that the son customarily inherited the same estate from his father, but it was not a given. So, land was leasehold, or *laenland*. When Oswald first rewarded his bishop, Aidan, with land to endow a monastery, the *laenland* system could not apply. The monks held their lands for a service that was 'commuted to prayer'; and that service was everlasting, as were their prayers for the founding patron. The king could not ask for monastic land back (later kings tried; Henry VIII succeeded). So this became *bocland*: the origins of medieval freehold. The profound implications of this for the future

of British society are considered in Chapter IX.

cantref. See under *tech.*

ceorl. The *ceorl* (pronounced 'churl', as in churlish) is troublesome; historians cannot agree how free he was, but perhaps he was something like a peasant farmer; neither the *ceorl* nor the *dreng* (q.v.) belonged to the elite warrior caste of *gesiths* (q.v.) or *ealdormen* (see under *duguth*).

dreng. The *dreng* seems to have been a free man holding property in return for services to his lord; possibly the rough equivalent of the squire in the later medieval period.

duguth, geoguth. The Anglo-Saxons distinguished between the rank of untried man or *geoguth* of the king's host, and the older veteran, the *duguth*. The young bucks of the noble rank, eager to prove themselves to their lord, might enter the army's ranks at sixteen. If they survived until the age of about twenty-five and had shown themselves skilful and worthy, they might then be rewarded with lands 'suitable to their rank' so that they could marry and raise the next generation of warriors. They would then graduate to the rank of *duguth*, a senior companion of the king. *Ealdormen* is a later term for those whose record fitted them to be the king's councillors. Oswald, in exile among the Scots, would have been both *atheling* and *geoguth* when fighting for Eochaid Buide.

gesith, **thane / thegn.** I have used the Anglo-Saxon term *gesith* for the caste of free-born, property-qualified nobility whose status is defined by their weapon-bearing place in the king's host, or army. The name originally derives from words for 'ash spear' and 'shield'. The Roman or

Latin equivalent is *comes*: companion. Thane, or thegn, is a later usage for the same caste.

hide. Generations of historians have argued over this very difficult term. If the *vill* (q.v.) is a place, a real piece of land with boundaries, fields, settlements, then the hide (Bede used the term *familiarum*) was a unit of render from the farms within a *vill*. But there is no arithmetical equivalent, no standard number of hides in a *vill*. The hide was a concept used to calculate how much such and such a settlement or kingdom owed in tribute or render; it was also used as a shorthand for value, but that value depended, naturally enough, on the productive surplus and wealth of that land. (See pp.217–218 for a discussion of the hide.)

laenland. See bocland.

metreth, cornage, truncage, heriot, merchet. Apart from the military service required of noble-born males, various services were rendered to the king from each estate or *vill* (q.v.)—essential in a cashless society. *Metreth* and *cornage* relate to the number of cattle owed each year to the king or the lord of an estate. Cattle were the fundamental means of measuring the wealth of a farmer. *Truncage* was a render of timber, *heriot* a death duty and *merchet* a marriage tax; there seem to have been several others. There are few references to them in contemporary literature, but the names are very ancient and, fortunately, they survived as anachronistic terms into the later medieval period when administrators were keen to record what kings and great lords were owed; or what they believed they were owed. The Domesday Book and Boldon Book

(the latter a twelfth-century survey of the bishopric of Durham) record many of these archaic services.

sept. See under *tech*.

shire. See under *vill*.

tech/tref, cantref/sept. Equivalents in Wales and in Scottish Dál Riata for the *vill* (q.v.) and shire are problematic. The *tech* was a unit of military render in Dál Riata (see p.71); but we do not know whether it relates to the size of a land-holding, the number of working people, or a notional family unit. It might either loosely equate to a smaller version of the English *vill*, the basic unit of agricultural and military render, something like a small farming establishment; or to the hide (q.v.). It is probably best to think of the *tech* in contemporary terms as a unit of render based on a king's power to exact tribute in the form of food-rent and military service with only a notional size equivalent. In Wales the *tref* is a rough equivalent; *trefs* were nominally grouped into hundreds and termed *cantref*; the *sept* is the Dál Riatan equivalent. We might think of these divisions as something like the English 'shire'.

vill, shire. The *vill* was the fundamental territorial unit of the Anglo-Saxon rural economy. In the North of Britain these have survived as townships; in the South they equate roughly to, but predate, the old parishes. The *vill* or *tref* (q.v.) was the customary unit from which services might be rendered; in time, the term *vill* was applied to the settlement or central place at the heart of its territory, and the name of the *vill* was applied to the place. We infer that a *vill* would have a *dreng*'s (q.v.) establishment, such as Thirlings, at its heart (see pp.221–4). Shires, unlike the counties with which they have been conflated in the modern period, were groups of estates with an important central place, belonging to a lord of at least the rank of *gesith* (q.v.). Sprouston on the River Tweed might represent the estate centre of a shire (see p.269). The *villa regia*, or royal estate centre, is most magnificently shown at Yeavering in Northumberland (see pp.275–6).

A NOTE ON PLACE-NAME ELEMENTS

Our maps are still full of names whose origins lie deep in our cultural and linguistic past. Many of our rivers— Avon, Ouse, Derwent, Eden, to name but a few—have names with Brythonic roots. There are hundreds of names of Anglo-Saxon origin ending in *-ham*, *-ton*, which denote the settlements or farms which are later called *vills*. Often these start with a personal name— *Acklington*, for example, which was the settlement named for a man, a *dreng* perhaps, called Eadlac. The Old English ending *-wic* is particularly interesting. It means farm, as in Keswick (cheese farm) in Cumbria, or Goswick (goose farm) in Northumberland; but it might also denote a periodic, opportunistic beach market (see p.170)—for example *Lundenwic* (London), *Gypeswic* (Ipswich) and so on. A surviving place-name element much loved by archaeologists is *eccles*: Eccles in Lancashire, famous for its liquorice cakes, and Ecclefechan in Dumfriesshire are examples. The Welsh equivalent is *egwlys*. Both derive directly from the Latin *ecclesia*, which identifies the place as the site of a Romano-British church. Not all *eccles* names are ancient in origin, which confuses matters slightly. The Anglo-Saxon suffix *-botl*, as in Harbottle or Shilbottle, denotes a (probably stone) building (the words *bastle* and *bastille* are later versions); *-ley* means a clearing in a wood and *-shaw* is the wood itself. The large numbers of *-ing* and *-ingaham* names refer to settlements claimed by Anglo-Saxon settlers. Ovingham in the Tyne Valley is the 'farm of Ova's people'; while a mile up the road Ovington is the 'village of Ova's people's farm'. Modern English offers examples of pleonastic (or tautological) place-names, built up from the same word in different languages and reflecting successive waves of cultural influence. Torpenhow in Cumbria (pronounced 'Trepenor') means 'hill hill hill' in Brythonic, Welsh and Old English. Place-names are one of our cultural treasures, an open-source book that offers a fascinating window on to early medieval Britain.

NB how can mean/lot riverside meadow - often in island

NOTES TO
THE TEXT

ABBREVIATIONS

HB Nennius's *Historia Brittonum*

EH Bede's Ecclesiastical History

ASC Anglo-Saxon Chronicle

LC Life of Colomba

HA Historia Abbatum

WLG Whitby Life of Gregory

AC Annales Cambriae

PLC Bede's Prose Life of St Cuthbert

VW Vita Wilfridi

HTSC Historia Translationum Sancti Cuthberti auctore anonymo

HSC Historia de Sancto Cuthberto

CHAPTER I

1 Nennius: *Historia Brittonum (HB)* 70; ed. J. Morris 1980.

2 Rackham 2006, 150.

3 *Beowulf* trans. and ed. Alexander 2014–31.

4 Ecclesiastical History of the English People

(EH) (*Historia Ecclesiastica*) III.5.

5 EH II.5.

6 *HB* 57; Anglo-Saxon Chronicle (ASC) Recension E sub anno 617.

7 Groves 2011.

8 Retrieved from an online article by Project Director Graeme Young: *www.btinternet. com/~graemeyoung/ BowlHole.htm* 13.07.2012.

9 Young 2003, 18.

10 Tolkien 1936.

11 *Henry IV Part I*, Act I, Scene I.

CHAPTER II

12 EH V.15.

13 Life of Columba (LC) (*Vita Columbae*) I.37.

14 Sharpe 1995, note 127.

15 Fleming 1998.

16 EH I.34.

17 Retrieved from the admirable Staffordshire hoard website: *www. staffordshirehoard. org.uk.*

18 *Current Archaeology* 236: The Inscriptions.

CHAPTER III

19 Caesar *De Bello Gallico* V.14.

20 Yorke 1990, 27 and Brooks 1989a, following Alan Everitt.

21 EH II.3.

22 *HB* 31.

23 *HB* 37.

24 EH II.1.

25 Hodges 1982, 69.

26 For example, the most recent analysis of imported pottery and glass in Campbell 2007, 109–24.

27 EH I.25.

28 EH I.26 Colgrave and Mynors 1969.

29 EH I.26; *Historia Abbatum (HA)* I.

30 EH I. 30. Colgrave and Mynors 1969, 108–9.

31 The Law of the Northumbrian Priests, usually attributed to Archbishop Wulfstan II, who died in 1023. Trans. Thorpe 1840, Volume 2, 291–302.

32 Eagles 2003.

33 EH II.2.

34 Chester Archaeological Society report: online at *www. chesterarchaeolsoc. org.uk/heronbridge. html.*

CHAPTER IV

35 Charles-Edwards 2000, 69.
36 Barry 1964.
37 EH III.4.
38 Sharpe 1995, 360ff.
39 LC II.3 Trans. Sharpe 1995.
40 LC II.45.
41 LC I.10.
42 LC III.5.
43 LC I.9.
44 LC III.5. Quoted by Adomnán from a lost work by Abbot Cumméne the White. Sharpe 1995.
45 Bartlett 2003.
46 Dickinson 2005.
47 Alcock 2003, 166ff; see also discussions by Cessford (1993), Hooper (1993) and Higham (1991).
48 Edited with an invaluable commentary by Bannerman (1974).
49 Bannerman 1974, 146ff.
50 Bannerman 1974, 149.
51 Campbell 2007, 116–17.
52 LC I.28; Sharpe 1995, 54.

CHAPTER V

53 EH II.12 Colgrave and Mynors 1969.
54 Quoted by Marsden 1992.
55 Morris 1980, 46.
56 Morris 1980, 46.
57 EH II.15.
58 EH II.12. Colgrave and Mynors 1969.
59 EH II.12.
60 EH II.12. Bede's internal quote is from Virgil's *Aeneid* iv.2. Colgrave and Mynors 1969, 179.
61 EH II.12.
62 Whitby Life of Gregory (WLG) 16.
63 *Beowulf* lines 1142–5.
64 Underwood 1999.
65 Myres and Southern 1973; Mortimer 1905, 247ff.
66 Oppenheimer 2007.
67 Fowler 1997, 245ff.
68 Powlesland 1997, 105ff.
69 Adams 1984.
70 Cramp 1995, 24.
71 Higham 1995, 156; Kirby 2000, 9.
72 Higham 1993, 89.
73 Roberts 2010.
74 Sherlock and Welch 1992.

CHAPTER VI

75 Bruce-Mitford 1968, 25.
76 *HB* 63; *Annales Cambriae* (*AC*) sub anno 616; Colgrave and Mynors 1969, 410.
77 Breeze 2009, 123.
78 EH II.9, Colgrave & Mynors 1969, 163.
79 Sidonius Apollinaris, *Letters*. Trans. by O. M. Dalton (1915)

vol. 2: 138–75 Book 8, Letter 6.
80 EH II.9.
81 Koch 2006, 671.
82 EH II.10.
83 EH II.11.
84 EH II.9.
85 In an essay submitted for the Award in Continuing Education programme, Centre for Lifelong Learning, University of Sunderland, 2009.
86 ASC sub anno 626.
87 EH II.9 Colgrave and Mynors 1969, 167.
88 EH II.12. Colgrave and Mynors 1969, 183.
89 EH II.13 Colgrave and Mynors 1969, 185.
90 EH II.16.
91 Hope-Taylor 1977, 67–9; 200–1.
92 Hope-Taylor 1977; for a modern appreciation and critique of his work see Frodsham and O'Brien 2005.
93 Barnwell 2005, 177.
94 EH II.16.
95 The latest investigation of this theatre has not yet been published in detail; information accessed from *www.pasthoriz onspr.com/index.php/ archives/04/2011/ canterburys-roman-*

theatre-revealed, April 2011.

96 Barnwell 2005, 180ff.

97 EH II.16.

CHAPTER VII
....

98 EH II.20 Colgrave and Mynors 1969, 203.

99 Higham 1993, 89.

100 EH II.20 Colgrave and Mynors 1969, 203.

101 For definitive surveys, now a little out of date, see Cramp 1988 and Higham 1993; Alcock 2003.

102 Collins 1977, 41.

103 EH III.1. Colgrave and Mynors 1969, 213.

104 EH III.1. Colgrave and Mynors 1969, 213.

105 *Y Gododdin* stanza 51, with poetic trans. Clancy 1970.

106 EH II.20.

107 EH II.9.

108 Bede's Prose Life of Saint Cuthbert (PLC): 27. Farmer 1983, 79.

CHAPTER VIII
....

109 National Maritime Museum, Greenwich: image A0765.

110 *Red Book of Hergest* 15, trans. William Skene; there are

various websites offering annotated versions.

111 I am indebted to Dr Hermann Moisl for this information.

112 Fairless 1984.

113 An example is illustrated from a buckle plate in grave 95 at Finglesham, Kent. Wilson 1992, 118.

114 Wilmott 2010.

115 LC I.1.

116 Wallace-Hadrill 1988, 89.

117 EH III.2.

118 EH III.2.

119 Woodfield 1965.

120 Wallace-Hadrill 1988, 90.

121 I quote from the work of the late Hexham historian Tom Corfe (1997), who did much to explore and clear up the difficulties surrounding the site and context of the battle.

CHAPTER IX
....

122 EH III.5.

123 EH III.5.

124 Todd and Reeves 1864, 231.

125 EH III.2.

126 O'Sullivan and Young 1995, 41: figure 21.

127 LC I.1.

128 Colgrave and Mynors 1969, 229.

129 EH III.3.

130 LC I.1.

131 EH III.4; Colgrave and Mynors 1969, 221.

132 EH III.16.

133 Brown 2006, 159.

134 O'Sullivan and Young 1995, 41.

135 EH III.17; McClure and Collins 1995, 137.

136 EH III.5.

137 EH III.12.

138 EH III.6.

139 EH III.6; Colgrave and Mynors 1969, 231.

140 EH III.2.

141 Gregory of Tours, *History of the Franks* II.38; I am indebted to Colm O'Brien for an interesting discussion on the potential significance of Oswald's gesture.

142 Lanigan 1822, 433.

143 Colm O'Brien, personal communication.

144 De Paor 1997, 218.

145 McCormack 1972, 730.

146 Thomas 1981, 291.

147 Thomas 1981, 263–5; Stancliffe 1995, 78.

148 South 2002.

149 Joliffe 1926.

150 O'Brien and Adams 2012.

CHAPTER X
....

151 EH II.20; Colgrave and Mynors 1969, 205.

152 EH IV.14.
153 Eagles 1989.
154 Stancliffe 1995, 60.
155 Brooks 1989b, 161.
156 EH II.20.
157 Brooks 1989b, 167.
158 *Y Gododdin*, stanza LXXX; trans. Project Gutenberg.
159 *HB* 56.
160 Campbell 1979.
161 Higham 1995, 26.
162 *Vita Wilfridi* (*VW*): LX; Colgrave 1927, 131.
163 Sawyer 1977, 148; 153.

CHAPTER XI

164 Joliffe 1926, 41.
165 EH III.17.
166 Adams 1999; O'Brien and Adams 2012.
167 Wilmott 2010; Roberts 2010; see also the paper by Rob Collins 2012.
168 Collins 2012, 19.
169 Stuart Laycock, *Britannia: The failed state*. The History Press 2008.
170 EH II.14.
171 Attenborough 1922, 59.
172 EH III.4; EH II.9.
173 For example, Higham 1995, 240ff.
174 EH IV.23.
175 O'Brien and Miket 1991.

CHAPTER XII

176 EH III.12; Colgrave and Mynors 1969, 251.
177 See Sawyer 1977.
178 Cambridge 1995, 147; Binns 1995, 268 Figure 8.
179 EH III.9.
180 EH III.14.
181 *Beowulf* lines 3137–46. Penguin edition, trans. Michael Alexander.
182 *Beowulf* lines 3168–82.

CHAPTER XIII

183 EH III.12
184 EH III.9. Colgrave and Mynors 1969, 243.
185 EH III.9; Colgrave and Mynors 1969, 243.
186 Campbell 1986.
187 EH III.10; Colgrave and Mynors 1969, 245.
188 Rollason 1989, 10.
189 WLG XXI; Colgrave 1968, 111.
190 EH III.10; Colgrave and Mynors 1969, 245.
191 EH III.10; Colgrave and Mynors 1969, 245.
192 Cubitt 2002.
193 Chaney 1970, 13.
194 EH IV.14; Colgrave and Mynors 1969, 381.

CHAPTER XIV

195 Smith 1962.
196 Brooks 1989a, 66.
197 EH III.15; Colgrave and Mynors 1969, 261.
198 EH III.24; Colgrave and Mynors 1969, 259.
199 PLC III; Wood 2008, 19.
200 Anonymous Life of Cuthbert VII; Colgrave 1940, 73.
201 EH III.16; Colgrave and Mynors 1969, 263.
202 EH III.24.

CHAPTER XV

203 EH III 21.
204 EH III.21.
205 Walker 1976.
206 EH III.22.
207 *HB* 64 and 65. *Id est Artbret Iudeu.*
208 EH I.12.
209 EH III.24; Colgrave and Mynors 1969, 291.
210 EH III.24.
211 EH III.24.
212 Wood 2008, 20.

CHAPTER XVI

213 EH III.25; Colgrave and Mynors 1969, 295.
214 *VW* XXII; Colgrave 1927, 47.
215 EH III.26; Colgrave and Mynors 1969, 311.

216 PLC VII.

217 PLC VIII; Colgrave 1940, 181.

218 EH III.26.

219 EH III.25; Colgrave and Mynors 1969, 297.

220 Cummian, *De Controversia Paschali*; Cotton Vitell. A. xii; Healy 1912.

221 Abels 1983.

CHAPTER XVII
....

222 EH III.27; Colgrave and Mynors 1969, 311.

223 Cowan Duff, personal communication.

224 Cramp 1976; Rahtz 1976.

225 Abels 1983, 12ff.

226 PLC VIII.

227 EH III.25; Colgrave and Mynors 1969, 299.

228 EH III.25; Colgrave and Mynors 1969, 301.

229 *VW* X.

230 EH III.25; Colgrave and Mynors 1969, 308–9.

231 Richardson 1961, 107.

CHAPTER XVIII
....

232 EH IV. 4; Colgrave and Mynors 1969, 347.

233 EH IV.4; Colgrave and Mynors 1969, 349.

234 EH III. 26; Colgrave and Mynors 1969, 309.

235 EH IV.19.

236 *VW* XIX; Colgrave 1927, 43.

237 *VW* XXIV; Colgrave 1927, 49.

238 EH III.11; Colgrave and Mynors 1969, 247.

239 EH III.11; Colgrave and Mynors 1969, 247.

240 EH IV.26.

241 *VW* XXIV.

242 WLG XVIII; Colgrave 1968, 103.

243 *VW* XIX; Colgrave 1927, 105.

244 *VW* XXIV.

245 *VW* XXXIV.

246 *VW* XXXVII.

247 Jones 1990.

248 EH IV.22.

249 *VW* XXXIX; Colgrave 1927, 79.

CHAPTER XIX
....

250 *Libellus de Exordio atque Procursu istius, hoc est Dunelmensis, Ecclesie*. Stevenson 1993.

251 *Historia Translationum Sancti Cuthberti auctore anonymo* (*HTSC*). Battiscombe 1956, 99.

252 *HTSC*. Battiscombe 1956, 103.

253 ALC XIV; Colgrave 1940, 131.

254 ALC XIV; Colgrave 1940, 133.

255 PLC XLII; Colgrave 1940, 295.

256 I *Corinthians* 15: 51–53.

257 EH III.19.

258 EH IV.19.

259 EH III.8.

260 Boddington et al. 1987; Reeve and Adams 1993; Hunter et al. 1996.

261 Tapp, E. and O'Sullivan, D., 'St Bees Man: the Autopsy', Proceedings of the Palaeopathology Association, 4th European Meeting, Middleburg 178–82, 1982

262 Janaway 1996, 77.

263 Holder 2011, 57; 95.

264 EH III.25.

265 Carver 2006, 101.

266 Garmonsway 1972, 55–6.

267 Alcuin: Letter to King Æthelred AD 793. Whitelock 1955, 775–7.

268 Alcuin: Letter to Higbald, bishop of Lindisfarne AD 793. Whitelock 1955, 844.

269 For a detailed consideration of this see Bailey 1995.

270 *Historia de Sancto Cuthberto* (*HSC*) XX.

271 *HTSC*, Battiscombe 1956, 100.

272 *HTSC*, Battiscombe
1956, 101.
273 *HTSC*, Battiscombe
1956, 108.
274 Bailey 1995, 200.
275 Alcuin: *Sanctis
Euboricensis Ecclesiæ*.
Godman 1982, 35.
276 ASC sub anno 909.
277 Bonser 1935.
278 Bailey 1995, 202.
279 Thacker 1995, 103.
280 Cambridge 1995,
155ff.
281 Michelle Ziegler
runs an impressive
blog called
Heavenfield at
*hefenfelth.wordpress.
com/*. She is also
the founder of
the online journal
The Heroic Age,
dedicated to Early
Medieval matters.
282 Cambridge 1995,
128.
283 For a review see the
relevant chapters
in Stancliffe and
Cambridge (eds)
1995.

CHAPTER XX

284 PLC XXIV;
Colgrave and
Mynors 1940, 235.
285 PLC XXIV;
Colgrave and
Mynors 1940, 237.
286 According to
Symeon of Durham;
Yorke 2009.
287 For example
Marsden 1992,
208–12.
288 EH IV 26.
289 Wood 2010, 91.
290 Bede, Letter to
Egbert. McClure
and Collins 1994,
344–5.
291 Bede, Letter to
Egbert. McClure
and Collins 1994,
345.
292 Bede, Letter to
Egbert. McClure
and Collins 1994,
347.
293 EH V.23; Colgrave
and Mynors 1969,
561.

294 Bede, Letter to
Egbert. McClure
and Collins 1994,
350.
295 Bede, Letter to
Egbert. McClure
and Collins 1994,
350–1.
296 Bede, Letter to
Egbert. McClure
and Collins 1994,
351.
297 EH IV 25.
298 *HSC* VI, VII.
299 *HSC* VIII.

APPENDIX A

300 Jackson 1964, 22.
301 Breeze 2009.
302 *HB* 63.
303 *HB* 63.
304 *HB* 63.
305 Hunter Blair 1950.

BIBLIOGRAPHY

ABELS, R.P., 'The Council of Whitby: a study in early Anglo-Saxon politics', *Journal of British Studies,* 23.1: 1–25, 1983

——*Lordship and military obligation in Anglo-Saxon England*, London: British Museum Press, 1988

ADAMS, M., 'Linear earthworks of land division on the Yorkshire Wolds', unpublished BA thesis, Department of Archaeology, University of York, 1984

——'Excavation of a pre-Conquest cemetery at Addingham, West Yorkshire', *Medieval Archaeology,* 40: 151–91, 1996

——'Beyond the Pale: some thoughts on the later prehistory of the Breamish Valley'. In Bevan, B. (ed.), *Northern Exposure: interpretive devolution and the Iron Ages in Britain*, Leicester Archaeology Monographs 4: 111–22, 1999

——'The haunt of saints and shamans', the *Northumbrian*, April/May 2002: 23–26

——*Admiral Collingwood: Nelson's own hero*, London: Weidenfeld and Nicholson, 2005

ALCOCK, L., 'The activities of potentates in Celtic Britain, AD 500–800: a positivist approach'. In Driscoll, S.T. and Nieke, M.R. (eds), 1988: 22–39 .

——*Arthur's Britain*, 2nd edition, London: Penguin, 2001

——*Kings and warriors, craftsmen and priests in Northern Britain AD 550–850*, Edinburgh: Society of Antiquaries of Scotland, 2003

ALEXANDER, M. (trans. and ed.), *Beowulf*, London: Penguin, 1973

ANDERSON, A.O., *Early sources of Scottish history AD 500 to 1286*, Edinburgh: Oliver and Boyd, 1922

ARNOLD, C.J., *An archaeology of the early Anglo-Saxon kingdoms*, London: Routledge, 1988

ARNOLD, T. (ed.), *Symeonis monachi opera omnia*, London: Longman, 1922

ATTENBOROUGH, F.L., *The laws of the earliest English kings*, Cambridge University Press, 1922

BAILEY, R., 'St Oswald's heads'. In Stancliffe, C. and Cambridge, E. (eds.), 1995: 195–209

BANNERMAN, J., *Studies in the history of Dalriada*, Edinburgh: Scottish Academic Press, 1974

BARNWELL, P.S., *Anglian Yeavering: a continental perspective*. In Frodsham, P. and O'Brien, C.F. (eds), 2005: 174–84

BARRY, J., *Joyful pilgrimage: The voyage of the Iona curragh*, Company of the Iona Curragh, 1964

BARTLETT, R. (ed.), *The miracles of Saint Æbbe of Coldingham and Saint Margaret of Scotland*, OUP: Oxford Medieval Texts, 2003

BASSETT, S. (ed.), *The Origins of Anglo-Saxon kingdoms*, Leicester University Press, 1989

——'In search of the origins of early Anglo-Saxon kingdoms'. In Bassett, S. (ed.), 1989: 3–27

BATTISCOMBE, C.F., *The relics of St Cuthbert*, Oxford University Press, 1956

BELL, T., 'Churches on Roman buildings: Christian associations and Roman masonry in Anglo-Saxon England', *Medieval Archaeology,* 42: 1–18, 1998

BIELER, L., 'Ireland's contribution to the culture of Northumbria'. In Bonner, G. (ed.), 1976: 210–28

BINNS, A., 'Pre-Reformation dedications to St Oswald in England and Scotland: a gazeteer'. In Stancliffe, C. and Cambridge, E. (eds), 1995: 241–71

BISHOP, M.C. and Dore, J.N., *Corbridge: Excavations of the Roman fort and town 1947–1980*, London: English Heritage, 1988

BODDINGTON, A., Garland, A.N. and Janaway, R.C., *Death, decay and reconstruction: approaches to archaeology and forensic science*, Manchester University Press, 1987

BONNER, G. (ed.), *Famulus Christi: Essays in commemoration of the thirteenth centenary of the birth of the Venerable Bede*, London: SPCK, 1976

BONSER, W., 'The magic of Saint Oswald', *Antiquity*, 9.36: 418–23, 1935

BREEZE, A., '*Din Guoaroy*, the Old Welsh name of Bamburgh', *Archaeologia Aeliana Series*, 5.38: 123–7, 2009

BREEZE, D.J., *The Northern frontiers of Roman Britain*, London: Batsford, 1982

BREEZE, D.J. and DOBSON, B., *Hadrian's Wall*, 4th edition, London: Penguin, 2000

BROOKS, N., 'The creation and early structure of the kingdom of Kent'. In Bassett, S. (ed.), 1989: 55–74

—— 'The formation of the Mercian kingdom'. In Bassett, S. (ed.), 1989: 159–70

BROWN, M., *How Christianity came to Britain and Ireland*, Oxford: Lion Books, 2006

—— '"Excavating" Northumbrian manuscripts: reappraising regionalism in insular manuscript production'. In Petts, D. and Turner, S. (eds) 2012: 267–82

BRUCE-MITFORD, R.L.S., *The Sutton Hoo ship burial: A handbook*, London: British Museum Press, 1968

CAMBRIDGE, E., 'Archaeology and the cult of St Oswald in pre-Conquest Northumbria'. In Stancliffe, C. and Cambridge, E. (eds), 1995: 128–63

CAMPBELL, A. (ed.), *Æthelwulf: De Abbatibus*, Oxford: Clarendon Press, 1967

CAMPBELL, E., *Continental and Mediterranean imports to Atlantic Britain and Ireland, AD 400–800*, Council for British Archaeology Research Report 157, 2007

CAMPBELL, J., *Bede's reges and principes*, Jarrow Lecture, Jarrow: St Paul's Church, 1979

—— *Essays in Anglo-Saxon history*, London: Hambledon Press, 1986

—— 'Secular and political contexts'. In DeGregorio, S. (ed.), 2010: 25–39

CARVER, M., *The cross goes north: processes of conversion in northern Europe, AD 300–1300*, San Marino: Boydell Press, 2006

CESSFORD, C., 'Cavalry in early Bernicia: A reply', *Northern History*, 29: 185–7, 1993

—— 'The death of Æthelfrith of Lloegr', *Northern History*, 30: 179–83, 1994

—— 'Relations between the Britons of Southern Scotland and Anglo-Saxon Northumbria'. In Hawkes, J. and Mills, S. (eds), 1999: 150–60

CHADWICK, N.K. (ed.), *Celt and Saxon: Studies in the early British Border*, Cambridge University Press, 1964

—— 'The Battle of Chester: A study of sources'. In Chadwick, N.K. (ed.), 1964: 167–85

—— 'The conversion of Northumbria: a comparison of sources'. In Chadwick, N.K. (ed.), 1964: 138–66

——'The Celtic background of Early Anglo-Saxon England'. In Chadwick, N.K. (ed.), 1964: 323–52

CHANEY, W., *The cult of kingship in Anglo-Saxon England*, Manchester University Press, 1970

CHARLES-EDWARDS, T.M., 'The distinction between land and moveable wealth in Anglo-Saxon England'. In Sawyer, P.H. (ed.), *English medieval settlement*, London: Edward Arnold, 1979

——'Early medieval kingship in the British Isles'. In Bassett (ed.), 1989: 28–39

——*Early Christian Ireland*, Cambridge University Press, 2000

CLANCY, J., *The earliest Welsh poetry*, London: Macmillan, 1970

CLEMOES, P., *The Cult of St Oswald on the Continent*, Jarrow Lecture, Jarrow: St Paul's Church, 1983

COLGRAVE, B., *The life of Bishop Wilfrid by Eddius Stephanus*, Cambridge University Press, 1927

——*Two Lives of Saint Cuthbert*, Cambridge University Press, 1940

——'The earliest Life of St Gregory the Great, written by a Whitby monk'. In Chadwick, N.K. (ed.), 1964: 119–37

——*The earliest life of Gregory the Great by an anonymous monk of Whitby*, Cambridge University Press, 1968

COLGRAVE, B. and Mynors, R.A.B. (eds), *Bede's Ecclesiastical History of the English People*, Oxford Medieval Texts, Oxford: Clarendon Press, 1969

COLLINS, R., 'Julian of Toldeo and the royal succession in late seventh-century Spain'. In Sawyer, P.H. and Wood, I. (eds), 1977: 30–49

——'Military communities and the transformation of the Frontier from the fourth to the sixth centuries'. In Petts, D. and Turner, S. (eds), 2012: 15–34

COLLINS, R. and ALLASON-JONES, L. (eds), *Finds from the frontier: Material culture in the 4th–5th centuries*, Council for British Archaeology Research Report 162, 2010

CORFE, T., 'The Battle of Heavenfield', *Hexham Historian*, 7: 65–86, 1997

CORNING, C., 'The baptism of Edwin, King of Northumbria: a new analysis of the British tradition', *Northern History*, 36.1: 5–15, 2000

CRAMP, R., 'Monastic sites'. In Wilson, D.M. (ed.), 1976: 201–52

——'Northumbria: the archaeological evidence'. In Driscoll, S.T. and Nieke, M.R. (eds), 1988: 69–78

——'The making of Oswald's Northumbria'. In Stancliffe, C. and Cambridge, E. (eds), 1995: 17–32

CUBITT, C., 'Universal and local saints in Anglo-Saxon England'. In Thacker, A. and Sharpe, R. (eds), 2002: 423–53

DEGREGORIO, S. (ed.), *The Cambridge Companion to Bede*, Cambridge University Press, 2010

DE PAOR, L., *St Patrick's World*, University of Notre Dame Press, 1997

DICKINSON, T.M., 'Symbols of Protection: The Significance of Animal-ornamented Shields in Early Anglo-Saxon England,' *Medieval Archaeology*, XLIX: 109–63, 2005

DRISCOLL, S.T. and Nieke, M.R. (eds), *Power and politics in early medieval Britain and Ireland,* Edinburgh University Press, 1988

DRISCOLL, S.T., 'Ad Gefrin and Scotland: the implications of the Yeavering excavations'. In Frodsham, P. and O'Brien, C.F. (eds), 2005: 161–73

DUMVILLE, D.N., 'The Anglian collection of royal genealogies', *Anglo-Saxon England*, 5: 23–50, 1976

——'Kingship, genealogies and regnal histories'. In Sawyer, P.H. and Wood, I. (eds), 1977: 72–104

——'On the North British section of the Historia Brittonum', *Welsh History Review*, 8.3: 345–54, 1977

——'The ætheling: a study in Anglo-Saxon constitutional history', *Anglo-Saxon England*, 8: 1–33, 1979

——'The origins of Northumbria: some aspects of the British background'. In Bassett, S. (ed.), 1989: 213–22

EAGLES, B., 'Lindsey'. In Basset (ed.), 1989: 202–12

——'Augustine's Oak', *Medieval Archaeology*, 47: 175-8, 2003

EDEL, D., 'Early Irish queens and royal power: a first reconnaissance'. In Richter, M. and Picard, J-M (eds), 2002: 1–19

EDMONDS, F., 'The practicalities of communication between Northumbrian and Irish churches *c.* 635–735'. In Graham-Campbell, J. and Ryan, M. (eds), 2009: 129–47

ENRIGHT, M.J., 'Further reflections on royal ordinations in the *Vita Colombae*'. In Richter, M. and Picard, J-M (eds), 2002: 20–35

FAIRLESS, K.J., 'Three religious cults from the Northern frontier region'. In Miket, R. and Burgess, C. (eds), 1984: 224–42

FARMER, D.H. (ed.), *The Age of Bede*, Harmondsworth: Penguin, 1983

FERGUSON, C., 'Re-evaluating Early Medieval Northumbrian contacts and the "Coastal Highway"'. In Petts, D. and Turner, S. (eds), 2012: 283–302

FLEMING, A., *Swaledale: Valley of the wild river*, Oxford: Oxbow Books, 1998

FLETCHER, E., 'The influence of Merovingian Gaul on Northumbria in the seventh century', *Medieval Archaeology* 24: 69–86, 1980

FLETCHER, R., *Who's who in Roman Britain and Anglo-Saxon England*, London: Shepheard-Walwyn, 1989

FOOT, S., 'Church and monastery in Bede's Northumbria'. In DeGregorio, S. (ed.), 2010: 54–68

FOWLER, P.J., 'Farming in Early Medieval England: some fields for thought'. In Hines, J. (ed.), 1997: 245-60

FRODSHAM, P. and O'Brien, C.F. (eds), *Yeavering: People, power and place*, Stroud: Tempus, 2005

GARMONSWAY, G.N. (ed.), *The Anglo-Saxon Chronicle*, London: J.M. Dent, 1972

GATES, T., and O'BRIEN, C., 'Cropmarks at Milfield and New Bewick and the recognition of Grubenhauser in Northumberland', *Archaeologia Aeliana*, Series 5.6: 1–9, 1988

GELLING, M., 'English place-names derived from the compound *wicham*', *Medieval Archaeology*, 11: 87–104, 1967

GODMAN, P., 'Alcuin: The bishops, kings and saints of York', *Oxford Medieval Texts*, Oxford: Clarendon Press, 1982

GRAHAM-CAMPBELL, J. and Ryan, M. (eds), 'Anglo-Saxon/Irish relations before the Vikings', *Proceedings of the British Academy*, 157, 2009

GROVES, S., 'Social and biological status in the Bowl Hole Early Medieval burial ground, Bamburgh, Northumberland'. In Petts, D. and Turner, S. (eds), 2012: 241–66

HALL, R.A., 'Recent research into Early Medieval York and its hinterland'. In Petts, D. and Turner, S. (eds), 2012: 71–84

HART, C., 'Byrhtferth's Northumbrian Chronicle', *English Historical Review*, 97: 558–82, 1982

HAWKES, J. and MILLS, S. (eds), *Northumbria's Golden Age*, Stroud: Alan Sutton, 1999

HEALY, Rev. J., 'Insula sanctorum et doctorum: or Ireland's ancient schools and scholars', Dublin: Sealy, Bryers and Walker, 1912

HERBERT, M., *Iona, Kells, and Derry: the history and hagiography of the monastic familia of Columba*, Oxford: Clarendon Press, 1988

HIGHAM, N.J., *The Northern Counties to AD 1000*, Harlow: Longman, 1986

—— 'Cavalry in early Bernicia', *Northern History*, 27: 236–41, 1991

—— *The kingdom of Northumbria AD 350-1100*, Stroud: Alan Sutton, 1993

—— *The English conquest: Gildas and Britain in the fifth century*, Manchester University Press, 1994

—— *An English Empire: Bede and the early Anglo-Saxon kings*, Manchester University Press, 1995

—— 'Dynasty and cult: the utility of Christian mission to Northumbrian kings between 642 and 654'. In Hawkes, J. and Mills, S. (eds), 1999: 95–104

—— *(Re-)Reading Bede: The Ecclesiastical History in context*, Abingdon: Routledge, 2006

HINES, J. (ed.), *The Anglo-Saxons from the Migration period to the eighth century: an ethnographic perspective*, San Marino: The Boydell Press, 1997

HODGES, R., *Dark Age Economics*, London: Duckworth, 1982

HOLDER, A., 'The Venerable Bede: On the Song of Songs and selected writings', *Classics of Western Spirituality Series*, Mahwah: Paulist Press International, 2011

HOLLIS, S., *Anglo-Saxon women and the church*, Woodbridge: The Boydell Press, 1992

HOOKE, D., 'The Anglo-Saxons in England in the seventh and eighth centuries: aspects of location in space'. In Hines, J. (ed.), 1997: 65–100

HOOPER, N., 'The Aberlemno stone and cavalry in Anglo-Saxon England', *Northern History*, 29: 188–96, 1993

HOPE-TAYLOR, B., *Yeavering: An Anglo-British centre of Early Northumbria*, London: HMSO, 1977

HUGHES, K., *The church in early Irish society*, London: Methuen, 1966

HUNTER, J.R., Roberts, C.A. and Martin, A.L., *Studies in crime: an introduction to forensic archaeology*, London: Batsford, 1996

HUNTER BLAIR, P.H., 'Some observations on the Historia Regum attributed to Symeon of Durham'. In Chadwick, N.K. (ed.), 1964: 63–118

—— *Northumbria in the days of Bede*, Felinfach: Llanerch, 1976

—— 'The Moore Memoranda on Northumbrian History'. In Fox, C. and Dickens, B., *The Early cultures of North-west Europe*, 245–57, Cambridge University Press, 1950

HUTTON, R., *The pagan religions of the Ancient British Isles*, Oxford: Blackwell, 1993

JACKSON, K.H., *Language and history in early Britain: a chronological survey of the Brittonic languages, 1st to 12th c. A.D.*, Edinburgh University Press, 1953

—— 'On the Northern British section in Nennius'. In Chadwick, N.K. (ed.), 1964: 20–62

JAMES, E., *The Franks*, Oxford: Blackwell, 1988

—— 'The origins of barbarian kingdoms'. In Bassett (ed.), 40–52, 1989

JANAWAY, R.C., 'The decay of buried human remains and their associated materials'. In Hunter et al. (eds), 1996: 58–85

Jansen, A., 'The development of St Oswald legends on the Continent'. In Stancliffe, C. and Cambridge, E. (eds), 1995: 230–40

Joliffe, J.E.A., 'Northumbrian institutions', *English Historical Review*, XLI:CLCI: 1–42, 1926

Jones, G.R.J., 'Broninis', *Bulletin of the Board of Celtic Studies*, 37: 125–32, 1990

Kapelle, W.E., *The Norman conquest of the North*, London: Croom Helm, 1979

Karkov, C.E., 'Whitby, Jarrow and the commemoration of death in Northumbria'. In Hawkes, J. and Mills, S. (eds), 1999: 126–135

Kemp, R.L., 'Anglian settlement at Fishergate, York', Council for British Archaeology: Archaeology of York series, 7/1: 46–54, 1996

Kirby, D.P., 'Bede and Northumbrian chronology', *English Historical Review*, 78: 514–27, 1963

Kirby, D.P., *The earliest English kings*, London: Routledge, 2000

Koch, J. T., *Celtic Culture: A Historical Encyclopedia*, Oxford: ABC-CLIO, 2006

Lanigan, J., *An ecclesiastical history of Ireland from the first introduction of Christianity among the Irish to the beginning of the 13th century*, Dublin: Graisberry, 1822

Lapidge, M., 'Byrhtferth of Ramsey and the early sections of the Historia Regum attributed to Symeon of Durham', *Anglo-Saxon England*, 10: 97–122, 1982

Loyn, H.R., *The governance of Anglo-Saxon England 500–1087*, London: Edward Arnold, 1984

Lucy, S., 'Early medieval burial at Yeavering: a retrospective'. In Frodsham, P. and O'Brien, C.F. (eds), 2005: 127–44

Lunn, A., *Northumberland*, New Naturalist series, London: Collins, 2004

Maitland, F.W., 'Northumbrian tenures'. In Fisher, H.A.L. (ed.), *The collected papers of Frederic William Maitland*, Volume 2, Cambridge University Press, 1911

Marsden, J., *Northanhymbre Saga*, Felinfach: Llanerch, 1992

Mayr-Harting, H., *The coming of Christianity to Anglo-Saxon England*, London: Batsford, 1972

McCarthy, M., 'Rheged: an Early Historic Kingdom near the Solway', *Proceedings of the Society of Antiquaries of Scotland*, 132: 357–81, 2002

——'The kingdom of Rheged: a landscape perspective', *Northern History*, 48.1: 9–22, 2011

McClure, J. and Collins, R. (eds), *Bede: The Ecclesiastical History of the English People*, Oxford World Classics, 1994

McCormack, S., 'Change and continuity in late Antiquity: the ceremony of *Adventus*', *Historia*, 21: 721–52, 1972

Meaney, A.L., 'Woden in England: a reconsideration of the evidence', *Folklore*, 77.2: 105–15, 1966

Mhaonaigh, M., 'Of Saxons, a Viking and Normans: Colmán, Gerald and the monastery of Mayo'. In Graham-Campbell, J. and Ryan, M. (eds), 2009: 329–66

Miket, R. and Burgess, C. (eds), *Between and beyond the walls: Essays on the prehistory and history of North Britain in honour of George Jobey*, Edinburgh: John Donald, 1984

Moisl, H.L., 'The Bernician royal dynasty and the Irish in the seventh century', *Peritia*, 2: 103–26, 1983

Moisl H.L., 'Das Kloster Iona und seine Verbindungen mit dem

Kontinent im siebenten und achten Jahrhundert'. In *Virgil von Salzburg: Missionar und Gelehrter: Beiträge des Internationalen Symposiums, Salzburger Residenz: Amt der Salzburger Landesregierung*, 1985

MORRIS, C.D., 'Northumbria and the Viking settlement: the evidence for land-holding', *Archaeologia Aeliana*, Series 5.5: 81–103, 1977

MORRIS, J. (ed.), *Arthurian Period Sources vol. 8: Nennius', British History and the Welsh Annals*, London: Phillimore, 1980

MORRIS, R.K., *Churches in the landscape*, London: Phoenix, 1989

——*Journeys from Jarrow*, Jarrow Lecture, Jarrow: St Paul's Church, 2004

MORTIMER, J.R., *Forty years' researches in the British and Anglo-Saxon burial mounds of East Yorkshire*, London: A. Brown & Sons, 1905

MURRAY, M.A., 'The divine king in Northumbria', *Folklore*, 53.4: 214–15, 1942

MYRES, J.N.L. and Southern, W.H., *The Anglo-Saxon cemetery at Sancton, east Yorkshire*, Hull: Hull Museums, 1973

NELSON, J.L., 'Inauguration rituals'. In Sawyer, P.H. and Wood, I. (eds), 1977: 50–71

NEWTON, R., *The making of the English landscape: the Northumberland landscape*, London: Hodder and Stoughton, 1972

NIEKE, M.R. and DUNCAN, H.B., 'Dalriada: the establishment and maintenance of an Early Historic kingdom in northern Britain'. In Driscoll, S.T. and Nieke, M.R. (eds), 1988: 6–21

O'BRIEN, C., 'The Early medieval shires of Yeavering, Breamish and Bamburgh', *Archaeologia Aeliana*, Series 5. 30: 53–73, 2002

——'The great enclosure'. In Frodsham, P. and O'Brien, C.F. (eds), 2005: 145–52

——'Gefrin: organisation, abandonment, aftermath'. In Frodsham, P. and O'Brien, C.F. (eds) 2005: 189–92

——'The emergence of Northumbria: artefacts, archaeology and models'. In Collins, R. and Allason-Jones, L. (eds), 2010: 110–19

O'BRIEN, C. and ADAMS, M., *Some observations on monastic estates in Northumbria*, paper delivered to the Royal Archaeological Institute Conference at Durham, September 2012

O'BRIEN, C. and Miket, R., 'The Early Medieval settlement of Thirlings, Northumberland', *Durham Archaeological Journal*, 7: 57–91, 1991

Ó CARRAGÁIN, É., *The city of Rome and the world of Bede*, Jarrow Lecture, Jarrow: St Paul's Church, 1994

Ó CRÓINÍN, D., *Early medieval Ireland, 400–1200*, London: Longman, 1995

Ó RIAIN-RAEDEL, D., 'Edith, Judith, Mathilda: the role of royal ladies in the propagation of the Continental cult'. In Stancliffe, C. and Cambridge, E. (eds), 1995: 210–29

O'SULLIVAN, D. and Young, R., *The English Heritage Book of Lindisfarne Holy Island*, London: Batsford, 1995

OPPENHEIMER, S., *The origins of the British: a genetic detective story*, London: Robinson, 2007

PETTS, D., 'Coastal landscapes and early Christianity in Anglo-Saxon Northumbria', *Estonian Journal of Archaeology*, 13.2: 79–95, 2009

PETTS, D. and Turner, S. (eds), *Early Medieval Northumbria: Kingdoms and communities AD 450–1100*, Turnhout: Brepols, 2012

PLUMMER, C., *Venerabilis Baedae: Historiam Ecclesiasticum Gentis Anglorum*, Oxford: Clarendon Press, 1896

POWLESLAND, D., 'Early Anglo-Saxon Settlements, Structures, Form and Layout'. In Hines, J. (ed.), 1997: 101–24

——'The Anglo-Saxon settlement at West Heslerton, North Yorkshire'. In Hawkes, J. and Mills, S. (eds), 1999: 55–65

PROUDFOOT, E. and Aliaga-Kelly, C., 'Aspects of settlement and territorial arrangement in South-east Scotland in the Late prehistoric and Early-Medieval periods', *Medieval Archaeology*, 41: 33–50, 1997

RACKHAM, O., *Woodlands*, New Naturalist series, London: Collins, 2006

RAHTZ, P.A., 'The building plan of the Anglo-Saxon monastery of Whitby Abbey'. In Wilson, D.M. (ed.), 1976: 459–62

REEVE, J. and ADAMS, M., 'The Spitalfields Project: The excavations', Council for British Archaeology Research Report 84, 1993

RICHARDSON, J., *My Dearest Uncle: Leopold I of the Belgians*, London: Jonathan Cape, 1961

RICHTER, M. and Picard, J-M (eds), *Ogma: Essays in Celtic Studies,* Dublin: Four Courts Press, 2001

ROBERTS, B.K., 'The land of Werhale – landscapes of Bede', *Archaeologia Aeliana,* Series 5.37: 127–59, 2008

——'Northumbrian origins and Post-Roman continuity: an exploration'. In Collins, R. and Allason-Jones, L. (eds), 2010: 120–32

ROLLASON, D.W., *Saints and relics in Anglo-Saxon England,* Oxford: Blackwell, 1989

ROLLASON, D.W., 'St Oswald in pre-Conquest England'. In Stancliffe, C. and Cambridge, E. (eds), 1995: 164–77

ROLLASON, D. (ed.), *The Durham Liber Vitae and its context*, Woodbridge: Boydell Press, 2004

ROSS, A., 'The human head in insular pagan Celtic religion', *Proceedings of the Society of Antiquaries of Scotland,* 92: 10–47, 1958

SAWYER, P.H. and Wood, I. (eds), *Early medieval kingship*, University of Leeds, 1977

SAWYER, P.H., 'Kings and merchants'. In Sawyer, P.H. and Wood, I. (eds), 1977: 139–58

SCULL, C., 'Post-Roman Phase I at Yeavering: A reconsideration', *Medieval Archaeology,* 35: 51–63, 1991

SHARPE, R. (trans. and ed.), *Adomnán of Iona: Life of Saint Columba*, London: Penguin, 1995

SHERLOCK S. J. and Welch, M. G., *An Anglo-Saxon cemetery at Norton, Cleveland*, Council for British Archaeology Research Report 82, 1992

SHIPPEY, T., *Poems of Wisdom and Learning in Old English*, Cambridge: D. S. Brewer, 1976

SKENE, W.F., *The Four Ancient Books of Wales*, Edinburgh: Edmonston and Douglas, 1868

SMITH, A.W., 'The luck in the head: a problem in English folklore', *Folklore,* 73.1: 13–24, 1962

——'The luck in the head: some further observations', *Folklore,* 74.2: 396–8, 1963

SMITH, I.M., 'Sprouston, Roxburghshire: an early Anglian centre of the eastern Tweed basin', Proceedings of the Society of Antiquaries of Scotland, 121: 261–94, 1991

SOUTH, T. J. (ed.), *Historia de Sancto Cuthberto: A History of Saint Cuthbert and a Record of His Patrimony*, Anglo-Saxon Texts 3, Cambridge: D.S. Brewer, 2002

STANCLIFFE, C. and CAMBRIDGE, E. (eds), *Oswald: Northumbrian king to European saint*, Stamford: Paul Watkins, 1995

STANCLIFFE, C., 'Oswald: "Most holy and most victorious king of the Northumbrians"'. In Stancliffe, C. and Cambridge, E. (eds), 1995: 33–83

—— 'Where was Oswald killed?' In Stancliffe, C. and Cambridge, E. (eds), 1995b: 84–96

—— 'British and Irish contexts'. In DeGregorio, S. (ed.), 2010: 69–83

STENTON, Sir F.M., *The Oxford History of England: Anglo-Saxon England*, 3rd Edition, Oxford: Clarendon Press, 1970

STEVENSON, J. (ed.), *Liber vitae ecclesiae Dunelmensis*, Surtees Society, 1841

STEVENSON, J. (trans.), *Simeon's History of the Church of Durham*, Felinfach: Llanerch, 1993

TAYLOR, S., 'Seventh-century Iona abbots in Scottish place-names'. In Brown, D. and Clancy, T.O. (eds), *Spes Scotorum, Hope of Scots: Saint Columba, Iona and Scotland*, Edinburgh: T.&T. Clark, 1999

THACKER, A., '*Membra disjecta*: The division of the body and the diffusion of the cult'. In Stancliffe, C. and Cambridge, E. (eds), 1995: 97–127

THACKER, A. and SHARPE, R. (eds), *Local saints and local churches in the early medieval West*, Oxford University Press, 2002

THOMAS, C., *The Early Christian Archaeology of North Britain*, Oxford University Press, 1971

—— *Bede, archaeology and the cult of relics*, Jarrow Lecture, Jarrow: St Paul's Church, 1973

—— *Christianity in Roman Britain to AD 500*, London: Batsford, 1981

—— 'The early Christian inscriptions of Southern Scotland', *Glasgow Archaeological Journal*, 17: 1–10, 1992

THORPE, B., *Ancient Laws and Institutes of England*, London: The Commissioners of Public Records, 1840

TODD, J.H. and REEVES, W., *The martyrology of Donegal: A calendar of the saints of Ireland*, Dublin: Irish Archaeological and Celtic Society, 1864

TOLKIEN, J.R.R., *Beowulf; the monster and the critics*, British Academy: Sir Israel Gollancz memorial lecture, 1936

TUDOR, V., 'REGINALD's *Life of St Oswald*'. In Stancliffe, C. and Cambridge, E. (eds), 1995: 178–94

UNDERWOOD, R., *Anglo-Saxon weapons and warfare*, Stroud: Tempus, 1999

WADDINGTON, C., 'Lanton Quarry: new evidence in northern Northumberland', *Current Archaeology*, 239: 12–21, 2010

WADE-EVANS, A.W., *Nennius's "History of the Britons"*, London: SPCK, 1938

WALKER, R.F., *The origins of Newcastle upon Tyne*, Newcastle upon Tyne: Thorne's Student Bookshop, 1976

WALLACE-HADRILL, J.M., *Bede's Ecclesiastical history of the English people: a historical commentary*, Oxford: Clarendon Press, 1988

WARE, C., 'The social use of space at Gefrin'. In Frodsham, P. and O'Brien, C.F. (eds), 2005: 153–60

WHITELOCK, D. (ed.), *English historical documents c.500–1042*, London: Eyre and Spottiswoode, 1955

WILMOTT, T., 'The late Roman frontier: the structural background'. In Collins, R. and Allason-Jones, L. (eds), 2010: 10–19

WILSON, D.M. (ed.), *Archaeology in Anglo-Saxon England*, Cambridge University Press, 1976

—— *Anglo-Saxon paganism*, London: Routledge, 1992

WILSON, P., 'Early Anglian Catterick and Catraeth', *Medieval Archaeology*, 40: 1–61, 1996

WINTERBOTTOM, M., *Arthurian period sources, volume 7: Gildas: The ruin of Britain and other works*, London: Phillimore, 1978

WOOD, I., 'Kings, kingdoms and consent'. In Sawyer, P.H. and Wood, I. (eds), 1977: 6–29

—— 'Before and after the Migration to Britain'. In Hines, J. (ed.), 1997: 41–64

—— 'An historical context for Hope-Taylor's Yeavering'. In Frodsham, P. and O'Brien, C.F. (eds), 2005: 185–8

—— 'Monasteries and the geography of power in the age of Bede', *Northern History*, XLV.1: 11–25, 2008

—— 'The foundation of Bede's Wearmouth-Jarrow'. In DeGregorio, S. (ed.), 2010: 84–96

WOOD, M., 'Bernician transitions: place-names and archaeology'. In Petts, D. and Turner, S. (eds), 2012: 35–70

WOODFIELD, C.C., 'Six turrets on Hadrian's Wall', *Archaeologia Aeliana*, 4th Series 43: 87–200, 1965

WOODING, J., 'Communication and commerce along the Western sealanes AD 400–800', BAR International Series 654, 1996

WOOLF, A., 'Cædualla *Rex Brittonum* and the passing of the Old North', *Northern History*, 41.1: 5–24, 2004

—— 'Dun Nechtain, Fortriu and the Geography of the Picts', *The Scottish Historical Review*, 85: 182–201, 2006

YORKE, B., *Kings and kingdoms of early Anglo-Saxon England*, London: Seaby, 1990

—— *Rex Doctissimus: Bede and King Aldfrith of Northumbria, Jarrow Lecture,* Jarrow Lecture, Jarrow: St Paul's Church, 2009

YOUNG, G., *Bamburgh Castle: The archaeology of the fortress of Bamburgh, AD 500 to AD 1500*, Alnwick: The Bamburgh Research Project, 2003

ACKNOWLEDGEMENTS

I must firstly thank the **Trustees of the Royal Literary Fund** for their generous award of a three-year fellowship at the University of Newcastle upon Tyne in the Department of English, without which I could not have completed this project.

My interest in Oswald and my thoughts on his extraordinary significance in English and European history have been stimulated by the students of the **North East Centre for Lifelong Learning**. Many have indulged my enthusiasms long enough to know how I value their ideas and thoughts. In particular I want to mention the members of the **Bernician Studies Group**, who will not let me get away with my wilder flights of fancy: I am indebted.

My friend and colleague **Colm O'Brien** has been a constant source of critical interest, of immense knowledge and equal passion for seventh-century Northumbria, and I owe him a great debt of gratitude, not least for reading proofs of the text and spotting significant errors.

Other friends and colleagues whom I would like to thank include **Dr Hermann Moisl** for his knowledge of the Irish material and his kindness in indulging what must have seemed some rather stupid questions; and **Professor Diana Whaley** for kindly putting my (almost non-existent) Old English right. The translations of the Anglo-Saxon maxims that head each chapter are derived from those of **Tom Shippey**, with a few amendments.

Dr Brian Roberts kindly gave me access to his own research on several aspects of the geography of the Northeast in Oswald's day.

Eleanor Carr not only translated from the German for me but also provided support, a good ear and many other kindnesses when the going was tough.

My son **Jack**, as always, has put up with more than most with amiable good humour and patience.

Ian Drury and **Richard Milbank** have been unstinting champions of Oswald.

Bernard of Clairvaux said, long before Newton stole the idea, that if we see further than our predecessors it is because we sit on the shoulders of giants. The scholarship of the Early Medieval period in Europe is, and has been, of a very high order. The work of **Dr Brian Hope-Taylor, Peter Hunter-Blair, Dame Rosemary Cramp, Professor Nick Higham, Professor Charles Thomas, Dr Brian K. Roberts, Professor David Rollason, Dr Clare Stancliffe** and the late **Professor Philip Rahtz** (not the least of whose talents were those of a brilliant teacher) stands out, as does the immense contribution made by the Bedan scholars **Charles Plummer, Bertram Colgrave** and **R. A. B. Mynors**.

This book is for lifelong learners everywhere, with a plea to short-sighted governments not to write us all off after the age of twenty-five. My oldest student, **Sybil Durno**—I hope she will not mind me mentioning her—is over ninety years of age. She has limited vision and does not hear every word. She never misses a class, is as sharp as a tack and a huge inspiration to all those who know her. This book is dedicated particularly to her and to another learner for life, my aunt **June Kempster**.

PICTURE CREDITS

Maps
Jeff Edwards

Plate section
1. Bamburgh Castle: Brian Kerr / Getty Images
2. Oswald's Gate: Max Adams
3. Iona Abbey: Ullsteinbild / TopFoto
4. Anglo-Saxon Chronicle entries for the years 824 to 833, Abingdon, mid-eleventh century, British Library Cotton MS Tiberius B.i, f.128. 27: British Library
5. Franks Casket: akg-images / Erich Lessing
6. Sutton Hoo Bronze Bowl: akg-images / Erich Lessing
7. Edwin's palace at Yeavering: Dr Brian Hope-Taylor, copyright HMSO
8. Yeavering Bell: Max Adams
9. Finglesham buckle: Yorke Digital Library / Jane Hawkes; with the kind permission of The Lord Northbourne
10. Heavenfield cross: Max Adams
11. The horned war-god Belatucadros / Cernunnos: Senhouse Museum
12. St Oswald and St Aidan, by Ford Madox Brown: Lady Lever Art Gallery, National Museums Liverpool / The Bridgeman Art Library
13. Lindisfarne Priory: Max Adams
14. Bede's World, Jarrow: Max Adams
15. Thirlings manor plan: Colm O'Brien and Roget Miket
16. Oswald's Well: Janet & Colin Bord / Fortean Picture Library / Topfoto
17. Hexham crypt: by kind permission of the Hexham Abbey Shop
18. Gold strip with biblical inscription from the Staffordshire hoard: Birmingham Museums Trust
19. Whitby Abbey: Lindsey Parnaby / AFP / Getty Images
20. The opening of Cuthbert's tomb: British Library
21. Cuthbert gospel: British Library
22. Lindisfarne Gospels: akg-images / British Library
23. Hildesheim relic: akg-images
24. Seventh-century coin from Kent: Fitzwilliam Museum, Cambridge
25. Seventeenth-century silver Kreuzer from Zug, Switzerland: courtesy of the Money Museum, Zürich
26. Stained-glass window from the church of St John Lee: Dave Webster

INDEX

а

X

Y

Z